THE IRA IN BRITAIN, 1919–1923
'IN THE HEART OF ENEMY LINES'

The IRA in Britain, 1919–1923

'In the Heart of Enemy Lines'

GERARD NOONAN

Liverpool University Press

First published 2014 by
Liverpool University Press
4 Cambridge Street
Liverpool
L69 7ZU

British Library Cataloguing-in-Publication data
A British Library CIP record is available

ISBN 978-1-78138-026-0 cased
ISBN 978-1-78694-013-1 limp

Typeset by Carnegie Book Production, Lancaster
Printed and bound by CPI Group (UK) Ltd, Croydon CR0 4YY

Contents

List of Illustrations

Cover illustration: IRA O/C London Reginald Dunne (with bandaged head) in police custody, June 1922 (Courtesy of Mercier Archives, Mercier Press Ltd., Cork)

List of Tables

List of Graphs

List of Abbreviations

O/C	Officer in Command
QM	Quartermaster
QMG	Quartermaster General
RIC	Royal Irish Constabulary
ROIA	Restoration of Order in Ireland Act (1920)
SPI	Socialist Party of Ireland
TD	Teachta Dála
WSPU	Women's Social and Political Union

Used in the Footnotes

In addition to those mentioned above

ABLP	Andrew Bonar Law Papers (PAHL)
ACC	Assistant Chief Constable
AÓBP	Art Ó Briain Papers (NLI)
ASS	Assistant Secretary of State
ASSI	Assizes File (TNA)
BMHCD	Bureau of Military History Contemporaneous Document(s) (MAI)
BMHWS	Bureau of Military History Witness Statement(s) (MAI)
CAB	Cabinet File (TNA)
CC	Chief Constable
CO	Colonial Office File (TNA)
CRIM	Central Criminal Court File (TNA)
DDAF	Department of Defence Administration File (MAI)
DÉ	Dáil Éireann File (NAI)
DIB	*Dictionary of Irish Biography* (Cambridge: Cambridge University Press, 2009)
DLGP	David Lloyd George Papers (PAHL)
DLIP	Durham Light Infantry Papers (Durham County Record Office)
DMFP	Desmond and Mabel Fitzgerald Papers (UCDA)
DPP	Director of Public Prosecutions File (TNA)
D/T	Department of the Taoiseach File (NAI)

ECP	Eithne Coyle Papers (UCDA)
EdeVP	Eamon de Valera Papers (UCDA)
EMP	Eamonn Mooney Papers
EO'ML	Ernie O'Malley Letters (UCDA)
EO'MN	Ernie O'Malley Notebooks (UCDA)
FGP	Frank Gallagher Papers (NLI)
FIN	Department of Finance File (NAI)
FO'DP	Florence O'Donoghue Papers (NLI)
FWWF	First World War File (NAS)
GAAA	Gaelic Athletic Association Archives
GCPP	George Count Plunkett Papers (NLI)
Hansard 5	Parliamentary Debates, 5th Series
HO	Home Office/Home Office File (TNA)
IHS	*Irish Historical Studies*
II	*Irish Independent*
INAVDFP	Irish National Aid and Volunteer Dependents' Fund Papers (NLI)
IT	*Irish Times*
JUS	Department of Justice File (NAI)
MAI	Military Archives of Ireland
MCP	Michael Collins Papers (MAI)
MEPO	Metropolitan Police Office File (TNA)
MG	*Manchester Guardian*
MSPB	Military Service Pensions Board
MSPC	Military Service Pensions Collection (MAI)
MTP	Maurice Twomey Papers (UCDA)
NAI	National Archives of Ireland
NAPLB	National Army Prisoner Location Books (MAI)
NAS	National Archives of Scotland
NHI	*A New History of Ireland* (9 vols, Oxford: Clarendon Press/ Oxford University Press, 1976–2005)
NLI	National Library of Ireland
ODNB	*Oxford Dictionary of National Biography* (Oxford: Oxford University Press, 2004)

PAHL	Parliamentary Archives, House of Lords
PBP	Piaras Béaslaí Papers (NLI)
PG/ECP	Provisional Government/Executive Council Papers (NAI)
PR	Police Records (Tyne and Wear Archives)
PSGF	Police Services General File (NAS)
RMP	Richard Mulcahy Papers (UCDA)
'RROUK'	'Report on Revolutionary Organisations in the United Kingdom'
SHP	Sighle Humphreys Papers (UCDA)
SO'MP	Seán O'Mahoney Papers (NLI)
TNA	The National Archives, Kew
TT	*The Times*
UCDA	University College, Dublin, Archives
USS	Under Secretary of State
WO	War Office File (TNA)

Acknowledgements

This book is based largely on my PhD thesis and I would therefore like to thank all those who assisted in the research and writing of the initial thesis and subsequent book. My supervisor, Professor Eunan O'Halpin, was a source of advice and constructive criticism. I am similarly indebted to Professor David Fitzpatrick and Dr Emmet O'Connor. I am grateful to Dr Anne Dolan for counsel on the structure of the thesis. Dr Eve Morrison generously shared her knowledge of the Bureau of Military History. Cathleen Knowles-McGuirk graciously granted me access to the private papers of her father, Eamonn Mooney, and I would also like to thank Dr Máirtín Seán Ó Catháin for introducing me to Mrs Knowles-McGuirk. Patrick Brennan kindly shared some valuable records too. Thanks also to the staff in the Trinity College Dublin (TCD) History Department office and in the Graduate Studies Office.

TCD's Graduate Studies Committee (College Awards) granted me a three-year Postgraduate Research Studentship. From Limerick County Council, I received a three-year maintenance grant. From the TCD Trust and the TCD History Department's Grace Lawless Lee Fund, I also obtained grants to cover the expense of research trips to archives in Britain. Without these financial supports, I could not have undertaken this project and I am very grateful to all the funding organizations for their generosity.

As well as thanking Patrick Brennan, Cathleen Knowles-McGuirk and Rosemaire Pinkman for permission to quote from copyrighted material, I am indebted to the staff at the following institutions for their helpful service and permission to cite from archives in their care: the British Library, Durham County Record Office, the Gaelic Athletic Association Archives, Limerick City Library, Limerick County Library, Limerick Studies, the Military Archives of Ireland, the National Archives in Kew, the National Archives of Ireland, the National Archives of Scotland, the National Library of Ireland, the Parliamentary Archives in the House of Lords, TCD library, Tyne and Wear Archives, University College, Dublin, Archives (including the

UCD-OFM Partnership for permission to access and quote from the Eamon de Valera Papers) and library and the Wiltshire and Swindon History Centre.

The first set of files from the Military Service Pensions Collection was released while I was correcting the proofs of this book. Unfortunately, therefore, I was able to make only the most cursory use of these records in this study.

Excerpts from 'The Waste Land' from *Collected Poems 1909–1962* by T.S. Eliot. Copyright 1936 by Houghton Mifflin Harcourt Publishing Company. Copyright © renewed 1964 by Thomas Stearns Eliot. Reprinted by permission of Houghton Mifflin Harcourt Publishing Company. All rights reserved. I am also grateful to Faber & Faber Ltd.

I owe a debt to Liverpool University Press for agreeing to publish the following pages. In particular, I would like to thank Alison Welsby and Patrick Brereton, along with Sue Barnes and the team at Carnegie Book Production. Gratitude is also due to the two anonymous readers for their suggested improvements.

In addition, I would like to thank my friends inside and outside the academy: their convivial company helped to preserve my sanity during this solitary scholarly pursuit.

Parts of Chapter 2 were published as 'Supplying an Army: IRA Gunrunning in Britain during the War of Independence', *History Studies: University of Limerick History Society Journal*, 12 (2011), pp. 80–92. Meanwhile, sections of Chapter 3 appeared as 'Republican Terrorism in Britain, 1920–1923', in David Fitzpatrick (ed.), *Terror in Ireland 1916–1923* (Dublin: Lilliput Press, 2012), pp. 236–48.

I dedicate this book to my parents, Gerard and Mary, whose support has been indispensable.

Introduction

This book studies the activities of Irish physical force republican organizations in Britain from the outbreak of the war of independence in 1919 to the conclusion of the civil war in 1923. The Irish Volunteers or Irish Republican Army (IRA) is the main focus of study, though the Irish Republican Brotherhood (IRB) or 'Fenians', the Cumann na mBan and Na Fianna Éireann are also accorded attention. Other organizations associated with these physical force groups, such as the Irish Self-Determination League of Great Britain (ISDL) and Sinn Féin, are given consideration as well.

The activities of republicans in Britain during this period are virtually bookended by the escape of Sinn Féin president Eamon de Valera and others from Lincoln prison in February 1919 and by the arrest and deportation to Ireland of over 110 anti-treaty activists in March 1923. In the interim, republicans were involved in a variety of activities, most importantly gunrunning and attacks on property.

Conspiratorial Irish republicanism in Britain was nurtured by the culture of Irish immigrants who settled in England, Scotland and Wales in the nineteenth century. Such immigration is usually associated with the Great Famine of 1845–51. The Irish were already a familiar sight in Britain prior to this, but the repeated destruction of the potato crop precipitated a dramatic increase in emigration to Britain, a trend that was sustained for a long period thereafter by the lack of economic opportunities in Ireland. By 1861, the Irish-born population of Britain numbered 805,717, scattered mainly in urban areas of northern England and Scotland. Thereafter, except for a slight increase in the 1870s, it began to decline until it numbered just under 524,000 at the height of republican activity in Britain in 1921.[1] If second- and

---

1   David Fitzpatrick, "'A Peculiar Tramping People': The Irish in Britain, 1801–70', in W.E. Vaughan (ed.), *A New History of Ireland [NHI], Vol. V: Ireland Under the Union, Vol. I, 1801–70* (Oxford: Clarendon Press, 1989), pp. 627, 658;

third-generation Irish are included, the Irish Catholic population as a whole in Britain probably exceeded 2,000,000 by then. Many native Britons feared and loathed the Irish, distaining their Catholic religion and strange customs. A number of anti-Irish riots occurred in the period from the 1830s to the 1860s.[2] However, most Irish in Britain did not experience such violence. If they did suffer discrimination, it was usually of a more subtle kind, such as difficulties in finding employment. As time progressed, the majority assimilated into British society, a process encouraged by the Catholic Church and facilitated by the acquisition of skilled employment.[3] Still, many retained an interest in Ireland's plight and supported politicians such as Daniel O'Connell and Charles Stewart Parnell in their peaceful campaigns for the abolition of the Union of 1800 which welded Ireland to Britain. A small minority believed that only violence could achieve Irish independence and it was this tradition that fostered the growth of the IRA and IRB in Britain.

Diaspora nationalism played a significant role in the evolution of Irish nationalism. The political geographer Adrian Mulligan has argued that the greater interconnectedness between the British Isles and the United States of America in the mid- to late-nineteenth century, in terms of travel, communications and the media, saw the development of a 'transatlantic Irish nationalist world'. Fenianism was a product of this new world. For immigrants in America, Irish nationalism was the vehicle that enabled them to cope with their new surroundings and at the same time retain a connection with Ireland. The 'New Departure' and the 'Skirmishing Fund' are examples of this transatlantic nationalism in action. In 1879, Irish-American Fenians decided to lend their support to both land agitation in Ireland and the constitutional attempt by the Irish Parliamentary Party (IPP) to secure a measure of autonomy for Ireland within the British Empire. This New Departure, Mulligan contends, was 'a crucial intervention in the transatlantic development of Irish nationalism [which] could only have been made by those outside of Ireland'. It strengthened Irish nationalism by linking the physical

---

David Fitzpatrick, 'Irish Emigration in the Later Nineteenth Century', *Irish Historical Studies [IHS]*, 22.86 (1980), p. 126; David Fitzpatrick, 'The Irish in Britain, 1871–1921', in W.E. Vaughan (ed.), *NHI, Vol. VI: Ireland Under the Union, Vol. II, 1870–1921* (Oxford: Clarendon Press, 1996), p. 690

2   Fitzpatrick, "A Peculiar Tramping People", pp. 639–44

3   Alan O'Day, 'Varieties of Anti-Irish Behaviour in Britain, 1846–1922', in Panikos Panayi (ed.), *Racial Violence in Britain, 1840–1950* (Leicester: Leicester University Press, 1993), pp. 38–40; Fitzpatrick, "A Peculiar Tramping People", pp. 656–57; Fitzpatrick, 'The Irish in Britain', pp. 688–89

force movement with both the constitutional movement and the widespread demand for changes in the terms of land tenure in Ireland. The Skirmishing Fund involved Irish immigrants in America donating money which allowed groups of Fenians to mount bomb attacks in Britain in the 1880s.[4] Irish nationalism, then, was not limited to the inhabitants of Ireland itself. Rather, it was an international phenomenon, one which the republican movement would call upon during the revolutionary period of 1916–23.

The Irish Revolution occurred against a backdrop of international war and revolution. The First World War unleashed forces which sustained violence long after the armistice of November 1918. In Eastern Europe, with the collapse of the Austro-Hungarian, Ottoman and Russian empires, nationalist and ethnic tensions exploded into fierce violence. In Africa and Asia too, nationalist movements challenged the British Empire. Added to this was the new threat of social revolution emanating from the nascent Soviet Union, the world's first communist state. In his celebrated poem 'The Waste Land', first published in 1922, T.S. Eliot described the beleaguered post-war world, a world haunted by death and destruction, with 'hooded hordes swarming | Over endless plains, stumbling in cracked earth', and where 'the city over the mountains | Cracks and reforms and bursts in the violent air', with 'falling towers' in the world's capitals presenting an 'unreal' spectacle.[5]

The activities of Irish republicans in Britain in the nineteenth- and late twentieth-centuries have been the subject of significant scholarly attention. In contrast, very little has been written on the activities of the IRA and the IRB there during the war of independence and civil war, a result perhaps of contemporaneous events in Ireland having overshadowed those in Britain. No book has been written on the topic. Moreover, many accounts of the Irish Revolution accord little or no space to republicanism in Britain. The most significant piece of research to date is an article by the historian Peter Hart entitled 'Operations Abroad: The IRA in Britain', first published in the *English Historical Review* in 2000. An article by the same author, entitled 'Michael Collins and the Assassination of Sir Henry Wilson', initially published in *Irish Historical Studies* in 1992, examines a controversial event involving

---

4 Adrian N. Mulligan, 'A Forgotten "Greater Ireland": The Transatlantic Development of Irish Nationalism', *Scottish Geographical Journal*, 118.3 (2002), pp. 219–34; Adrian N. Mulligan, 'Absence Makes the Heart Grow Fonder: Transatlantic Irish Nationalism and the 1867 Rising', *Social & Cultural Geography*, 6.3 (2005), pp. 439–54

5 T.S. Eliot, 'The Waste Land', in T.S. Eliot, *The Waste Land and Other Poems* (London: Faber & Faber, 1940), p. 37

IRA men in London that contributed to the outbreak of the civil war. A third article by Hart, 'The Social Structure of the Irish Republican Army', originally published in the *Historical Journal* in 1999, also contains some relevant research. Iain Paterson's article 'The Activities of Irish Republican Physical Force Organisations in Scotland, 1919–21', published in the *Scottish Historical Review* in 1993, discusses republican activity in Scotland during the war of independence.

Patterson argues that the contribution of republicans in Scotland, and by implication that of their comrades in England and Wales, to the IRA's campaign in Ireland during the war of independence was 'slight'.[6] This author disagrees. The weapons smuggled to Ireland by republicans in Britain were of great importance to the IRA units in the field. Moreover, while it is true that the amount of violence perpetrated by Volunteers in Britain pales in comparison to that of their most active comrades in Ireland, it should be remembered that the republican campaign was not spread evenly throughout 'John Bull's other island'. Some areas, such as west Munster and Dublin city, were significantly more active than other areas, such as the majority of Leinster. Taking this into account, we can see that the IRA in parts of Britain was actually more active than Volunteers in some parts of Ireland.[7] After all, as a senior IRA commander told the Volunteers in Liverpool in November 1920, the Volunteers in Ireland were 'in the front line trenches', while the men in Britain were 'in the heart of enemy lines'.[8] Or, as another put it, '… in a manner of speaking, our people in England are only the auxiliaries of our attacking forces'.[9] In other words, republicans in Britain were adjuncts to the Volunteers in Ireland, auxiliaries to the main attacking forces in the campaign for Irish independence. I would argue that this was indeed the case. Through gunrunning and violence, republicans in Britain made a significant contribution to the IRA's campaign during the war of independence. And they did the same during the civil war, again through the provision of weapons but more significantly with the provision of recruits to both sides in the conflict.

6   Iain D. Patterson, 'The Activities of Irish Republican Physical Force Organisations in Scotland, 1919–21', *Scottish Historical Review*, 72.193 (1993), p. 46

7   On the level of violence in Irish counties, 1917–23, see Peter Hart, 'The Geography of Revolution in Ireland', in Peter Hart, *The IRA at War 1916–1923* (Oxford: Oxford University Press, 2003), p. 35

8   Quoted in Edward M. Brady, *Ireland's Secret Service in England* (Dublin: Talbot Press, 1928), p. 26

9   Michael Collins to Art O'Brien, 6 June 1921 (National Archives of Ireland [NAI], Dáil Éireann file [DÉ] 2/330)

In writing this book, I have adopted an analytical approach. Separate chapters on different topics allow for the detailed and concentrated exploration impossible in a strict chronological approach. The prologue traces the history of the Volunteers in Britain from its founding in 1913 to the outbreak of the war of independence in 1919, while also examining the history of Irish republicanism in Britain. Chapter 1 discusses how IRA and IRB units were organized in Britain during the war of independence, examining how they were run, the type of people who became members and their reasons for joining. It also studies the wider republican movement, especially the ISDL and Sinn Féin. The second chapter focusses on gunrunning, the acquisition and smuggling of munitions into Ireland. This was the most important activity of republicans in Britain. All aspects of the weapons-smuggling process are examined including the types of munitions acquired and the means by which they were obtained, run into Ireland and distributed to IRA units. Chapter 3 examines the violence perpetrated by Volunteers in Britain during the war of independence, discussing its aims, character and effectiveness. The fourth chapter focusses on republican activities in Britain during the period of the truce, the treaty and the slide towards civil war in Ireland. Chapter 5 examines the IRA in Britain during the civil war in terms of organization, munitions-smuggling and violence. It also follows the course of the war in Ireland through the eyes of those formerly connected with the movement in Britain. The sixth chapter analyses the response of the authorities – politicians, police, courts and prisons – to the republican threat.

Writing in the 1970s, a veteran of the Glasgow Cumann na mBan lamented that, with the deaths of fellow members, 'the history of the Scottish Brigade [IRA], which was immense & interesting, will never now be completed'.[10] This study cannot pretend to completeness. However, it is the hope of the author that it will provide an insight into the bloody birth of independent Ireland from a relatively neglected vantage point.

---

10 Anonymous memoir, 1972–73 (University College, Dublin, Archives [UCDA], Eithne Coyle Papers [ECP], (P61/4[65–66]))

Map 1: Britain and Ireland with the major places mentioned in the text.

Prologue

I

Irishmen hae [i.e. have] now for the first time in over a hundred years the opportunity of arming and learning the use of arms, and the hot blood of our dead and gone warrior sires will surge so in their veins as they see things militant materialise that they must sooer [i.e. sooner] or later "fall in" in their places amongst the manhood of Erin, and that is now assuredly in the ranks of the Irish Volunteers.

So wrote the secretary of the nascent 1st Glasgow and West of Scotland Regiment of the Irish Volunteers in early March 1914.[1] The outfit, also known as the Sarsfield Regiment, in honour of Patrick Sarsfield, an Irish military leader who fought in the Williamite Wars of 1689–91, initially numbered ten 'skeleton companies'. By August, it had expanded to the districts of Stirlingshire, Lanarkshire, Renfrewshire and Ayrshire, and boasted an estimated membership of 2,590.[2] The Volunteer organization also spread through England and Wales. The Rhondda Valley soon had over 1,000 members, Tyneside almost 700, Cardiff at least 560, Manchester a 'very large number', London at least 480 and Wigan 100. One of the founders of the Volunteers on Merseyside later claimed that the membership there quickly reached 1,200. Units also existed in Sheffield, Bolton, Glamorgan and Swansea Valley.[3] 'England and Scotland are both dotted with corps drilling

---

1 *Irish Volunteer*, 7 Mar. 1914
2 *Irish Volunteer*, 21 Feb., 18 July 1914; Máirtín Seán Ó Catháin, *Irish Republicanism in Scotland 1858–1916: Fenians in Exile* (Dublin: Irish Academic Press, 2007), appendix 2
3 *Irish Volunteer*, 4, 18 Apr., 9, 16, 30 May, 6, 20, 27 June, 4, 11, 25 July, 8, 15, 22 Aug., 12 Sept. 1914; Bureau of Military History Witness Statement [BMHWS] 510, Frank Thornton, p. 1 (Military Archives of Ireland [MAI])

and making ready,' noted the *Irish Volunteer* newspaper, 'and a few enthusiasts have spread the flame from coast to coast.'[4]

The flame had been lit in Dublin in November 1913 when a group of nationalists, led by Eoin MacNeill, the founder of the Gaelic League, established the Volunteers. They were reacting to the Ulster Unionists who – in opposition to the British government's plan to grant a limited form of autonomy or 'home rule' to Ireland – had established a paramilitary outfit, the Ulster Volunteer Force, and threatened rebellion. Enraged by the Unionists' success in forcing the government to contemplate the partitioning of Ireland into nationalist and unionist blocs, the nationalists in Dublin hoped that a paramilitary army of their own, the Irish Volunteers, would intimidate the government into honouring its pledge for all-Ireland home rule. The men of Ireland were enjoined to 'to enrol and arm themselves in order to secure and maintain the rights and liberties of the Irish people'.[5] Within a short period of time, thousands of Irishmen had joined the organization in Ireland and Britain.

The Irish Volunteers was not the first manifestation of radical Irish nationalism in Britain. The presence there of Irishmen prepared to use violence to achieve Irish freedom usually only revealed itself at times when their fellow nationalists in Ireland were willing to do likewise. The history of physical force republicanism in Britain, therefore, is intimately linked with the Irish rebellions of 1798, 1803, 1848 and 1867.

The 1798 rebellion was the work of the Society of the United Irishmen, the first expression of modern Irish republicanism. Inspired by the French Revolution, the organization was founded with the aim of reforming the Irish political system. The government, however, alarmed at events in France, viewed the body as revolutionary and violently obstructed its attempts at peaceful reform. In 1798, boasting members in London, Manchester and Birmingham, the United Irishmen and comrades in the United Britons resolved to aid a French invasion of the British Isles. However, their plans were disrupted by the arrest of prominent members in Britain. The rebellion went ahead in Ireland that same year. However, poorly armed, lacking effective communications and riven with dissension, the rebels proved little opposition for the British army.[6]

4 *Irish Volunteer*, 27 June 1914
5 The O'Rahilly, *The Secret History of the Irish Volunteers* (Dublin: Irish Publicity League, 1915), pp. 3–6
6 Marianne Elliott, 'Irish Republicanism in England: The First Phase, 1797–9',

The United Britons re-organized the following year. In concert with remnants of the United Irishmen, they drew up plans once again for the outbreak of insurrections in Britain and Ireland upon the landing of a French invasion force. The plan, however, was thrown into confusion in July 1803 by the precipitate outbreak of rebellion in Dublin. A pathetic affair, the revolt, headed by Robert Emmet, was crushed before the United Britons and the French had the opportunity of aiding it.[7]

Violent Irish nationalism next appeared in Britain in 1848, the year in which the Young Ireland movement launched what transpired to be another feeble rebellion. Frustrated with nationalist leader Daniel O'Connell's sectarianism and absolute renunciation of the use of violence to overturn the Act of Union, the Young Irelanders established the Irish Confederation. Branches of the organization were founded in British cities, including London, Liverpool and Manchester. There, they entered into a wary alliance with the Chartist movement, a mass organization dedicated to achieving constitutional reform in Britain. The British authorities viewed the alliance with alarm, fearing the spread of revolution to the United Kingdom. Their fear was justified for, as well as engaging in public agitation, many confederates clubs were secretly arming themselves. Dreading a Chartist-confederate rebellion in Lancashire, between April and August 1848 the authorities made a number of arrests and seized quantities of munitions, including pikes, swords and guns. The remaining confederates in England resolved to aid the imminent rebellion in Ireland. By threatening disorder, they hoped to prevent the despatch of troops across the Irish Sea. However, when the rebellion was launched in late July, the confederates had neither the organization nor the arms necessary to mount diversions. In any event, troops from Britain were not required to ensure the rebellion's suppression.[8]

The next year of rebellion in Ireland was 1867. The revolt was launched by the IRB. Akin to secret societies on the European continent, such as

in Thomas Bartlett and D.W. Hayton (eds), *Penal Era and Golden Age: Essays in Irish History 1690–1800* (Belfast: Ulster Historical Foundation, 1979), pp. 204–21; E.W. McFarland, *Ireland and Scotland in the Age of Revolution: Planting the Green Bough* (Edinburgh: Edinburgh University Press, 1994); Nancy Curtain, *The United Irishmen: Popular Politics in Ulster and Dublin, 1791–1798* (Oxford: Clarendon Press, 1994), pp. 254–89

7 Marianne Elliott, 'The "Despard Conspiracy" Reconsidered', *Past & Present*, 75.1 (1977), pp. 46–71

8 W.J. Lowe, 'The Chartists and the Irish Confederates: Lancashire, 1848', *IHS*, 24.94 (1984), pp. 172–96

Blanqui's Society of the Seasons and Mazzini's Young Italy, the Fenians hoped to foment a rebellion by the Irish masses to overthrow British rule. The actual rebellion itself was effectively stillborn due to a lack of munitions and training, poor planning, bad leadership and ineffective communications.[9] What was significant about 1867 for our purposes was the activities of the IRB in Britain. The historian Máirtín Seán Ó Catháin asserts that 'the Fenian movement was essentially an overseas movement'. By 1860, the IRB had established itself in a number of British cities, its membership in Scotland five years later being around 8,000.[10] The Fenians in England played a significant role in planning the 1867 rebellion. In January that year, frustrated with the delay in fixing a date for an insurrection, they decided to establish a directory to plan an immediate revolt. The directory plotted for simultaneous uprisings to take place in Ireland, London and Liverpool on 11 February. This plan, however, was quickly shelved. Instead, the Fenians decided to seize arms from Chester Castle, a military fortress on the England–Wales border. The scheme called for the arms to be transported via commandeered train and steamboat to Ireland, where their landing would signal the beginning of the rebellion.[11] On 11 February, between 600 and 1,500 Fenians from various towns in England converged on Chester. However, having been warned of the IRB's plan by an informer, the authorities had reinforced the town's garrison. Taking fright, the Fenians abandoned the proposed raid and fled the town. Many were arrested as they attempted to travel to Ireland.[12] Nevertheless, before the year was out, Britain experienced two remarkable IRB operations. On 18 September, a policeman was killed during the rescue of two Irish-American Fenians from a prison van in Manchester. Three Irishmen, William O'Meara Allen, Michael Larkin and Michael O'Brien, were convicted of the policeman's murder. Hanged on 23 November, they became known as the 'Manchester

---

9   Peter Hart, 'The Fenians and the International Revolutionary Tradition', in Fearghal McGarry and James McConnel (eds), *The Black Hand of Republicanism: Fenianism in Modern Ireland* (Dublin: Irish Academic Press, 2009), pp. 194–95; Shin-inchi Takagami, 'The Fenian Rising in Dublin, March 1867', *IHS*, 29.115 (1995), pp. 340–62

10   Ó Catháin, *Irish Republicanism in Scotland*, pp. 31, 47, 247

11   Martha Ramón, *A Provisional Dictator: James Stephens and the Fenian Movement* (Dublin: University College Dublin Press, 2007), p. 226; Takagami, 'Fenian Rising', pp. 340–41; Brian Jenkins, *The Fenian Problem: Insurgency and Terrorism in a Liberal State, 1858–1874* (Toronto: McGill-Queen's University Press, 2008), pp. 80–81

12   Ramón, *Provisional Dictator*, p. 227; Jenkins, *Fenian Problem*, p. 81

martyrs' and quickly entered the pantheon of nationalist heroes. Three months later, the inept employment of gunpowder during an unsuccessful attempt to rescue another Irish-American Fenian from a prison in London caused the deaths of seven civilians and injured dozens more. Convicted of murder, an Irishman named Michael Barrett was hanged on 26 May 1868; it was the last public execution to take place in Britain.[13]

The last manifestation of violent Irish nationalism in Britain prior to the founding of the Irish Volunteers in 1914 occurred in the 1880s. Unlike previous episodes of violence in Britain, it was not accompanied by rebellion in Ireland. For a period of six years, beginning in 1881, and again in 1890, rival groups of Irish-American Fenians, some of whom had been born in Ireland and Britain, conducted a bombing campaign in London, Liverpool and Glasgow. Some used gunpowder in their devices, while others employed the newly invented dynamite. The aim, in the words of Jeremiah O'Donovan Rossa – one of the leaders of the campaign – was to inflict so much damage in Britain as to convince the government that 'she [i.e. England] will lose more than she can gain by holding Ireland'.[14] One civilian was killed in the attacks, a seven year-old boy, as were three bombers, while hundreds of people were injured and thousands of pounds of damage was caused to property. In the event, however, while the campaign did cause panic and alarm amongst the public, the security establishment and the government, it failed to affect a change in the government's Irish policy.[15]

The Irish Volunteer companies that were founded in Britain in 1914 were staffed by a significant number of men from Ireland but also by British-born men of Irish descent. Hundreds of 'little Irelands' existed

13 Jenkins, *Fenian Problem*, chapters 4–7; Elaine McFarland, 'A Reality and Yet Impalpable: The Fenian Panic in Mid-Victorian Scotland', *Scottish Historical Review*, 77.2 (1998), pp. 199–223; Gary Owens 'Constructing the Martyrs: The Manchester Executions and the Nationalist Imagination', in Lawrence W. McBride (ed.), *Images, Icons and the Irish Nationalist Imagination* (Dublin: Four Courts Press, 1999), pp. 18–36

14 Quoted in Lindsay Clutterbuck, 'The Progenitors of Terrorism: Russian Revolutionaries or Extreme Irish Republicans?', *Terrorism and Political Violence*, 16.1 (2004), p. 164

15 K.R.M. Short, *The Dynamite War: Irish-American Bombers in Victorian Britain* (Dublin: Gill & Macmillan, 1979); Ó Catháin, *Irish Republicanism in Scotland*, pp. 126–39, 155–56, 180; Niall Whelehan, *The Dynamiters: Irish Nationalism and Political Violence in the Wider World, 1867–1900* (Cambridge: Cambridge University Press, 2012), chapters 2–4

throughout Britain. These areas of concentrated Irish settlement gave rise to the formation of clubs and societies based around politics, religion, sport and general conviviality. It was the members of these bodies who founded the Volunteers. Alongside sporting and cultural bodies such as the Gaelic Athletic Association (GAA) and the Gaelic League, there also existed the United Irish League and the Ancient Order of Hibernians (AOH), both associated with the IPP, the organization which had dominated Catholic nationalist politics in Ireland since the 1880s.[16] More marginal political organizations were involved too. Sinn Féin, founded in 1907 and led by the prolific journalist Arthur Griffith, argued that Ireland should emulate Hungary. Through passive resistance and abstention from the Westminster parliament, the Irish would affect the same revolution in their relationship with Britain as the Hungarians had achieved in relation to Austria. This complicated dual monarchist policy made little headway against the IPP's more straight-forward home rule platform. Nevertheless, the term 'Sinn Féin' became associated with radical politics, partly due to the party's advocacy of cultural nationalism, such as the learning of the Irish language and the playing of Irish sports, but also due to it containing a number of IRB members. Branches of Cumann na nGaedheal, a precursor to Sinn Féin, had been established in Liverpool, London, Manchester and Glasgow by 1902 and IRB men soon came to dominate the organization, as they did Sinn Féin itself when it was founded in Britain a few years later.[17] Fenians were also involved in the Volunteers. The failure of the 1867 rebellion had prompted the IRB to change its strategy from one focussed on openly fomenting mass insurrection in Ireland to one where it sought to secretly infiltrate other organizations and use them for its own purposes.[18] From its foundation in 1913, the Irish Volunteers was penetrated by Fenians in Ireland and Britain.[19] Arthur Agnew remembered that when a Volunteer company was formed in Bootle, Liverpool, IRB officers instructed their men to join it in order to

---

16   *Irish Volunteer*, e.g. 7 Mar., 30 May, 6, 20 June, 11 July, 8 Aug. 1914

17   Michael Laffan, *The Resurrection of Ireland: The Sinn Féin Party 1916–1923* (Cambridge: Cambridge University Press, 1999), pp. 16–18, 26; Máirtín Ó Catháin, 'A Winnowing Spirit: Sinn Féin in Scotland, 1905–38', in Martin Mitchell (ed.), *New Perspectives on the Irish in Scotland* (Edinburgh: John Donald, 2008), pp. 116–21, 234 n. 12; *Irish Volunteer*, 3 Oct. 1914; BMHWS 285, Eamon O'Connor, p. 1

18   Hart, 'The Fenians and the International Revolutionary Tradition', p. 202

19   Marnie Hay, *Bulmer Hobson and the Nationalist Movement in Twentieth Century Ireland* (Manchester: Manchester University Press, 2009), pp. 109–27

secure the key positions. Indeed, most of the Merseyside Volunteers were Fenians, he claimed. Joseph Furlong, a member of the London Volunteers, described the Fenians as the 'Back Bone [sic]' of the organization in the capital. Likewise, 'as far as possible, the [Glasgow] Volunteers were officered and trained by the I.R.B.,' recollected Daniel Branniff.[20]

Established alongside the Volunteers were branches of the Cumann na mBan or League of Women. At least two branches of the organization existed in Britain in 1914: one in Liverpool and the other in London.[21] There already existed a scouting movement for boys, Na Fianna Éireann. In Britain, Glasgow seems to have been the only place to boast Fianna 'sluaigh' or troops in earnest, founded by members of the Gaelic League and the IRB, though there is mention of an attempt to establish a troop in London in 1914.[22] In 1903, Belfast-born Joseph Robinson arrived in Glasgow. A veteran of Na Fianna in his native city, Robinson soon immersed himself in the organization on Clydeside. In 1911, Séamus Reader, born in Glasgow but of Irish descent, joined the Willie Nelson troop, named after a 16 year-old County Antrim boy executed in the 1798 rebellion. As he had been a patrol leader in Baden Powell's scouts, Reader quickly became a scout leader in the troop and later became captain. In the autumn of 1914, there were two or three troops in Glasgow, with a combined membership of 150. As well as attending Gaelic League classes, Na Fianna organized camping trips in Ireland. Fianna officers such as Joe Robinson, Alec Carmichael and James McGallogly were members of the IRB and Reader followed them into the Fenians in 1914. When the Volunteers were founded on Clydeside, they immediately signed up and Robinson soon became Secretary of the Regimental Committee.[23]

The Irish Volunteers' main activity was drill practice. '[W]e drilled in the crypt of the Church in Bermondsey – with just dummy guns', remembered London's Fintan Murphy.[24] In Glasgow, some Volunteers used miniature rifles, while a 'good number' had revolvers and automatics. Route marches

---

20 BMHWS 152, Arthur Agnew, pp. 1–2; BMHWS 335, Joseph Furlong, p. 3; BMHWS 272, Daniel Branniff, p. 1

21 *Irish Volunteer*, 3 Oct. 1914; BMHWS 945, Sorcha Nic Diarmada, p. 2

22 BMHWS 1108, Jeremiah O'Leary, p. 3; Marnie Hay, 'The Foundation and Development of Na Fianna Éireann, 1906–16', *IHS*, 36.141 (2008), pp. 53–71

23 BMHWS 627, Séamus Reader, pp. 1–5; BMHWS 244, John McGallogly, pp. 1–2; Séamus Robinson Statement, p. 58 (National Library of Ireland [NLI], Frank Gallagher Papers [FGP], MS 21,256); *Irish Volunteer*, 22 Aug., 12 Sept., 17 Oct. 1914

24 BMHWS 370, Fintan Murphy, p. 1

also took place.[25] However, some members got involved in a more clandestine activity: gunrunning, the smuggling of weapons to the Volunteers in Ireland. In July 1914, Arthur Lynch, MP for West Clare, addressed a meeting of the Volunteers in London. 'We have got the men – we must get the rifles – and we will get them', he said:

> We think of the days of '98 [i.e. 1798] with a thrill of enchantment, when arms poured into our country, and wish for such opportunities to-day … There is scope to-day for the smugglers of old, and some means will probably be found again for landing rifles on Irish shores.[26]

Lynch was sabre-rattling. Nevertheless, some Volunteers, especially those involved in the IRB, took him at his word. The Fenians had a long history of gunrunning in Britain. In the run-up to the 1867 rebellion, munitions were procured in London, Birmingham and Liverpool and then smuggled to Ireland.[27] As we have seen, on 11 February that year, English Fenians attempted to steal materiel from Chester Castle. However, the raid miscarried, and this played a significant role in the ultimate failure of the rebellion in Ireland the following month.[28] In the decades following 1867, IRB men in Britain continued to procure small amounts of weapons and send them to their comrades in Ireland in the hope that they would someday be used to fight for Irish independence.[29] In 1914, Séamus Reader, Na Fianna leader, Volunteer and Fenian, carried detonators to Ireland from Glasgow.[30] On one occasion, Joe and Matthew Furlong, Wexford-born IRB men and Volunteers in London, smuggled a rifle to the veteran Fenian Thomas Clarke in Dublin.[31] The 'chief purpose' of the capital's Cumann na mBan was 'to provide arms and also, of course, to collect money for the purchase of arms', remembered Sorcha McDermott. Along with Grace O'Sullivan and others, McDermott smuggled weapons to Dublin too.[32]

In October 1914, the Volunteer movement split. The previous month,

25 BMHWS 222, Daniel Branniff, p. 3
26 *Irish Volunteer*, 4 July 1914
27 Mark Ryan, *Fenian Memories* (Dublin: M.H. Gill & Son, 1945), p. 38
28 Takagami, 'Fenian Rising', pp. 340–62
29 Ryan, *Fenian Memories*, pp. 40, 47, 61; T.W. Moody, *Davitt and Irish Revolution 1846–82* (Oxford: Clarendon Press, 1984 edition), pp. 53–116
30 BMHWS 627, Séamus Reader, p. 4
31 BMHWS 335, Joseph Furlong, p. 3
32 BMHWS 945, Sorcha Nic Diarmada, pp. 2–3

in response to the outbreak of the Great War, John Redmond, leader of the IPP, had called on Irishmen to 'account themselves as men not only in Ireland itself but wherever the firing line extends'.[33] The IPP, perceiving the Volunteers as a threat to its hegemony in Irish nationalist politics, had gained control of the organization's provisional committee the previous June. Now, however, MacNeill and some other founding members rejected Redmond's call on Volunteers to serve in the British army. The IPP leader responded by establishing a new force, the National Volunteers. The ranks of the Irish Volunteers emptied as its members swelled the new organization.[34] Only about 100 men remained in Glasgow's Sarsfield Regiment, one-quarter of its peak membership. Joe Robinson reacted by re-organizing the men into one unit, 'A' Company. He became the Officer in Command (O/C) and Séamus Reader a lieutenant.[35] On Merseyside, only about 50 stayed in the Irish Volunteers, though the membership increased subsequently. They were organized into two companies: 'A' Company in Bootle, with Corkman Seán Hennessey as O/C, later succeeded by Thomas Craven, and 'B' Company in Duke Street, Liverpool, under the County Louth-born Frank Thornton.[36] The organization in London also experienced a large decline in membership, with some following Redmond's advice to join the British army and others simply losing interest in the cause. The remnants consolidated by amalgamating the North and South London companies.[37] By October 1915, Patrick Pearse, the Volunteers' director of organization, was reduced to finding solace in the continued existence of the Volunteers in London and Liverpool, implying that the organization had virtually ceased to exist elsewhere in Britain.[38]

Those that remained continued to apply themselves to drill practice and gunrunning. In a basement on Liverpool's Scotland Road, the Duke Street Volunteers learned the use of revolvers and miniature rifles.[39] They

33 *Irish Times* [*IT*], 21 Sept. 1914
34 O'Rahilly, *Secret History*, pp. 8–9, 17
35 BMHWS 627, Séamus Reader, p. 5
36 BMHWS 510, Frank Thornton, p. 3; Thomas Craven, 'A Brief Personal Narrative of The Six Days Defence of the Irish Republic, Easter, 1916, by a Captain of the Dublin Division, I.R.A.' (MAI, Bureau of Military History Contemporaneous Document [BMHCD] 141/4, Thomas Craven, p. 4)
37 Joe Good, *Enchanted by Dreams: Journal of a Revolutionary*, ed. Maurice Good (Dingle: Brandon, 1996), pp. 10, 12; BMHWS 335, Joseph Furlong, p. 3; BMHWS 1108, Jeremiah O'Leary, p. 9
38 *Irish Volunteer*, 16 Oct. 1915
39 BMHWS 510, Frank Thornton, p. 5

also acquired 'fairly substantial quantities' of munitions through purchase and theft. IRB men Neil Kerr Senior, Stephen Lanigan, Patrick Lively and Hugh Early Senior smuggled the weapons to Ireland, sometimes hidden in coffins.[40] 'The Glasgow Volunteers had many in their ranks who were working in munition [sic] factories and shipyards', remembered Séamus Robinson, younger brother of Joe Robinson. 'These men brought out information and keys, and the Fianna under Joe Robinson and Seamus Reader constantly raided for explosives.'[41] Collieries near Bothwell, Hamilton and Uddingston were just some of the places raided, and the explosives were then smuggled across the Irish Sea.[42] Just before Christmas 1915, Margaret Skinnider, a member of the Glasgow Cumann na mBan, travelled to Dublin with bomb detonators hidden in her hat.[43] However, in January 1916, after returning from a trip to Belfast and Dublin, where they delivered a 'large' quantity of gelignite and detonators, Joe Robinson and Séamus Reader were arrested in Glasgow and interned.[44] Meanwhile, on the instructions of Michael (known as 'The') O'Rahilly – the Volunteers' director of armaments – the London Volunteers also acquired munitions. Seán McGrath purchased revolvers and ammunition in Birmingham, while his comrades bought and stole rifles. These munitions were then smuggled to Dublin in luggage.[45]

II

Sometime in early 1916, the leaders of the Volunteer companies in Britain received notice to bring their men to Ireland. 'We knew there was going to be a fight', remembered Liverpudlian Arthur Agnew, 'but we did not know when or what it was going to be like.'[46] The fact that Volunteers in Britain were liable to be conscripted into the British army also proved a motivation in their relocation. A large contingent from Merseyside moved to Dublin and took up residence in a derelict mill at Larkfield, the Kimmage estate of Count George Plunkett, a scholar who flirted with separatist politics. Volunteers from

40   BMHWS 510, Frank Thornton, pp. 3–4
41   Séamus Robinson Statement, p. 60 (FGP, MS 21,265)
42   BMHWS 244, John McGallogly, pp. 1–2
43   Margaret Skinnider, *Doing My Bit for Ireland* (New York: The Century Co., 1917), p. 9
44   BMHWS 627, Séamus Reader, pp. 9–12; BMHWS 1767, Séamus Reader
45   Seán McGrath to Art O'Brien, 22 Mar. 1935 (NLI, Art Ó Bríain Papers [AÓBP], MS 8461/25); BMHWS 1108, Jeremiah O'Leary, p. 10
46   BMHWS 152, Arthur Agnew, p. 3

London, Manchester and Glasgow, the majority born in Britain, arrived soon afterwards to join the 'Kimmage Garrison', as it became known.[47]

It is difficult to be precise as to the number of men who lodged at Larkfield. Frank Thornton states that the Liverpool contingent alone numbered 127, but this seems an exaggeration.[48] Séamus Robinson says that there were 'fifty or sixty' members in total, though he then goes on to give the names of 91 men, 84 of whom were from units in Britain; of these, 38 were from Liverpool, 19 from Glasgow, 16 from London and 11 from Manchester.[49] London Volunteer Joseph Good estimates the garrison membership to have peaked at 64 or 84, with Liverpool being the place of origin of the greatest number and Manchester the smallest.[50] Arthur Agnew says that at its height the membership was 54.[51] It would seem, therefore, that the garrison numbered around 60.

The garrison was 'the first standing Army of the Irish Republic', noted Londoner Ernie Nunan.[52] When not drilling and parading, the Volunteers manufactured ammunition and explosives, including shot gun cartridges, lead pellets and hand grenades.[53] In early April, Patrick Pearse told the Kimmage men that 'they would be going into action in a short time, [and] that by a special honour the garrison would become a Company of the Headquarters Battalion of the High Command Staff of the Volunteers'.[54]

---

47 BMHWS 510, Frank Thornton, p. 3; Good, *Enchanted*, pp. 15–17

48 BMHWS 510, Frank Thornton, p. 3

49 BMHWS 156, Séamus Robinson, pp. 9–12. I have revised Robinson's list as it contains some errors: (1) Arthur Agnew was a member of the Liverpool Volunteers, not the Manchester Volunteers (BMHWS 152, Arthur Agnew, p. 1). (2) David Begley, Frank Kelly and John 'Blimey' O'Connor were members of the London Volunteers, not the Manchester Volunteers (Ernie Nunan, 'The Irish Volunteers in London', *An tÓglach*, 1.12 [1966], p. 4). (3) Joseph and Matthew Furlong were members of the London Volunteers, not the Manchester Volunteers. Moreover, they fought in the Rising as part of the Dublin Volunteers rather than the Kimmage Garrison (BMHWS 335, Joseph Furlong, p. 4). (4) Joseph Vize was not a member of the London Volunteers or any other Volunteer unit in Britain prior to the Rising and he fought in the rebellion in same unit as the Furlongs (BMHWS 335, Joseph Furlong, p. 4).

50 BMHWS 388, Joseph Good, p. 4

51 BMHWS 152, Arthur Agnew, p. 2

52 Ernie Nunan, 'The Kimmage Garrison, 1916', *An tÓglach*, 2.2 (1966), p. 9

53 BMHWS 388, Joseph Good, pp. 2–4

54 BMHWS 388, Joseph Good, p. 5; see generally Ann Matthews, *The Kimmage Garrison, 1916: Making Bill-Can Bombs in Larkfield* (Dublin: Four Courts Press, 2010)

At around 10.30 am on Easter Monday, 24 April 1916, about 60 men armed with rifles, shotguns, handguns, pikes, crowbars and pickaxes marched from Larkfield to Harold's Cross, where they took the tram to Dublin city centre. Outside Liberty Hall, they assembled with other Volunteer units and members of the Irish Citizen Army (ICA), a small workers' militia set up by the socialist republican James Connolly.[55] The rebellion began at 12 noon when a contingent of rebels, headed by Connolly, commandeered the General Post Office (GPO) on Sackville Street (now O'Connell Street). 'All civilians and Post Office staff were evacuated', remembered Ernie Nunan's brother Seán, 'and we proceeded to barricade all windows.'[56]

The majority of the men in the Kimmage Garrison spent the rebellion in the area around Sackville Street, including Londoners Seán McGrath, Liam O'Kelly, Jeremiah O'Leary, Joe Good and Ernie and Seán Nunan, Liverpool's Frank Thornton, Arthur Agnew, Patrick Caldwell and Tom Craven, and Glasgow's Séamus Robinson, John McGallogly, Seán Hegarty, Brian McMullan and Cormac Turner.[57] Members of the Liverpool Cumann na mBan saw service in this area too, working as cooks and despatch-carriers.[58] Some Kimmage men went into action elsewhere, including Londoners David O'Leary and Eamon O'Tierney, who fought in St Stephen's Green with the ICA and in North King Street and the Four Courts respectively.[59] Glasgow's Margaret Skinnider, who did not stay at Larkfield, also attached herself to the ICA contingent at St Stephen's Green and worked as a scout, despatch-carrier and sniper. 'Every shot we fired was a declaration to the world that Ireland, a small country but large in our hearts, was demanding her independence', she later wrote. However, on Easter Wednesday she was wounded by sniper fire while attempting to set fire to a building on Harcourt Street and was incapacitated for the remainder of the revolt.[60] Meanwhile, some veterans

---

55 BMHWS 638, Patrick Caldwell, p. 5; BMHWS 156, Séamus Robinson, p. 14

56 BMHWS 1744, Seán Nunan, p. 2

57 BMHWS 1108, Jeremiah O'Leary pp. 16–18; BMHWS 1744, Seán Nunan, pp. 2–5; Good, *Enchanted*, pp. 23–76; BMHWS 510, Frank Thornton, pp. 13–22; BMHWS 638, Patrick Caldwell, pp. 5–11; BMHWS 152, Arthur Agnew, pp. 3–7; Craven, 'A Brief Personal Narrative' (BMHCD 141/4, Tom Craven); BMHWS 156, Séamus Robinson, pp. 14–23; BMHWS 244, John McGallogly, pp. 6–9; Eamonn Mooney to Joseph Robinson, n.d. but *c.* 1938 (ECP, P61/13[24–29])

58 BMHWS 655, Nora Thornton, pp. 1–2

59 BMHWS 1108, Jeremiah O'Leary pp. 15, 18–19

60 Skinnider, *Doing My Bit*, pp. 102–49 (quote pp. 137–38)

of the London Volunteers fought with Dublin units. Joe and Matt Furlong served with 'D' Company, 2nd Battalion, Dublin Brigade in Jacob's biscuit factory.[61] Fintan Murphy went into battle at the GPO with the 4th Battalion's 'E' Company.[62] Michael Collins, a staff officer attached to Volunteer General Headquarters (GHQ), fought in the post office too.[63]

Members of the Kimmage Garrison were among those killed and injured in the fighting. Four London Volunteers lost their lives: Seán Hurley, Patrick Shortis, Michael Mulvihill and Jimmy Kingston. (A fifth, Donal Sheehan, had drowned in a car accident near Killorglin, County Kerry, three days before the rebellion commenced. This happened during a journey to Caherciveen to steal a radio set from the Atlantic Wireless College which was to be used to make contact with the German vessels carrying munitions to the rebels.)[64] Meanwhile, Glasgow's Charles Carrigan was killed on Moore Street.[65]

A significant number of Scottish IRB men failed to mobilize for the rebellion. They later claimed that they had not received any notice. The 'first intimation of the Rising the [Motherwell IRB] members had was the report in the papers of Easter Tuesday morning', averred Patrick Mills. Responsibility was later ascribed to John Mulholland, Scottish representative on the IRB Supreme Council, and he and a few other senior Scottish Fenians were forced to resign their positions. In the autumn of 1914, Mulholland had apparently opposed plans for a rebellion during the Great War. Despite the Supreme Council approving the idea, he remained opposed and kept the Scottish IRB in ignorance of the preparations. Sometime in April 1916, a meeting of Motherwell and Wishaw IRB circles took place, with Mulholland in attendance. One account of the meeting states that Mulholland failed to provide definite details about the timing of the rebellion, resulting in no one from the three circles taking part in the Rising. Another account argues that Mulholland arrived so late to the meeting, held on 22 April, that the news that the rebellion was scheduled to begin the following day left the attendees with insufficient time to travel to Ireland.[66] The Scottish Fenians and Volunteers who

---

61 BMHWS 335, Joseph Furlong, pp. 6–8

62 BMHWS 370, Fintan Murphy, pp. 1, 6–11

63 Peter Hart, *Mick: The Real Michael Collins* (London: Macmillan, 2005), pp. 87, 91–95

64 Nunan, 'The Irish Volunteers in London', p. 4; BMHWS 110, Denis Daly, pp. 2–3

65 Eamonn Mooney to Joseph Robinson, n.d. but *c.* 1938 (ECP, P61/13[24–29])

66 BMHWS 777, Patrick Mills, p. 1; BMHWS 828, James Byrne, pp. 1–2; Máirtín

did participate in the rebellion seem to have come mainly from Glasgow.[67] Even here, however, a measure of confusion was evident. With the Rising expected to take place throughout Ireland, preparations were made for the Scots to be posted to Belfast. Glasgow IRB man Dan Branniff was despatched to the city and charged with ensuring that the Volunteers were sent to County Tyrone to join up with their Belfast comrades. The Glasgow men, however, opted to travel to Dublin instead. Failing to link-up with the Scottish contingent, the Belfast Volunteers retreated.[68] The confusion surrounding Scotland's involvement in the 1916 Rising was to be a source of controversy in subsequent years.[69]

In the aftermath of the rebellion, about 3,200 people were arrested throughout Ireland; 2,519 of these were then transported to Britain for internment in prisons in Glasgow, Knutsford (in Cheshire), Lewes (East Sussex), Stafford (Staffordshire), Wakefield (Yorkshire), Wandsworth (London) and Woking (Surrey). Another 141 people, found guilty by courts-martial of involvement in the revolt, were also imprisoned in England, at Dartmoor (in Devon), Portland (Dorset), Aylesbury (Buckinghamshire) and Wormwood Scrubs (London).[70] General Sir John Maxwell, the commander of British forces in Ireland, insisted for security reasons that the internees be prevented from communicating with each other. Initially, therefore, the men in all the prisons were confined to their cells for all but 30 minutes a day. In Knutsford, Joe Good found the regime trying, due to the lack of reading material, the 'constant gnawing of hunger' and 'the loss of the sky'. After three weeks, however, the government relaxed the regime, allowing the internees to associate with each other, smoke tobacco and receive parcels from outside.[71] In May, it was decided to transfer the internees to Frongoch internment camp, near Bala in north Wales. A ramshackle set-up, Frongoch consisted of two sections: a north camp, comprising 27 huts, and a south camp, a former

Seán Ó Catháin, 'A Land Beyond the Sea: Irish and Scottish Republicans in Dublin, 1916', in Ruan O'Donnell (ed.), *The Impact of the 1916 Rising: Among the Nations* (Dublin: Irish Academic Press, 2008), pp. 38–39

67 BMHWS 244, John McGallogly, pp. 2–3

68 BMHWS 222, Daniel Branniff, pp. 3–7; Robert Lynch, *The Northern IRA and the Early Years of Partition 1920–1922* (Dublin: Irish Academic Press, 2006), pp. 13–14

69 Correspondence between Joe Vize and Michael Collins, 20 Feb., 3 Mar. 1920 (UCDA, Richard Mulcahy Papers [RMP], P7/A/11)

70 Seán McConville, *Irish Political Prisoners, 1848–1922: Theatres of War* (London: Routledge, 2003), pp. 451, 455, 509

71 Good, *Enchanted*, pp. 82–83; McConville, *Irish Political Prisoners*, pp. 455–56

whiskey distillery building divided into five large dormitories. Conditions in both sections were spartan: the north camp was muddy and cold, while the south camp was infested by vermin and lacked proper ventilation. In charge was Colonel Frederick Heygate-Lambert, and his peremptoriness quickly led to a constant state of virtual warfare between the inmates and the authorities. The men reacted to Heygate-Lambert's petty edicts and disproportionate punishments with provocative behaviour and defiance, thus goading the bumptious commandant to greater heights of officiousness. '[I]t would all have been so easy and simple if they had left us our rags of uniforms and called us prisoners of war,' reflected Joe Good, 'but they regarded us as a mob and, by God, they got a mob.'[72]

Protests against Heygate-Lambert's officiousness and conditions in the camp became embroiled with those against conscription. Under the Military Service Act 1916, Irishmen aged between 18 and 41, unmarried and ordinarily resident in Britain on or after 15 August 1915 became liable to compulsory military service. (Ireland was excluded from conscription at the time.) The Kimmage men had anticipated this during the Rising when Patrick Pearse agreed to the surrender of the rebel forces on 29 April. 'They said that if they were in danger of being shot as deserters [from the British armed forces] they would prefer to be killed still fighting the British army', remembered Good. 'Many others believed that they would be conscripted if captured, and anything would be preferable to that.' However, senior IRB man Seán McDermott persuaded them against continuing the fight, arguing that the worst punishment they were likely to receive would be a few years in prison. 'The thing that you must do, all of you, *is to survive!*' he said. The rebel leaders would be executed, he continued, but they would die happy in the knowledge 'that there are still plenty of you around who will finish the job'.[73] The authorities calculated that about sixty-something Frongoch internees were liable under the Act. However, as they had not matched the names with the faces, roll-calls were held at which the men were ordered to identify themselves. Seán Nunan remembered the absurdity of the situation: 'It struck me as rather naive for the British to expect us to join their forces after having taken up arms against them only a few weeks previously – but that's the way the official mind works!'[74] In solidarity with their British-born colleagues and to frustrate the authorities' attempt to identify the 'deserters', many of the

---

72 McConville, *Irish Political Prisoners*, pp. 466–70; Good, *Enchanted*, p. 99
73 Good, *Enchanted*, pp. 66–69; original emphasis
74 BMHWS 1744, Seán Nunan, p. 6

Irish-born rebels joined their comrades in refusing to answer to their names at roll-call. '[I]f some of them [i.e. the British-born internees] are allowed to be taken away [i.e. conscripted] without an unmistakeable protest', explained Michael Collins in a letter smuggled out of Frongoch, 'a stupid Government Department may consider it an equally simple matter to foist conscription on our countrymen at home.'[75] From 2–4 November, 201 men staged a hunger-strike in protest at the threat of conscription. At roll-call on 7 November, Heygate-Lambert responded by flooding the camp with armed soldiers, telling the internees' hut leaders that 'he meant to have discipline in the camp even though the place contained nothing but dead bodies'. When 342 persisted in refusing to acknowledge their names, they were sent to the south camp and their privileges were cut off, while 15 hut leaders were court-martialled.[76]

Such solidarity was not always evident, however. A rumour began to circulate in the camp that the surrender of the rebels in Moore Street had been orchestrated by members of the Kimmage Garrison. Hurt and indignant, Joe Good responded by asking his fellow Kimmage men to identify themselves to the camp authorities 'rather than adhere to a body of men who could believe such gossip and deliberate lies'. However, fearful of a split in the ranks of the internees, Michael Collins assembled the men together to scotch the rumour. Collins 'spoke with passion of the particular sacrifice of the English-born Irishmen during the Rising', remembered Good,

> and put stress on our being chosen to fight in direct defence of the Commander-in-Chief [Patrick Pearse]. He was particularly emphatic when he came to their 'special courage and fierce reluctance to surrender at all!'

Collins' speech quashed the rumour.[77]

The internees' war against conscription continued at the Advisory Committee, a body established by the government and to which the rebels could make representations against their detention without trial. Their innocence soon established, many of the men were quickly released. Most of the dedicated rebels, however, refused to appeal. The authorities, therefore, decided to force the remaining men to appear before the committee. When

75 Michael Collins to Art O'Brien, 13 Oct. 1916 (AÓBP, MS 8429/17)
76 Collins to O'Brien, 19 Nov. 1916 (AÓBP, MS 8429/17); McConville, *Irish Political Prisoners*, p. 472
77 Good, *Enchanted*, pp. 91–93

he came before it, Joe Good stuck to the internees' 'agreed tactics' and refused to divulge his identity and place of birth.[78]

Despite the internees' silence, however, the authorities succeeded in identifying about 50 of the sixty-odd 'deserters'.[79] After eventually identifying himself at roll-call on 1 September, Hugh Thornton, a member of the Liverpool Volunteers and brother of O/C Frank Thornton, was removed from Frongoch and sent to Wrexham where Michael Collins believed he was 'serving a sentence of two years [sic] hard labour for refusing to serve'.[80] On 2 November, Fintan Murphy was recognized and court-martialled too, though his lodging an appeal delayed the commencement of his prison sentence.[81] Soon afterwards, the King brothers, John, George and Patrick, members of the Liverpool Volunteers, were also identified. Proceedings, however, were apparently only brought against the latter two. Refusing to serve in the forces, George and Patrick were court-martialled. Found guilty of desertion, they were incarcerated in Stafford military prison. When they declined to perform drill there, they were court-martialled a second time.[82] Ernie and Seán Nunan were placed into military custody after appearing before the Advisory Committee. Passed medically fit for service, Seán Nunan was assigned to the 6th Battalion City of London Regiment. Convicted of desertion, he was sentenced to 112 days' imprisonment with hard labour. Due to good behaviour, his sentence was reduced. However, his prison experience did not blunt his defiant attitude and a second court-martial on 11 November sentenced him to nine months plus the 54 days that he had been remitted from his first sentence. In Devizes military prison, he remained unbowed:

> I would get an order, e.g., to fall-in on parade, and, on refusing, would be brought before the Colonel for a Regimental Court Martial, and get X days confinement, with bread and water.
> When that period was up I would get another order which would

---

78 Good, *Enchanted*, pp. 82, 90

79 McConville, *Irish Political Prisoners*, p. 497

80 Michael Collins to Art O'Brien, 13 Oct. 1916 (AÓBP, MS 8429/17); BMHWS 510, Frank Thornton, p. 9; BMHWS 1043, Joseph Lawless, p. 201

81 George Gavan Duffy to the Judge Advocate General, 15 Nov. 1916; minutes of meeting of Irish National Aid and Volunteer Dependents Fund [INAVDF] Sub-Committee, 3 Jan. 1917 (AÓBP, MS 8445/24); BMHWS 1043, Joseph Lawless, p. 202

82 Duffy to Sir Reginald Herbert Brade, 30 Dec. 1916 (AÓBP, MS 8445/24)

get another refusal, followed by another Court Martial and another period of bread and water.[83]

Meanwhile, at his first court-martial Ernie Nunan, who was enrolled in the 11th County of London Regiment, was sentenced to six months' hard labour, while at his second he received two years'.[84]

Thomas O'Donoghue, a Dubliner who had been a member of the London Volunteers but fought in the ICA during the Rising, was released from Frongoch in July 1916, only to be re-arrested in Ireland soon afterwards. Returned to London for court-martial, he was sentenced to 112 days' hard labour, followed by 21 months' hard labour.[85] Proceedings were also brought against Liverpool's Neil Kerr Junior.[86]

In February 1917, however, perhaps wearying of the internees' dogged defiance, the government announced that 'men who have been imprisoned or interned in consequence of having been concerned in the Irish rebellion are not to be enlisted in the British Army'.[87] Hugh Thornton had been discharged from the army two months previously, seemingly on humanitarian grounds.[88] Now the Kings, Nunans and Thomas O'Donoghue were set free, while proceedings were dropped against Fintan Murphy, Neil Kerr Junior and the other internees.[89] The whole episode proved that 'all the might of the Empire

---

83 BMHWS 1744, Seán Nunan, pp. 5–8; Michael Collins to Art O'Brien, 13 Oct., 19 Nov.; Duffy to the Judge Advocate General, 15 Nov.; Duffy to Brade, 15 Dec. 1916; minutes of meeting of INAVDF Sub-Committee, 17 Jan. 1917 (AÓBP, MS 8429/17, 8445/24); John (i.e. Seán) Nunan's Record of Service, 22 June 1916 (The National Archives, Kew [TNA], War Office file [WO], 364 piece 2729)

84 Minutes of meeting of INAVDF Sub-Committee, 3 Jan.; Duffy to O'Brien, 5 Feb. 1917 (AÓBP, MS 8445/24); Ernest Nunan's Record of Service, 29 July 1916 (WO, 364 piece 2729)

85 Michael Collins to O'Brien, 13 Oct.; Duffy to the Judge Advocate General, 15 Nov. 1916; Duffy to O'Brien, 16 Jan. 1917 (AÓBP, MS 8429/17, 8443/4, 8445/24); BMHWS 1687, Harry Colley, p. 30

86 Minutes of meeting of INAVDF Sub-Committee, 3 Jan. 1917 (AÓBP, MS 8445/24)

87 *Hansard 5* (*Commons*), xc, col. 628 (14 Feb. 1917): Sir Ian MacPherson

88 J. Barwick Thompson to George Gavan Duffy, 16 Dec. 1916; minutes of meeting of INAVDF Sub-Committee, 3 Jan. 1917 (AÓBP, MS 8445/24)

89 Minutes of meeting of INAVDF Sub-Committee, 14 Feb.; Art O'Brien to J.A. Smyth, 7 Mar. 1917 (AÓBP, MS 8445/24, 8443/4)

could not break an Irishman's spirit or will', declared London Volunteer John 'Blimey' O'Connor.[90]

Victories such as these buoyed the Frongoch men and helped to forge an *espirit de corps* that was to prove important for the future. 'I am fully convinced that Frongoch made our whole organization into what it eventually reached', Kerry Volunteer William Mullins later argued:

> The comradeship that developed in Frongoch and the knowledge we got of each other from different parts of the country, the military aspect of things and being brought into close contact with men whom we used only hear about previous to that was a binding force for the future. John Bull made an awful blunder when he put us all together there.[91]

Glasgow's John McGallogly was one of the 141 people sent to penal servitude in British prisons. Court-martialled after the Rising, he was originally sentenced to death but this was immediately commuted to ten years in prison. After some months in Portland prison, McGallogly was transferred to Lewes prison. Lacking leadership, the Irish prisoners in Portland obeyed the rules without protest. McGallogly recalled that at Lewes, however, they were more defiant and 'gradually began to break down prison discipline'. In May 1917, Eamon de Valera, the prisoners' leader and one of the most senior surviving commanders of the Easter Rising, led the men in a protest in pursuit of prisoner of war status. The inmates refused to obey orders given by prison officials and declined to do any work except for their own cooking and laundry. In response, they were confined to their cells. 'When we commenced breaking the windows with the table or stool', remembered McGallogly, 'everything in the cell was taken from us, and we took our food sitting on the floor.' After almost two weeks, some of the prisoners were transferred to other prisons, where they continued the protest. Soon afterwards, however, they were released.[92]

Organizations sprang up in Ireland and Britain to alleviate the plight of the prisoners and the internees as well as their families. Republicans in London established the Irish National Relief Fund (INRF) while the rebellion was still ongoing in Dublin, and soon branches of the organization had been

---

90 John T. ('Blimey') O'Connor, 'Some Have Come from a Land Beyond the Sea', *An tÓglach*, 1.12 (1966), p. 6

91 BMHWS 801, William Mullins, p. 1

92 BMHWS 244, John McGallogly, pp. 10–16

founded in Manchester and Glasgow.[93] Meanwhile, three committees vied for supremacy on Merseyside, including one apparently established by the city's remaining Volunteers.[94] Each week, the Manchester Committee supplied the men in Frongoch with cocoa, sugar, rice, fresh fruit and sultanas, the Glasgow organization sent 'periodicals and magazines, together with any occasional requests for books, games, materials for study etc', and the London outfit provided the inmates with cash and also supplied financial aid to the other committees.[95] In November 1916, the London Committee become a branch of the Dublin-based Irish National Aid and Volunteer Dependents' Fund (INAVDF).[96] The London organization fund-raised at least £846 0s. 4d. in 1916, £405 18s. 6d. in 1917 and £345 13s. 2d. in 1918.[97]

III

In December 1916, the internees were released unconditionally from Frongoch. Those who returned to Ireland received a rapturous welcome. The government's perceived heavy-handed reaction to the Rising had led the populous to revise its initial hostility to the rebellion. The Volunteers returning home to Britain received a similar reception. Séamus Reader recalls that he and Joe Robinson 'got a tremendous welcome from the I.R.B. and Republicans' when they returned to Glasgow from internment in Reading Jail. 'I was invited to house parties and ceilis [i.e. dances] all over Scotland,' he remembered.[98] Despite the party being uninvolved, the authorities labelled the Rising a 'Sinn Féin rebellion'. Therefore, when the insurrection underwent retrospective sanctification among the mass of the people, Arthur Griffith's Sinn Féin party experienced an explosion in popularity and it proceeded to win a number of by-elections in Ireland. Joe McGuinness won South Longford for the party, despite being incarcerated in Lewes prison. A few months later, and after his release from Lewes, de Valera triumphed in East Clare. Soon afterwards,

---

93 Art O'Brien to 'A chailín uasail', 8 June; O'Brien to Fred Allen, 10 July 1916 (NLI, Irish National Aid and Volunteer Dependents' Fund Papers [INAVDFP], MS 24,324/1)

94 O'Brien to Allen, 1, 8 Nov., 28 Dec. 1916 (INAVDFP, MS 24,324/1; AÓBP, MS 8435/31)

95 O'Brien to the Honorary Secretary of the INAVDF, 15 Oct. 1916 (AÓBP, MS 8435/31); O'Brien to Allen, 1 Nov. 1916 (INAVDFP, MS 24,324/1)

96 O'Brien to Allen, 22 Nov. 1916 (AÓBP, MS 8435/31)

97 INRF Ledger, entries for 10 May 1916–23 Dec. 1918 (AÓBP, MS 8458/6)

98 BMHWS 933, Séamus Reader, p. 1

William Cosgrave, a veteran of Frongoch, tasted victory in Kilkenny City. At its convention in October 1917, de Valera was elected president of Sinn Féin. In order to prevent a split between moderates such as Griffith and radicals such as de Valera, the party's aim became, rather confusingly, the achievement of a republic with the proviso that the Irish people would subsequently be allowed to choose between a republic and a monarchy.[99]

As well as involving themselves in Sinn Féin, many of the former internees and prisoners soon set to work re-organizing the Volunteers and the IRB in Ireland. At the Volunteer convention in October 1917, held the day after the Sinn Féin conference, de Valera was elected president, while Michael Collins was appointed director of organization and Richard Mulcahy director of training. The following March, the Volunteers established a GHQ staff. Mulcahy became chief of staff (C/S) and Collins adjutant general. By then Collins was also the treasurer of the IRB Supreme Council as well as its south of England representative.[100] Fintan Murphy associated with Collins and sometime in 1918 or 1919 served as Volunteer Quartermaster General (QMG) for a time.[101] Frank Thornton returned to County Louth and began organizing the Volunteers there as well as in south Down and south Armagh. Hugh Thornton and Séamus Robinson set about similar work in west Cork and south Tipperary respectively.[102]

Re-organization was also under way in Britain. In January 1917, Joe Robinson re-established 'A' Company on Clydeside. However, disgusted with the failure of the city's Fenians to participate in the Easter Rising in respectable numbers, he resigned from the IRB. Three local veterans of the rebellion – Alec Carmichael, Bernard Friel and Paddy Moran – quit in sympathy with him. Séamus Reader, however, disagreed with Robinson's actions and proceeded to establish companies around IRB circles. John Carney, O/C of the Sarsfield Regiment in 1914, became O/C 'C' Company.

99　Laffan, *Resurrection*, pp. 96–103, 106–13, 118

100　Hart, *Mick*, pp. 157, 172; Charles Townshend, *Easter 1916: The Irish Rebellion* (London: Allen Lane, 2005), p. 334; BMHWS 4, Diarmuid Lynch, p. 9; BMHWS 183, Liam Gaynor, p. 15

101　Fintan Murphy interview (UCDA, Ernie O'Malley Notebooks [EO'MN], P17b/107); BMHWS 865, John Plunkett, p. 16

102　BMHWS 510, Frank Thornton, pp. 43, 54; BMHWS 1603, Michael Crowley, p. 2; BMHWS 1721, Séamus Robinson, pp. 22–23; BMHWS 1474, Eamon O'Dwyer, pp. 2–25; Liam Deasy, *Towards Ireland Free: The West Cork Brigade in the War of Independence 1917–21*, ed. John E. Chisholm (Cork: Royal Carbery Books, 1973), pp. 14, 20, 58

In 1918, after Carmichael succeeded Robinson as O/C 'A' Company, IRB men Seán McGarry and Frank Kearney arrived from Dublin and persuaded him to end the feud between his company and the Fenians.[103]

The only other place in Britain to boast a Volunteer organization between the Rising and the outbreak of the war of independence seems to have been Liverpool. As we have seen, in 1916 it appears that Volunteers in the city established an organization to cater for the Easter Rising internees and prisoners. In 1917 or 1918, a number of people, including Thomas Kerr, brother of Neil Kerr Junior, son of gunrunner Neil Kerr Senior and an Easter Week veteran in his own right, re-established a company in earnest.[104]

The IRB in Britain was also re-organized. Joe Gleeson and Patrick McCormack became the representatives of northern England and Scotland respectively on the Supreme Council. Both, however, were soon succeeded: Gleeson by Neil Kerr Senior and McCormack by Dan Branniff.[105] The south of England, as we have seen, was represented by Michael Collins.

In 1917, a new Cumann na mBan branch was founded in Glasgow, named after Anne Devlin, an associate of Robert Emmet. Having talked her way out of custody at the end of the Easter rebellion, Margaret Skinnider returned to Glasgow, became captain of the branch and helped to instruct the members in gun practice, first aid, signalling and collecting money for the purchase of arms by the Volunteers of 'A' Company, to which the branch was attached.[106]

As well as re-establishing the Volunteers, the Cumann na mBan and the Fenians, the Easter veterans soon resumed their gunrunning activities. In 1917, Micheal Collins instructed Seán McGrath to recommence gun-smuggling in London. Every fortnight, McGrath travelled to Birmingham with Manchester Fenian Tom McCormack to purchase munitions. According to McCormack, the average purchase on each occasion was 'about 70 guns and corresponding ammunition'. The duo would then travel to Liverpool and hide the armaments in the house of IRB man William Geraghty, wherefrom they were smuggled to Ireland.[107] In Glasgow, similar activity was organized by Joe Robinson. Michael O'Carroll was one of those who worked under Robinson. Born in Dublin in

103 BMHWS 933, Séamus Reader, pp. 2–4; *Irish Volunteer*, 22 Aug. 1914
104 BMHWS 824, Paddy Daly, p. 1
105 BMHWS 367, Joseph Gleeson, p. 11; BMHWS 339, Patrick McCormack, pp. 10–11
106 Anonymous memoirs, 1972–73 (ECP, P61/4[65–69]); Skinnider, *Doing My Bit*, pp. 177–96
107 Seán McGrath interview (EO'MN, P17b/100); Tom McCormack to the Military

1901, he too had been 'out' in 1916. O'Carroll spent his weekends acquiring explosives in the mining districts. 'Each week I would return to Glasgow with a package weighing up to seven or ten pounds in gelignite', he remembered. He made frequent trips to Dublin with parcels of explosives. 'There was always a consignment for the Citizen Army', he recalled, 'and always one for the Volunteers.' However, on 25 November 1917, O'Carroll and another boy named Seán Nelson, aged 15, were arrested in Belfast while journeying to Dublin with a box containing gelignite, blasting powder and detonators. Implicated, Robinson pleaded guilty to possessing munitions in Glasgow for an unlawful purpose and to removing explosives to Ireland without a permit. However, he emphasized that his crime was political in nature. 'He and his party claimed the right of Irishmen to determine for themselves the form of government for Ireland', Robinson's counsel explained. The judge, however, dismissed this excuse and sentenced Robinson to ten years in prison.[108]

Gunrunning continued under Alec Carmichael's direction. On 12 March 1918, however, the authorities struck again. Bernard Friel was apprehended aboard a Glasgow steamer bound for Dublin with 18.5 lbs (8.4 kg) of compressed gunpowder and 3.5 oz (0.1 kg) of gunpowder. According to his counsel, Friel's view 'and the view of his party was that, his opponents [i.e. the Ulster Unionists] having armed themselves with munitions and guns, his party was entitled to take means to protect themselves'. He was sentenced to three years' imprisonment.[109] Volunteer John McGallogly remembers that Carmichael kept the details regarding gunrunning activities quite secret. Frustrated by this secrecy, a Volunteer named Michael O'Callaghan set up his own gunrunning operation. However, on 12 July 1918, he was arrested with seven others as they waited at Ardrossan harbour to board a boat to Belfast with suitcases full of munitions. Five were found guilty. O'Callaghan was sentenced to three years' imprisonment, while the four others received sentences of three or six months.[110]

In March 1918, the German army launched a massive offensive on

Service Pensions Board [MSPB], 22 Oct. 1942 (UCDA, Ernie O'Malley Letters [EO'ML], P17a/154)

108 John Cooney, 'The Irish Republican Brotherhood in Scotland: The Untold Stories of Andrew Fagen and Michael O'Carroll', in T.M. Devine and J.F. McMillan (eds), *Celebrating Columba: Irish-Scottish Connections 597–1997* (Edinburgh: John Donald, 1999), pp. 141–42; *Glasgow Herald*, 2 Feb. 1918

109 *Glasgow Herald*, 1 May 1918; all metric figures are rounded to the first decimal place

110 BMHWS 244, John McGallogly, pp. 17–18; *The Times* [*TT*], 11 Sept. 1918

the Western front. The British government judged the situation sufficiently grave to warrant the introduction of a new military service bill, the terms of which included a provision for the extension of conscription to Ireland. The prospect of coercing Irishmen into the British army aroused immediate and fierce opposition in Ireland, and for a period of five weeks the country was convulsed as all section of society – political parties, trade unions and the Catholic Church – came together to agitate against the government's policy. About 12 members of the Glasgow Volunteers, including John McGallogly, travelled to Ireland to aid the resistance. After about three weeks, when 'it seemed unlikely that conscription would be tried', McGallogly returned to Glasgow.[111]

As well as Volunteers in Britain travelling to Ireland, however, the conscription crisis led Volunteer headquarters in Dublin to send some men to London on a special mission: to assassinate the British cabinet before the Order in Council ratifying Irish conscription could be signed. Cathal Brugha, head of the Volunteer Executive, led the 11-man squad. Amongst them were veterans of the London Volunteers, Joe Good and Matt Furlong, as well as Tom Craven from Liverpool. It was 'a very dangerous job', Brugha told his men, 'and I have not much hope of you getting back from it [alive]'. While Brugha lived with his daughter in a large house near Regent's Park, the men lodged with sympathizers such as the Nunans.[112] Brugha conducted a lottery for the allocation of a cabinet minister to each man and discussed the operation with them individually. Good was assigned Andrew Bonar Law, the Chancellor of the Exchequer. 'I had nothing against Bonar Law except that he was fond of matinees', remembered Good:

> We were to be often at the theatre together and I got to know his habits well, though he, of course, was unaware of the existence of his escort. And I was many times close to Bonar Law's heels as he walked from Downing Street to the Houses of Parliament. It seemed to me that he was singularly incautious, considering all that he had done and proposed to do in Ireland. It seemed that he had no sixth sense. He could not have had the experience of living dangerously. It's surprising how safe public figures in England felt then.[113]

111   Laffan, *Resurrection*, pp. 128–42; BMHWS 244, John McGallogly, p. 18
112   Good, *Enchanted*, pp. 130–36; BMHWS 369, William Whelan, pp. 5–6
113   Good, *Enchanted*, p. 137

On two occasions, William Whelan accompanied Brugha to the House of Commons for reconnaissance. In the public gallery, as the session went on below, Brugha informed Whelan that his role in the assassinations was to repulse any attempted interference while he, Brugha, fired onto the floor of the chamber. During the second visit, with Matt Furlong, the trio were armed with handguns.[114]

As the men waited impatiently for Dublin to authorize the assassinations, they passed their time shadowing their quarry, walking aimlessly around the city, reading and rowing. Mobilization orders were often issued, only to be cancelled at the last moment. Final authorization never came. Faced with overwhelming opposition to its plans and fearful that the predominantly Catholic police force would prove unreliable in enforcing conscription, the government changed tack, calling instead for the voluntary enrolment of 50,000 Irish recruits by the following September. By then, however, the German offensive had dissipated. After three frustrating months in London, Brugha and his men returned home.[115]

In the December 1918 general election, Sinn Féin annihilated the IPP, winning 73 of the 105 Irish seats at Westminster. A significant number of the victorious candidates were in prison once again, having been among the 73 people arrested the previous May on suspicion of involvement in a 'German Plot' to mount a rebellion in Ireland akin to the Easter Rising of two years previously. 63 of these, including de Valera, were deported to Britain and interned in Gloucester and Usk prisons.[116] Nevertheless, on 21 January 1919, in fulfilment of their election pledge to abstain from Westminster, those Sinn Féin MPs – or Teachtaí Dála [TDs] in Irish – who were still at liberty met in Dublin and founded an Irish parliament, Dáil Éireann. English rule in Ireland was 'based upon force and fraud and maintained by military occupation against the declared will of the people', asserted the Dáil's 'Declaration of Independence'. Ratifying the establishment of the republic declared at Easter 1916, the declaration went on to state that 'foreign government' was 'an invasion of our national right' to independence and demanded 'the evacuation of our country by the English Garrison'. This was the only way that the 'state of war' which existed between Ireland and

---

114 Good, *Enchanted*, pp. 138–39; BMHWS 369, William Whelan, p. 7

115 Good, *Enchanted*, pp. 137–42; BMHWS 369, William Whelan, p. 7; Eunan O'Halpin, *The Decline of the Union: British Government in Ireland 1892–1920* (Dublin: Gill & Macmillan, 1987), p. 159

116 *TT*, 20 May 1918; McConville, *Irish Political Prisoners*, pp. 624–26

England could be terminated, added the 'Message to the Free Nations of the World'.[117] Coincidently, that same day, two Royal Irish Constabulary (RIC) men were killed while escorting a cart of gelignite near the village of Soloheadbeg by members of the South Tipperary Brigade of the Volunteers, headed by Séamus Robinson. The war of independence had begun.[118]

117   Dáil Éireann Debates, vol. 1, cols. 16, 20 (21 Jan. 1919), accessed at http://historical-debates.oireachtas.ie/D/DT/D.F.O.191901210008.html and http://historical-debates.oireachtas.ie/D/DT/D.F.O.191901210013.html, on 13 Mar. 2012; translated from the Irish

118   BMHWS 1721, Séamus Robinson, pp. 25–28

CHAPTER 1

'On a Solid Footing': Organizing Republicanism in Britain, January 1919–July 1921

I

Following their release in late 1916 and 1917, the Easter Rising veterans were intent on continuing militant opposition to British rule in Ireland. They therefore quickly set to work re-organizing the republican movement. However, the war of independence had almost broken out in January 1919 before similarly serious efforts began in Britain. IRA GHQ 'fully realise the necessity of making provision in countries outside Ireland', declared Michael Collins, commending recruitment activities in Scotland.[1] This chapter examines the means by which republicanism established itself in Britain and the fortunes it enjoyed there. Through an in-depth discussion of organizing efforts in Glasgow, section II provides an insight into the creation of Volunteers units in Britain. Section III introduces the main people involved in republican affairs. Section IV describes the means by which IRA units were founded and the roles of the IRB, the Cumann na mBan and Na Fianna Éireann. Sections V, VI and VII discuss the milieu in which these organizations existed, the type of people who became members and their motivations for joining. Section VIII focuses on how IRA units were run, while section IX concludes.

II

Sometime around 21 January 1919, Joseph Vize, the newly appointed Irish Volunteer organizer in Scotland, wrote to Michael Collins from Glasgow. There, he had found two Volunteer companies riven with animosities. 'A' Company, he reported, was 'composed of a good number of undesirables and

---

1 Michael Collins to Joe Vize, 1 Oct. 1919 (RMP, P7/A/11)

mixed citizen army & vol[unteer]s. trying to run the whole movement here'. It thus constituted a dangerous impediment to the development of the Volunteer organization in Scotland's biggest city. 'B' Company, however, proved more promising even though its members were somewhat disordered and frustrated by 'little differences between themselves'. He wrote to Collins:

> I am happy to report that I have re-organized B. [Company] by taking on myself the authority to issue a special mobilization order in the name of headquarters (Dublin [sic] and hope I have not done wrong in doing so,) and settled all little differences between them, had a meeting of about 60 members together, formed the company in sections, appointed N.C.O.s [i.e. Non-Commissioned Officers], and made same with Captains & Lieut[enant]s. into a committee for to carry on the company's work, the said committee are all of right type, so that B. Co[mpany]. is now on a solid footing …

With 'B' Company members 'greatly pleased' with the re-organization, Vize proposed to attempt reconciliation and amalgamation with its rival company. Failing that, he intended to call a meeting of all Glasgow Volunteers with the aim of re-organizing the whole movement in the city, for 'there are quite a number of willing men here to help in that work and very anxious that something like it will take place at once'.[2]

The following month, however, with 'A' Company still proving recalcitrant, Vize was forced to undertake a complete re-organization of the Volunteers in Glasgow and its surrounding districts on the basis of a seven-point system drawn up by himself. The first and most important point stated that the 'Volunteer movement in Glasgow [is] to be controlled by Dublin Headquarters, who will issue <u>all</u> orders for the management of same'. The re-constitution of the movement according to the system was proceeding 'to the entire satisfaction of all here', reported a pleased Vize.[3] 'A' Company still proved an irritant, however. By early September, Vize was contemplating suspending the whole company for not 'running straight'.[4] Specifically, he complained that Liam Gribbon, who had apparently succeeded Alec Carmichael as Company O/C, repeatedly ignored orders. Also, the

---

2 Vize to Collins, n.d., but marked 'Recd 5.2.19' (RMP, P7/A/11)

3 'Outlines of my new system', part of missing letter, Vize to Collins, *c.* Feb./ Mar. 1919 (RMP, P7/A/11); original emphasis

4 Vize to Collins, 5 Sept. 1919 (RMP, P7/A/11)

company refused to give Vize access to its accounts. Vize was confident that suspension of the unit would stop the rot in Glasgow, at the expense of losing only about 20 men.[5]

Over three months later, however, Vize had yet to receive authorization from Dublin to suspend 'A' Company. The fact that Gribbon was planning a fund-raising event, entitled 'A Night of Surprises', made Vize anxious that immediate action be taken for 'nobody will see a penny out of it'. Vize, however, had already taken steps to frustrate 'A' Company's plans. As well as moving to deprive it of the usual venue for holding such events, he intended to enlist the services of a local priest and other Volunteer leaders to expose Gribbon and his associates as fraudsters. Anticipating a challenge to his authority, Vize beseeched Collins to immediately send him his official appointment as organiser for Scotland, as well as an order for the disbandment of 'A' Company. Without such ammunition, he warned, 'Gribbon will get hold of Edinburgh and we will be powerless to stop him'.[6] Taking the warning to heart, Collins duly sent authorization for the suspension of 'A' Company, on the grounds of failing to conform to the battalion requirements of the Volunteers' *General Scheme of Organisation*.[7] Vize fails to record whether 'A' Company was actually suspended. In any event, the company's 'Night of Surprises' went ahead at the end of March 1920, only to be disrupted by a group of Volunteers.[8] A week later, Vize tried to have Gribbon stripped of his job as distribution agent for an Irish newspaper in Scotland.[9]

III

Joe Vize was just one person in the ranks of Irish republicanism in Britain in the period 1919–21. His influence straddled the military and the civilian sides of the republican movement. Vize was a military man involved in organizing units of the Volunteers (or IRA as they were becoming known), but in order to do this effectively it was necessary for him to engage with the civilian side of the movement too. Peter Hart states that it was the IRA's 'mobilization of deep communal and personal loyalties' that gave it its strength.[10] This was

5 Vize to Collins, 24 Oct. 1919 (RMP, P7/A/11)
6 Vize to Collins, 7 Feb. 1920 (RMP, P7/A/11); original emphasis
7 Collins to Vize, 14 Feb. 1920 (RMP, P7/A/11)
8 Vize to Collins, 15 Feb., 26 Mar. 1920 (RMP, P7/A/11)
9 Vize to Collins, n.d., but *c.* 7 Apr. 1920 (RMP, P7/A/11)
10 Peter Hart, 'The Thompson Submachine Gun in Ireland Revisited', in Hart, *IRA at War*, p. 193

especially true of the republican movement in Britain, where Vize in Glasgow and others like him in London, Liverpool, Manchester and elsewhere gathered about themselves small groups of like-minded people.

Vize was born in Wexford town in 1881, the son of a bank manager. He trained as an engineer. In 1905, when Seán McDermott founded an IRB circle in the town, Vize joined with his friends Joe and Matt Furlong, future members of the London Volunteers. After a period spent working in Scotland, he served in the merchant marine during the First World War. In December 1915, while travelling from Melbourne to England, his ship, the *Clan Davidson*, was torpedoed off Malta by a German u-boat. Four months later, Vize fought alongside the Furlong brothers in the Easter Rising, seeing action at Jacob's factory and the College of Surgeons.[11]

In Scotland, Vize surrounded himself with a number of lieutenants. Séamus Reader, O/C 'B' Company, continued his work organizing new companies. In early 1920, he was elected O/C Scottish Brigade, but the following October he became brigade intelligence officer (I/O) and director of organization.[12] John Carney, O/C of 'C' Company in 1918, became O/C 1st Battalion. An American army veteran now working as a barber, he succeeded Reader as O/C Scottish Brigade in the autumn of 1920.[13] Patrick Clinton, a recent arrival from Dublin, took command of 2nd Battalion.[14] Hugh McGorry, Seán O'Mara and Michael O'Callaghan served as brigade adjutant at different periods during the war of independence (or 'the war' as I shall henceforth call it).[15] Meanwhile, Andrew Fagan was brigade quartermaster (QM) from 1920 onwards.[16]

In Liverpool, activities centred on the Kerr family and Steve Lanigan. Born in County Armagh in around 1862, Neil Kerr Senior moved to

11 Clipping from *Wicklow People*, 10 Jan. 1959 (Eamonn Mooney Papers [EMP], file 1/A/72; papers in the possession of Cathleen Knowles-McGuirk); BMHWS 335, Joseph Furlong, pp. 1, 4, 5–8

12 BMHWS 933, Séamus Reader, pp. 4–5; Joe Vize to Michael Collins, 28 May 1919 (RMP, P7/A/11)

13 Membership roll, 'C' Company, 1st Battalion, Scottish Brigade IRA, n.d., but *c.* 1940s/1950s (EMP, 3/C/13); John Carney to C/S, 22 Feb. 1922 (NLI, Seán O'Mahoney Papers [SO'MP], MS 24,474); *Glasgow Herald*, 15, 16 Aug. 1921

14 BMHWS 933, Séamus Reader, p. 4

15 Membership roll, 'B' Company, 1st Battalion; membership roll, 'E' Company, 1st Battalion, Scottish Brigade IRA (EMP, 3/C/13)

16 Membership roll, 'C' Company, 2nd Battalion, Scottish Brigade IRA (EMP, 3/C/13)

Liverpool with his wife in 1887. A foreman in the Cunard Shipping Company, he was Head Centre of the Liverpool IRB and north of England representative on the Supreme Council. He was an experienced gunrunner. His three sons Tom, John and Neil Junior participated in the Easter Rising, and Tom had helped to re-establish the Volunteers in the city in 1917 or 1918. Lanigan, a senior Fenian and 'something of an agnostic', worked as a customs official.[17]

In London, the major figures were Reginald Dunne, Seán McGrath, Sam Maguire and Art O'Brien. Dunne, O/C London IRA, was born in the capital in 1898, the son of a former British army bandmaster. In 1916, he joined the Irish Guards. Fighting in the Great War, he rose to the rank of corporal. However, after suffering a bad wound to his knee, he was discharged. He then began training as a school-teacher.[18] IRB man Seán McGrath, as noted, had joined the London Volunteers in 1914 and helped to smuggle weapons to Ireland. He fought in the Easter Rising and was interned at Frongoch. During the war, the railway clerk served as I/O of the London Volunteers and was heavily involved in gunrunning. Elizabeth MacGinley, then known as Lily Brennan, was an associate of McGrath and described him as 'a wonderful worker and organiser'.[19] Sam Maguire was born into a Protestant family in County Cork in 1877. He worked for many years in the central sorting office of the London postal service. A prominent figure in the London GAA, captaining the city's teams in the All-Ireland football finals in 1901 and 1903, Maguire also joined the IRB. He later initiated fellow post office employee Michael Collins into the organization. During the war, Maguire served as head of the London Fenians. MacGinley remembered him as 'a wonderful man' who devoted almost all his time to the cause of Irish freedom.[20] Arthur ('Art') O'Brien was born in London in 1872 to an Irish father who served in the British army and an English mother and he studied civil and electrical

17   Memorandum on Neil Kerr Senior, 3 Mar. 1925 (MAI, Department of Defence Administration File [DDAF], A/13648); BMHWS 814, Patrick Daly, pp. 5, 14–15, 17–18, 25

18   Martin Wallace, 'Reginald Dunn [sic] and Joseph O'Sullivan', *An tÓglach*, 1.7 (1963), p. 1

19   Seán McGrath interview (EO'MN, P17b/100); McGrath to Art O'Brien, 22 Mar. 1935 (AÓBP, MS 8461/25); *TT*, 29 Jan. 1919; BMHWS 860, Elizabeth MacGinley, p. 3

20   Marie Coleman, 'Maguire, Sam', in James McGuire and James Quinn (eds), *Dictionary of Irish Biography* [*DIB*] (Cambridge: Cambridge University Press, 2009), accessed at http://dib.cambridge.org on 1 Dec. 2009; BMHWS 860, Elizabeth MacGinley, p. 2

engineering. He then worked as an engineer in England, France and Spain. In 1898, he joined the London Gaelic League and became its president in 1914. He also enrolled in the Irish Volunteers and the IRB. He was one of the prime movers in the establishment of the INRF and worked as one of its honorary secretaries. Around the same time, he became president of the Sinn Féin organization in England and Wales. In December 1918, he agreed to a request from a delegation of recently elected Sinn Féin TDs, including Michael Collins, to assume the full-time position of Irish representative in Britain. In that role, O'Brien sought to publicize Ireland's right to freedom by disseminating propaganda. In support of this, he helped found the ISDL in March 1919, and went on to serve as its vice-president. With American president Woodrow Wilson recommending national self-determination as the means of avoiding a recurrence of the world war which had wrought so much destruction over the previous four years, the ISDL hoped to secure the application of the principle to Ireland.[21] O'Brien developed contacts with fellow anti-colonial radicals, such as Burmese and Egyptian nationalists and the Indian-born communist Shapurji Saklatvala, as well as representatives of the officially anti-imperialist Soviet Union.[22] MacGinley worked as O'Brien's secretary for a period in 1920–21. She remembered him as a very difficult person, due to his prickly personality.[23]

In Manchester, the comparable figures were Patrick O'Donoghue, William ('Liam') McMahon, Matthias ('Matt') Lawless and later Glasgow's John McGallogly. O'Donoghue worked as a grocer and was a founding member and secretary of the Richardson Street Sinn Féin Club. In 1919, he became IRA O/C Manchester. Born in 1878, Limerick man McMahon, who worked 'in the bacon trade', was a senior member of the Manchester IRB, involved in the purchasing and smuggling of weapons to Ireland. After the Easter Rising, he worked with the INAVDF. During the war, he served as I/O

21   Keiko Inoue, 'O'Brien, Arthur Patrick Donovan', in *DIB*, accessed at http://dib. cambridge.org on 1 Dec. 2009; autobiographical sketch (AÓBP, MS 8461/31); Erez Manela, *The Wilsonian Moment: Self-Determination and the International Origins of Anti-Colonial Nationalism* (Oxford: Oxford University Press, 2007)

22   E.g. Art O'Brien to Michael Collins, 2 Oct. 1920 (AÓBP, MS 8426/11); Shapurji Saklatvala to O'Brien, 30 Dec. 1919 (AÓBP, MS 8433/46); O'Brien to Collins, 29 July 1920 (DÉ, 2/322); Mike Squires, 'Saklatvala, Shapurji (1874–1936)', in H.C.G. Matthew and Brian Harrison (eds), *Oxford Dictionary of National Biography* [*ODNB*] (Oxford: Oxford University Press, 2004), online edition, accessed at http://www.oxforddnb.com/view/article/35909, on 14 June 2010

23   BMHWS 860, Elizabeth MacGinley, p. 4

in the Manchester IRA. McGallogly was born near Bothwell, in Lanarkshire, Scotland, in 1898. He and his older brother James joined the IRB, Sinn Féin and the Irish Volunteers and were involved in gunrunning activities. Veterans of the Easter Rising, they moved to Manchester in 1920 and became involved in activities there.[24]

Few of these figures remained in charge of the republican movement in Britain for the whole course of the war. In early 1919, Seán McGrath was sent to prison for six months for illegal possession of munitions. Dennis Kelleher, a 20 year-old civil servant at the Board of Education, became more involved in matters in London when McGrath was arrested once again in February 1921, this time in connection with the IRA's campaign of violence in Britain.[25] In July 1920, Scotland's Joe Vize returned to Ireland to assume the new position of Volunteer director of munitions. (In the event, he was arrested in Dublin in mid-October and interned.)[26] GHQ then sent Joe Furlong to Scotland. In early 1921, Furlong was in turn succeeded by D.P. Walsh, a Tipperary man who had escaped with five other Volunteers from Strangeways prison in October 1919 with the help of the Manchester IRA. A few months later, Walsh and John Carney, O/C Scottish Brigade, were arrested and put on trial in connection with the killing of a policeman in Glasgow.[27] Arrests in the aftermath of the IRA's arson attack on Merseyside warehouses and timber yards in November 1920 led to the internment and imprisonment of the Kerrs and Steve Lanigan. The leadership was then assumed by Paddy Daly, a native of County Offaly who had immigrated to Liverpool in 1918.[28] In April 1921, O/C Manchester Paddy O'Donoghue was arrested by police investigating arson attacks in the city centre. In his absence, McGallogly became O/C 'A' Company.

24 BMHWS 847, Patrick O'Donoghue, pp. 5–6; BMHWS 274, Liam McMahon, pp. 1–3; BMHWS 244, John McGallogly, pp. 1–18; Paddy Daly interview (EO'MN, P17b/136); Paddy O'Donoghue to Michael Collins, 29 Sept. 1920 (RMP, P7/A/10); Paddy Daly to Collins, 22 June 1921 (RMP, P7/A/6); *Manchester Guardian [MG]*, 6 Apr. 1921

25 Seán McGrath interview (EO'MN, P17b/100); Collins to Art O'Brien, 1 Mar. 1921 (DÉ, 2/328); Denis Kelleher to O'Brien, 18 Feb. 1922 (AÓBP, MS 8424/13)

26 Captain 'P' Section to Commandant, Military Barracks, 9 Apr. 1921, enclosing list of prisoners (MAI, Michael Collins Papers [MCP], A/0619/73)

27 BMHWS 776, Joseph Booker, p. 5; BMHWS 777, Patrick Mills, pp. 5–6; BMHWS 828, James Byrne, pp. 6–7; *Glasgow Herald*, 23 July 1921; see Chapter 3

28 BMHWS 814, Patrick Daly, pp. 1, 21–22

However, he too was soon arrested.[29] Despite all these arrests and changes, the Volunteers in Britain remained relatively intact as an organization. The injunction from Michael Collins that 'the enemy must not be allowed to break up our organisation, no matter whom he takes' was therefore obeyed.[30]

For republicans in Britain, Collins was the most important figure in the leadership in Dublin. Born in County Cork in 1890, he worked in London from the age of 15 to 25, first in the post office savings bank, then in a stockbroker's and finally in a bank. It was while in the English capital that he became associated with advanced nationalist politics. He joined the IRB, the Irish Volunteers, Sinn Féin, the Gaelic League and the GAA. He met many of the people who would lead the republican movement in Britain during the war, including Sam Maguire, Seán McGrath, Art O'Brien and Neil Kerr Senior. In 1916, Collins was one of a number of London Volunteers who travelled to Ireland and fought in the Rising. After being released from Frongoch at Christmas 1916, he set about helping to re-establish the republican movement and rose rapidly through its ranks. During the war, he occupied a number of offices. On the military side, he was, at one time or another, director of the IRA's departments of organization and intelligence, as well being adjutant-general. He was also south of England representative, treasurer and then president of the IRB. On the political side, he served on the executive of Sinn Féin, represented the constituency of South Cork in Dáil Éireann, and was minister for finance in the Dáil's underground government.[31] Collins did not confine his activities to these offices, however, for his zeal and energy lead him to involve himself in virtually every aspect of the republican movement that interested him. As Fintan Murphy observed, 'Collins [,] whatever job he held [,] was running the show. Collins would tell Dick Mulcahy [,] who was C/S [,] what he was to do'.[32] It was mainly in his capacity as a senior IRB member that Collins involved himself in the activities of republicans in Britain.

As the war progressed, other members of IRA GHQ staff became associated with republican activity across the Irish Sea. Roderick ('Rory')

29 BMHWS 847, Patrick O'Donoghue, pp. 13–15; BMHWS 244, John McGallogly, p. 20

30 Michael Collins, 'Memo to Liverpool', 9 Dec. 1920 (RMP, P7/A/3)

31 Hart, *Mick*, pp. 3, 23, 26, 61, 157, 185, 188, 203; Peter Hart, 'Collins, Michael (1890–1922)', in *ODNB*, online edition, Jan. 2008, accessed at http://www.oxforddnb.com/view/article/32506 on 15 July 2010; McGrath to O'Brien, 22 Mar. 1935 (AÓBP, MS 8461/25); Piaras Béaslaí, *Michael Collins and the Making of a New Ireland* (2 vols, London: G.G. Harrap & Co., 1926), i, p. 217

32 Fintan Murphy interview (EO'MN, P17b/109)

O'Connor was appointed O/C Britain in August 1920. Born in Dublin in 1883, he qualified as an engineer and spent four years working on the Canadian railways before returning to Ireland. A militant nationalist, his engineering expertise led to his being placed in charge of instructing the Kimmage Volunteers in bomb-making prior to the Easter Rising. Imprisoned for his involvement in the rebellion, O'Connor later became involved in Sinn Féin. In March 1918, upon the establishment of GHQ, he was appointed director of engineering.[33] In November 1920, following the arrest of Joe Vize, Liam Mellows became director of (munitions) purchases (D/P). He was born to Irish parents in Ashton-under-Lyme in Lancashire in 1892. His father was a soldier in the British army. Raised in counties Cork and Dublin, Mellows joined Na Fianna Éireann in 1911 and later became a full-time organizer for the movement. He also joined the IRB and the Irish Volunteers and during the 1916 Rising he led the Volunteers in Galway, one of the few places outside of Dublin to see action. Avoiding the subsequent police dragnet, Mellows escaped to New York. There, as well as being involved in gunrunning activity, he was associated with Eamon de Valera's American tour of 1919–20, which attempted to raise support for Irish self-determination.[34] Both O'Connor and Mellows and their staffs visited Britain on a regular basis in 1920–21. Nevertheless, Collins remained an important figure for republicans there throughout the war.

IV

Compared to the Irish Volunteers in Ireland, the re-organization of the IRA in Britain in the years following the Easter Rising was somewhat delayed. Whereas reformation efforts in Ireland were well under way in 1918, due to the threat of conscription, on the other side of the Irish Sea such activities did not commence in earnest until the following year.[35] Across Britain itself, there was variation in the timing and pace of re-organization work. In Scotland, GHQ appointed Joe Vize to take charge in early 1919. In England and Wales, however, organization seems to have been dependent on the initiative of people on the spot.

---

33 Lawrence William White, 'O'Connor, Roderick ('Rory')', in *DIB*, accessed at http://dib.cambridge.org on 1 Dec. 2009
34 Marie Coleman and William Murphy, 'Mellows, William Joseph ('Liam')', in *DIB*, accessed at http://dib.cambridge.org on 1 Dec. 2009
35 Michael Hopkinson, *The Irish War of Independence* (Dublin: Gill & Macmillan, 2004), pp. 16–17

When Vize began his re-organization work in Scotland, the aims of the Irish Volunteers, essentially the same as those set out at the outfit's first convention in 1914, were:

1. To secure and maintain the rights and liberties common to all the people of Ireland.

2. To train, discipline and equip for this purpose an Irish Volunteer Force.

3. To unite, in the service of Ireland, Irishmen of every creed and of every party and class.[36]

Its organizational structure was also similar. The *General Scheme of Organisation* declared that the 'tactical unit' of the organization was the company. In theory, the company was to consist of four sections, each with a membership of between 19 and 25. The total membership of each company, therefore, would number between 76 and 100. Command was vested in the O/C or captain. He was to be assisted by a 1st and a 2nd lieutenant, an adjutant and a QM. The O/C possessed ultimate responsibility for every aspect of his company, including 'discipline, organisation, equipment, training and general efficiency'. He was to command the company in 'peace and war'. Both the 1st and 2nd lieutenants were responsible for the efficiency of their respective half-companies, composed of two sections each. The adjutant acted as an assistant to the O/C. He was to keep a register detailing attendance at parades and drill practice. In addition, he was charged with supervising general drill operations and the instruction of new recruits. The QM's task was to ensure the security and maintenance of the company's munitions and equipment, as well as their distribution and collection as required. He was also responsible for company funds, including the collection and recording of the weekly subscription from members. The next unit in the organizational hierarchy was the battalion, composed of between four and seven companies. Battalion officers included the commandant, vice-commandant, adjutant and QM. Three or more battalions constituted a brigade, which had its own commandant, vice-commandant, adjutant and QM.[37]

As well as using the *General Scheme* as a guide, Vize used his seven-point

---

36 Irish Volunteers, *General Scheme of Organisation* (MCP, A/0032A, Group 2, Item 2)

37 Irish Volunteers, *General Scheme of Organisation* (MCP, A/0032A, Group 2, Item 2)

system to aid his organizational efforts. This placed ultimate control of the Volunteers in the hands of GHQ in Dublin. GHQ was to arrange a programme of work for each company and in addition every company was to be inspected by a member of GHQ staff twice or three times a year. New companies were to be established through Sinn Féin clubs.[38]

However, a central feature of Vize's approach to organization work was missing from both the *General Scheme* and his own seven-point system, namely his reliance on the IRB. As he and his men moved about Scotland, from Motherwell to Mid Lanarkshire, Glasgow to Edinburgh, Vize organized new Volunteer companies around local IRB circles and swore the new officers into the organization. In Motherwell, for example, membership of the new company, initially numbering 40, was confined to the IRB. Subsequently, non-IRB men were permitted to join. Throughout, however, the company officers were always members of 'the Organisation', as the IRB was known to initiates.[39] Many Irish nationalists admired the Fenians for their indefatigable commitment to Irish freedom. While politics in late nineteenth- and early twentieth-century Ireland was dominated by the IPP's peaceful attempt to secure home rule, the IRB, though small in number, remained committed to the use of physical force to achieve complete freedom. For Michael O'Leary, a Kerry-born member of the Liverpool IRA during the war, the establishment of the Irish Volunteers in 1913 'not only fanned the dying embers of the Fenian fires' in Ireland and, by extension, amongst the Irish in Britain, 'but also 'resurrected the dormant spirit of freedom in the hearts' of Irishmen.[40]

As part of its re-organization in the aftermath of the Easter Rising, the IRB adopted a new constitution. Apart from minor changes in 1920, this document served the organization until its dissolution in 1924. The aim of the IRB was 'to establish and maintain a free and independent Republican Government in Ireland'. The means of achieving this was by 'force of arms'. Membership was open to every Irishman 'irrespective of class or creed, whose character for patriotism, truth, valour, sobriety and obedience to superior officers can bear scrutiny'.[41]

The basic unit of the IRB was the 'circle', led by a centre, a sub-centre and a treasurer. The circle was divided into sections of up to ten members each and

38 'Outlines of my new system', *c.* Feb./Mar. 1919 (RMP, P7/A/11); original emphasis

39 BMHWS 777, Patrick Mills, p. 2

40 BMHWS 797, Micheál Ó Laoghaire, pp. 3–4

41 IRB, *Constitution as Revised to Date 1920* (NLI, Florence O'Donoghue Papers [FO'DP], MS 31,233), p. 1

headed by a section leader. The organization's overall governing institution was the Supreme Council, a body which the constitution declared to be 'in fact, as well as by right, the sole Government of the Irish Republic'. Its enactments, therefore, were to be recognized as the laws of the Irish Republic until a republican government was established after Ireland had secured its freedom from Britain. (In 1920, the IRB recognized Dáil Éireann as the government of the Irish Republic.) Membership of the Supreme Council was to consist of 15 people, including three divisional centres from Britain, representing the south of England, the north of England and Scotland. Until the IRB's recognition of the Dáil in 1920, the president of the Supreme Council was 'in fact as well as by right, President of the Irish Republic'.[42] The tenure of Michael Collins as south of England representative may have extended into the war period. Who, if anyone, succeeded him in that position is not known. Until his arrest in November 1920, Neil Kerr Senior represented the north of England. He was succeeded by Paddy Daly. Scotland was represented by Dan Branniff.[43] No authoritative membership figures exist for the IRB in Ireland or Britain during the war. A total membership of around 2,000 has been suggested, though James Byrne estimated that there were around 600 Fenians in Scotland's Mid Lanarkshire area alone.[44]

Vize discovered that it was not always possible to ensure IRB control of newly founded Volunteer units. Sending Michael Collins the names and addresses of officers in four of Glasgow's five companies, he commented that most were 'of the right kind', that is to say Fenians. However, the fact that non-IRB members held such important positions shows the limits of his power to fashion the Volunteers to his liking and the importance of local politics. Their holding office 'for the present … cannot be avoided', he wrote, but '… steps will be taken when an opportunity presents itself to remedy this'.[45] Another obstacle to Vize's plans was the unexpected opposition the Volunteers encountered from the local Sinn Féin clubs. His system had simply assumed that new Volunteer companies would be established through such clubs. Now,

42 IRB, *Constitution as Revised to Date 1920* (FO'DP, MS 31,233), pp. 2–3, 6, addenda

43 BMHWS 814, Patrick Daly, p. 32; BMHWS 272, Daniel Branniff, p. 2

44 John O'Beirne-Ranelagh, 'The Irish Republican Brotherhood in the Revolutionary Period, 1879–1923', in D.G. Boyce (ed.), *The Revolution in Ireland, 1879–1923* (Dublin: Gill & Macmillan, 1988), p. 144; Joseph M. Curran, 'The Decline and Fall of the IRB', *Éire-Ireland*, 10.1 (1975), p. 16; BMHWS 828, James Byrne, p. 2

45 Joe Vize to Michael Collins, 28 May 1919; 'Outlines of my new system', *c.* Feb./Mar. 1919 (RMP, P7/A/11)

however, Vize condemned the club members as 'a rotten lot', 'good only for singing and dancing', and asked Collins to intervene immediately to rectify the situation.[46]

In England, the re-organization of the Volunteers seems to have been a more informal affair than in Scotland. No organizer was sent there by GHQ. At the start of the war, the only place in Britain besides Glasgow to boast a Volunteer company was Liverpool. Tom Craven, O/C of one of the Liverpool companies before the Easter Rising, became commander once again. However, it was May 1919 before the company applied for affiliation with GHQ.[47]

The establishment of the Volunteers in Manchester occurred in the aftermath of the successful rescue from Lincoln prison on 3 February 1919 of Eamon de Valera, president of Sinn Féin and the Volunteers, Seán Milroy, Sinn Féin's director of elections, and Seán McGarry, an IRB man. The operation saw Paddy O'Donoghue, Liam McMahon and some fellow nationalists aid Michael Collins and others in planning and executing the jail-break, arranging accommodation for the fugitive prisoners and later accompanying them to Liverpool, whence they returned to Ireland as stowaways. (In October, under the command of Rory O'Connor, the Manchester men would repeat their success by helping six IRA men to escape from Strangeways prison.[48]) In one of only two references in its pages to the Volunteers in Britain, *An t-Óglác* ('The Volunteer'), the IRA's in-house journal, described the operation as 'a brilliant example of Volunteer courage, skill and efficiency'. At least one IRA company was established in the aftermath of the escape.[49] The following year saw William O'Keeffe and a few fellow Connacht natives found a company in nearby Salford. They subsequently made contact with O'Donoghue's organization.[50] Also in 1920, frustration with the English public's indifference to the war in Ireland led Tyneside ISDL officials Gilbert Barrington and Richard Purcell to begin organizing Volunteer companies. Only in November 1920,

---

46　Vize to Collins, 28 May, 6 June 1919; 'Outlines of my new system', *c.* Feb./ Mar. 1919 (RMP, P7/A/11)

47　Tom Craven to Collins, 25 May 1919 (RMP, P7/A/1[57])

48　See Chapter 6

49　BMHWS 274, Liam McMahon, pp. 4–9; BMHWS 847, Patrick O'Donoghue, pp. 1–5; John McGallogly to The Secretary, Military Service Pensions, 11 Oct. 1937, enclosing Patrick O'Donoghue's account of the Manchester IRA (MAI, Military Service Pensions Collection [MSPC], File RO/608); *An t-Óglác*, 27 Mar. 1919; for a detailed account of the escape, see The Earl of Longford and Thomas P. O'Neill, *Eamon de Valera* (London: Hutchinson, 1970), pp. 81–87

50　BMHWS 1678, William O'Keeffe, p. 7

after making cautious enquiries about how to link up with IRA units in other parts of Britain, did the Tyneside men come into contact with Volunteer officialdom, in the form of Manchester's Liam McMahon and O/C Britain Rory O'Connor.[51] 1920 also saw the establishment of the IRA in Birmingham by a number of Irishmen, formerly members of the Volunteers in Ireland, who were working on a housing scheme in West Bromwich. As with their Tyneside comrades, it was late 1920 before they made contact with GHQ. Prior to this, however, they did affiliate themselves with the Liverpool IRA.[52] The establishment of the Volunteers in the Sheffield area also seems to have been done on local initiative and without any reference to Dublin.[53] GHQ did have an input in the re-formation of the Volunteers in London in 1919. That summer, 'a number of young men met in East London and took the oath of allegiance to the Irish Republic', remembered Martin Wallace. A few months later, however, Seán McGrath complained about the existence of 'a great many wild young chaps' in the capital's IRA. In order to bring them under discipline, he asked Michael Collins for permission to appoint a committee to take charge of the Volunteers for a six-month period. Collins responded by recommending the appointment of an O/C and two lieutenants, as recommended by the *General Scheme of Organisation*. In March the following year, GHQ was informed that the London Volunteers were 'very anxious' to affiliate with Dublin.[54]

While organizing in Scotland, Joe Vize ensured that IRB circles and Sinn Féin clubs played a central role in the establishment of the Volunteers. In England, the picture is mixed. True, Paddy O'Donoghue in Manchester was president of a Sinn Féin club, but he does not mention club members taking a leading part in Volunteer affairs in the city. IRB man Liam McMahon says that all the officers in the IRA, apart from O'Donoghue, were appointed on his recommendation, perhaps indicating that he ensured that Fenians alone occupied such positions of leadership.[55] Newcastle's Gilbert Barrington states that he and five others were sworn into the IRB by Mick McEvoy, a member of Rory O'Connor's staff. This, however, seems to have taken place after the

51 BMHWS 773, Gilbert Barrington, pp. 1–2

52 BMHWS 922, James Cunningham, pp. 1, 5, 15

53 O/C Britain to C/S, 15 Oct. 1921 (RMP, P7/A/29[264–73])

54 Wallace, 'Reginald Dunn', p. 1; Seán McGrath to Michael Collins, c. Sept./Oct. 1919 (MCP, A/0457, Group VIII, Item 1); Collins to McGrath, 9 Oct. 1919 (AÓBP, MS 8429/11); Art O'Brien to Collins, 27 Mar. 1920 (DÉ, 2/321)

55 BMHWS 847, Patrick O'Donoghue, pp. 1, 5; BMHWS 274, Liam McMahon, p. 3

Tyneside men had already established Volunteer units. Previous to this, while the Fenian organization did exist in the district, it was 'virtually dead'.[56] The main exception to this informality seems to have been Liverpool. There, according to Michael O'Leary, IRB control of the re-established Volunteers was ensured from the beginning. He claims that the IRB moved to control the Council of Irish Societies, a body which co-ordinated the activities of Liverpool's various Irish organizations, such as the GAA and the Gaelic League. The societies were invited to affiliate with the council and appoint representatives thereon. Fenians within each society ensured that only fellow IRB men were appointed as representatives. 'In this way,' O'Leary boasts, 'we were able to solidly unite all Irish organisations and speak as one body.'[57]

The apotheosis of this informal Volunteer organizing in England was found in the operation of companies unaffiliated with GHQ. Affiliation was mainly about money. It involved the payment of an annual fee to Dublin, as well as a yearly levy of two shillings (2s.) per Volunteer.[58] In July 1920, Neil Kerr Senior complained that a new Volunteer unit had been established on Merseyside. The O/C, a man named Pevoy, claimed to have received authorization from Dublin, but Kerr had his doubts. '[T]his man is under suspicion and very much at present', he warned Michael Collins, asking him to make enquiries on the matter.[59] That same year, a company was formed in the Irish Club, Erskine Street, Hulme, with Charles Harding as O/C. They operated 'more or less "on their own" and were not working in harmony with the main [Manchester IRA] Company [under Paddy O'Donoghue]', Collins was informed.[60] Specifically, they engaged in unauthorized gunrunning to Dublin and Drogheda in County Louth and refused to share with O'Donoghue any details regarding the matter.[61] The response from Collins was tart:

> If they [i.e. the Erskine Street Company] don[']t want to act as organized disciplined Volunteers they are of course at liberty to do what they like, and if they do want to act as disciplined Volunteers, they must

56 Mary Barrington, *The Irish Independence Movement on Tyneside 1919–1921* (Dublin: Dun Laoghaire Genealogical Society, 1999), p. 9

57 BMHWS 797, Micheál Ó Laoghaire, pp. 18–23

58 Michael Collins to Tom Craven, 6 June 1919 (RMP, P7/A/1[56]); Collins to Seán McGrath, 9 Oct. 1919 (AÓBP, MS 8429/11)

59 Neil Kerr to Collins, n.d., but *c.* 6 July 1920 (RMP, P7/A/2)

60 Paddy Daly to Collins, 18 Apr. 1921 (RMP, P7/A/5)

61 Paddy O'Donoghue to Collins, 11 Nov., 3 Dec. 1920 (RMP, P7/A/10)

obey orders and get themselves into line with the requirements of the organisation.[62]

Members of the Erskine Street Company were later tried and sentenced for mounting an arson attack on Manchester city centre in April 1921.

As well as working with the IRB, the IRA also received assistance from the Cumann na mBan. According to its 1918 constitution, this organization was 'an independent body of Irishwomen pledged to work for the Irish Republic, by organising and training the women of Ireland to take their place by the side of those who are working and fighting for its recognition'. In pursuit of its aims – among others, to 'secure international recognition of the Irish Republic' and the evacuation of Ireland by the British 'Army of Occupation' – the Cumann na mBan aimed to develop 'military activities in conjunction with the I.R.A.'.[63] The organization's prescribed activities included administrating first aid, nursing wounded Volunteers, intelligence work, carrying despatches, hiding munitions, mounting prison rescues, commandeering supplies and disseminating propaganda.[64] Units of the Cumann na mBan were to be organized into areas corresponding with those of IRA battalions. The basic unit of organization was the branch or squad and every IRA company was to have a branch or squad attached to it, each headed by a captain, a secretary and a treasurer.[65]

As Joe Vize travelled around Scotland organizing the Volunteers in 1919–20, he also established branches of the women's auxiliary.[66] The membership in Scotland during the war has been estimated at 130. Figures for other parts of Britain are not known.[67] However, by October 1920, there were 21 branches in England and Scotland affiliated with headquarters in Dublin.[68] During the subsequent 12 months, headquarters received £201 in subscription fees from branches in Britain: £89 of this came from 11 branches in Scotland; Manchester paid £70; Liverpool and St Helens £22; and London £20. By

---

62 Collins to O'Donoghue, 26 Nov. 1920 (RMP, P7/A/10)

63 Constitution of Cumann na mBan, n.d., but *c.* 1918 (UCDA, Sighle Humphreys Papers [SHP], P106/1126[1–2])

64 Constitution of Cumann na mBan (SHP, P106/1126[1–2])

65 Cumann na mBan, *Scheme of Organisation*, n.d., but *c.* 1918 (SHP, P106/1126[3–4])

66 Joe Vize to Michael Collins, 15 Feb. 1920 (RMP, P7/A/11)

67 Calculations of company memberships, Scottish Brigade IRA (EMP, 3/C/13)

68 British army pamphlet, *The Irish Republican Army (From Captured Documents Only)* (1921), p. 11 (WO, 141/40)

way of comparison, £478 was paid by branches in Ireland, of which £69 10*s*. came from Connacht and £26 10*s*. from Ulster.[69] A list of branches that paid affiliation fees between November 1920 and October 1921 indicates that there were at least six branches of the organization in London. In Manchester, there were four branches. There seemed to be two branches in the Merseyside area, one in Birkenhead and the other in St Helens. Tyneside boasted three branches, one each in Newcastle-upon-Tyne, Jarrow and Chester-le-Street. Scotland possessed 16 branches, seven of which were in Glasgow.[70] Sorcha McDermott remembered that the main activity of the Cumann na mBan in London during the war was sending garments to those who suffered violence at the hands of Crown forces in Ireland. Individually, some members also smuggled weapons and money across the Irish Sea. In the capital, the organization went under the title of the Irish Ladies Distress Committee, as the members were fearful that they would be refused halls for social events if they used their Irish title.[71]

Finally, there was Na Fianna Éireann. Unfortunately, little information exists on this organization in Britain during the war. It seems to have been confined to Glasgow, and its membership there was later estimated at 40, though this figure included those who graduated to the IRA.[72]

As in the period before the Easter Rising, the motive behind most of this organization work – of Volunteer companies, IRB circles, Cumann na mBan branches and Na Fianna troops – in Scotland and England during 1919–21 was the desire to acquire munitions and smuggle them to Ireland. Vize told the officers of the 2nd Scottish Battalion that gunrunning was their main task, and he presumably told other Volunteer units the same.[73] A desire to help supply the IRA in Ireland with materiel also informed the establishment of Volunteer companies upon local initiative in Manchester, Tyneside, Birmingham and Sheffield.[74]

---

69 Subscription to GHQ Organization Funds, probably for 1920–21, n.d. (SHP, P106/1130[11–12]); the National Archives' Historical Currency Convertor estimates that £1 in 1920 would be worth £21 21*s*. in 2005: accessed at http://www.nationalarchives.gov.uk/currency/default0.asp#mid on 6 Nov. 2012

70 'List of those who have paid affiliation fees', Nov. 1920–Oct. 1921 (SHP, P106/1132[1–16])

71 BMHWS 945, Sorcha Nic Diarmada, pp. 5–6

72 'List of Fianna Boys in Glasgow 1908–1921 Willie Nelson Sluagh' (EMP, 3/B/4)

73 BMHWS 828, James Byrne, p. 1

74 BMHWS 847, Patrick O'Donoghue, pp. 1–6; BMHWS 773, Gilbert Barrington, pp. 1–2; BMHWS 922, James Cunningham, pp. 1, 5, 15

However, some Volunteers in Britain entertained the idea of travelling to Ireland to fight with the IRA there, just as some had done in 1916 and again in 1918. In 1920, Liverpool's John Pinkman, impatient with the lack of activity on Merseyside, was tempted to join to the IRA in Dublin. However, fearful of his mother's reaction to him quitting his engineering apprenticeship, he dismissed the idea.[75] Plans were drawn up for the Volunteers in Scotland to join their comrades across the Irish Sea for, in March 1920, an informant told the police that a meeting of the organization in Glasgow resolved that IRA units should travel to Ireland 'as originally arranged' once orders had been received from Dublin. The informant added that the Volunteers preferred service in Ireland to that in Scotland.[76] In 1921, Liverpool's Edward Brady asked Rory O'Connor for permission to transfer to Ireland. There, he believed, his skills would be put to better use. Moreover, the war in Ireland was much more exciting than that in England. O'Connor, however, refused the request. Brady possessed the skills necessary to successfully operate in Britain, he argued, and such skills were invaluable to the organization for 'no matter how efficient a gunman might be in Ireland, he was hopelessly at sea when it came to carry out operations in England'. Reluctantly, Brady accepted O'Connor's decision.[77]

The size of the IRA organization in Britain seems to have peaked sometime in the autumn of 1921. When O'Connor was appointed O/C Britain in August 1920, the Volunteers boasted eight companies in three areas: Liverpool, London and Manchester. By September the following year, that number had increased to 31 and the organization had spread to other areas of Britain. Liverpool – designated no. 1 area – hosted two companies, one in the city itself, the other in St Helens. The combined membership of the two companies was 100. (Small companies also existed in Birkenhead, Earlstown, Wigan and Preston for a time. These units do not appear in O'Connor's report, indicating perhaps that they had disappeared by the time of his visit.)[78] Manchester was named no. 2 area. The number of companies here was not recorded. Instead, it was noted that there were '[n]ominally 35 men'. However, Paddy O'Donoghue later stated

75 John Pinkman, *In the Legion of the Vanguard*, ed. Francis E. Maguire (Cork: Mercier Press, 1998), p. 25

76 'Report on Revolutionary Organisations in the United Kingdom' ['RROUK'], no. 48, 30 Mar. 1920 (TNA, Cabinet file [CAB] 24/103)

77 Brady, *Secret Service*, pp. 56–57

78 O/C Britain to C/S, 9 Sept. 1921 (RMP, P7/A/24[63-65]); BMHWS 824, Paddy Daly, p. 18; BMHWS 1535, Hugh Early, p. 10; 'LIVERPOOL', n.d. (MSPC, RO/604)

that at one time three companies existed, with a combined membership of about 100.[79] No. 3 area, Tyneside, boasted 12 companies based in Newcastle-upon-Tyne and its environs, including Durham, Hull and Middlesbrough (where William Whelan, a veteran of Brugha's 1918 assassination squad was an officer). Individual company memberships ranged between seven in Ashlington and 61 in Jarrow. The total membership was 335.[80] London, no. 4 area, had four companies, based on compass points: south-west and west, south-east, north and north-west, and east. Membership ranged between 16 in the South-West and West Company and 46 in the South-East Company. The area had a total membership of 106. No. 5 area was Birmingham, where two companies, one in the city itself and the second in Coventry, had a combined membership of 42. A company boasting a membership of five existed in nearby Rugby. Sheffield, no. 6 area, had eight companies located in the city and the surrounding area, along with Doncaster. Each company, however, had a rather small membership, ranging between three each in the Mexborough and Rotherham companies and 17 in the Barnsley Company. The area's total membership was 59. The combined membership of the six areas and Rugby was 682.[81]

IRA membership in Scotland at this time was significantly higher. John Carney claimed that when he became O/C Scottish Brigade in the autumn of 1920, the organization consisted of three battalions, totalling 21 companies, with an average strength of 30 men in each. His organizing efforts over the course of the following year saw the number of companies in the 1st Battalion increase from seven to ten. The 2nd and 3rd Battalions expanded too, from six to 14 and eight to 16 companies respectively. He had also established a 4th Battalion, consisting of eight companies, and a 5th Battalion with one company. The average strength of each company now stood at 50. Carney boasted that the total strength of the Scottish Brigade was 4,000.[82] More realistically, another member estimated membership to have been around 2,000 at the time of the truce in July 1921.[83]

79 O/C Britain to C/S, 9 Sept. 1921 (RMP, P7/A/24[63–65]); BMHWS 847, Patrick O'Donoghue, p. 5

80 O/C Britain to C/S, 9 Sept. 1921 (RMP, P7/A/24[63–65]); BMHWS 369, William Whelan, p. 8; Barrington, *Irish Independence Movement*, p. 17

81 O/C Britain to C/S, 9 Sept. 1921 (RMP, P7/A/24[63–65])

82 John Carney to C/S, 22 Feb. 1922 (SO'MP, MS 24,474); it should be noted that Carney's membership figures do not add up. He claimed to have expanded the Scottish Brigade to 49 companies. If their average membership was 50 each, as he claims, then the total membership would be 2,450, not 4,000.

83 S. Fullerton to Minister for Defence, 31 Aug., 6 Sept. 1922 (MCP, A/06181)

For detailed information on the various companies in the Scottish Brigade and their areas of operation, we are dependent on the imperfect and incomplete recollections of those involved. According to these records, compiled in the decades following the end of the Irish Revolution by Eamonn Mooney, an officer in the Scottish IRA, the outfit contained five battalions. The majority of the nine companies in the 1st Battalion, established in 1914 and re-established in the period 1917–19, was based in Glasgow city and its suburbs. Two of the companies, however, were based outside the city: one in Uddingston and Mossend, the other in the area encompassing Dumbarton, Renton, Alexandria, Cardross and Kirkintilloch. The battalion's total membership was estimated at around 700.[84] The 2nd Battalion, established in 1918–19 and numbering eight companies with a total membership of about 775, was based in Lanarkshire, incorporating such towns and villages as Hamilton, Motherwell, Coatbridge, Bothwell, Calderbank, Bellshill and Mossend (again).[85] The 3rd Battalion seems to have been founded in 1919. Composed of five companies and an estimated 130 men, it was spread across Edinburgh city, West Lothian, Mid- and West-Calder and Sterlingshire.[86] The 4th Battalion contained at least four companies, but details have survived of only two. The first, 'B' Company, with an estimated membership of 200, was seemingly established in 1920 in Greenock and its districts of Gourock and Port-Glasgow. Meanwhile, Dundee hosted the second, 'D' Company, of which 31 members are listed.[87] 62 men served in the 5th Battalion, though the number of companies they were divided into and their locations are not recorded.[88] Finally, a company existed in Fife, encompassing Buckhaven, Methilhill, Lochgelly, Cowdenbeath and Lochore, along with Kinrosshire. This company, with its small membership, does not seem to have been allocated to any particular battalion in the Scottish Brigade.[89] According to this source, the total membership of the brigade in July 1921 was between 1,600 and 1,900.[90]

Therefore, the total membership of the IRA in Britain in the autumn of 1921 was somewhere between 2,282 and 2,582.

---

84 Membership roll, 1st Battalion, Scottish Brigade IRA (EMP, 3/C/13)
85 Membership roll, 2nd Battalion, Scottish Brigade IRA (EMP, 3/C/13)
86 Membership roll, 3rd Battalion, Scottish Brigade IRA (EMP, 3/C/13)
87 Membership roll, 4th Battalion, Scottish Brigade IRA (EMP, 3/C/13)
88 Brigade membership calculations, Scottish Brigade IRA, 15 Aug. 1953 (EMP, 3/C/13)
89 Membership roll, Buckhaven Company, Scottish Brigade IRA (EMP, 3/C/13)
90 Calculations of company memberships, Scottish Brigade IRA (EMP, 3/C/13)

Why was the membership of the IRA in Scotland over two-and-a-half times greater than that in England? Two factors may have contributed to the disparity. Anti-Irish and anti-Catholic sectarianism may have been more pronounced in Scotland than in England, thus motivating Irish-born and Scottish-born second generation Irish to join the Volunteers.[91] Class conflict may have been another factor. James Connolly, the trade union leader and Marxist theorist, was born in an Edinburgh slum. Following his execution in the aftermath of the Easter Rising, Connolly acquired great status amongst the politically-active Irish in Scotland. As Joe Vize discovered when he set about organizing the Volunteers in Glasgow in 1919, Connolly's ICA retained a presence in Scotland even while it was disappearing in Ireland.[92]

V

Joe Vize, as noted, had sought to organize Volunteer companies in Scotland around Sinn Féin clubs. The number of clubs in Britain during the war is unknown. However, by the end of 1921, there were 65 branches in Scotland affiliated with Dublin. Membership subscriptions for the year amounted to £4,045.[93] Sinn Féin's aim was the achievement of the 'absolute and complete independence of Ireland', a speaker declared at a public meeting of the party's Kilcaldy branch in November 1919. 'The authority of Britain in Ireland, [sic] is null and void, so far as the people are concerned', he continued. 'It is usurped authority, and usurped authority is against the Divine Ordinance of God.' A 'state of War' existed between Ireland and England.[94] England and Wales had only eight Sinn Féin branches, but boasted subscriptions of £4,711.[95] Here,

91 See Stewart J. Brown, "Outside the Covenant': The Scottish Presbyterian Churches and Irish Immigration, 1922–1938', *Innes Review*, 42.1 (1991), pp. 19–45; Richard J. Finlay, 'Nationalism, Race, Religion and the Irish Question in Inter-War Scotland', *Innes Review*, 42.1 (1991), pp. 46–67

92 Joe Vize to Michael Collins, n.d., but marked 'Recd 5.2.19' (RMP, P7/A/11); Brian Hanley, 'The Irish Citizen Army after 1916', *Saothar: Journal of the Irish Labour History Society*, 28 (2003), pp. 37–47

93 Report of Honorary Secretary, Sinn Féin Ard Comhairle, 12 Jan. 1922 (DÉ, 2/486)

94 Chief Constable [CC] of Kilcaldy to Under-Secretary for Scotland, 29 Nov. 1919, enclosing report of meeting (National Archives of Scotland [NAS], First World War File [FWWF], HH31/34/18)

95 Report of Honorary Secretary, Sinn Féin Ard Comhairle, 12 Jan. 1922 (DÉ, 2/486)

however, the main republican political organization was not Sinn Féin but the ISDL. This body was part of a general attempt by Dáil Éireann to harness the Irish outside of Ireland in support of Irish freedom. Following his escape from Lincoln jail in February 1919, de Valera made arrangements to travel to the United States in order to get American support for Irish self-determination. However, before he departed from Liverpool disguised as a sailor, he 'planned the aims and the constitution' of the ISDL.[96] 'The land of your forefathers is still in bondage', he declared in an appeal to the Irish in England on St Patrick's Day 1919. 'She is suffering today as she suffered through the centuries.' With men and women in Ireland having revolted 'against the tyranny', it was incumbent on the '[c]hildren of the Irish race in England' to 'unite and assist them' in achieving the aim of 'government of the people of Ireland by the people of Ireland for the people of Ireland'.[97] Soon afterwards, the ISDL was formally inaugurated in Manchester. The aims of the league were:

> To gather together the Irish residents in Great Britain, in order that they shall as a body support their compatriots in Ireland, and use every means in their power to secure the application of the principle of self-determination for Ireland, and in the meantime to render all and every assistance to Irish political prisoners in Ireland or Great Britain.[98]

Believing that it was 'the duty of the exiled Irish everywhere to aid their kindred at home' in securing international recognition of Ireland's right to self-determination, the founders of the ISDL believed that the organization provided 'a common platform for all Irish Residents in Great Britain, who admit that Ireland is a nation, and [who] endorse her demand that she shall be so recognised by all other nations'. Membership of the organization was confined to those of Irish birth or descent. P.J. Kelly, an Irish nationalist councillor in Liverpool and a native of County Tyrone, became ISDL president. Art O'Brien occupied the vice-presidency, while Seán McGrath was later appointed general secretary.[99]

---

96   Eamon de Valera, 'General Note', n.d. (UCDA, Eamon de Valera Papers [EdeVP], P150/620)

97   De Valera, 'To the Irish in England', 17 Mar. 1919 (EdeVP, P150/630)

98   ISDL, *Constitution and Rules* (1921), p. 3 (AÓBP, MS 8438/13)

99   Poster, 'IRISH SELF-DETERMINATION LEAGUE OF GREAT BRITAIN', dated, in handwriting, 5 June 1919; ISDL, *Constitution and Rules* (1921), p. 3 (AÓBP, MS 8427/42, 8438/13); Sam Davies, ''A Stormy Political Career': P.J. Kelly and Irish Nationalist and Labour Politics in Liverpool, 1891–1936',

Due, perhaps, to the proliferation of Sinn Féin branches in Scotland, the Irish there proved unresponsive to the ISDL. According to British police intelligence, which monitored the organization, by April 1920 the ISDL boasted 9,017 members in 98 branches.[100] By the end of the following September, membership had increased to 23,943. Manchester boasted 4,348 members, London 4,192, Tyneside 3,208, Liverpool 2,597, South Wales 1,770, Teesside 1,383, Leeds 1,248, Sheffield 1,245, Wigan 1,241, Bradford 1,151, north-west Lancashire 711, Birmingham 445, north Staffordshire 298, Nottingham 70 and Leicester 36.[101]

The ISDL's most striking activity consisted of mass meetings and demonstrations, sometimes addressed by TDs from Ireland. In February 1920, for example, an overflowing audience of over 10,000 people attended a rally in the Albert Hall, London, to hear speeches by Arthur Griffith and Eoin MacNeill.[102] The organization's more workaday occupations included attending to the needs of Irishmen in British prisons, along with collecting money for various Irish causes such as the INAVDF and selling bonds for the Dáil loan, the republican government's fund-raising scheme.

As Máirtín Ó Catháin observes, the support which the Irish in Scotland gave to Sinn Féin during the 1919–23 period demonstrated 'the depth of [their] rootedness to Ireland'. Unlike the IPP and other political organizations, Sinn Féin did not seek to redress the difficulties, socio-economic and otherwise, being experienced by the Irish in Scotland. Rather, it was focused exclusively on affairs in Ireland.[103] The same could be said of those who supported the ISDL in England and Wales.

The IRA in Britain developed a close relationship with the ISDL and Sinn Féin. Thomas McDonnell, a senior member of Scottish Sinn Féin, remembered that the organization's branches allowed for the recruitment of men to the IRA and the Fenians.[104] Likewise, Gilbert Barrington, secretary of the ISDL's Tyneside District Council and an IRA organizer in the area, recalled that

Transactions of the Historic Society of Lancashire and Cheshire, 148 (1999), pp. 147–89

100 'RROUK', no. 50, 15 Apr. 1920 (CAB, 24/103)

101 'RROUK', no. 83, 2 Dec. 1920 (CAB, 24/116)

102 *Freeman's Journal,* 12 Feb. 1920; see generally Keiko Inoue, 'Dáil Propaganda and the Irish Self-Determination League of Great Britain during the Anglo-Irish War', *Irish Studies Review,* 6.1 (1998), pp. 47–53

103 Ó Catháin, 'A Winnowing Spirit', pp. 122–23

104 Thomas McDonnell's statement to the MSPB, 4 July 1939 (EMP, 2/A/9)

As a general rule, the prime movers in the formation of a branch of [the] I.S.D.L. were also prominent in the recruitment of Volunteers. Not a great deal of pressure was necessary to encourage the formation of new branches; on the contrary, it was usual for the initiative to be taken locally. Similarly, it was not long after a branch of the I.S.D.L. was formed until endeavours would be made by some of the members to get in touch with responsible officers of the I.R.A. with a view to the establishment of a Company in the district ... In this way, the personnel in contact with each I.S.D.L. branch was, in general, the same as controlled the activities of the I.R.A. in the area.[105]

Hence, branches of the ISDL and Sinn Féin functioned as recruiting pools for the Volunteers. In 1920, Edward Roche, who was very active in the London ISDL, was introduced to two men who asked him if he would 'link up' with the IRA. Roche agreed, and in a house on Baker Street he was sworn into the Volunteers. He was then assigned the task of raising a Volunteer unit in the Richmond, Kew and Hounslow areas of south-west London.[106] Edward Brady, an Ulsterman living in Liverpool, similarly got involved in the IRA through constitutional politics. After attending a public meeting in 1919 which demanded the release of Irish political prisoners, Brady met with an acquaintance and was prevailed upon to join Sinn Féin, and remembered later:

His arguments seemed so to impress the mind of one politically ignorant of the significance of the state of affairs, or of the logical outcome of the movement with which he was obsessed, that at his request, I gave him permission to nominate me as a member of his club.

In addition to Sinn Féin, Brady became involved in other groups advocating the Irish cause, including the ISDL. Through involvement in such activities as fund-raising for the Dáil loan and disseminating propaganda, Brady became aware of the existence of the Volunteers, drilling and arming themselves with the aim of starting hostilities in Britain. Invigorated by the exciting atmosphere and the righteousness of the cause, he joined the IRA's Birkenhead Company.[107]

British cities also boasted branches of the GAA and the Gaelic League,

105 BMHWS 773, Gilbert Barrington, pp. 9–10
106 Edward Roche to MSPB, 4 Aug. 1937 (EO'ML, P17a/154)
107 Brady, *Secret Service*, pp. 16–23

manifestations of cultural nationalism, the desire to preserve and celebrate Ireland's distinctive culture. By 1921, there were at least seven GAA clubs in London, and an unknown number existed in the rest of Britain.[108] The London Gaelic League, founded in 1898, was dedicated to the 'preservation, teaching, and extension of Irish as a spoken language', as well as to 'the cause of an Irish-Ireland'. In 1919, the organization had 466 paid-up members, 1,100 in 1920 and 903 in 1921.[109] The Manchester IRA recruited some of its members from the Gaelic League.[110]

As well as having overlapping memberships, therefore, the ISDL, Sinn Féin, the GAA and the Gaelic League constituted the milieu within which the IRA, the IRB, the Cumann na mBan and Na Fianna Éireann existed. Often, there was little distinction between the organizations. Séamus Reader remembered that the Fenians, the Volunteers and the Sinn Féin organization were 'very much mixed up' in Glasgow, and Art O'Brien wrote likewise about London.[111] Events such as dances enabled Volunteers to socialize with supporters and sympathizers. While such supporters may not themselves have been members of the ranks of violent republicanism, they did prove of some service to those who were. Some allowed their addresses to be used in the clandestine postal system that enabled Michael Collins and other GHQ leaders in Dublin to communicate with Volunteer and IRB men in Britain. Some sheltered fugitive IRA men from Ireland or escapees from British prisons. Others allowed their houses to be used as arms dumps. As Collins noted, 'people who were not prepared to go out and fight' nevertheless had 'some uses' and 'might be of great value to the actual fighters themselves'.[112] Indeed, the first mobilization of the London IRA, in April 1920, was for the

---

108 'A Call from Ireland', n.d., but *c.* 1918–21 (AÓBP, MS 8436/5); attendance at GAA Annual Congresses, 1921–23 (GAA Archives [GAAA], Central Council Minute Book, 1911–25, GAA/CC/01/02[537, 572, 639]); *Report and Balance Sheet 1924*, p. 60 (GAAA, Annual Reports, Balance Sheets and Motions for Congress, 1911–28)

109 Art Ó Briain, 'Gaedhil Thar Sáile: Some Notes on the History of the Gaelic League of London', *Capuchin Annual*, (1944), p. 117; Gaelic League of London, *Constitution* (1919), p. 1; *Annual Report of the Gaelic League of London, 1921* (1921), p. 14 (AÓBP, MS 8436/5)

110 John McGallogly to The Secretary, Military Service Pensions, 11 Oct. 1937, enclosing Patrick O'Donoghue's account of the Manchester IRA (MSPC, RO/608)

111 BMHWS 933, Séamus Reader, p. 7; 'IRB', n.d., but *c.* 1930s (AÓBP, MS 8427/22)

112 Michael Collins to Art O' Brien, 13 June 1921 (DÉ, 2/330)

purpose of protecting Irish men and women from the violent attentions of an English crowd which took exception to their demonstration in support of hunger-striking IRA men in Wormwood Scrubs.[113] One hunger-striker later told reporters:

> The last thing we expected was an Irish demonstration outside the prison in the heart of the enemy's country. [It] was a tremendous encouragement to us in our fight to know that our people in London were sympathising with us. It was simply splendid, and put great heart into the boys.[114]

Later that year, Volunteers acted as stewards at the large public meetings addressed by Daniel Mannix, the Roman Catholic Archbishop of Melbourne and staunch Irish republican.[115] Participation in such activities of the wider republican movement inculcated a sense of camaraderie and reinforced republicans' belief in the righteousness of their cause. Michael O'Leary stated that rallies in Liverpool 'helped to swell the Sinn Féin membership and afterwards to bring self-determination into operation'.[116]

Security was often a concern when accepting new recruits into the Volunteers. John Pinkman, a Merseyside IRA man, states that admittance to the city's ranks was dependent on a standing member vouching for the new recruit's integrity. Such a procedure was adopted to prevent the organization being infiltrated by Irishmen working as British spies. If, despite his surmounting this obstacle, a doubt still remained about the advisability of admitting a new recruit, especially one from Ireland, subterfuge would be employed to verify his bona fides. The recruit would be told that his joining the city's Volunteers was contingent upon him becoming a member of the health benefit scheme of the Irish National Foresters, a benevolent society. Once he had filled out the scheme's application form, his details were secretly forwarded to IRA GHQ in Dublin, which, in turn, would make enquiries regarding the recruit from the I/O in his home area.[117]

Some procedures, if not specifically these ones, seem to have been

---

113 *Freeman's Journal*, 29 Apr.; *IT*, 29, 30 Apr.; *TT*, 29 Apr. 1920; 'London Battalion IRA' (EO'ML, P17a/51)

114 *Freeman's Journal*, 10 May 1920

115 BMHWS 696, Henry O'Hagan, p. 6; BMHWS 797, Micheál Ó Laoghaire, pp. 33–35

116 BMHWS 797, Micheál Ó Laoghaire, p. 25

117 Pinkman, *Legion*, pp. 21–22

adopted by IRA companies in other parts of Britain too. Nevertheless, at least two incidents of spying by Volunteers did occur in Britain. The most serious concerned Manchester's Erskine Street Company. Following an IRA arson attack upon the city centre on 2 April 1921, police raided the company's headquarters, the Irish Club in Hulme. One man was shot dead and a number of others were arrested. When they were subsequently put on trial on charges of treason felony, one of their number, Charles Murphy, a former member of the Belfast Volunteers, turned King's evidence and testified against his fellow members. As a result, 16 of the defendants were found guilty and imprisoned for up to ten years each.[118] Edward Brady later stated that Murphy was a spy who was admitted to the Manchester Volunteers after failing to gain entry to the Liverpool IRA. Murphy, he wrote, 'apparently acted as an *agent provocateur*' in encouraging the mounting of the arson attack.[119] Murphy, however, denied this at his trial, stating that he only took part in the operation out of fear of being court-martialled by his Volunteer colleagues and that it was his uneasy conscience that led him to confess all to the police.[120] Michael Collins thought it 'a positive disgrace' that the Manchester men took Murphy into their confidence so quickly. Murphy was 'not one bit more guilty [of the prosecutions] than the men who were responsible for such a thing [i.e. admitting him to the organization so hastily],' he continued. '... We must certainly fix the responsibility for accepting him as a member and detailing him for work.'[121]

The second incident ended with an execution on Ashford golf course in Middlesex on 3 April 1921, the day after the Manchester arson attack. On a piece of paper placed near the body was written: 'Let spies and traitors beware – IRA'. At the inquest, the victim was identified as Vincent Fouvargue, a 20 year-old clerk book-keeper. Under the name Richard Stanton, Fouvargue had attended ISDL dances at Kelvedon Hall, Fulham. He had been at one such dance on the night of his death. The jury, some of whom had received threatening letters, reached a verdict of wilful murder against some person or persons unknown.[122] Fouvargue had been the I/O of Dublin's 4th Battalion for a short time. Captured by the British, he seems to have divulged information relating to his fellow Volunteers, perhaps after

118 *TT*, 4 Apr.; *MG*, 28 Apr., 15, 17 July 1921
119 Brady, *Secret Service*, pp. 11–12; original emphasis
120 Deposition of Charles Murphy, 27 Apr. 1921, pp. 17–18, 20–23 (TNA, Assizes File [ASSI], 52/331 Part 1)
121 Michael Collins to Art O'Brien, 23 May 1921 (DÉ, 2/330)
122 *TT*, 4, 5, 7, 21 Apr. 1921

being tortured. The British then staged an ambush so as to let Fouvargue escape from their custody and re-join the IRA, where he would continue to spy for them. He subsequently moved to London and attempted to ingratiate himself with the Volunteers there. Brady states that his activities led to the arrest of a police sergeant secretly working for the IRA. It was then that Fouvargue's former comrades in the Dublin Volunteers became suspicious of him and alerted the IRA in London.[123]

Volunteer recruitment took place on a continuous basis during the war. As we have seen, in August 1920, the IRA boasted just eight companies in England, spread across Liverpool, London and Manchester. By September the following year, it had expanded to 31 companies, encompassing Tyneside, Birmingham and Sheffield, along with the three original areas.[124] In Scotland too, over the same period, the Volunteers expanded numerically, from 21 to 49 companies, and geographically.[125]

VI

Before a new recruit was admitted to the Volunteers, he was usually required to swear the following oath:

> I, the undersigned, desire to be enrolled for service in Ireland as a member of the Irish Volunteer Force. I subscribe to the Constitution of the Irish Volunteers, and pledge my willing obedience to my superior officers. I declare that in joining the Irish Volunteer Force I set before myself the stated objects of the Irish Volunteers, and no others.[126]

What motivated people to join the Volunteers and swear such an oath? Membership of the IRA was, after all, fraught with danger. Most of the British populace seems to have followed the prime minister, David Lloyd George,

---

123   Ernie O'Malley, *On Another Man's Wound* (Dublin: Anvil, 2002 edition), p. 317; Brady, *Secret Service*, pp. 12–13; BMHWS 380, David Neligan, p. 4; BMHWS 615, Frank Thornton, p. 42; BMHWS 476, Joseph Kinsella, pp. 15–17; 'Report on the Intelligence Branch of the Chief of Police', in Peter Hart (ed.), *British Intelligence in Ireland, 1920–21: The Final Reports* (Cork: Cork University Press, 2002), p. 82

124   O/C Britain to C/S, 9 Sept. 1921 (RMP, P7/A/24[63–65])

125   John Carney to C/S, 22 Feb. 1922 (SO'MP, MS 24,474)

126   Irish Volunteers, *General Scheme of Organisation* (MCP, A/0032A, Group 2, Item 2)

in viewing the IRA in Ireland as a 'murder gang', 'assassins' terrorizing the country.[127] For the Volunteers in Britain, 'in the heart of enemy lines', the danger could only be worse. On a less demanding level, membership entailed spending hours at drill practice and the payment of a weekly membership fee.[128] Why, then, were people willing to devote time, money and energy to the Volunteers, as well as, *in extremis*, putting their lives at risk?

Unfortunately, of the almost 2,600 people who joined the Volunteers in Britain, only a small minority have left accounts of their activities. Of this minority, just a few have left memoirs containing the detail necessary for a competent discussion of the factors motivating their involvement in the Volunteers. Therefore, the following discussion relies on the testimony of 15 people who served in the IRA in Britain. Ten of these were born or grew up in Britain, the remainder in Ireland. Before we examine these accounts, however, it is necessary to briefly discuss the history of the Irish in Britain.

As we have seen, by 1921 the Irish-born population of Britain was a little under 524,000, but when the second- and third-generations are taken into account the number of Irish Catholics would probably have exceeded 2,000,000.[129] Excepting those emigrants who fled Ireland during the Great Famine, most Irish immigrated to Britain for economic reasons. However, lacking valuable skills, they tended to be limited to working in menial jobs, such as labouring in factories and on railway- and building-construction projects. Native British workers often viewed the Irish as a threat to their living standards, accusing them of driving down wage levels. A number of anti-Irish riots ensued, in such workplaces as the Pontypool ironworks in 1834, Penrith railway works in 1846 and the mines and factories of Dunfermline in 1850.[130] However, employment and wages were rarely the sole causes of these violent confrontations. Other factors were at work. Many native Britons despised the Irish as feckless and violent. Their Catholicism was seen as particularly objectionable, for, despite the emancipation of Catholics, Britain in the nineteenth century was a self-consciously Protestant nation. 'It was their common investment in Protestantism [in the sixteenth and seventeenth centuries] that first allowed the English, the Welsh and the Scots to become fused together, and to remain so, despite their many cultural divergences', notes the historian Linda Colley. Britain's many wars with Catholic France

---

127 *TT*, 11 Oct. 1920

128 Michael Collins to Tom Craven, 6 June 1919 (RMP, P7/A/1[56]); Collins to Seán McGrath, 9 Oct. 1919 (AÓBP, MS 8429/11)

129 See Introduction

130 Fitzpatrick, "A Peculiar Tramping People", pp. 639–44

in the seventeenth and eighteenth centuries then cemented the Protestant religion's place in the country's national self-identity.[131] In the 1850s and 1860s, anti-Catholic and anti-Irish riots occurred in British towns and cities, including London, Cardiff, Birkenhead, Stockport, Blackburn and Oldham. Rome's restoration of the Catholic hierarchy in England was a significant factor in these outbreaks of violence, as were British acclaim and Irish detestation of Garibaldi's assault on the Papal States during the wars of Italian re-unification, preacher William Murphy's anti-Catholic crusade and the violence of Fenian revolutionaries. After the 1860s, such anti-Irish violence declined in frequency. Yet it appeared again in Lancashire, particularly in 1903–09, where Conservative and Protestant domination of municipal politics mixed with the militant Protestant crusade of Pastor George Wise to create a combustible situation.[132] Moreover, anti-Catholicism played a fundamental role in popular British opposition to Irish home rule, with perhaps up to one million people attending rallies throughout the country in 1912–14 in support of the Ulster Unionists, and some promising to fight alongside their fellow Protestants if home rule was imposed on them.[133]

With this background in mind, we will now analyse the biographical accounts of ten Volunteers born or raised in Britain. Born in Liverpool around 1890, Tom Craven became O/C of one of the city's two Volunteer companies in early 1916 and went on to fight in the Easter Rising. A member of Cathal Brugha's assassination squad in 1918, he resumed his Liverpool command in 1919. In September that year, however, he resigned from the force and moved to New York.[134] Seán Nunan was born in London in 1890. He joined the North London Volunteers in 1914 and, as we saw earlier, fought in the GPO during the Rising. While interned in Frongoch, the authorities attempted to conscript him and his brother into the British army. After his release, Nunan returned to Ireland and resumed his Volunteer activities. After serving as a clerk at the first meeting of the Dáil on 21 January 1919, he went to America

---

131 Linda Colley, *Britons: Forging the Nation 1707–1837* (New Haven: Yale University Press, 1992), pp. 367–68

132 Fitzpatrick, "A Peculiar Tramping People", pp. 645–51; O'Day, 'Varieties of Anti-Irish Behaviour', pp. 29–36

133 Daniel M. Jackson, *Popular Opposition to Irish Home Rule in Edwardian Britain* (Liverpool: Liverpool University Press, 2009), pp. 9–14, 81, 119, 155, 174–75, 243

134 Craven, 'A Brief Personal Narrative …' (BMHCD 141/4, Thomas Craven); Craven to Michael Collins, 25 May; Neil Kerr to Collins, 25 Sept. 1919 (RMP, P7/A/1[5, 24–25])

with de Valera, where he was involved in Dáil loan affairs and gunrunning.[135] Nunan's fellow Londoner Joe Good was born in Soho in 1895. In 1914, he joined the Volunteers, serving in the same company as Michael Collins. After being released from Frongoch, following his involvement in the Easter rebellion, Good participated in various IRA activities, including gunrunning and the planned assassination of British cabinet ministers.[136] John Pinkman, born in Liverpool in 1902, joined the city's Volunteers in 1919 and participated in the IRA's campaign of violence.[137] Gilbert Barrington was born in Blackburn, Lancashire, in 1889. He helped found IRA companies in the Tyneside area in 1920–21 and took part in arson attacks and gunrunning activities.[138] Brothers Eamonn and Seán (or Séamus) Mooney, born in Ireland and Scotland respectively, joined the Scottish Volunteers in 1914, fought in the Easter Rising and served in Scotland during the war.[139] Born in Glasgow in 1897 or 1898, Séamus Reader, as we have seen, joined Na Fianna Éireann, the IRB and the Irish Volunteers. He helped to re-organize the Volunteers in Glasgow from 1917 onwards, and served as O/C Scottish Brigade for a period.[140] Born in Belfast, Joe and Séamus Robinson moved with their family to Glasgow in 1903. Involved in Na Fianna and the IRB, Joe Robinson, as we saw earlier, took charge of the Volunteers in the aftermath of the 1914 split and would have participated in the 1916 Rising but for his arrest. His brother Séamus fought in the rebellion and subsequently organized the IRA in south Tipperary. After his release from internment Joe, on the other hand, returned to Glasgow to direct gunrunning activity but was arrested and imprisoned in 1918.[141]

A number of themes are common in the biographies of these men. Family background was a major factor in their becoming Irish nationalists. Craven's parents were natives of Ulster. He credited his mother as the source

135   BMHWS 1744, Seán Nunan

136   Good, *Enchanted*, pp. x–xi, 9, 14–99, 130–44, 174–76, 182–85

137   Pinkman, *Legion*, pp. 9–10, 18–19, 32–53

138   Barrington, *Irish Independence Movement*, pp. 4, 10; BMHWS 773, Gilbert Barrington, pp. 2–9

139   Interview with Cathleen Knowles-McGuirk, Eamonn Mooney's daughter, 6 Aug. 2009

140   BMHWS 627, 933, Séamus Reader; Stephen Coyle, *High Noon on High Street: The Story of a Daring Ambush by the IRA in Glasgow in 1921* (Glasgow: Clydeside Press, 2008), p. 68

141   Séamus Robinson statement (FGP, MS 21,256); Marie Coleman, 'Robinson, Séamus', in *DIB*, downloaded from http://dib.cambridge.org on 1 Dec. 2009

of his 'love of Ireland and hatred of Britain'. In her native County Tyrone, she had been a member of the Ladies Land League and later in Liverpool she joined various nationalist organizations. The pro-Boer sympathies of Craven's father were so pronounced during the South African War of 1899–1902 as to lead to the family home being attacked and wrecked by mobs on four occasions. His own pro-Boer stance and refusal to salute the Union Jack or wear a Queen Victoria button resulted in the young Craven being beaten up. Outside of the Boers, as a young boy playing at soldiers Craven imagined himself fighting for Ireland, sometimes as Theobald Wolfe Tone and Robert Emmet.[142] Seán Nunan's parents, natives of County Limerick, were 'intensely national – of Fenian stock' and were members of various Irish organizations in London. 'It was no wonder, therefore, that I also took a deep interest in all things Irish', he reflected.[143] Joe Good's father, like Craven's, was sympathetic to the Boers, but his parents generally were supporters of the IPP, treating the family to loud renditions of Irish MPs' speeches from the newspapers every Sunday. Good's sister, Agnes, became active in an Irish political society and also joined the Gaelic League.[144] Pinkman, despite his unusual name, traced his ancestry to County Fermanagh. His family home was a repository of Irish culture. His father was a devout Catholic, while his mother treasured and practised Irish customs and traditions. Both were Irish-speakers and nationalists. Irish song and dance provided entertainment at regular get-togethers, all of which took place under the gaze of engravings and pictures of former IPP leader Parnell and famous Fenians. Bernard Meehan, a cousin of Pinkman's, fought in the Easter Rising, and while he was imprisoned in Frongoch Pinkman's mother sent him food parcels. Following his release, Meehan lodged with the Pinkmans until he found a job in the city. Disgust at the executions of the Rising's leaders motivated Pinkman's refused to salute the Union Jack at his school's Empire Day celebrations in 1916.[145] Gilbert Barrington's family had a long association with Irish nationalism. Family tradition stated that some ancestors had participated in the 1798 Rebellion. Barrington's paternal grandfather was a member of the IRB. Although Barrington's father had been sworn into the Fenians by his father, he objected to violence and therefore his politics took the form of moderate nationalism.

---

142 Craven, 'A Brief Personal Narrative …', pp. 1, 4 (BMHCD 141/4, Thomas Craven)

143 BMHWS 1744, Seán Nunan, p. 1

144 Good, *Enchanted*, pp. 6–7, 13

145 Pinkman, *Legion*, pp. 9–10, 14, 18

He joined the AOH in South Shields, as did Gilbert. Educated by the Irish Sisters of Mercy near Bath, Barrington's mother was intensely nationalistic.[146] The Mooney parents were republicans, with one of their parents in turn said to have been a founding member of the IRB. Both parents were also cultural nationalists, with the father working as an Irish language translator.[147] Séamus Reader came from 'a good national background'. Rebel songs, such as 'The Wearing of the Green' and 'Who Fears to Speak of '98?', were sung at home, while pictures of Robert Emmet and the battle of Fontenoy (1745) – where an Irish Brigade in the French army helped to defeat an Allied force that included Great Britain – hung on the walls. Reader joined Baden Powell's Scouts. However, when his younger brother taunted him that the scouting organization he had joined, Na Fianna Éireann, was better than Séamus's because 'they had swords' and attractive uniforms, Séamus switched to the Willie Nelson troop.[148] While Joe and Séamus Robinson were growing up, their family professed moderate nationalism. However, when Séamus was about 30 years old he learned that a grandfather of theirs had fought in the 1848 rebellion. According to Séamus, his brother was the first person to enrol when the Fianna were established in Belfast in 1902 and Séamus joined soon afterwards. 'Joe had always been determined to devote his life to the Fenian ideal …', remembered Séamus.[149]

The historian Gearóid Ó Tuathaigh has argued that nationalism may have served 'an important and complex psychological function' for Irish immigrants in nineteenth-century Britain. It gave 'an exalted sense of purpose to lives that were otherwise spent in adverse social circumstances'. Moreover, 'by demanding freedom for the homeland', nationalism allowed immigrants 'to engage in a kind of revolt by proxy against their own depressed condition'.[150] Immigrants sometimes passed on these sentiments to their children.

The powerful influence which family relations had in the moulding of a nationalist consciousness is evident in the significant number of siblings in the ranks of the Volunteers and the IRB in Britain. During the war, the London IRA included at least four sets of brothers: Seán and Michael McGrath,

---

146 Barrington, *Irish Independence Movement*, pp. 4, 10; BMHWS 773, Gilbert Barrington, pp. 2–9

147 Interview with Cathleen Knowles-McGuirk

148 BMHWS 627, Séamus Reader, pp. 1–2

149 Séamus Robinson statement, p. 58 (FGP, MS 21,256)

150 Quoted in Mark Boyle, 'Towards a (Re)Theorization of the Historical Geography of Nationalism in Diasporas: The Irish Diaspora as an Exemplar', *International Journal of Population Geography*, 7.6 (2001), p. 435

Denis and Joseph Carr, Charles and William Robinson and Joseph and Patrick O'Sullivan.[151] As well as the Kerr brothers, the Liverpool Volunteers had the membership of Jimmy and Paddy Lowe and Michael O'Leary and his brother.[152] At least 22 sets of brothers existed in the Scottish ranks.[153] As well as Joe and Séamus Robinson and Eamonn and Seán Mooney, there was John and James McGallogly and the McGovern brothers, Michael, Patrick and Thomas. Séamus Reader's younger brother was still involved in the Volunteers in 1917 and may have continued his membership during the war as well.[154] Fathers sometimes joined their sons in the Volunteers too. 'B' Company of the 2nd Battalion boasted three sets of fathers and sons: Kelly, Rafferty and Sullivan.[155] Given the number of members sharing the same surnames, 'A' Company, 2nd Battalion, seems to have been a veritable family affair.[156]

A second factor in motivating involvement in the Volunteers – explicitly mentioned in only two cases but probably significant in many more – was the influence of friends. In 1918, John Pinkman and Bernie Meehan regularly attended dances at the local Sinn Féin club. There, they learned from Niall Lively, a neighbour with whom Pinkman had attended hurling matches, that an IRA company was about to be founded in the area. About six or eight men attended the inaugural meeting of the company, the 17 year-old Pinkman among them. 'More than anyone else,' he later wrote, 'Niall Lively … was responsible for my joining the Company.'[157] Gilbert Barrington stated that, family influence apart, his involvement in the IRA on Tyneside was motivated by the sincere patriotism of Father Vaughan, the Catholic parish priest of South Shields.[158] The historian Charles Townshend has argued that the persistence of opposition to British rule in Ireland 'cannot be explained

151 Seán McGrath interview (EO'MN, P17b/100); Reginald Dunne to Art O'Brien, 24 Apr. 1922; O'Brien to whom it may concern, 27 Apr. 1935 (AÓBP, MS 8427/22, 8432/21); Wallace, 'Reginald Dunn', p. 1

152 Pinkman, *Legion*, p. 165; BMHWS 797, Micheál Ó Laoghaire, p. 47

153 Membership rolls, Scottish Brigade IRA (EMP, 3/C/13)

154 Interview with Cathleen Knowles-McGuirk; membership roll, 'A' Company, 1st Battalion; membership roll, 'H' Company, 1st Battalion, Scottish Brigade IRA (EMP, 3/C/13); BMHWS 933, Séamus Reader, p. 3

155 Membership roll, 'B' Company, 2nd Battalion, Scottish Brigade IRA (EMP, 3/C/13)

156 Membership roll, 'A' Company, 2nd Battalion, Scottish Brigade IRA (EMP, 3/C/13)

157 Pinkman, *Legion*, pp. 18–19

158 Barrington, *Irish Independence Movement*, p. 11

by the intellectual or even the emotional power of republican ideology, but only by an inheritance of communal assumptions validating its methods as much as its ends'.[159] Family and friends constituted the most important media by which such communal thinking was passed on to the next generation, especially among those who felt themselves 'exiled' from Ireland, forced to emigrate due to British misrule or malevolence. ('It was my misfortune to be born in exile', lamented Craven.[160]) Indeed, Máirtín Ó Catháin argues that the 'very shape and nature of Fenianism grew out of an Irish exile colloquy …'.[161]

If families and friends constituted important influences in the development of an Irish nationalist outlook in these men, so too did popular books, newspapers and ballads. Craven eagerly read Irish history and remembered Father Patrick Kavanagh's *A Popular History of the Rebellion of 1798* (1870) as being the first book he ever read outside of school books. Aged 14, he then came across an advertisement for Arthur Griffith's *United Irishman* newspaper. Intrigued by the title, Craven decided to buy a copy. Impressed by Griffith's argument that Ireland could expect little help from Britain, he became a regular reader of the publication.[162] Aged about 15, Joe Good, solitary and imaginative, began to read Irish history. Soon afterwards, he encountered Irish songs and ballads for the first time when his sister Agnes brought home a Gaelic League songbook. He became enchanted by the romantic works of Thomas Davis, James Clarence Mangan and Thomas Moore. The sentiments of such poems as Mangan's 'Dark Rosaleen' and John O'Hagan's 'Dear Land' resonated with Good, as he later remembered: 'These were thoughts which had run in my head since childhood, and that I had never heard expressed – till now'. Following his sister into the Gaelic League, Good was introduced to *An Claidheamh Soluis* ('The Sword of Light'), the movement's newspaper. Here again, he found laid out in black and white sentiments and arguments regarding 'direct action' and 'physical force' which reverberated with him. Walking about with the newspaper in his pocket, Good felt conspiratorial,

---

159 Charles Townshend, *Political Violence in Ireland: Government and Resistance Since 1848* (Oxford: Clarendon Press, 1983), pp. viii–ix

160 Craven, 'A Brief Personal Narrative …', p. 1 (BMHCD 141/4, Thomas Craven)

161 Ó Catháin, *Irish Republicanism in Scotland*, pp. 247, 254; Enda Delaney, 'Narratives of Exile and Displacement: Irish Catholic Emigrants and the National Past, 1850–1914', in Terence Dooley (ed.), *Ireland's Polemical Past: Views of Irish History in Honour of R.V. Comerford* (Dublin: University College Dublin Press, 2010), pp. 102–22

162 Craven, 'A Brief Personal Narrative …', p. 1 (BMHCD 141/4, Thomas Craven)

like 'a small Guy Fawkes'.[163] John Pinkman, too, was influenced by his reading Irish history, learning of 'the cruelties suffered by the Irish people in the past'. The Great Famine of 1845–51 was particularly instructive:

> My father was born less than ten years after the Great Famine when nearly two million [sic] Irish people were allowed to die of starvation. Irish people were dying on the roadsides eating grass while grain was being shipped out of Dublin to pay rents to absentee English landlords.

His reading and the nationalism of his parents, therefore, inculcated in Pinkman a hatred of British imperialism and its malign influence on Ireland.[164] For Irish immigrants, argues Adrian Mulligan, Ireland 'operated as a symbolic anchor often imagined from afar'.[165] By consuming popular media, such as books and newspapers, Craven, Good and Pinkman were doing exactly this.

A fourth factor, somewhat connected to the last, was the influence of cultural nationalist organizations. The arguments in Griffith's *United Irishman* seem to have motivated Tom Craven to become active in 'all phases of the Irish-Ireland and Anti-Parliamentarian Movement'. He joined the Gaelic League, the GAA and Sinn Féin.[166] From a young age, Seán Nunan was a Gaelic Leaguer and he joined the GAA too.[167] Joe Good, as we have seen, joined the Gaelic League. He also attended GAA matches and may have joined the organization.[168] Aged 16, Pinkman joined the Roger Casement Sinn Féin Club in Litherland. He considered his membership 'natural' in light of the 'strong Irish atmosphere' in which he grew up. He also attended hurling matches with friends, as we have seen.[169]

A fifth factor, in Pinkman's case at least, was that of sectarianism. Discrimination against the Irish and Catholics was evident in Liverpool, especially in the area of employment. Noting that he was one of only about six Catholic boys who attended the junior day technical school in Bootle, Pinkman, an altar boy in his youth, believed that Catholics were admitted reluctantly and only as a concession to the town's large Catholic population. In general, he believed that 'Catholics, especially Irish Catholics, were treated

---

163 Good, *Enchanted*, pp. 5–8

164 Pinkman, *Legion*, p. 18

165 Mulligan, 'Absence Makes the Heart Grow Fonder', pp. 451–52

166 Craven, 'A Brief Personal Narrative ...', p. 1 (BMHCD 141/4, Thomas Craven)

167 BMHWS 1744, Seán Nunan, p. 1

168 Good, *Enchanted*, pp. 7–8

169 Pinkman, *Legion*, pp. 18–19

like dirt' on Merseyside. For Pinkman, such treatment was of a part with the oppression suffered by the Irish at the hands of British imperialism in Ireland.[170] Another environmental factor, class struggle, was credited by Barrington as contributing to the rebelliousness of the Irish on Tyneside.[171]

For the Irish-born in Britain or those who grew up in Britain, the decision to join the Volunteers, therefore, can be seen as having been influenced by perhaps five factors, namely their families' attitude towards nationalism, the involvement of friends in nationalist movements, consumption of nationalist popular media, membership of cultural nationalist organizations and experience of sectarian discrimination.

Due to the lack of comprehensive membership lists for the Volunteers in Britain, the proportion of Irish-born as opposed to British-born men active in the force cannot be stated with precision. However, the surviving evidence indicates a very significant proportion, if not a majority, of the Volunteers active in Britain during the war were born in Ireland. Gilbert Barrington stated that those who were 'active [in the Tyneside IRA] were mostly Irish born'.[172] According to Paddy Daly, membership of the Liverpool Volunteers was 'mostly composed of labouring men coming across from Ireland'.[173] Irish-born men also seem to have constituted a significant proportion of the IRA in London, as well as that of the 2nd Scottish Battalion.[174] The factors that led Irish-born men to join the Volunteers were the same as those in the cases of British-born Volunteers. Family background was an important influence. Joe Furlong, a member of the pre-Rising Volunteers in London sent to Scotland in 1920, was born into a republican family in County Wexford. His father had been imprisoned during the Land War of 1879–81.[175] An immigrant from County Mayo, Patrick Mills joined his uncle in the Motherwell IRB in 1912.[176] Born in County Galway in 1899, William O'Keeffe, later a member of the Manchester IRA, remembered the nationalist tales his mother used to tell him and his siblings when they

170 Pinkman, *Legion*, pp. 12–15, 18
171 Barrington, *Irish Independence Movement*, p. 9
172 Barrington, *Irish Independence Movement*, p. 7
173 BMHWS 814, Patrick Daly, p. 18
174 Reginald Dunne to O/C Britain, 24 Oct. 1921 (RMP, P7/A/27[49–50]); BMHWS 828, James Byrne, pp. 2–3; membership rolls of Scottish Brigade IRA, esp. 'H' Company, 2nd Battalion, 'C' Company, 3rd Battalion, 'B' Company, 4th Battalion (EMP, 3/C/13)
175 BMHWS 335, Joseph Furlong, p. 1
176 BMHWS 777, Patrick Mills, p. 1

were young. Their favourite stories concerned local happenings during the United Irishmen's rebellion:

> … the landing of the French at Killala on the 22nd August, 1798, and the battle at Castlebar on the 27th August which resulted in a humiliating defeat for the English – known as "The Races of Castlebar"; the return of the English soldiers to Mayo after the capture of the [French leader] General Humbert, when they pillaged and plundered and slaughtered the old, the infirm and the young who were unable to escape; also how Father Manus Sweeney of Lahardane was hanged in Castlebar after a mock trial because he shook hands with a French officer.

In 1917–18, O'Keeffe's older brother aided the Claremorris Volunteers in carrying despatches.[177] Louth-born Frank Thornton remembered that his mother 'preached Fenianism' to her children.[178] Such romantic reverence for physical force and those who wielded it against British rule was not confined to incorrigible separatists. Rather, the mass of the Irish Catholic population, along with its political representative the IPP, sympathized with such a view, informed as it was by a popular nationalism that portrayed Ireland as a righteous victim of British oppression.[179]

Furlong attests to the influence of his schooling in the formation of his nationalist outlook. He particularly remembered the Irish history lessons of his Christian Brothers teacher, Brother Collins. Due to the influence of Collins and his own parents, Furlong 'grew up a Rebel'.[180] O'Keeffe evidences the influence of neighbours. Joe Brennan, the founder of the Claremorris Volunteers in the post-Rising period, 'was the Irish boy's ideal of what an Irishman should be', O'Keeffe remembered, 'a splendid athlete, great step dancer, powerful swimmer, captain of our football team, organiser of céilís and patriotic plays, and last, but not least, a strict teetotaller'.[181] It was at the insistence of some of his workmates that Furlong joined the Wexford IRB in 1908.[182]

---

177 BMHWS 1678, William O'Keeffe, pp. 1–2, 5–6
178 BMHWS 510, Frank Thornton, p. 1
179 Michael Wheatley, *Nationalism and the Irish Party: Provincial Ireland 1910–1916* (Oxford: Oxford University Press, 2005), pp. 79–84; Jonathan Githens-Mazer, *Myths and Memories of the Easter Rising: Cultural and Political Nationalism in Ireland* (Dublin: Irish Academic Press, 2006)
180 BMHWS 335, Joseph Furlong, p. 1
181 BMHWS 1678, William O'Keeffe, pp. 5–6
182 BMHWS 335, Joseph Furlong, p. 1

In addition to the influence or family, friends, neighbours and teachers, that of cultural nationalism is also evident. Furlong states that he joined the Wexford Gaelic League immediately upon its establishment in the town.[183] Liam McMahon joined the Gaelic League when he moved to Liverpool from his native Limerick in 1878. His membership of the GAA led to an invitation to join the IRB.[184] Historians of the IRA in counties Cork, Limerick, Longford and elsewhere have confirmed the importance of family, friends, schooling and inchoate nationalism in motivating Volunteer membership.[185]

We can see, therefore, that membership of the Volunteers in Ireland was often motivated by the same factors that prompted second generation Irish immigrants in Britain to join the Volunteers there, namely their families' political outlook, influence of teachers, neighbours and friends and membership of cultural nationalist organizations. These factors combined to form a defiant nationalism that refused to accept the legitimacy of British rule in Ireland. The government's perceived indulgence of the Ulster Unionists' violent opposition to home rule in 1912–14 exacerbated hostility to British rule, as did its reaction to the 1916 Rising and its attempt to impose conscription in 1918.[186]

Why, however, did these Irish-born men join the Volunteers in Britain? In the majority of cases, economic necessity motivated temporary or permanent immigration to Britain. In the remaining cases, immigration was prompted by their being charged with carrying out IRA activities in Britain. Those who immigrated because of the lacks of jobs in Ireland often had some association with advanced nationalist politics prior to their moving. Paddy Daly, for example, senior Liverpool gunrunner during the latter part of the war, was

---

183 BMHWS 335, Joseph Furlong, p. 1
184 BMHWS 274, Liam McMahon, p. 1
185 Peter Hart, *The IRA and Its Enemies: Violence and Community in Cork, 1916–1923* (Oxford: Clarendon Press, 1998), pp. 202–13; Hart, 'Geography', pp. 30–61; Joost Augusteijn, *From Public Defiance to Guerrilla Warfare: The Experience of Ordinary Volunteers in the Irish War of Independence 1916–1921* (Dublin: Irish Academic Press, 1996), pp. 364–67; John O'Callaghan, *Revolutionary Limerick: The Republican Campaign for Independence in Limerick, 1913–1921* (Dublin: Irish Academic Press, 2010), pp. 204–08; Marie Coleman, *County Longford and the Irish Revolution 1910–1923* (Dublin: Irish Academic Press, 2003), pp. 159–61
186 Joost Augusteijn, 'Motivation: Why did they Fight for Ireland? The Motivation of Volunteers in the Revolution', in Joost Augusteijn (ed.), *The Irish Revolution, 1913–1923* (Basingstoke: Palgrave, 2002), pp. 107–17

a member of the Offaly Volunteers before moving to Merseyside in 1918 in order to take up a job as a clerical worker.[187] Meanwhile, Joe Furlong was a member of the IRB before joining the Volunteers in London in 1914.[188]

VII

Moving away from the issue of motivation, what can we say about the social make-up of the IRA in Britain?

Peter Hart has analysed a large sample of Volunteer members from throughout Ireland during the period 1917–23 and has identified a number of characteristics to create a Volunteer typology. Almost certainly a Roman Catholic, the Volunteer was probably under 30 years of age, likely to be unmarried and probably unpropertied. He most likely lived in an urban setting, was educated and was at the beginning of his career in a skilled occupation.[189] While agreeing with Hart on the issues of religion, age, marital status and wealth, other studies of IRA membership at the county level have emphasized the rural origins of most Volunteers.[190]

No comprehensive membership lists exist of the IRA in Britain. Therefore, information allowing us to construct a social profile of the Volunteers has to be gathered from newspaper reports of trials, memoirs and other scattered archives.

What was the age profile of the IRA in Britain? An analysis of the ages of a sample of Volunteer officers and rank and file is presented in Table 1. As we can see, officers were, on average, over two years older than the men under their command.

An analysis of the occupations of officers and men is presented in Table 2. The most popular occupations among the officers were clerking and school teaching, while among the men they were labouring, engineering and clerking. The British civil service seems to have been the employer of a

187 BMHWS 814, Patrick Daly, p. 1

188 BMHWS 335, Joseph Furlong, p. 3

189 Peter Hart, 'The Social Structure of the Irish Republican Army', in Hart, *IRA at War*, p. 131

190 O'Callaghan, *Revolutionary Limerick*, pp. 183–90; Coleman, *County Longford*, pp. 149–50; Fergus Campbell, *Land and Revolution: Nationalist Politics in the West of Ireland 1891–1921* (Oxford: Oxford University Press, 2005), pp. 259–62; Augusteijn, *Public Defiance*, pp. 353–62; David Fitzpatrick, *Politics and Irish Life 1913–1921: Provincial Experience of War and Revolution* (Cork: Cork University Press, 1998 edition), pp. 169–70, 184–85

Table 1: Ages of Volunteers in Britain, 1919–1921

	Officers	*Men*
Sample	**34**	**63**
	%	%
<20 years of age in 1921	11.8	15.9
20–24 years of age in 1921	32.4	53.9
25–29 years of age in 1921	32.4	12.7
30–39 years of age in 1921	14.7	9.5
40–49 years of age in 1921	5.9	3.2
50–59 years of age in 1921	2.9	3.2
>60 years of age in 1921	0	1.6
Median Age	25 years	22 years
Average Age	26.9 years	24.7 years

Sources: Barrington, *Irish Independence Movement*; BMHWS; exhibits 12, 22 & 25 (TNA, Central Criminal Court file [CRIM], 1/190/1); lists of prisoners amnestied in Feb. & Apr. 1922 (Home Office [HO], 144/4645); Pinkman, *Legion*; membership rolls of Scottish Brigade IRA (EMP, 3/C/13); *Evening News* (London), *Freeman's Journal, Glasgow Herald, IT, Liverpool Courier, MG, Newcastle Daily Chronicle, Pall Mall Gazette* (and its successor, the *Pall Mall and Globe*), *The Observer, TT,* 1919–21; 1911 Census of Ireland accessed at www.nationalarchives.ie/ on 21 Feb. 2012; 1911 Census of England and Wales accessed at www.1911census.co.uk/ on 21 Feb. 2012; figures are rounded to the first decimal place

significant number of London Volunteers.[191] Indeed, when Seán McGrath was re-organizing the IRA in the capital in late 1919, he asked Michael Collins about the necessity of new recruits swearing the oath of allegiance to the Dáil, particularly those who, as civil servants, had taken a similar oath to the British government.[192] Michael O'Leary states that the majority of the Liverpool City Volunteers worked as dockers.[193] James Byrne noted that the preponderance of men in the 2nd Scottish Battalion laboured as miners and steel workers.

191 BMHWS 1584, Patrick Murray, p. 20
192 Seán McGrath to Michael Collins, n.d., but *c.* Sept. 1919 (MCP, A/0457, Group VIII, Item 1)
193 BMHWS 797, Micheál Ó Laoghaire, p. 28

Table 2: Occupations of Volunteers in Britain, 1919–1921

	Officers	*Men*
Sample	29	81
	%	%
Lower Professionals	13.8	0
Employers	6.9	0
Clerical Workers	17.2	11.1
Skilled Manual Workers	34.5	26
Semi-skilled Manual Workers	24.1	23.5
Unskilled Manual Workers	0	37
Unemployed	3.5	2.5

Sources: Barrington, *Irish Independence Movement*; BMHWS; exhibits 12, 22 & 25 (CRIM, 1/190/1); lists of prisoners amnestied in Feb. & Apr. 1922 (HO, 144/4645); Pinkman, *Legion*; membership rolls of Scottish Brigade IRA (EMP, 3/C/13); *Evening News* (London), *Freeman's Journal*, *Glasgow Herald, IT, Liverpool Courier, MG, Newcastle Daily Chronicle, Pall Mall Gazette* (and its successor, the *Pall Mall and Globe), The Observer, TT,* 1919–21; 1911 Census of Ireland accessed at www.nationalarchives.ie/ on 21 Feb. 2012; 1911 Census of England and Wales accessed at www.1911census.co.uk/ on 21 Feb. 2012; figures are rounded to the first decimal place; I have followed the categorization in Guy Routh, *Occupation and Pay in Great Britain, 1906–60* (Cambridge: Cambridge University Press, 1965)

Miners dominated the Falkirk Company, part of the 3rd Scottish Battalion.[194] Mining also seems to have been the occupation of a majority of men in such Lancashire towns as St Helens, Earlstown and Wigan.[195] According to Gilbert Barrington, the Tyneside IRA was composed mainly of artisans, semi-skilled workers and small tradesmen, along with a few teachers and businessmen. 'It seems that the relatively better educated, who understood the issues involved, were more active', he posits. Many of these men were recent emigrants, leading Barrington to suggest that 'their resentment at having to emigrate [from Ireland] had not had time to die'. By remaining in contact with relatives in Ireland, they kept abreast of events there.[196]

At least six members of the sample served in the British army during

194 BMHWS 828, James Byrne, pp. 2–3; BMHWS 696, Henry O'Hagan, p. 4
195 BMHWS 1535, Hugh Early, p. 10
196 Barrington, *Irish Independence Movement*, pp. 8–10

the Great War. Service in British uniform seems to have featured in the career history of a considerable number of Volunteers. Enough former British soldiers sought membership of the London IRA in 1919 for Seán McGrath to ask Collins about the necessity of their swearing the oath of allegiance to the Dáil too.[197] Gilbert Barrington states that ex-soldiers constituted a significant proportion of Tyneside IRA's membership, Barrington himself having served in the Royal Army Medical Corps during the Great War.[198] Members of the Nottingham and Sheffield IRA were former soldiers as well.[199]

Finally, from scattered references in Volunteers' memoirs, it would appear that the overwhelming majority of IRA men in Britain were practising Roman Catholics and that they were unmarried.[200]

The above data was culled from an accidental sample, in that it is taken from memoirs as well as from newspaper reports of people who happened to be arrested by the police on suspicion of such illegal activities as gunrunning and arson attacks. Therefore, it does not give a representative picture of the IRA in Britain. However, given the absence of comprehensive membership lists, the data can be used to give a tentative picture of the Volunteers' makeup. The data suggest that, as Hart has argued, the average member of the IRA in Britain was a Roman Catholic single male in his mid-twenties from the working and lower middle classes.[201]

How do Volunteer members compare with the wider Irish community in Britain? According to the census of 1911, the occupations which accounted for the largest number of Irish male workers in Scotland were iron and metal manufacturing (33.7 per cent), mining (16.2 per cent), general labouring (8.2 per cent) and the building trade (6.7 per cent). Manual labour, therefore, dominated the occupations of the Irish in Scotland.[202] While a majority of Volunteers in our sample held manual occupations, a significant minority were clerical and professional workers. Occupationally, therefore, it would seem that IRA members were, on average, broadly representative of the Irish community in Britain.

---

197 Séan McGrath to Michael Collins, n.d., but *c*. Sept. 1919 (MCP, A/0457, Group VIII, Item 1)

198 Barrington, *Irish Independence Movement*, pp. 4–5, 7

199 O/C Britain to C/S, 15 Oct. 1921 (RMP, P7/A/29[264–73])

200 See the memoirs mentioned in Section VI; e.g. Pinkman, *Legion*, pp. 66–67, 77–78

201 Hart, 'Social Structure', pp. 127–28

202 *Report on the Twelfth Decennial Census of Scotland, iii* [Cd. 7163] (1913), pp. v–vi

VIII

How was a Volunteer company run? The *General Scheme of Organisation* outlined the formal government of the company. The O/C and his two lieutenants, the senior company officers, were to be elected by the company members. The other officers, including NCOs, were then to be appointed by the O/C.[203] Such rules, however, were not always followed.

Upon the initial foundation of a Volunteer company, the organizers usually dispensed with elections and appointed the officers themselves, especially when GHQ was involved. As noted earier, Michael Collins approved the appointment of three officers to bring the 'many wild young chaps' of the London IRA under discipline. Joe Vize acted similarly in Glasgow.[204] Meanwhile, Rory O'Connor appointed a brigade staff on Tyneside in November 1920.[205] Thereafter, as the membership became more disciplined, GHQ allowed the replacement of company leaders to proceed through elections. On the other hand, the Birmingham Volunteers, established without any reference to Dublin, elected their own officers from the beginning.[206] Although GHQ retained the right to withdraw the commissions of the elected officers, the provision for elections effectively gave the rank and file the major role in deciding the company leadership. However, Dublin did not always approve of the officers elected this way. The arrest of a large number of IRA men in Manchester following the arson operation of April 1921 led Michael Collins to complain of a 'general looseness' in the city's Volunteer organization: the leadership exuded an irritating, laid-back, 'happy-go-lucky air', he wrote.[207]

The Liverpool City Company provides an example of the rank and file initiating an election to change the O/C. Sometime around September 1919, Michael O'Leary was elected company commander, replacing the America-bound Tom Craven. Soon, however, the men became disgruntled with O'Leary's leadership. His lectures were placing too much emphasis on political matters at the expense of such straightforwardly military issues as street fighting. Some feared that O'Leary's leadership was causing the men to lose interest in the Volunteers. Fearful that the company would continue to

---

203 Irish Volunteers, *General Scheme of Organisation* (MCP, A/0032A, Group 2, Item 2)

204 Joe Vize to Michael Collins, 27 Sept. 1919 (RMP, P7/A/11)

205 BMHWS 773, Gilbert Barrington, p. 2

206 BMHWS 922, James Cunningham, pp. 1, 5, 15

207 Michael Collins to Art O'Brien, 23 May, 6 June 1921 (DÉ, 2/330)

haemorrhage members as long as O'Leary remained in charge, John Pinkman and others called for an election. Tom Kerr, 1st lieutenant, was elected O/C and a suitable martial tone was re-introduced into Volunteer matters.[208]

Where possible, the election of the 1st lieutenant to the O/C position seems to have been the usual procedure in the event of the commanding officer proving unsatisfactory or being incapacitated. This was the case in Liverpool at any rate, which suffered the highest leadership turnover of any IRA unit in Britain. Following Tom Kerr's arrest in November 1920, in connection with arson attacks in Liverpool city and Bootle, Peter Roland became O/C. The following month, however, Roland, his 2nd lieutenant and five other Volunteers were arrested in a public house.[209] Hugh Early, Roland's successor, was arrested in June 1921 in connection with the sabotage of communications infrastructure. Edward Brady, 1st lieutenant, was then appointed acting O/C until another candidate was appointed, Michael Collins having stated that an election was unnecessary.[210] A few days later, however, Brady, his 2nd lieutenant and three other Volunteers were arrested in another wire-cutting operation. Denis Fleming, 1st lieutenant, 'about the best man left, and also the most suitable for the position', was then appointed O/C without an election.[211]

Once the companies, battalions and brigades had been established and their officers appointed or elected, their association with GHQ depended on their involvement in gunrunning. As soon as they got involved in smuggling activities, Dublin instituted close contact.[212]

Unlike the IRA in Ireland, the Volunteers in Britain were never formally recognized by Dáil Éireann. In March 1921, over two years after the outbreak of the war, de Valera, President of the Dáil, declared that the revolutionary government was '*responsible for the actions*' of the IRA. Although belated, his comments elevated the IRA in Ireland to 'a national army of defence'.[213] Such recognition did not extend to the Volunteers in Britain, an army of offense. Like de Valera, *An t-Óglác* feigned ignorance in regard to Volunteer activities across the Irish Sea. Despite widespread press coverage of the Volunteers'

---

208 Pinkman, *Legion*, pp. 19–20; it should be noted that O'Leary himself claims that he retired from the leadership because he realised that he possessed neither the time nor the energy that he considered necessary to fulfil the role of O/C: BMHWS 797, Micheál Ó Laoghaire, pp. 41–42

209 Paddy Daly to Michael Collins, n.d., but *c.* 31 Dec. 1920 (RMP, P7/A/3)

210 Correspondence between Daly and Collins, 6, 9 June 1921 (RMP, P7/A/5)

211 Daly to Collins, 13, 20 June 1921 (RMP, P7/A/5)

212 See Chapter 2

213 *An t-Óglác*, 15 Apr. 1921; original emphasis

campaign of violence in Britain in 1920–21, the official organ of the IRA failed to address the matter. Indeed, its only references to the Volunteers in Britain were in relation to the jailbreaks of 1919 which witnessed the escapes of, among others, de Valera from Lincoln prison and *An t-Óglác* editor Piaras Béaslaí from Strangeways prison.[214]

We can see then that the relationship between IRA units in Britain and GHQ in Dublin varied. This was also the case in Ireland. It was only in February 1920, 13 months after the shooting dead of two policemen by members of the IRA at Soloheadbeg that *An t-Óglác* came out unambiguously in favour of offensive warfare. In the interim, 19 policemen and officials had been killed by the Volunteers. Therefore, as the historian David Fitzpatrick observes, 'The great mass of provincial Volunteers had drifted imperturbably towards revolution, oblivious to the whistlings of their leaders, governed by the logic of local experience.'[215] Joost Augusteijn, however, argues that GHQ played a large part in spreading that violence throughout Ireland.[216] Nevertheless, Dublin's inability to supply provincial units with adequate amounts of munitions had the effect of limiting its influence over them.[217]

In August 1920, the IRA in Britain became the responsibility of an O/C Britain. The first person to occupy this post was Rory O'Connor. His mandate was 'to organise and carry out operations in Enemy Territory'.[218] O'Connor and members of his staff frequently visited Volunteer units. A 'Mr F.' travelled to Liverpool in April 1921 in order to plan operations with the local company.[219] 'Flan' and 'M. R.' spent some time in London the following June. They seem to have been involved in some sort of re-organization of the Volunteers there, for Michael Collins feared that Flan lacked 'the comprehensive outlook [necessary] for directing and ordering an organisation over a large area'.[220] Mick McEvoy visited Tyneside in 1920–21 to confirm leadership appointments and inspect the various companies.[221] IRA units sometimes

214   *An t-Óglác*, 27 Mar., 15 Dec. 1919

215   Fitzpatrick, *Politics*, p. 179; *Return Showing by Monthly Periods the Number of Murders of Members of the Royal Irish Constabulary and of the Dublin Metropolitan Police … from the 1st Day of January, 1919, to the 30th April, 1920* [Cmd. 709] (1920), p. 2

216   Augusteijn, *Public Defiance*, p. 183

217   Fitzpatrick, *Politics*, pp. 172–73; O'Callaghan, *Revolutionary Limerick*, p. 193

218   O/C Britain to C/S, 9 Sept. 1921 (RMP, P7/A/24[63–65])

219   Paddy Daly to Michael Collins, 23, 27 Apr. 1921 (RMP, P7/A/5)

220   Collins to Art O'Brien, 6 June 1921 (DÉ, 2/330)

221   BMHWS 773, Gilbert Barrington, p. 2

Figure 1:
IRA O/C Britain
Rory O'Connor
(Courtesy of the
National Library
of Ireland)

received visits from Joe Furlong, D.P. Walsh and Liam Mellows too. However, these officers mainly concerned themselves with gunrunning rather than Volunteer affairs per se.[222]

The historian Iain Patterson has argued that the republicanism in Scotland suffered 'deep internal divisions' which 'depleted the movement's morale and organisational effectiveness'.[223] By way of evidence, he points to the existence of unruly Volunteers in Glasgow, IRB men apparently more interested in supplying the ICA with weapons than sending them to GHQ and to controversy regarding the Scottish gunrunning accounts. The latter

---

222 BMHWS 828, James Byrne, pp. 2–3; Michael Collins to Art O'Brien, 13 June
     1921 (DÉ, 2/330)
223 Patterson, 'Activities', p. 46

two issues will be discussed later. However, while acknowledging the existence of such divisions, this author believes that Patterson has exaggerated their singularity and the consequences which flowed from them. As we have seen, the existence of a rebellious Volunteer company under Liam Gribbon in Glasgow did not prevent Joe Vize from organizing companies in other parts of Glasgow and Scotland. Even the most active IRA units in Ireland suffered similar problems, mainly as a result of bad organization.[224] Such problems did not diminish their morale and neither did it that of the Scottish IRA to any great extent. Undoubtedly, the Volunteers in Scotland, and by extension those in England and Wales too, were not as active as their most energetic comrades in Ireland. This, however, was not due to internal divisions but rather to the fact that, as we shall see, their role was limited to gunrunning, with the mounting of a violent attacks being of only secondary importance.

Just as their relationship with Dublin varied, so did that between the different IRA units themselves. Rory O'Connor stated that the eight companies which existed in England in August 1920, in London, Liverpool and Manchester, were acting autonomously and in isolation from one another. In October the following year, he judged that an improvement had come about in communications between the units, now numbering 31 companies and spread across a wider area.[225] We noted already that the Birmingham Volunteers affiliated themselves with the Liverpool IRA. Birmingham's James Cunningham fails to explain what such an affiliation specifically involved.[226] Presumably, however, it entailed close contact between the two units. Outside of such affiliations, relations between IRA centres were fostered by the complicated business of gunrunning. With Liverpool seen as the safest port from which to smuggle the munitions to Ireland, the Merseyside men received regular visits from their London, Birmingham, Manchester and Glasgow comrades.

The IRB seems to have had a significant role in the command of the Liverpool Volunteers. However, Fenian control was dependent on the compliance of the commanding officer. By April 1921, the O/C, Hugh Early, although an IRB member, had 'fallen away somewhat' from the control of the local Fenian executive, Paddy Daly told Michael Collins. Such an alteration in

---

224 'SERIOUS DEFICIENCIES IN COUNTRY UNITS', 7 Mar. 1921 (RMP, P7/A/19[169])

225 O/C Britain to C/S, 9 Sept., 15 Oct. 1921 (RMP, P7/A/24[63–65], P7/A/29 [264–73])

226 BMHWS 922, James Cunningham, pp. 1, 5, 15

the relationship between the IRB and the Volunteers on Merseyside had been caused by the institution of direct communications between Early and Rory O'Connor, along with the innovation whereby the former was now planning operations solely in consultation with the O/C Britain's representative in Liverpool. Having 'acquired this power', Early proceeded to collect a significant amount of money from various Irish organizations, including the Cumann na mBan. His refusal to reveal the amount he had collected reinforced suspicions which already existed against him in the minds of the IRB regarding the lenient treatment he had received from the authorities in connection with a recent arson attack. Taken as a whole, 'things look very "fishy"', Daly noted. He himself, however, did not believe that anything nefarious was afoot. Still, he suggested that the O/C Britain's representative should take complete control of the Volunteers. Under such an arrangement, he hoped that the rules and constitution of the IRA would be fully observed, implying that this was not the case under Early. Such procedures would ensure that

> the O/C and the other officers meet at periodical times to discuss volunteer matters, that an adjutant be appointed, and that a quarter-master be appointed to look after the funds and any fire-arms belonging to the Co[mpan]y.

O'Connor's representative taking charge of the Volunteers did not need to involve his remaining permanently on Merseyside, Daly added. Rather, the Company O/C would be answerable to him, sending him regular reports on the situation. Alternatively, Daly proposed that a member of the Liverpool IRB executive, appointed by his colleagues and ratified by GHQ, assume the position of 'sub director' of the Liverpool IRA. This man would then act as an intermediary between Dublin and the Company O/C and would be involved in the planning of operations with other IRA officers.[227] The sources do not say if Daly's suggestions were implemented. However, Michael Collins told Daly that IRB man Seán McGarry would 'deal with all local questions, and fix up things on a firm basis'. McGarry did spend some time in Liverpool the following month, but the nature of his reforms, if any, are not recorded.[228]

Early later stated that he had found the IRB to be of little use and was only a nominal member.[229] This raises questions about the importance of the

---

227 Paddy Daly to Michael Collins, 27 Apr. 1921 (RMP, P7/A/5)
228 Correspondence between Collins and Daly, 5, 11 May 1921 (RMP, P7/A/5)
229 BMHWS 1535, Hugh Early, p. 11

Fenians. Augusteijn states that the re-organization of the Volunteers in Ireland in the period between the Easter Rising and the 1918 General Election saw a decline in the importance of the IRB. For the military-minded, the Fenian organization was superfluous as the Volunteers were now openly defying the British authorities. De Valera and Cathal Brugha, who later became minister for defence, subscribed to this, believing that secret societies were no longer necessary.[230] Nevertheless, in Cork city and county it was militant IRB men who forced the pace from 1917 onwards by mounting unauthorized attacks on policemen.[231] Marie Coleman contends that while IRB membership in County Longford was small and that its influence among ordinary Volunteers was minimal, Fenianism was 'an important motivating factor for the leaders of republicanism' in the county.[232]

In Britain, the position of the IRB was ambiguous. Ordinary Volunteers were sometimes kept in ignorance of the organization's existence. Yet, leaders like Joe Vize used the Fenians as bedrock for the re-establishment of the Volunteers. Others, however, were sceptical of the IRB's value. Liverpool's Paddy Daly found his Fenian colleagues little help with gunrunning matters. Moreover, due to his youth, they balked at Daly succeeding Neil Kerr Senior as centre for the north of England and consistently tried to undermine his position. In the latter part of the war, the IRB's 'power as a secret organisation was very much on the decline', Daly later wrote.[233] Seán McGrath captured the ambiguity of the organization when he stated in later life that he was 'suspicious of some of the men who were in the I.R.B. It was an organisation joined without serious thought', an indication perhaps that some members viewed Fenianism as a social outlet rather than a serious revolutionary force.[234]

IX

In Ireland, the ranks of violent republicanism began to re-organize themselves in earnest in 1917. It was 1919 before similar efforts commenced in Britain, with the re-founding of the Irish Volunteers, the IRB, Cumann na mBan and

---

230   Augusteijn, *Public Defiance*, p. 86
231   Hart, *IRA and Its Enemies*, pp. 240–42
232   Coleman, *County Longford*, pp. 163–64
233   BMHWS 814, Patrick Daly pp. 29–30, 32–33
234   Seán McGrath interview (EO'MN, P17b/100); see R.V. Comerford, 'Patriotism as Pastime: The Appeal of Fenianism in the Mid-1860s', *IHS*, 22.86 (1980), pp. 239–50

Na Fianna Éireann. Joe Vize led the way in Scotland and was soon followed by fellow IRB men in Liverpool and London. Later, new organizations were founded in Birmingham, Manchester, Sheffield and Tyneside, often on the initiative of people who had little previous connection with physical force republicanism. At its peak in the autumn of 1921, the membership of the IRA lay somewhere between 2,282 and 2,582. Those of the other three republican organizations are unknown but were probably in the hundreds. The Volunteer rank and file was made up of men born in Ireland and those born in Britain to Irish immigrants. Their reasons for joining the IRA can usually be traced to such factors as having imbibed a nationalist outlook from their family relations, the consumption of nationalist media, membership of cultural nationalist organizations and experience of sectarian discrimination. As in Ireland, the Volunteers in Britain sometimes suffered problems including loose organization and bad leadership.

In November 1920, discussing the nascent Tyneside IRA, London's Seán McGrath agreed with Michael Collins's connection that organizing Volunteer companies in Britain was his most important task. The Tyneside men were 'only waiting [for] a visit from me to enable them to get direct[ly] in touch with you', McGrath wrote.[235] What motivated Collins's interest in the establishment of Volunteer organization in Britain was the opportunity it afforded for gunrunning, the clandestine acquisition and despatch to Ireland of munitions of war. It is to that topic that we now turn.

235 McGrath to Michael Collins, 13 Nov. 1920 (RMP, P7/A/8)

CHAPTER 2

Supplying an Army: Gunrunning in Britain, January 1919–July 1921

I

The retrospective political success of the Easter Rising encouraged those who re-formed the Volunteers and the IRB in 1917 to continue the struggle to overthrow British rule in Ireland. The acquisition of weapons, therefore, became of paramount importance. The attack at Soloheadbeg, the opening shots of the war, was motivated by a desire to acquire explosives.[1] However, with only a limited amount of munitions available for purchase or theft in Ireland itself, rebels were forced to source materiel abroad. Britain was the main source of armaments procured overseas, and gunrunners there engaged in illegal and dangerous activities in order to provide munitions to their comrades in Ireland. As the Liverpool gunrunner Paddy Daly expressed it: 'I always have it before me that we have got to help supply an army …'.[2] This chapter discusses such gunrunning. Section II introduces the main figures involved. Section III follows gunrunners on missions to secure armaments. Section IV deals with the sources tapped, along with the types and quantities of materiel acquired. Section V notes the arrangements made for the storage of such armaments, while section VI describes the transport of weapons to Ireland and their distribution there. Section VII concludes.

II

Scarcity of weapons was a persistent problem for the IRA in Ireland. In 1917, in order to raise funds to buy arms, Volunteers held concerts, dances and collections. However, the number of firearms purchased with these funds was

---

1 BMHWS 1721, Séamus Robinson, pp. 21–22
2 Paddy Daly to Michael Collins, 28 Sept. 1921 (RMP, P7/A/7)

small.[3] The following year, during the Conscription Crisis, many Volunteers began to acquire weapons by raiding private houses, despite Sinn Féin prohibiting such operations. In 1918, 311 civilians had their houses raided. In 1919, the figure was 196; in addition, the police suffered 12 raids and the military 15. In September 1920, IRA GHQ finally authorized the raiding of houses; 2,802 such operations took place that year.[4] However, despite these and other attempts to acquire weapons, the IRA was forced to exploit sources abroad in order to augment its arsenal.

In this, the Volunteers were following in the footsteps of the IRB. In the run-up to the 1867 rebellion, Fenians procured munitions in London, Birmingham and Liverpool, and smuggled them to Ireland.[5] Also, on 11 February that year, they unsuccessfully attempted to steal materiel from Chester Castle. Over the course of subsequent decades, IRB men continued to send small amounts of weapons to Ireland for use when England's difficulty would be Ireland's opportunity.

At the beginning of the war in 1919, a handful of people dominated the Fenian movement in each of the four major centres of Irish activity in Britain. In London, Seán McGrath and Sam Maguire were assisted by, among others, Denis and Joe Carr, Eamon O'Tierney, Martin Walsh, Martin Geraghty and Art O'Brien.[6] Gunrunning was one of the responsibilities of Joe Vize and he chose a number of lieutenants to aid this work. Patrick Clinton and James Quinn were chief amongst them, evidenced by the fact that Vize nominated them, successively, to take charge of 'war material' in the event of his arrest.[7] Andrew Fagan became QM of the Scottish Brigade and Seán Flood was appointed QM of the 1st Battalion and later Assistant Brigade QM.[8] On Merseyside, the Kerrs and Steve Lanigan were

3 Augusteijn, *Public Defiance*, pp. 72–73

4 Augusteijn, *Public Defiance*, pp. 75–76, 93–94; Fitzpatrick, *Politics*, pp. 177, 186; *Return Showing by Monthly Periods the Number of Murders of Members of the Royal Irish Constabulary and of the Dublin Metropolitan Police … from the 1st Day of January, 1919, to the 30th April, 1920* [Cmd. 709] 1920, p. 2

5 Ryan, *Fenian Memories*, p. 38

6 John J. Sherlock Statement, pp. 1–3 (NLI, MS 9,873); O'Brien to the Committee investigating London cases in regard to the Military Pensions Act, 17 Apr. 1941 (AÓBP, MS 8461/26); Martin Walsh to the MSPB, n.d.; Martin Geraghty to the MSPB, 20 May 1937 (EO'ML, P17a/154)

7 Joe Vize to Michael Collins, 15 Feb., 26 Mar. 1920 (RMP, P7/A/11)

8 Andrew Fagan reference, 15 May 1939; Vize to the Secretary, MSPB, 29 Sept. 1944 (EMP, 2/A/3, 2/A/8)

in charge.[9] In Manchester, Paddy O'Donoghue, Liam McMahon and Matt Lawless managed operations.[10]

As the war progressed, some changes occurred in the gunrunning personnel. In February 1919, London's Seán McGrath was sentenced to six months' imprisonment for purchasing munitions without a permit. Released in July, he quickly resumed clandestine activities.[11] In July 1920, Joe Vize returned to Ireland to take up the new position of D/P. His gunrunning duties in Scotland were then assumed by Joe Furlong. In early 1921, Furlong departed for Dublin and became involved in the manufacture of munitions for GHQ.[12] He was succeeded in Scotland by D.P. Walsh, the assistant QMG.[13] In early 1920, John and James McGallogly took up employment in Manchester and became involved in gunrunning there.[14] The Volunteers' arson attack on Merseyside in November 1920 led to the internment and imprisonment of Neil Kerr Senior and Tom Kerr, as well as Steve Lanigan. The leadership was then assumed by Paddy Daly.[15] In February 1921, Seán McGrath was arrested again, this time in connection with IRA attacks in the London area. Interned in Ireland, his shoes were filled by Art O'Brien and Dennis Kelleher.[16] Three months later, the Carr brothers were arrested as part of the police investigation into attacks on the relatives of RIC men. Seán Golden, a Dublin Volunteer who became QM of the London IRA, then took charge of gunrunning in the capital.[17]

Until December 1920, the gunrunners received their orders from the IRB in Dublin, the leadership of which during the war was dominated by Michael Collins. Visits to Britain by Collins and other Fenian leaders such as Seán McGarry and periodic trips to Ireland by the gun-smugglers themselves ensured that the Dublin leadership and the gunrunners remained

---

9   BMHWS 814, Patrick Daly, pp. 16–17

10 BMHWS 847, Patrick O'Donoghue, pp. 5–6; BMHWS 274, Liam McMahon, pp. 2–3; BMHWS 244, John McGallogly, pp. 17–18; Paddy Daly interview (EO'MN, P17b/136)

11 *TT*, 29 Jan., 7 Feb. 1919; Seán McGrath interview (EO'MN, P17b/100)

12 BMHWS 664, Patrick McHugh, p. 45

13 BMHWS 777, Patrick Mills, p. 5; BMHWS 1100, John Sharkey, p. 18

14 BMHWS 244, John McGallogly, pp. 18–19

15 BMHWS 814, Patrick Daly, pp. 1, 21–22

16 Correspondence between Michael Collins and Art O'Brien, 28 Feb., 1 Mar. 1921 (DÉ, 2/328); Denis Kelleher to O'Brien, 18 Feb. 1922 (AÓBP, MS 8424/13)

17 Martin Walsh to the MSPB, n.d. (EO'ML, P17a/154); correspondence between O'Brien and Collins, 18, 27 Nov. 1919 (AÓBP, MS 8429/11)

in face-to-face as well as written contact.[18] In the summer of 1920, GHQ was re-organized and some new departments were created. Among them was a department of (munitions) purchases, headed by a D/P. Joe Vize was the first D/P. However, upon his arrest in October 1920, he was succeeded by Liam Mellows.[19] Despite Mellows and his lieutenants making regular visits to gunrunning centres in Britain in 1921, Michael Collins continued to send orders to Liverpool and London. Paddy Daly states that he succeeded in working with both IRA and IRB leaders in gunrunning matters.[20]

The appointment of Mellows as D/P in 1920 coincided with and stimulated the IRA's increased involvement in gunrunning in Britain. Previous to this, Volunteer companies established in 1919 and 1920 in London, Liverpool and Manchester had been involved in munitions-smuggling only under the auspices of the IRB.[21] Now IRA companies were becoming involved in their own right. This was apparent in the development of Tyneside, South Wales and Birmingham as centres of procurement. In the former, operations were run by the O/C Tyneside Brigade Richard Purcell, QM Gilbert Barrington and adjutant J.P. Connolly.[22] The procurement of munitions there had begun on the initiative of the men themselves without direction from GHQ or the other gunrunning centres. In late February or early March 1921, at about the same time that the brigade began mounting arson attacks on property, Barrington was summoned to Dublin to meet Mellows. The D/P gave him instructions and money for the purchase of arms.[23] When Connolly later moved to South Wales to open up new sources of munitions, he was replaced as adjutant by David Fitzgerald.[24] In Birmingham too, gunrunning had begun without the involvement of GHQ. A number of Irish immigrants, including James Cunningham, established their own Volunteer company. Initially, they sent their munitions to the 3rd Dublin Battalion. The Dublin men were so impressed with the supply that they advised GHQ to exploit Birmingham more

18 Collins to 'Donal', 13 Apr. 1919 (RMP, P7/A/1[72]); Seán McGrath interview (EO'MN, P17b/100); O'Brien to Collins, 23 May 1921 (DÉ, 2/330); BMHWS 814, Patrick Daly, pp. 21–22

19 Captain 'P' Section to Commandant, Military Barracks, 9 Apr. 1921, enclosing list of prisoners (MCP, A/0619/73); Béaslaí, *Michael Collins*, ii, p. 161

20 BMHWS 814, Patrick Daly, pp. 5, 14–15, 25

21 BMHWS 922, James Cunningham, p. 1; BMHWS 847, Patrick O'Donoghue, pp. 5–6

22 Barrington, *Irish Independence Movement*, p. 13

23 BMHWS 773, Gilbert Barrington, pp. 8–9

24 Barrington, *Irish Independence Movement*, p. 13

fully. Cunningham duly travelled to Dublin in early 1921 and met Michael Collins and QMG Seán McMahon. Impressed with Birmingham's potential, they appointed Cunningham as full-time gunrunning agent in the city.[25]

How was gunrunning organized? Cunningham remembered the enormity of the job he had undertaken: 'I had a Herculean task ahead of me', he later wrote,

> when one realises that the only organisation we had was the haphazard one which a few working men had built up in the comparatively short time which had elapsed from our initial meeting in the parochial hall attached to St. Michael's Church at Meeting House Lane.

He decided to set up a clandestine gunrunning network separate from the city's Volunteers. Even Patrick O'Neill, the O/C, was kept in ignorance of gun-smuggling matters. 'I considered that the people with whom I was to work should, as far as possible, be inconspicuous in Irish affairs', he commented. Two recruits were 'real finds': Dan O'Malley, a third generation Irishman who had fought in the British army, and Tom Gilmore, a gunsmith who owned a small factory. Gilmore's factory became a warehouse and packing centre, while O'Malley took charge of despatching the consignments to Liverpool for the onward journey to Ireland.[26]

By arranging matters in such a way, Cunningham was probably following the advice of Merseyside's Paddy Daly, whom he visited on his return journey from Dublin. Daly sought to guarantee that the management of gunrunning activity in Liverpool in 1921 was confined to himself and his assistant, initially a man named Hogan and later Tim O'Sullivan. '[W]e rarely had to call on other members of the I.R.B.', he remembered, 'so that a considerable number of people in the Volunteers did not know that such an organisation [i.e. gunrunning] was in existence at all.'[27] Daly, in turn, was following in the footsteps of the Kerrs, who had placed paramount importance on secrecy. Indeed, ignorance regarding the existence of Fenian gun-smuggling in Liverpool during Neil Kerr Senior's time had led Volunteer John Pinkman and some friends to raid a gunsmith's shop in 1920. Frustrated by the apparent inactivity of the IRA in Liverpool, they intended to send the munitions to Ireland to help the 'real soldiers'. The raid proved successful, with the gang

25 BMHWS 922, James Cunningham, pp. 1–4
26 BMHWS 922, James Cunningham, pp. 4–6
27 BMHWS 814, Patrick Daly, p. 25

seizing 12 revolvers and hundreds of rounds of ammunition. However, O/C Tom Kerr reproached the men. 'We have special [gunrunning] channels from England to Ireland; we've had them for years and they've never been discovered', he declared. Mounting such a raid ran the risk of the police launching sweeps through Irish neighbourhoods, perhaps leading to the discovery of arms dumps. Kerr concluded by warning the Volunteers that they were to steer clear of gunrunning unless specifically ordered to do otherwise.[28] Indeed, Daly may have placed even more of a premium on secrecy than the Kerrs, for he even refused to take other senior members of the Liverpool IRB into his confidence. The assistance of such men was 'unnecessary as far as activities in connection with arms were concerned', he argued.[29]

III

Gunrunning was 'a very ticklesome job and any slip-up would reveal the whole system of smuggling such items to the enemy', wrote one Liverpool Volunteer.[30] It was, of course, illegal. The Explosives Act 1875 made the unauthorized transportation of explosives a criminal offence.[31] Under the Explosive Substances Act 1883, it was illegal to make or keep explosives with the intent to endanger life or property. Section five of the Act criminalized anyone who 'by the supply of or solicitation for money, the providing of premises, the supply of materials, or in any manner whatsoever, procures, counsels, aids, abets, or is accessory to, the commission of any crime under this Act'. Such a person would be charged with felony and would 'be liable to be tried and punished for that crime, as if he had been guilty as a principal'.[32] Meanwhile, the Firearms Act 1920 made it an offence to possess a gun without a certificate from the police, restricted the sale and repair of arms and ammunition to authorized dealers and laid down that the conveyance and export of firearms required police authorization.[33] In Ireland, meanwhile, legislation introduced during the Great War and continued

28 Pinkman, *Legion*, pp. 22–28
29 BMHWS 814, Patrick Daly, pp. 32–33
30 BMHWS 1535, Hugh Early, pp. 9–10
31 Explosives Act 1875 (38 & 39 Victoria), accessed at http://www.opsi.gov.uk/RevisedStatutes/Acts/ukpga/1875/cukpga_18750017_en_1 on 7 Dec. 2009
32 Explosive Substances Act 1883 (46 & 47 Victoria), accessed at http://www.opsi.gov.uk/RevisedStatutes/Acts/ukpga/1883/cukpga_18830003_en_1 on 7 Dec. 2009
33 Firearms Act 1920 (10 & 11 George V) accessed at http://www.opsi.gov.uk/acts/acts1920/pdf/ukpga_19200043_en.pdf on 7 Dec. 2009

into peacetime in the face of the IRA insurgency made the ownership and carrying of most weapons subject to increasing restrictions, until, in December 1920, the unauthorized ownership of a firearm was made a capital offence in martial law areas.[34]

Gunrunning in Britain was a cloak-and-dagger affair, involving the cultivating of contacts, the pursuit and evaluation of leads, the testing of munitions offered for sale, the organization of arms dumps and the transporting of weapons to Ireland. The smugglers were sometimes aided in the task by people from outside the ranks of the Volunteers and the IRB. Michael O'Leary recalled that ISDL members often provided the IRA with valuable intelligence concerning the location of weapons.[35] The league was also sometimes used to provide cover for gunrunning operations. In September 1920, Seán McGrath used the pretext of organizational work as ISDL general secretary to locate some new sources of munitions on the north-east coast of Britain.[36] When Newcastle-upon-Tyne's J.P Connolly moved to South Wales in 1921 to procure weapons, he did so under the guise of an ISDL organizer.[37] The '[r]emoval and care of arms and ammunition' was one of the Cumann na mBan's 18 prescribed activities, and members of the women's auxiliary helped with the procurement and storage of munitions.[38] More generally, Paddy Daly remembered that Irishmen throughout the north of England were always 'on the lookout for weapons that would be of use irrespective of whether they were in an [Irish] organisation or not'.[39] Sometimes GHQ in Dublin passed on unsolicited offers of help it had received from people in Britain. In November 1919, for example, Countess Markievicz, President of the Cumann na mBan, told Michael Collins that she had learned from an ex-soldier that at least 700 rifles were stored in an unused aerodrome in Georgetown, over 11 kilometres from the Scottish town of Paisley. Collins passed the information on the Joe Vize, 'for what it is worth'.[40] The sources do not record the upshot of this lead.

---

34   'Measures Taken To Prevent Hostile Organisations Obtaining Arms and Ammunition', n.d., but *c.* 1917; see also proclamations from 1918–19 (TNA, Colonial Office file [CO], 904/29 [336–40, 447, 458–59, 486, 518, 544]); *TT*, 14 Dec. 1920; Fitzpatrick, *Politics*, pp. 177, 274 n. 21–22

35   BMHWS 797, Micheál Ó Laoghaire, p. 28

36   Michael Collins to Neil Kerr, 23 Sept. 1920 (RMP, P7/A/3)

37   Brian O'Kennedy to J.P. Connolly, 25 Feb. 1921 (AÓBP, MS 8442/5)

38   Constitution of Cumann na mBan (SHP, P106/1126[1–2]); BMHWS 773, Gilbert Barrington, p. 8

39   BMHWS 814, Patrick Daly, pp. 15–16

40   Michael Collins to Joe Vize, 14 Nov. 1919 (RMP, P7/A/11)

Some leads proved to be very time-consuming, complicated, worrying and ultimately fruitless. '[W]e are now on a few good lines that I expect to work with good results very soon', Vize told Collins in early May 1919. One line of enquiry concerned a big army stores containing machine guns, revolvers, rifles and grenades. The rifles were broken down into their constituent parts. All the parts were included except the wooden sections, which could be manufactured in Ireland. He concluded: '[I] intend to give it extra attention and try to strike something good.'[41] Two-and-a-half weeks later, Vize was emphatic: 'We've struck oil'.

> There is now passing into our hands 500 Revolvers and 200,000 rounds of .303 [ammunition], don't think I've made a mistake in the figures, it[']s right, I'm making speeding up arrangements so that it will be in our hands as soon as possible … I expect this to be extra good and intend working for it for all its worth, I'm going down there on Wed[nesday]. night to speed up things (It is outside the City) Send over what money you can by [Paddy] Nolan [the seafarer], to have on hand. This first lot will cost nothing only what I spent as bait about £30 or £40 up to now, but they will be expecting a present when all is got through before making another deal[.]

The first raid was scheduled for Wednesday night, 4 June. Further raids would be mounted every subsequent night until all the materiel had been removed.[42]

The following week, however, the raid was re-arranged for Tuesday night, 10 June. Between 25,000 and 30,000 rounds of .303 ammunition were to be removed by motor car, along with revolvers by hand. Six dumps were arranged to receive the projected haul. The motor car would distribute the munitions between the dumps in the country, while a horse and cart would do likewise in the city. Vize did not know the number of revolvers in the store as the storekeeper 'is not a man you could buy over, so we must take it as he dets [i.e. debts] us'. Moreover, the storekeeper had not yet indicated how or when he wanted to be rewarded for his co-operation. Still, Vize and his men expected to get a large haul of munitions: 'Everything is looking the best for us, (unless something unforeseen happens) and I have great hopes of doing something extra big for you (God grant it).' Meanwhile, he had carried out reconnaissance on two army shooting ranges. Raids on

---

41 Vize to Collins, 10 May 1919 (RMP, P7/A/11)
42 Vize to Collins, 28 May 1919 (RMP, P7/A/11); original emphasis

these would be 'dead easy', he boasted, but fearing that an attack on them might alert the authorities at the army stores, he decided to postpone any operations.[43]

It would seem that the IRA never mounted the raid on the army stores, for almost two weeks after the operation was scheduled to take place Vize noted that the storekeeper was continuing to smuggle out small quantities of rifle parts.[44] Perhaps the shooting ranges proved a more tempting target, for Vize authorized a raid on one of them. However, 'meeting our old luck', the operation was cancelled. The day before the scheduled raid, Vize's agent, the army range keeper, was sentenced to 30 days' imprisonment for pawning army boots, while his wife was given three weeks to vacate the family's lodgings at the base. Vize hoped that they might be able to acquire some of the munitions within that period. Nevertheless, he was keenly disappointed. '[T]he worst part of it is filling you and the boys with such hopes only to be dashed to the ground', he confessed to Collins, 'it has not been for the want of working up the job I can assure you, we could only do our best'.[45]

Another affair fraught with danger concerned the gunrunner John Byrnes. Art O'Brien seems to have first met Byrnes, a passionate communist who supported Irish self-determination, in early 1919. Byrnes offered his services, claiming that he was in a position to procure arms for the IRA. On one occasion he handed a dozen .45 revolvers to Seán McGrath.[46] By the middle of June, O'Brien was offering to pay the expenses involved in Byrnes spending a week or a fortnight procuring materiel. Byrnes declined the offer, but evidently continued to supply small amounts of munitions to O'Brien, McGrath and Sam Maguire, for Collins agreed to his request for an interview in November.[47] Collins had already met Byrnes, describing him as likeable and straight-forward.[48] In early December, Byrnes, by now using the alias John Jameson, travelled to Dublin and met Collins.[49] Over the following few weeks, Jameson travelled back and forth between London and Dublin, making arrangements for gunrunning. However, Tom Cullen, a senior member of Collins's intelligence staff, expressed a strong dislike of Jameson. Frank Thornton, by now the deputy assistant director

43 Vize to Collins, 6 June 1919 (RMP, P7/A/11); original emphasis
44 Vize to Collins, 22 June 1919 (RMP, P7/A/11)
45 Vize to Collins, 22 June 1919 (RMP, P7/A/11)
46 Seán McGrath interview (EO'MN, P17b/100)
47 Art O'Brien to Michael Collins, 22 May, 18 June 1919 (AÓBP, MS 8429/11)
48 Collins to O'Brien, 6 June 1919 (AÓBP, MS 8429/11)
49 Collins to O'Brien, 9 Dec. 1919 (AÓBP, MS 8426/6)

of intelligence, agreed to set a trap in order to ascertain his bona fides. Thornton arranged for Jameson to deliver a batch of munitions to an address on Dublin's Bachelors' Walk. Meanwhile, Jim McNamara, a sympathizer in the RIC's detective division, was asked to alert Thornton if he heard of any imminent police activity in the area. Jameson appeared at the address carrying a portmanteau of munitions, which he claimed he had secured from communist sources in Britain and smuggled into the country. Soon afterwards McNamara contacted Thornton to say that the police were planning a raid on premises on Bachelors' Walk. This pointed to Jameson being a spy.[50] Suspicions were heightened over the following weeks by similar police raids on IRA safe-houses which Jameson had visited. Volunteers also found incriminating evidence in his hotel room.[51] Using a friend of his, Seán McGrath learned that the address which Jameson had supplied him was not that of a business as Jameson had said but merely an accommodation address.[52] Taken as a whole, these incidents 'proved conclusively that this man was a spy and it was decided that he should be eliminated', remembered Dublin IRA man Paddy Daly. In March 1920, lured to Glasnevin under the pretext of meeting Collins, Jameson was executed.[53]

Jameson was just one of many people executed as spies by the IRA in Ireland. In his case it transpired that he was indeed an agent. Working for A2 – a branch of military intelligence established in 1919 with the aim of countering communist attempts to penetrate the armed forces – Jameson donned the guise of a radical socialist and made contact with various revolutionary outfits, including those of the Irish republican movement.[54]

Gunrunners sometimes employed purchasing agents in order to maximize the quantity of munitions they acquired. In May 1919, Michael Collins recommended that Joe Vize take on J. Corbett as an agent as he claimed to be in a position to obtain gelignite and detonators in Scotland.[55] Vize demurred as he had previous dealings with Corbett and found him

50   BMHWS 615, Frank Thornton, pp. 38–40

51   'STATEMENT BY Major-General Patrick O'Daly, 41, Naas Road, Inchicore', p. 30, n.d., but *c.* 1965 (RMP, P7/D/8)

52   Seán McGrath interview (EO'MN, P17b/100)

53   'STATEMENT BY Major-General Patrick O'Daly', pp. 31–32 (RMP, P7/D/8); BMHWS 615, Frank Thornton, pp. 38–40; *TT*, 4 Mar. 1920; this Paddy Daly should not be confused with Liverpool's Paddy Daly.

54   Julian Putkowski, 'The Best Secret Service Man We Had: Jack Byrnes, A2 and the IRA', *Lobster 94: Journal of Parapolitics*, 28 (1994), pp. 1–38

55   Michael Collins to Joe Vize, 29 May 1919 (RMP, P7/A/11)

impetuous, greedy and over-inquisitive.[56] With detonators in short supply, however, Collins insisted on Corbett's employment. In fact, he agreed a deal with the gunrunner himself, whereby Corbett would supply detonators at a price of £1 for 100. 'That price is not too high', noted Collins, 'and if he _is_ willing to do business on that basis do it'. If Corbett was not so willing, Vize was to ascertain his new terms.[57] Vize responded by saying that Corbett still owed him £2 on a previous deal. If this debt was paid, he would be prepared to meet him and agree some arrangement for the procurement of detonators.[58] However, a few months later, Vize wrote that Corbett's association with the ICA in Dublin made him wary of employing him. Principally, he was concerned about security, finding Murray, another ICA man and associate of Corbett, worryingly indiscreet; he was not surprised to learn that he had recently been arrested. Vize hoped to secure Corbett's services exclusively for the IRA and, with this in mind, arranged a meeting with him. Stung in his dealings with the ICA, Corbett, a contractor with his own business, agreed to work for Vize. He immediately suggested that an Irishman, preferably from County Clare, be sent over to work for him as a miner: he would act as a conduit for the supply of gelignite and detonators between Corbett and Vize. This arrangement would enable Corbett to avoid storing munitions in his own house. Vize gave him £10 to get started.[59] Corbett held up his side of the deal with Collins, making at least one trip to Dublin with detonators costing £1 per 100.[60] The following year, Bernard McCabe, a provisions merchant in Glasgow, also began to help with gunrunning, allowing his shops on Duke Street, Dennistown, and Lindon Road, Bridgeton, to be used as munitions dumps.[61] However, McGovern, an agent sent to Glasgow by Michael Collins, proved unreliable. In late 1920, Seán O'Sheehan, the Sinn Féin organizer in Scotland, told Collins that McGovern was being very indiscreet about his activities. On one occasion, he declared his membership of the IRA at a public meeting. Moreover, there was evidence of misappropriation of gunrunning funds. 'He and his people are in a humble position in life and a few months back he was very shabby', Sheehan noted. '[Now] he seems to have left his job. Yet he has blossomed out into spending money lavishly.' In particular, he had

---

56   Vize to Collins, 6 June 1919 (RMP, P7/A/11)
57   Collins to Vize, 19 June 1919 (RMP, P7/A/11); original emphasis
58   Vize to Collins, 22 June 1919 (RMP, P7/A/11)
59   Vize to Collins, 5 Sept. 1919 (RMP, P7/A/11)
60   Collins to Vize, 8 July 1919 (RMP, P7/A/11)
61   Bernard McCabe's statement to the MSPB, n.d., but _c._ 1950s (EMP, 2/A/11)

acquired a taste for clothes and alcohol, and his recent wedding had cost at least £100.[62] Vize was disheartened to hear of the rumours regarding McGovern: 'he was one I would have trusted a long way, and I'm very much disappointed in him'.[63]

Corbett, McCabe and McGovern all had previous connections with the republican movement, to a greater or lesser degree. Other agents, such as a former sergeant-major in the British army employed by Vize in September 1919, had no previous association with the movement at all.[64]

While the number of people involved in gunrunning expanded as the war continued, so did the number of places tapped as sources for munitions. Michael Collins and GHQ regularly encouraged the development of sources in towns and cities outside the four original gunrunning centres of London, Liverpool, Manchester and Glasgow. In November 1920, Paddy O'Donoghue began sourcing munitions in Newcastle-upon-Tyne.[65] The following month, he noted that Liam Mellows and Rory O'Connor were travelling to Tyneside to investigate new channels of supply. He had promised them that he would try to uncover new sources in the districts surrounding Manchester.[66] O'Donoghue also had 'clients' in Bolton supplying him with materiel.[67] Meanwhile, noting that 'there was never a time when it was more important to get the goods', Collins asked Neil Kerr Senior if there was any possibility of finding new sources of armaments in Runcorn, a port town in Cheshire. Indeed, he suggested that any port where a motor boat could call would be worth investigating.[68] 'I wonder if we have any friends there [i.e. in Runcorn] at all', mused Collins a fortnight later. 'It is like a place that Irishmen would be working.'[69] Kerr visited the town with Rory O'Connor on 18 November. He was unimpressed. The fact that the Liverpool men had no contacts there seems to have frustrated Collins's idea of sourcing munitions in or despatching them from the town.[70] However, Birmingham's James Cunningham proved successful in making

---

62 Michael Collins to Joe Vize, 28 Oct. 1920 (NLI, Piaras Béaslaí Papers [PBP], MS 33,916[2])

63 Vize to Collins, n.d., but *c.* 22 Feb. 1921 (PBP, MS 33,916[2])

64 Vize to Collins, 27 Sept. 1919 (RMP, P7/A/11)

65 Paddy O'Donoghue to Collins, 29 Nov. 1920 (RMP, P7/A/10)

66 O'Donoghue to Collins, 3 Dec. 1920 (RMP, P7/A/10)

67 O'Donoghue to Collins, 13 Dec. 1920 (RMP, P7/A/10)

68 Collins to Neil Kerr, 8 Nov. 1920 (RMP, P7/A/3)

69 Collins to Kerr, 21 Nov. 1920 (RMP, P7/A/3)

70 Kerr to Collins, 27 Nov. 1920 (RMP, P7/A/3)

contacts in Coventry, Stoke-on-Trent, Purslow in Shropshire, Nottingham and Wolverhampton.[71]

Sources outside Britain were also tapped. In February 1920, Vize told Collins that he had two seafarers sourcing munitions for him in New York. One was Larry Ryan, a veteran of Frongoch. They were travelling on separate ships and Vize had given them £16 between them to ascertain the existence of any possible sources. With Ryan's ship scheduled to make only two trips between Glasgow and New York before plying between Liverpool and the 'Big Apple', Vize recommended that Ryan be introduced to the Merseyside men.[72] Collins, however, advised against Vize's sourcing of munitions in New York: '[W]hat we want', he wrote, 'is people who will bring the goods [to Ireland] rather than people who will get fresh supplies'. He therefore asked for details regarding Ryan and his accomplice, including the names of the boats they were travelling on, so that he could contact them.[73]

Both the Glasgow and the Liverpool men made arrangements to receive munitions from the German city of Hamburg. Joseph Booker, a Scottish gunrunner, remembered that a German ship arrived in Leith about every ten days:

> The captain would bring from twelve to fifteen parabellums or 'Peter the Painters' and ammunition, each trip. He would contact a barber whose name I cannot remember. He would in turn contact a Mr. Gordan, who, although not a Volunteer, was very friendly and used to buy guns for us whenever he got a chance. Mr. Gordan would send us a telegram when the ship had arrived. We were never allowed to have any direct contact with the captain or go near the ship. The arms were delivered by members of the crew to the barber's shop and collected by Mr. Gordan. At Gordan's house we oiled and greased the guns and packed them into suitcases ready for despatch to Liverpool.[74]

71   BMHWS 922, James Cunningham, p. 12
72   Joe Vize to Michael Collins, 7 Feb. 1920 (RMP, P7/A/11)
73   Collins to Vize, 14 Feb. 1920 (RMP, P7/A/11)
74   BMHWS 776, Joseph Booker, p. 2; 'Peter the Painter' was the nickname given to a German Mauser pistol due to its association with a group of alleged anarchists led by the mysterious Peter Piatkoff, a Latvian who masqueraded as a house painter. In December 1910, during an aborted robbery of a jewellery shop in London, the gang killed three policemen: Bernard Porter, 'Piatkoff, Peter (*fl.* 1910)', in *ODNB*, online edn, Sept. 2010, accessed at http://www.oxforddnb.com/view/article/92479, on 13 Oct. 2010

In mid-May 1920, Vize took delivery of one such batch from Hamburg, consisting of 17 revolvers and a quantity of ammunition, worth £64 in total. For the return journey he gave the seafarers £135, asking that they look out for bomb throwers and rifle grenades. '[T]hey promised to do everything possible to obtain all we want', he told Collins.[75] The following month, however, suspecting his agents of overcharging him, Vize secretly arranged for another ship to travel to Hamburg so that he could compare the prices he was being charged.[76]

Liverpool also received munitions from Hamburg. Steve Lanigan referred to the Hamburg source as the 'red villian [i.e. villain]', perhaps indicating that he was a communist. The first consignment of munitions reached Liverpool from Germany on 8 April 1920, and Lanigan later told Collins that deliveries could be made every fortnight.[77]

In March 1921, Liverpool received its first delivery of weapons from the Belgian city of Antwerp. On 7 March, Daly told Collins that a seafarer was travelling from Merseyside to Dublin with a batch of munitions from Antwerp.[78] Further munitions received from Belgium and despatched to Ireland that same month included 348 lbs (157.9 kg) of explosives, six Winchester rifles and four Owen guns.[79] Edward Brady, a member of the Liverpool Volunteers, remembered that he had inspected a consignment of munitions from Antwerp – .45 revolvers and 5,000 rounds of ammunition – just a few hours before he was arrested on charges of involvement in attacks on property in June 1921.[80]

Collins believed that 'good business' was possible if the Liverpool men succeeded in placing an agent on a ship stopping at Genoa, in Italy. To facilitate this he provided a letter of introduction to Donal Hales, the Dáil's representative in the city.[81] Paddy Daly later stated that munitions were received in Merseyside from Italy. However, the infrequency of ships plying between Liverpool and Genoa prevented the city from becoming a regular source of armaments.[82]

From time to time, Liverpool and London also received munitions from

75 Joe Vize to Michael Collins, 15 May 1920 (RMP, P7/A/11)

76 Vize to Collins, 11 June 1920 (RMP, P7/A/11)

77 Steve Lanigan to Collins, 8 Apr., 28 May 1920 (RMP, P7/A/2)

78 Paddy Daly to Collins, 8 Mar. 1921 (RMP, P7/A/4)

79 Daly to Collins, 11, 18 Mar. 1921 (RMP, P7/A/4)

80 Brady, *Secret Service*, p. 94

81 Michael Collins to Paddy Daly, 20 Dec. 1920, 13 Jan. 1921 (RMP, P7/A/3)

82 BMHWS 814, Patrick Daly, p. 11

New York, Berlin and Buenos Aires. These sources, however, were arranged by Collins and others in Dublin rather than by the gunrunners in Britain themselves.[83]

IV

The types and quantities of munitions acquired by gunrunners in Britain during the war varied through time due to a number of factors. These included the orders they received from Dublin, the financial resources at their disposal and the nature of the armament sources available. Michael Collins frequently made specific requests of his gunrunners in response to the demands of IRA units in the field. Many related to ammunition, the shortage of which was a constant problem for the IRA. 'There have also been a number of pressing enquiries sent [to] us here [in GHQ] for .303 [ammunition] and I shall consequently be glad if you will hurry forward delivery of at least some packages of this', Collins told Joe Vize in August 1919.[84] Shortage of ammunition was 'a haunting nightmare' for commanders of flying columns or Active Service Units (ASUs), full-time combat units composed of men on the run, remembered Tom Barry, O/C of the 3rd Cork Brigade flying column.[85] Florence O'Donoghue, I/O of the 1st Cork Brigade, claimed that the lack of ammunition was often the paramount factor in dictating the nature of engagements with Crown forces. 'In the best days, there was no possibility of sustaining a fight involving more than the expenditure of twenty to thirty rounds per man', he maintained. 'Actions therefore had to be short and sharp, and had to be broken off if not successful at an early stage.'[86] Tom Barry concurred, remembering that his flying column's limited supply of ammunition forced the Volunteers into 'a swift and intensive fight at close quarters' when they were surrounded by enemy forces at Crossbarry in March 1921.[87] When C/S Richard Mulcahy learned that a lack of money had led a Glasgow gunrunner to decline an offer of 9,000 rounds of .303 ammunition,

83   Andreas Roth, 'Gun Running from Germany to Ireland in the Early 1920s', *Irish Sword*, 22.88 (2000), pp. 209–20; Emmet O'Connor, 'Waterford and IRA Gun-Running, 1917–22', *Decies: Journal of the Waterford Archaeological & Historical Society*, 57 (2001), pp. 181–93; Hart, 'Thompson Submachine Gun', pp. 178–93

84   Michael Collins to Joe Vize, 25 Aug. 1919 (RMP, P7/A/11)

85   Tom Barry, *Guerrilla Days in Ireland* (Dublin: Anvil, 1981), p. 82

86   Florence O'Donoghue, *No Other Law* (Dublin: Anvil, 1986), p. 135

87   Barry, *Guerrilla Days*, pp. 125–26

he reproached Liam Mellows: 'there are people in this country [i.e. Ireland] who would lynch us if they thought that we were in any way responsible for missing stuff like this'.[88] The widespread shortage of ammunition led *An t-Óglác* to advise that controlling its expenditure during fire fights was of great importance.[89] The high consumption of ammunition by Volunteers during an attack on the RIC barracks in Kilmallock, County Limerick, on 28 May 1920 led to a reprimand from GHQ.[90] Documents recovered by the British in March or early April 1921 indicated that the Volunteers in Ireland had only 43 rounds of ammunition for each revolver they possessed, 21 rounds for each rifle and seven rounds of each shotgun.[91] Consequently, the supply of ammunition was a subject that continually exercised IRA leaders. 'Is there any chance of getting ammunition for these forty fives [i.e. .45 revolvers] [?]', Collins asked Manchester's Séamus Barrett. 'Of all things we want it more badly than anything else.'[92]

Of course, the provision of weapons themselves, in addition to the ammunition, was also a concern of the IRA leadership. By early 1921, the Volunteers in Ireland had 4,156 members but only 2,035 firearms – 569 rifles, 30 miniature rifles, 477 revolvers and 959 shotguns.[93] 'Don[']t fail to [be] keeping <u>all your eyes</u> open for arms', Collins told Steve Lanigan, '… we[']re awfully short of .45 [revolvers]'.[94] The O/C of a flying column reviewed a number of revolver and semi-automatic handguns in *An t-Óglác* in March 1921. Revolvers were so called due to the chamber containing the bullets rotating somewhat each time the trigger was pulled, thereby positioning another bullet for firing. In semi-automatics, the energy from the recoil of a shot caused the spent cartridge to be ejected and a live bullet to be positioned for firing. Handguns varied in the size of the bullet they fired, known as the calibre and measured in inches. The O/C declared that both the Webley and Smith & Wesson .45 calibre revolvers were 'ideal weapons for the average Volunteer'. Both revolvers could be used to deadly effect, provided of course that the Volunteer was a good marksman. They were also easy to clean. The

88 C/S to D/P, 22 Mar. 1921 (RMP, P7/A/19[23])

89 *An t-Óglác*, 22 July 1921

90 O'Callaghan, *Revolutionary Limerick*, pp. 126–27

91 L.K. Lockhart to Hemming, 11 May 1921 (TNA, Home Office file [HO], 317/60)

92 Michael Collins to Séamus Barrett, 24 Apr. 1919 (RMP, P7/A/9)

93 L.K. Lockhart to Hemming, 11 May 1921 (HO, 317/60)

94 Michael Collins to Steve Lanigan, 24 May 1919 (RMP, P7/A/1[66]); original emphasis

Colt .45 revolver, with its long barrel, was more powerful and accurate than the first two. A high standard of training was recommended for successfully handling the Colt .45 automatic due to the weapon's accuracy and speed of fire, and cleaning the gun's delicate mechanism also demanded skill.[95]

Such handguns were short range weapons, useful at distances up to 75 yards (69 m).[96] 'Sunday morning[']s work has been felt more by the English people here than anything that has happened yet', enthused Manchester's Paddy O'Donoghue, referring to the shooting dead of 14 suspected British intelligence officers by the IRA in Dublin on 21 November 1920, later dubbed 'Bloody Sunday'.[97] The victims were killed at close range, perhaps using handguns supplied by O'Donoghue and other gunrunners in Britain.

Rifles were long range firearms and Michael Collins considered them to be 'the best of all' weapons.[98] Most Volunteers agreed. County Clare's Michael Brennan remembered that 'the moral effect of one rifle' in mid-1919 'was greater than that of a hundred shotguns'.[99] In April 1921, the O/C 1st Brigade, 1st Northern Division, warned GHQ that 'a falling-off in the existing good spirit of the men' under his command was possible if his unit was not granted a batch of rifles.[100] Rifles facilitated accurate shooting at long distances due to the inside of the guns' barrels containing groves or rifling that caused the bullet – itself designed with corresponding threads – to spin as it travelled through the air. Like handguns, rifles varied in the calibre of bullet they employed. Types of rifles included the Winchester, Mauser, Martini-Henry and Remington. The most famous, however, was the Lee Enfield, the rifle acquired in the largest quantities by Irish gunrunners. The weapons-smugglers consistently failed to specify the models of Lee Enfield they obtained, but most were probably the Mark III .303 calibre with short magazine, the standard issue British army rifle during the Great War.[101] In October 1919,

95　*An t-Óglác*, 1 Mar. 1921; James Marchington, *Handguns & Sub-Machine Guns: Semi-Automatic Pistols & Revolvers* (London: Brassey's, 1997), pp. 32–33

96　*An t-Óglác*, 8 July 1921

97　Paddy O'Donoghue to Michael Collins, 23 Nov. 1920 (RMP, P7/A/10); Anne Dolan, 'Killing and Bloody Sunday, November 1920', *Historical Journal*, 49.3 (2006), pp. 789–810

98　Collins to Séamus Barrett, 24 Apr. 1919 (RMP, P7/A/9)

99　Michael Brennan, *The War in Clare: Personal Memoirs of the Irish War of Independence* (Dublin: Four Courts Press & Irish Academic Press, 1980), p. 38

100　C/S to QMG, 26 Apr. 1921 (RMP, P7/A/19[243])

101　Ian Skinnerton, *The British Service Lee: Lee-Metford and Lee-Enfield Rifles and Carbines 1880–1980* (London: Arms & Armour Press, 1982), pp. 99–115

when he learned that the gunrunners in Scotland had a number of short Lee Enfield rifles awaiting despatch to Ireland, Collins asked that Vize 'have them shipped to us as quickly as possible' as they were in 'persistent demand' from IRA units throughout the country.[102]

GHQ was also interested in new weapons that came on the market. The most famous was the Thompson sub-machine gun. In July 1921, *An t-Óglác* hailed the weapon as 'OUR LATEST ALLY' in the war against the British.[103] An attempt by IRA men in New York to smuggle 495 such guns directly to Ireland in one shipment in June 1921 failed due to incompetence.[104] Prior and subsequent to this, however, small quantities of Thompsons were smuggled to Ireland, some via Liverpool.[105] Gunrunners in Britain also attempted to acquire machine guns on their own bat. Such weapons were portable automatic firearms designed to fire bullets in rapid succession from a belt or magazine. A crew of men was usually required to effectively operate the gun. The shooting ranges of the Thompson, Lewis and Vickers machine guns varied between 2,500 ft (762 m) and 3,200 ft (975.4 m).[106] *An t-Óglác* held that the effective range of the machine gun was equal to that of the rifle. However, it boasted a number of advantages over the rifle. Experimentation had found that 'the fire of a machine gun is about twice as concentrated as that of riflemen firing an equal number of rounds at the same target'. Also, with the machine gun commanding a frontage of 1.8 m capable of delivering fire equal to that of 30 riflemen, it was a more effective and easily concealed weapon. Disadvantages included the fact that the concentrated nature of its fire required a higher level of marksmanship when operating the machine gun compared to the rifle. Machine guns were also more liable to temporary breakdowns. Moreover, the gun's peculiar noise and its habit of emitting steam when the water in the barrel casing reached boiling point meant that its position might be easier to locate by the enemy than that of a rifleman.[107]

As Peter Hart notes, the Thompson sub-machine gun failed to live up to expectations. During the war, the much-maligned shotgun was responsible

102 Michael Collins to Joe Vize, 23 Oct. 1919 (RMP, P7/A/11)
103 *An t-Óglác*, 22 July 1921; original emphasis
104 Hart, 'Thompson Submachine Gun', p. 181
105 Patrick Jung, 'The Thompson Submachine Gun During and After the Anglo-Irish War: the New Evidence', *Irish Sword*, 21.84 (1998), pp. 190–218; Paddy Daly interview (EO'MN, P17b/136)
106 *An t-Óglác*, 17 Feb. 1922
107 *An t-Óglác*, 5 Aug. 1921

for many more fatalities than the Thompson. Moreover, pistols and revolvers caused more deaths than the much sought-after rifle. The majority of fatalities inflicted by the IRA in Ireland occurred outside of ambushes or battles. Rather, 'death was more likely to come at point-blank range, on doorsteps and in ditches'. Shotguns, pistols and revolvers were much easier to use in such situations than rifles and bulky machine guns.[108]

Explosives were another form of munitions the sourcing of which was urged by Dublin. 'If there is any chance at all, go ahead as quickly as you can laying in the stuff [i.e. explosives]', Collins told Liverpool's Neil Kerr Senior in late 1920, adding that this should be relayed to the Glasgow gunrunners too.[109] Explosive materials such as gelignite, ammonite, dinitrobenzene and trinitrotoluene, along with chemicals such as potassium chlorate, were used in the manufacture of bombs. These were then employed in attacks on police stations and army barracks.[110]

IRA operations employing explosives were not always successful. In January 1921, the West Cork Volunteers mounted three attacks on RIC barracks in Kilbrittain and Innishannon. These operations were unsuccessful due to the failure of the homemade bombs to explode. Something similar happened at Drimoleague the following month. 'We were simply incapable of properly making a mine', remembered Tom Barry.[111] Bombs supplied by GHQ were sometimes little better. An attack on the barracks in Scariff, County Clare, in September 1920, was scuppered by the failure of the bombs to explode. It was later discovered that the bombs' striking pins were too short, hence preventing the detonators from exploding.[112] As the war progressed, however, both GHQ and provincial units became much more adept at manufacturing and handling explosives. (Matt Furlong, formerly of the London Volunteers, was involved in the manufacture of bombs for GHQ and died from injuries sustained in Dunboyne, County Meath, on 21 October 1920, when a prototype trench mortar exploded.[113]) Indeed, Hart contends that the IRA's 'real technological advance' in 1921 was not the acquisition of Thompson sub-machine guns but the use of industrial explosives in mines.

108 Hart, 'Thompson Submachine Gun', pp. 181–83, 187–89, 192–93

109 Michael Collins to Neil Kerr, 4 Nov. 1920 (RMP, P7/A/3)

110 BMHWS 1713, James O'Donovan, pp. 8–9; Rudolf Meyer, Josef Köhler and Axel Homburg, *Explosives* (Weinheim: Wiley-VCH, 2007), pp. 114, 147, 210–11, 260

111 Barry, *Guerrilla Days*, pp. 65–75, 93

112 Brennan, *War in Clare*, pp. 38–39

113 BMHWS 664, Patrick McHugh, pp. 4, 6, 12–17

Such mines inflicted far more casualties on Crown forces during the closing stages of the war than did the machine gun. For the IRA, gelignite and handguns were 'clearly superior' to machine guns as death-dealing weapons, he writes.[114]

The financial resources at the disposal of the gunrunners also influenced the types and quantities of munitions they acquired. As well as sending orders, Collins and GHQ provided the money to fund the purchase of the munitions, be they ammunition, firearms or explosives. Between April 1919 and September 1920, Collins sent at least £1,600 to Manchester.[115] By May 1921, the Ministry of Defence had sent £4,500 to Scotland, and this figure presumably included £1,000 and £500 that D/P Liam Mellows had sent to Glasgow and Edinburgh respectively in March that same year.[116]

On 20 January 1920, for example, Collins sent Vize £500. On 11 June, the Scottish gunrunner supplied the following list of munitions and equipment he had purchased with the money:

[Quantity]	[Item]	[Cost £ s. d.]	[Quantity]	[Item]	[Cost £ s. d.]
2	Lee Enfields & Brt [?]	13 – –	1	Winchester.22	2 10 –
1	Do Do & Do [i.e. ibid]	6 – –	1	Webley	3 – –
2	Do Do @ 4/10/0	9 – –	1	"	3 5 –
2	Do Do @ 4/10/0	8 – –	1	" & 43 Rds	5 – –
4	Bayonets @10/6	2 2 –	1	"	4 – –
1	Lee Enfield, Brt & Equip	5 – –	2	" @ 2/10/0	5 – –
8	Lee Enfields @ 3/0/0	24 – –	1	Am[erican]. Colt	4 – –
1	Do Do	3 – –	2	Webleys @ 3/-/-	6 – –
150	R[oun]ds [of] .303[ammunition]	1 10 –	2	Do @ 3/5/-	6 10
1	Equipment	1 – –	1	Do	4 – –
98	Rds .303	17 – –	2	Do @ 65 rds	6 – –
–	.303	[0] 12 –	1	German Auto[matic]	5 – –
2	Rifles 1 L.E. 1 German	9 – –	1	Do	4 10 –
2	Lee Enfields & Bts	10 5 –	1	Webley	4 – –
1	Do	4 – –	5	Do @ 4/5/0	21 5 –

114 Hart, 'Thompson Submachine Gun', p. 193

115 Correspondence between Michael Collins and the Manchester gunrunners, Apr. 1919–Jan. 1921 (RMP, P7/A/9–P7/A/10)

116 Cathal Brugha to Eamon de Valera, 16 May 1921 (EdeVP, P150/1387); D/P to Commandant Carney and Messrs Burke, Byrne and Fagan, 3 Mar. 1921 (RMP, P7/A/19[36–38])

1	Do & Bayonet	5 5 –		1	Do	4 – –
1	Lee Enfield	4 12 –		2	Do	8 – –
				1	German Auto	3 – –
				1	Do	3 10 –
				1	Am[erican?]. Colt	3 – –
				2	Special @ 2/0/0	4 – –
				5	Webleys @ 3/10/0	17 10 –
				2	Do @ 3/5/–	6 10 –
				13	Do @ 3/10/–	45 10 –
				4	Do @ 3/10/0	14 – –

500	Electric Deto[nator]s	5 – –		1	Revolver	3 – –
1	Parcel soft stuff [i.e. explosives]	1 – –		900	Rds. .38	9 – –
L. Ryan [an agent of Vize]		10 – –		450	Do.22 long	2 – –
16 lbs Soft stuff		1 4 –		1	Colt Auto	6 0 0
900	Ord. Detos	9 – –		1	Smith & Weston	3 – –
1	Range finder	3 – –		1	Webley	5 0 0
1	Field glasses	1 – –			Amm[unition]	1 10 –
1	Gas Helmet	– 5 –		3	Holsters	– 15 –
1	Pr[ism]. Glasses	2 10 –		1	Colt	4 10 –
1	Telescope	5 5 –		2	Webleys @ 3/10/–	7 – –
7	Weeks @ 4/4/0	29 8 –		2	Colts	7 10 –
800	E. Detos	8 0 0		103	Rds amm	– 15 –
12	lbs soft stuff	– 5 –		55	Do	– 10 –
73	Detos	– 12 2		1	Revolver	3 – –
34	Do	– 7 6		1	Sm[all]. Colt	4 10 –
1	Revolver.38	2 10 –		1	Webley	3 15 –
1	Do	3 5 –				

General Ex[pen]ses, for trains, trams etc　　　　7 – –

Eixes [i.e. Expenses] to Liverpool		
Mar	10th	£6 17 0
"	16th	£5 10 0
"	23rd	£9 3 4
"	30th	£6 0 0
April	6th	£6 0 0
"	8th	£4 15 0
"	14th	£10 0 0
Total		£48 15 4

£251 7 0 (To be allowed for £16 7 0 on next a/c of £1000)

$$£265 \ – \ –$$
$$\underline{£251 \ 7 \ –}$$
$$\underline{£516 \ 7 \ –}^{117}$$

The gunrunners did not always supply Collins with such clear accounts as this. In December 1919, Paddy O'Donoghue confessed that armaments were often despatched to Ireland from Manchester without being inspected, thus preventing the composition of accurate accounts. He promised that hereon in he would insist on all munitions being collected in a central location for accounting before being sent off.[118] Also, despite repeated instructions that the Liverpool men clearly distinguish munitions received from different gunrunning centres 'so that we can keep our accounts straight', the often indiscriminate despatch of munitions to Ireland via Merseyside made book-keeping a difficult task for GHQ.[119]

The lack of accurate and comprehensive accounts was to prove a source of contention. In 1920, Cathal Brugha, Michael Collins's superior, began to suspect that the IRB was wasting Volunteer money in its gunrunning operations in Britain. Worried about the finances of the Glasgow operations in particular, he demanded that Collins investigate the matter. 'So long as the generally accepted laws of Accounting are not deviated from, I am satisfied', Brugha wrote, implying that Collins's accounting was haphazard. 'My concern is to see that the Q.M.G. gets value in goods for the money I pay out.'[120] Stung by Brugha's accusations, Collins was disheartened to discover that at least £1,000 was indeed improperly accounted for.[121] Brugha returned to the issue a few months later, declaring: 'A very serious situation has arisen owing to a considerable amount of money I have paid out to "Purchases a/c" being unaccounted for'. £2,700 4s. 5d. had been wrongly recorded in the accounts. 'A certain person', probably Collins, had forced the QMG to pay £1,349 for munitions received from Liverpool. Meanwhile the IRA owed £459 10s. to people in Scotland, while agents there possessed £198 8s. 1d., money 'which may never be recovered'. Brugha asked de Valera to arrange a meeting with

117 Joe Vize to Michael Collins, 11 June 1920 (RMP, P7/A/11)

118 Paddy O'Donoghue to Collins, n.d., but date-stamped 24 Dec. 1919 (RMP, P7/A/9)

119 Collins to Steve Lanigan, 27 Jan. 1920; Paddy Daly to Collins, n.d., but *c.* 5 Dec. 1920 (RMP, P7/A/1, P7/A/3)

120 Comments of the Minister of Defence, 23 Mar. 1921 (RMP, P7/A/19[39])

121 Correspondence between Michael Collins and George McGrath, 15 Jan., 17, 21 Feb. 1921 (DÉ, 5/7, 5/15)

him and Collins to discuss the matter.[122] This may have led to the meeting which a colleague of Austin Stack, the minister for home affairs, later recalled:

> Collins came, he brought books and receipts and was able to account for all of it except maybe a hundred pounds … Collins was so upset by the accusation that he openly wept. 'Now', said de Valera, 'it is quite clear that these charges are groundless.' Brugha arose without a word and left the room. Stack rushed after him: 'Come in, shake hands'. But Brugha angrily turned from him; 'You'll find him out yet', he spat. He stamped out.[123]

Ó Catháin argues it was Collins's 'instinctive anglocentric view' – a product of his years in London – which resulted in the Scottish gunrunning operation degenerating into a mess whilst that in England, and by extension Wales, continued to work effectively.[124] Piaras Béaslaí, the IRA's director of publicity, later described Brugha's demands for 'strict and tabulated accounts' as 'eminently unreasonable', especially given that many of the men involved in gunrunning in Scotland were incommunicado, either in prison like Vize or on the run. The involvement of both the IRA and the IRB in gunrunning in Britain led to a certain amount of confusion, he conceded. However, the successful procurement of munitions required that agents be given 'plenty of funds and large scope and discretion'. Some agents had simply been unwise in their expenditure. Béaslaí speculated that Brugha's dislike of the IRB in general played a part in his attitude.[125] Richard Mulcahy later stated that Brugha had grown jealous of Collins and attempted to use the issue of the Scottish accounts to undermine him.[126] Collins himself seemed to sense this. Writing to Joe Vize about the issue, he stated that 'the whole thing has another motive, as you know very well'.[127] Vize agreed. 'What is the idea of

---

122 Cathal Brugha to Eamon de Valera, 16 May 1921 (EdeVP, P150/1387)

123 Quoted in Tim Pat Coogan, *Michael Collins: A Biography* (London: Hutchinson, 1990), p. 176

124 Máirtín Ó Catháin, 'Michael Collins and Scotland', in Frank Ferguson and James McConnel (eds), *Ireland and Scotland in the Nineteenth Century* (Dublin: Four Courts Press, 2009), pp. 169–70

125 Béaslaí, *Michael Collins*, ii, pp. 161–63

126 'Talk with Lieut. General Costello on the 23rd May 1963' (RMP, P7/D/3[23]), p. 1

127 Michael Collins to Joe Vize, 16 Mar. 1921, reprinted in Béaslaí, *Michael Collins*, ii, pp. 162–63

all this [accounting] work?' he asked irritably. '[C]an't they [i.e. Brugha etc.] give men a chance, there['s] no doubt everything will turn out all right if they only wait a little time. They know who got the money, and it will be accounted for in good time.'[128]

Collins saw Liam Mellows as an ally of Brugha and treated him somewhat frostily. When Mellows queried the different gunrunning accounts, Collins told Vize: 'If the D.P. wished, he knows perfectly well the difference between one account and the other – no one knows better than he does'.[129] When, in 1921, Liverpool's Paddy Daly complained of lacking money, Collins relished the opportunity of contrasting his management of gunrunning finances with that of Mellows:

> You will understand that I could forward you some money for your own use, but in the way things are going here at present, I don't like doing this. It is up to those people who are making so much fuss to attend to things. Nothing like it happened when I was in charge of certain details. It should not happen now either.[130]

Mellows soon began to reciprocate the animosity, complaining that Collins was attempting to monopolize the purchase of materiel in Britain just to spite him.[131] As Hart comments, however, this was improbable. Rather, it is more likely that Collins simply desired to continue to operate gunrunning in Britain as it had traditionally been run – through the IRB.[132]

As well as providing the funds, Dublin often advised on the prices to be paid for the weaponry. Thus, Collins directed one gunrunner: 'Never on any account give more than £6' without consulting his Liverpool colleagues. This applied to rifles, revolvers and automatics. A price greater than £6 might be agreed in the case of a German automatic complete with stock and 50 or 100 rounds of ammunition, he continued. Still if he were to be made such an offer, the gunrunner should confer with the Merseyside men before agreeing to it.[133] When Liverpool's Steve Lanigan seemed about to make a

128 Vize to Collins, n.d., but date-stamped 27 Apr. 1921 (PBP, MS 33,916[2])

129 Collins to Vize, 16 Mar. 1921, reprinted in Béaslaí, *Michael Collins*, ii, pp. 162–63

130 Correspondence between Paddy Daly and Collins, 28 Feb., 9 Mar. 1921 (RMP, P7/A/4)

131 BMHWS 624, Mary Woods, pp. 26–27

132 Hart, *Mick*, p. 261

133 Michael Collins to Séamus Barrett, 31 Jan. 1920 (RMP, P7/A/9)

deal in London in 1919, Collins advised him that £5 was the maximum he was to pay for rifles.[134] Around the same time, he approved the payment of 7s. 6d. per lb (0.5 kg) of gelignite and 1s. 1½d. per 55 ft (16.8 m) of fuse.[135] The following year Collins insisted that £5 10s. was the maximum price to be paid thereafter for individual munitions.[136]

Although the majority of the funds used to purchase munitions came from GHQ, some were raised in Britain through contributions from Volunteers themselves, as well as through the organization of dances, lotteries and collections patronized by the wider Irish community.[137] In the acquisition of materiel, funds were employed in two different ways. In some deals, money was simply handed over in return for weapons. Buying weapons from gunsmiths and British army soldiers recently returned from the world war were examples of such transactions. A Jewish gunsmith was one of the main sources of munitions for the London men.[138] Crucibles – large pots used in the mixing of chemicals for bombs – were bought by the Liverpool men from a firm named Rawltan Brothers. 'We found the Englishman always willing to do business', Paddy Daly recollected.[139] Other deals were more complicated, sometimes necessitating the incurring of expenses ever before the munitions were actually acquired. Asking Michael Collins for an additional £500, Joe Vize explained that he had spent all his funds pursuing many different channels of enquiry, each of which required deposits and outlays. 'I must have money in those places', he wrote in February 1920, '[for] if one of them start[s] on a large scale, I would like to be able to meet them without calling in money from the other places'.[140] The employment of agents so as to maximize the purchase of munitions was also costly, as it sometimes required the payment of something approaching a wage. 'I gave him to understand, if he wanted to make a few pounds, he was in the right place', Vize wrote, in reference to an ex-sergeant major who had offered his services.[141] Even the theft of munitions incurred costs. The weapons themselves were not purchased of course, but bribes had to be paid to facilitate the heist. We saw earlier that Vize spent £30 or £40 as 'bait' in preparing a raid on an

---

134　Collins to Steve Lanigan, 3 June 1919 (RMP, P7/A/1[58])

135　Collins to Joe Vize, 8 July 1919 (RMP, P7/A/11)

136　Collins to Paddy O'Donoghue, 7 Sept. 1920 (RMP, P7/A/10)

137　BMHWS 922, James Cunningham, p. 1

138　Dennis Kelleher interview (EO'MN, P17b/107); BMHWS 847, Patrick O'Donoghue, p. 6

139　BMHWS 814, Patrick Daly, p. 28

140　Michael Collins to Joe Vize, 15 Feb. 1920 (RMP, P7/A/11)

141　Vize to Collins, 27 Sept. 1919 (RMP, P7/A/11)

army stores. This was probably a bribe for his contact, the storekeeper. The raid was seemingly never mounted, but the storekeeper did pass a small amount of rifle parts to the IRA.[142]

The gunrunners themselves were often conscious of expenses too. As already noted, in mid-1920 seafarers on a boat plying between Glasgow and Hamburg agreed to procure munitions in Germany for Joe Vize. He, however, became dissatisfied with the prices they were charging, with revolvers costing on average £4 each and ammunition 30s. per 100 rounds. The seafarers attributed the cost to a number of factors, including the exchange rate between sterling and the German mark and the expense of 'getting stuff lifted'. The frugal Vize was unconvinced, however, and to ensure their honesty through price comparison, he made arrangements for another boat or two to work the same route.[143] Volunteer companies engaged in weapons-smuggling sometimes established purchasing committees in order to control costs. The Motherwell IRA's committee, for example, decided that £3 10s. and £4 10s. were the maximum prices they were willing to pay for individual revolvers and automatic handguns respectively.[144] In March 1921, in an attempt to solve problems relating to the financing of gunrunning in Glasgow and Edinburgh, Liam Mellows instructed John Carney and three other gun-smugglers to form a committee to control the procurement and despatch of munitions.[145]

As well as having to heed the orders received from Dublin and being limited by the financial resources at their disposal, the quantities and types of munitions acquired by the gunrunners was dictated by the nature of the weapons sources available to them. British army soldiers were a particularly fertile source as many brought munitions home with them as souvenirs when they were demobilized following the end of the Great War. Acting on initiative, individual Volunteers would approach the former soldiers and ask if they were willing to sell their weapons. Motherwell's James Byrne later stated that around 100 rifles and 'a couple of hundred revolvers', all costing between £3 and £3 10s. were purchased in this way, along with a small amount of ammunition.[146] Paddy O'Donoghue remembered that Séamus Barrett similarly secured 'a big number of revolvers' from soldiers in Manchester. 'There could

142 See pp. 91–92 above

143 Joe Vize to Michael Collins, 11 June 1920 (RMP, P7/A/11); see p. 97 above

144 BMHWS 777, Patrick Mills, p. 5

145 D/P to Commandant Carney and Messrs Burke, Byrne and Fagan, 3 Mar. 1921 (RMP, P7/A/19[36–38])

146 BMHWS 828, James Byrne, pp. 3–4, 8

not have been much of a check by the British Army authorities on these guns judging by the rather easy way they could be disposed of', he observed.[147] Ex-soldiers and seamen were also good sources in Newcastle-upon-Tyne, while in Middlesbrough weapons bought from seafarers were mainly used to arm the city's Volunteers.[148]

As well as selling their own munitions to them, soldiers often helped gunrunners to gain access to armaments held in army barracks. Such barracks, drill halls, shooting ranges and similar facilities – with their arsenals of firearms, ammunition and more – proved alluring. In July 1920, Joe Vize issued orders to all IRB centres in Scotland 'to report without delay any rifle ranges, drill halls or army stores in their districts'.[149] By then, he had already mounted a number of thefts. His first raid, on the army barracks in Hamilton, a town situated about 19 kilometres south-east of Glasgow, seems to have taken place in August 1919. Vize made contact with a quartermaster sergeant in the barracks. On the appointed night, a small group of Volunteers travelled to the barracks and, at a location arranged by the soldier, two of the party climbed over the wall. They soon return with the rifles and handed them to their colleagues, who hid them under their coats and fled the scene. Ten rifles were seized, along with a quantity of ammunition.[150]

The successful raid whetted Vize's appetite for mounting similar operations on barracks in Georgetown and Glasgow's Maryhill district, as well as resulting in a return visit being made to Hamilton. He was also interested in a large soldier demobilization station. He told Collins that ten new Webley revolvers had been secured there, while arrangements were being made to acquire some machine guns.[151] The following month, he noted that his contact in Maryhill barracks, a sergeant in the machine gun stores, was only waiting to place a sympathizer, properly bribed, on sentry duty before 'starting work for us'. Brand new the machine guns would each cost between £250 and £300; Vize was prepared to offer £50 to £70 for these second-hand models. 'I was never so sure of anything as I am of this lot', he boasted.[152] The sources do not record Vize's success in getting weapons from Maryhill. However, James

147   BMHWS 847, Patrick O'Donoghue, p. 6
148   BMHWS 773, Gilbert Barrington, p. 9; BMHWS 369, William Whelan, pp. 8–9
149   Joe Vize to Michael Collins, n.d., but date-stamped 7 July 1920 (RMP, P7/A/11)
150   BMHWS 777, Patrick Mills, p. 3; BMHWS 776, Joseph Booker, p. 3
151   Joe Vize to Michael Collins, n.d., but *c.* 18 Jan. 1920 (RMP, P7/A/11)
152   Vize to Collins, 7 Feb. 1920 (RMP, P7/A/11)

Fagan, O/C 'F' Company, 1st Battalion, and Volunteer Robert O'Donnell were later charged with soliciting a soldier to steal munitions from the barracks and were each sentenced to three years' imprisonment for conspiracy.[153]

Meanwhile, Hamilton barracks was 'just developing' as a source. Having secured ten rifles in the first raid, Vize expected many more.[154] When he learned that a sergeant working at one of the barracks was an Easter Rising veteran who had recently rejoined the British army, he hoped to arrange a meeting with him.[155] On 24 June, Vize and 30 Volunteers returned to the base. Having made arrangements with two soldiers, one of whom may have been the Easter Week veteran, they seized 40 German rifles and bayonets from the armoury and loaded them into a waiting taxi. The cost, probably in bribes, was £60.[156] Five months later, Vize and his men raided the Orange Hall on Glasgow's Cowdaddens Street. Five rifles and 1,000 rounds of ammunition were seized, along with an amount of money and some regalia. The graffito 'Commandeered for the Irish Republican Army' was written on the wall.[157]

Republicans in other parts of Britain mounted similar raids, although much less frequently. On one occasion, a priest helped James Cunningham to take 20 Martini-Henri rifles from a drill hall in the Pottery area of Birmingham.[158] In March 1921, after his meeting with Mellows in Dublin, Gilbert Barrington and his fellow officers in the Tyneside IRA began raids of their own. 'C' Company, led by E. Kerrigan and E. Costello, raided a drill hall in Gateshead and seized six rifles.[159] Four months later, the same company acquired three machine guns in a raid on Saltwell Park, a public park. In order to transport the guns from the scene, Barrington hired a horse and cart from 'a shady character', a member of the Askew Road gang. The machine guns, along with the rifles from the raid on the drill hall, were then transported to Liverpool.[160] Meanwhile, Denis Kelleher and other London gunrunners made

---

153 *IT*, 17, 21 Mar. 1921; membership roll, 'F' Company, 1st Battalion, Scottish Brigade IRA (EMP, 3/C/13)

154 Joe Vize to Michael Collins, 7 Feb. 1920 (RMP, P7/A/11)

155 Vize to Collins, 15 Feb. 1920 (RMP, P7/A/11)

156 Vize to Collins, 27 June 1920 (RMP, P7/A/11); BMHWS 828, James Byrne, pp. 4–5

157 Scottish Office to Carew-Robinson, HO, 20 Nov. 1922 (HO, 144/4645); Neil Kerr to Collins, 12 Nov. 1920 (RMP, P7/A/3); 'RROUK', no. 80, 11 Nov. 1920 (CAB, 24/114)

158 BMHWS 922, James Cunningham, p. 12

159 BMHWS 773, Gilbert Barrington, p. 9

160 BMHWS 773, Gilbert Barrington, p. 9

contact with a Sergeant Roche, a quartermaster in Chelsea Barracks, who smuggled some weapons out of the base for them.[161]

The black market was another big source of armaments. On his journeys into Birmingham's underworld, James Cunningham ensured that Dan O'Malley, his Birmingham-born right-hand man, accompanied him due to the byzantine layout of the city's dens, lanes, courts and squares. As well as a guide, however, he also used O'Malley as a virtual translator, as he found it very difficult to understand the slum dwellers' patois.[162]

Meanwhile, in the mining districts of Britain, especially Lanarkshire in Scotland and Lancashire in England, the large number of mining concerns presented conspicuous and attractive targets for the acquisition of explosives. In such areas, the local IRA company was often composed entirely of miners.[163] At the beginning of each day's work, they were usually given a quantity of explosives to blast the rock and coal. Each miner setting aside a small amount of his allocation and smuggling it out of the mine at the end of his shift meant that large quantities of explosives were acquired for little or no cost and without raising the suspicions of the mine owners.[164] During a coal strike in 1921, the St Helens Volunteers, numbering about 15 miners, decided to raid the mining depots for explosives. The strike provided cover for the raid, for it was common for out-of-work miners to steal explosives to use for blasting coal for their own domestic use. The Volunteers succeeded in seizing a considerable quantity of munitions, amounting to hundreds of pounds of gelignite, a vast quantity of fuse and thousands of electric detonators. Paddy Daly remembered it as one of the biggest consignments of explosives acquired during the war.[165] Michael Collins considered the St Helens Volunteers such a valuable source of munitions that he agreed to provide funds to relieve the hardship they were experiencing as a result of the strike.[166]

The inconspicuous nature of the activities of the St Helens miners meant that they escaped police attention. However, the occurrence of a number of overt raids on mining magazines did alert the police to the existence of Irish revolutionaries in Britain. On 26 July 1919, for example, three carts of gelignite and 100 detonators were stolen from Greenfoot quarry in Glenboig,

161   Dennis Kelleher interview (EO'MN, P17b/107)

162   BMHWS 922, James Cunningham, p. 6

163   BMHWS 777, Patrick Mills, p. 3

164   BMHWS 828, James Byrne, p. 3

165   Paddy Daly to Michael Collins, 17 May 1921 (RMP, P7/A/5); BMHWS 814, Patrick Daly, pp. 31–32

166   Collins to Daly, 20 May 1921 (RMP, P7/A/5)

Lanarkshire. On 24 April the following year, 225 lbs (102 kg) of gelignite, 9 lbs (4.1 kg) of gunpowder, 550 detonators and 30 lbs (13.6 kg) of fuse were taken from Robroyston Colliery, again in Lanarkshire. In all, police returns record 24 such thefts during the war, of which 21 took place in Scotland. Irishmen were convicted of involvement in only two cases, but in 17 others Irish involvement was presumed or considered probable.[167] For example, the police records note that the theft of 10 lbs (4.5 kg) of gelignite from a mine in Gavieside, West-Calder, Scotland, on 14 April 1921 was probably 'attributable to Irish agency', for 'Irish agencies were at the time very active in obtaining explosives in this manner' and 'no other reason' existed to explain the theft.[168]

The quantity of munitions smuggled to Ireland from Britain during the war is difficult to estimate accurately due to the absence of a complete set of primary source records and also because of the lack of precision in some of the extant correspondence. Of all the gunrunning centres, the best surviving evidence relates to Liverpool, but even here no records exist for the periods January–May 1919 and October 1919–February 1920, while some correspondence appears to be missing for the months June–August 1920. Therefore, the following figures constitute the *minimum* amount of munitions smuggled by gunrunners.[169]

In general, the despatch of munitions to Ireland from Liverpool increased in frequency as the war progressed. During the course of June 1919, for example, the Merseyside men sent munitions to Ireland on only one occasion.[170] The same month two years later saw two despatches.[171] Moreover, not only did the frequency of the despatches increase as the conflict continued, so did the size of the consignments. The batch sent in June 1919 amounted to 70 rounds of .303 and .45 ammunition. Both of the consignments sent the same month two years later were bigger. On 9 June, six .45 Colt revolvers, four .45 automatics, 600 Colt cartridges and 400 rounds of .45 Colt automatic ammunition were despatched. Meanwhile, the consignment of 16 June included 19 Webley revolvers, five Colt revolvers, four parabellum

167 Scottish Office to Carew-Robinson, HO, 20 Nov.; Assistant Chief Constable [ACC] of Lancashire to the Under Secretary of State [USS], HO, 27 Oct.; CC of the North Riding to the USS, HO, 16 Oct. 1922 (HO, 144/4645)

168 Scottish Office to Carew-Robinson, HO, 20 Nov. 1922 (HO, 144/4645)

169 The figures that follow supersede those given in Gerard Noonan, 'Supplying an Army: IRA Gunrunning in Britain during the War of Independence', *History Studies: University of Limerick History Society Journal*, 12 (2011), pp. 90–91

170 Michael Collins to Steve Lanigan, 27 June 1919 (RMP, P7/A/1[51])

171 Paddy Daly to Collins, 9, 16 June 1921 (RMP, P7/A/5, P7/A/6)

pistols, two Colt automatics, two Smith & Wesson revolvers, three miscellaneous .45 revolvers and 2,772 rounds of assorted ammunition. The increase in the quantity of munitions smuggled from Liverpool was due to the fact GHQ designated Merseyside the main port of despatch in 1920. Thus, the 70 rounds of .303 and .45 ammunition despatched in June 1919 were sourced by the Merseyside men themselves, while the 35 handguns and 2,772 rounds of ammunition sent two years later were procured in London and Glasgow.

The Glasgow gunrunners started to send munitions to Liverpool in early March 1920. In the ten months previous to this, the extant correspondence reveals that the Glasgow men despatched directly to Ireland 17 handguns, 108 sticks of gelignite, 246 detonators, 106 fuses, 230 rounds of ammunition and two unspecified batches of munitions.[172] In September 1920, while examining a consignment of munitions received from Glasgow, Tom Kerr accidently shot dead his brother Neil Kerr Junior.[173]

The amount of munitions despatched to Liverpool from Glasgow fluctuated as time went by. In February 1921, Michael Collins complained that the quantity being procured by the Clydeside men was declining. He reflected wistfully on what the situation had been 12 months previously when Scottish gunrunning was going 'well' and 'the stuff was coming inn [sic] at such a fine rate'. Now 'nothing' was being received. He blamed the deterioration on the fallout from the Bothwell incident and the arrest of Henry Coyle.[174] On 28 October 1920, a group of Volunteers from the 2nd Scottish Battalion had attempted to raid a territorial army drill hall in Bothwell, a town situated about 14 kilometres south-east of Glasgow. In the course of the raid, a policeman was shot. Subsequent arrests disrupted the battalion's gunrunning activities.[175] The arrest of senior Scottish gunrunners Henry Coyle and Charles McGinn after a car chase on 4 December compounded the difficulties.[176] In addition, John Carney was proving 'useless' as a director of gunrunning.[177] From his prison cell, Joe Vize recommended that Collins write a 'strong[ly]

---

172 Correspondence between Collins and Joe Vize, May 1919–Mar. 1920 (RMP, P7/A/11)

173 Collins to Neil Kerr, 6 Sept. 1920 (RMP, P7/A/3); Vize to Collins, n.d., but date-stamped 27 Apr. 1921 (PBP, MS 33,916[2])

174 Collins to Vize, 28 Feb. 1921 (PBP, MS 33,916[2])

175 Scottish Office to Carew-Robinson, HO, 20 Nov. 1922 (HO, 144/4645); BMHWS 828, James Byrne, p. 5; BMHWS 777, Patrick Mills, pp. 4–5; see Chapter 6

176 *MG*, 16 Mar. 1921

177 Michael Collins to Joe Vize, 28 Feb. 1921 (PBP, MS 33,916[2])

worded appeal' to the IRB's Scottish Executive and have Joe Furlong read it at a meeting of the body. He also recommended that Andrew Fagan, Michael Burke and James Byrne should be placed in charge of gunrunning operations in Scotland. Vize was confident that such an arrangement would have impressive results.[178] It is not known if Collins followed his advice. D.P. Walsh tried to rectify the problem by sending munitions directly to Dublin in crates but a number of these were intercepted by the authorities and at least three Volunteers were arrested and convicted.[179] In May, the situation worsened with police arrests and raids following the killing of a policeman during the IRA's failed attempt to rescue a comrade from a Glasgow prison van.[180]

The Manchester men sent some of their armaments to Ireland via Liverpool, especially from January 1920 onwards. However, in November that year, 'as every day becomes more and more pressing to us', Michael Collins ordered that small quantities of revolvers, automatics, rifles, .303 ammunition and .45 revolver ammunition be sent directly to Cork.[181] Records for the period previous to the Liverpool arrangement reveal that £223 6s. 6d. worth of munitions had been procured by four gunrunners in the year 1919: the armaments included revolvers, gelignite, fuse wire and fuse caps.[182] Between March 1920 and the truce in July 1921, at least 56 handguns and 4,197 rounds of ammunition, among other munitions, made their way from Manchester to Dublin via Liverpool.[183]

The extant records in relation to London indicate that 1919 saw the despatch of at least three rifles and nine handguns directly to Dublin, along with three consignments whose contents were unspecified.[184] In the first nine months of the following year, at least four handguns, 4,000 rounds of

178   Vize to Collins, n.d., written on the back of Collins to Vize, 28 Feb. 1921 (PBP, MS 33,916[2])

179   BMHWS 776, Joseph Booker, p. 5; BMHWS 777, Patrick Mills, pp. 5–6; BMHWS 828, James Byrne, pp. 6–7; list of IRA prisoners, no. 98, n.d. (MCP, A/0619/39); *Glasgow Herald*, 9 Aug. 1921; membership roll, 'D' Company, 4th Battalion, Scottish Brigade IRA (EMP, 3/C/13)

180   BMHWS 933, Séamus Reader, pp. 9–11; see Chapter 3

181   Michael Collins to Paddy O'Donoghue, 9 Nov. 1920 (RMP, P7/A/10)

182   Correspondence between Collins, O'Donoghue and Séamus Barrett, Apr. 1919–Mar. 1920, esp. O'Donoghue to Collins, n.d., but marked 'Recd 5.12.19' (RMP, P7/A/9)

183   Correspondence between Collins and Manchester and Liverpool gunrunners, Mar. 1920–11 July 1921 (RMP, P7/A/6, P7/A/10)

184   Correspondence between Collins and Art O'Brien, Mar.–Dec. 1919 (AÓBP, MS 8429/11)

ammunition and an indeterminate number of rifles were despatched.[185] From November 1920 onwards, munitions from the capital were sent to Ireland via Liverpool. Armaments sent by this route up to the truce included at least 26 rifles, 56 handguns and 7,400 rounds of ammunition, among other munitions.[186] However, this did not constitute the sum total of weapons purchased by the London men in 1920, for in late January the following year the munitions account was overdrawn to the tune of £663.[187]

The Tyneside IRA purchased hundreds of pounds worth of handguns and explosives. Again, these were sent to Ireland via Liverpool. Sometime in May or June 1921, two rifles, 200 rounds of ammunition and two cwt (101.6 kg) of high explosives were among a batch of munitions sent from Newcastle-upon-Tyne to Manchester, whence they were transported to Liverpool. On 2 July, the Tyneside men sent 15 handguns and 262 rounds of ammunition to Merseyside.[188]

Before they came under GHQ's control, gunrunners in Birmingham sent small quantities of munitions directly to the 3rd Dublin Battalion. Subsequently, they despatched their weapons via Liverpool. On 26 May 1921, for example, six Lee Enfield rifles, two .32 automatics, one parabellum, one .380 Webley revolver and one 'Peter the Painter', along with 85 rounds of .38 and .45 revolver ammunition and 20 .303 and .45 sporting cartridges – all from Birmingham – were despatched from Liverpool.[189]

Overall, the two-year period from June 1919 to the truce in July 1921 saw the Liverpool men smuggle to Ireland a minimum of 297 firearms, consisting of seven machine guns, 25 rifles and 265 handguns, along with 22,985 rounds of ammunition and 470.2 kg of explosives, mainly gelignite and ammonite.[190]

185 Correspondence between Collins, O'Brien and Seán McGrath, Mar.–Oct. 1920 (DÉ, 2/321–2/322; RMP, P7/A/8)

186 McGrath to Collins, 16 Nov. 1920 (RMP, P7/A/8); Paddy Daly to Collins, 21 Dec. 1920, n.d., but *c.* 4 Jan., 10 Jan., 21 Feb., 2, 18 Mar., 30 Aug. 1921 (RMP, P7/A/3, P7/A/4, P7/A/7)

187 Art O'Brien to Collins, 27 Jan. 1921 (DÉ, 2/327)

188 BMHWS 773 Gilbert Barrington, pp. 8–9; 'Sent to M.', n.d., but *c.* May/June 1921; untitled note by David Fitzgerald, 2 July 1921, reprinted in Barrington, *Irish Independence Movement*, pp. 24–25

189 BMHWS 922, James Cunningham, p. 2; Paddy Daly to Michael Collins, 27 May 1921 (RMP, P7/A/5)

190 Correspondence between Collins, Neil Kerr, Steve Lanigan and Daly, June 1919–July 1921 (RMP, P7/A/1–P7/A/7); Hart has slightly higher figures: Hart, 'Thompson Submachine Gun', pp. 183–84

Graph 1: Quantity of Firearms Despatched to Ireland through Liverpool, 11 Aug. 1919–11 July 1921

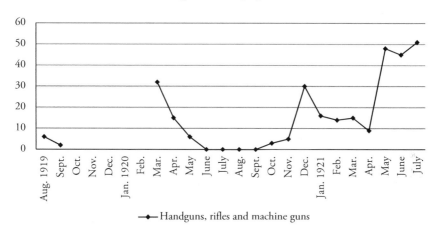

— Handguns, rifles and machine guns

Source: Correspondence between Michael Collins, Neil Kerr, Steve Lanigan and Paddy Daly, June 1919–July 1921 (RMP, P7/A/1–P7/A/7). Note that data are unavailable for the period Oct. 1919–Feb. 1920

Graph 2: Quantity of Ammunition Despatched to Ireland through Liverpool, 27 June 1919–11 July 1921

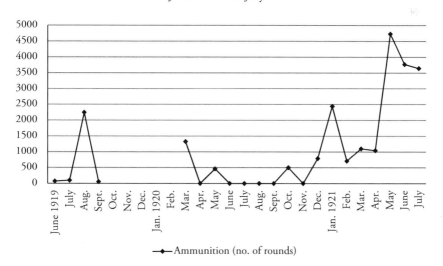

— Ammunition (no. of rounds)

Source: Correspondence between Michael Collins, Neil Kerr, Steve Lanigan and Paddy Daly, June 1919–July 1921 (RMP, P7/A/1–P7/A/7). Note that data are unavailable for the period Oct. 1919–Feb. 1920

Graph 3: Quantity of Explosives Despatched to Ireland through Liverpool, 30 Dec. 1920–11 July 1921

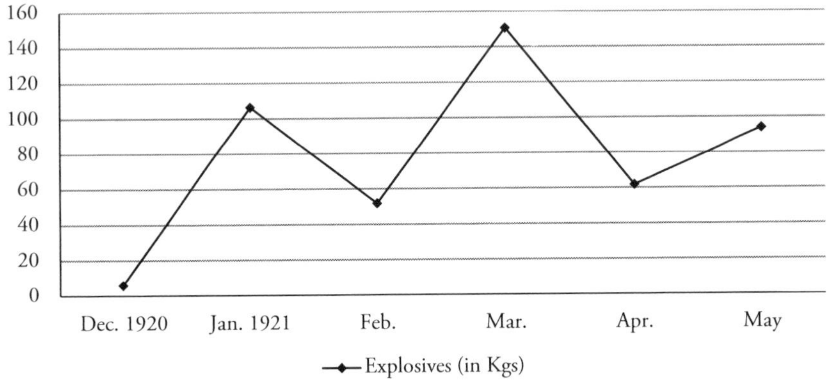

Source: Correspondence between Michael Collins, Neil Kerr, Steve Lanigan and Paddy Daly, June 1919–July 1921 (RMP, P7/A/1–P7/A/7)

These figures relate to munitions sent to Ireland from Liverpool. When the armaments transported straight to Dublin from London, Manchester and Glasgow in 1919 and 1920 are taken into account, the minimum amount of firearms sent to Ireland totals seven machine guns, 29 rifles and 300 handguns, along with 27,332 rounds of ammunition.[191]

As noted before, these figures are based on incomplete sources and therefore do not represent the total amount of munitions sent to Ireland by weapons-smugglers in Britain. In addition due to the activities of police and customs officials in Britain and Ireland, munitions despatched did not always reach IRA units in the field.[192]

Furthermore, some IRA men engaged in gunrunning outside the official channels of the IRA and IRB. Provincial units in Ireland were often dissat-isfied with the quantity of supplies they received from headquarters in Dublin. Michael Brennan made a number of trips to GHQ in order to plead for weapons. All he received, however, was 'a few revolvers occasionally'; he was

191 Correspondence between Collins, O'Brien and Seán McGrath, Mar.–Oct. 1920 (AÓBP, MS 8429/11, DÉ, 2/321–2/322; RMP, P7/A/8); correspondence between Collins, Séamus Barrett and Paddy O'Donoghue, Apr. 1919–Mar. 1920 (RMP, P7/A/9); correspondence between Collins and Joe Vize, May 1919–Mar. 1920 (RMP, P7/A/11)

192 See Chapters 4 and 6

never given any rifles. This caused great resentment among the Volunteers in Clare.[193] Many provincial units believed that Michael Collins, a Cork man, deliberately favoured his own county in terms of rifle distribution. To some extent their suspicions were correct. In March 1921, a GHQ staff memo noted that the counties of Cork, Kerry, Limerick and Tipperary constituted the 'war zone', the area in Ireland where the Volunteers and Crown forces clashed most frequently. Hence, the IRA in this area was 'entitled to supplies of all kinds and must be kept munitioned [sic] as fully as possible'.[194] Even so, the IRA in Cork often found itself short of munitions too. Historian John O'Callaghan states that GHQ was of 'limited assistance to the Limerick Volunteers in their efforts to procure arms and ammunition'. As well as undermining GHQ's authority in the provinces, Dublin's failure to supply adequate amounts of materiel had the effect of motivating some units to send their own representatives to Britain to obtain munitions.[195]

In September 1919, Joe Vize complained that a man named James O'Connell, claiming to be connected with GHQ, was receiving munitions from a member of Glasgow's 'B' Company. He asked Collins to confirm the bona fides of the arrangement, otherwise he was going to shut it down, for 'if those fellows are caught [by the police] it would mean the closing of our working channels, or perhaps worse'.[196] Two months later, Vize reported that a man named Patrick Connell or O'Connell was in Glasgow. As he too claimed to be working for GHQ, this was probably the same man as James O'Connell. Connell had tapped into one of Vize's sources and was offering inflated prices for munitions: £5 for 100 rounds of ammunition and £8 to £10 for rifles. '[H]e is doing great harm', Vize complained, urging Collins to have him 'looked up, or locked up'.[197] The following week, Collins informed Vize that there was no Patrick Connell working in Glasgow for GHQ and authorized his arrest.[198]

Connell/O'Connell proved to be just the first of many unauthorized gunrunners in Britain during the war. Collins took the position that such missions by inexperienced men ran the risk to disrupting the activities of the full-time gun-smugglers. News that a Volunteer from County Mayo had been

---

193 Brennan, *War in Clare*, p. 38
194 Brennan, *War in Clare*, p. 38; Staff Memo, 'THE WAR AS A WHOLE', 24 Mar. 1921 (RMP, P7/A/19[171–73])
195 O'Callaghan, *Revolutionary Limerick*, p. 193; Fitzpatrick, *Politics*, pp. 172–73
196 Joe Vize to Michael Collins, 5 Sept. 1919 (RMP, P7/A/11)
197 Vize to Collins, 16 Nov. 1919 (RMP, P7/A/11)
198 Collins to Vize, 22 Nov. 1919 (RMP, P7/A/11)

purchasing munitions in Liverpool led him to declaim that he 'would be better employed letting the people who are already at that work go ahead while he himself got on with his work in Mayo'.[199] A couple of months later, when he learned that an Alderman Lynch of Sligo was also acquiring armaments on Merseyside, Collins reminded Paddy Daly of GHQ's attitude towards such activity. 'You thoroughly understand don't you', he told the chief Liverpool gunrunner,

> than [i.e. that] any man working on his own is not to be facilitated unless authority is got from this side. People who have not a long experience in working these matters don't know the harm [they do] by spreading things about in a larg[e] circle.[200]

The permission of either the ministry of home affairs or GHQ was required for anyone to leave Ireland, he later wrote. Any person lacking such authorization was 'a deserter or a fugitive' and was to be shunned.[201] Despite these order from Collins, however, some gunrunners continued to help such rogue comrades from Ireland.

Some members of the IRA in Britain also engaged in unauthorized gunrunning. In late 1920, Paddy O'Donoghue told Michael Collins that No. 2 Company, Manchester Volunteers, was sending munitions to Dublin, sometimes via Drogheda and other times direct by train. The Volunteers themselves refused to divulge any details regarding the arrangements, so he asked Collins to clarify that the munitions were indeed being received in Dublin.[202] Collins replied that no such deliveries had arrived. He speculated that the weapons were being sent privately to individual Volunteers or IRA companies in Ireland, and if they were being sent through Drogheda they were effectively lost. Such private gun-smuggling 'is the sort of thing that always creates disorganisation and disturbance', he complained.[203] In a raid on the company's headquarters in Erskine Street on 2 April 1921, the police uncovered a large amount of munitions.[204] Meanwhile, the Scottish IRA allowed Seán Healy and Henry Coyle, representing brigades in Cork, Mayo

---

199   Collins to Paddy Daly, 23 Dec. 1920 (RMP, P7/A/3)
200   Collins to Daly, 5 May 1921 (RMP, P7/A/5)
201   Collins to Daly, 24 May 1921 (RMP, P7/A/5)
202   Paddy O'Donoghue to Collins, 11 Nov., 3 Dec. 1920 (RMP, P7/A/10)
203   Collins to O'Donoghue, 26 Nov. 1920 (RMP, P7/A/10)
204   List of ammunition and explosives found at the Irish Club, Erskine Street, Hulme, n.d. (HO, 144/4645)

and Sligo, to procure munitions in Scotland on the understanding that they would avoid encroaching on GHQ sources and would co-ordinate their prices with the Scottish Brigade's purchasing committee so as to avoid inflating the market. Coyle later became a member of the committee.[205] Iain Patterson has claimed that munitions received from Scotland had little impact on the IRA's campaign in Ireland during the war. However, while the quantity of Scottish armaments distributed by GHQ might have been small, the amount of materiel received by units through unofficial channels operated by Healy, Coyle and others should not be underestimated.[206]

In 1920, Richard Walsh, an organizer with the Mayo IRA, received permission from Collins to travel to Britain to procure munitions using funds raised by the men under his command. He succeeded in acquiring 'a considerable amount' of arms. Walsh despatched the munitions to Mayo via Dublin. However, GHQ commandeered the consignment and sent it to Munster instead. When a similar fate befell a second batch, a furious Walsh sought and was granted permission by his brigade to engage in gunrunning outside of GHQ channels: 'I knew that Brigades in Cork, Kerry, Tipperary and some of the midland counties had agents [in Britain] working in defiance of GHQ', he later wrote. Walsh then returned to Britain, accompanied by Pat Fallon, a fellow Mayo IRA member, and Joe Good, the London-born Volunteer who was now working as an electrician in Walsh's business. From February to July 1921, the trio travelled around England purchasing armaments. Visiting London, Birmingham, Bradford, Liverpool and Manchester, among other places, they acquired significant quantities of materiel. Despite the enterprise being unauthorized, Walsh received help from the Carr brothers in London, along with Hugh Early and the Mayo-born members of the Merseyside IRA. In London, they obtained a large number of weapons, but ammunition proved harder to procure. However, when Walsh learned that a gunrunner for the Cork IRA in London was suffering from a surfeit of ammunitions and a shortage of firearms, he agreed to an exchange, trading handguns in return for ammunition. 'Irish countrymen in England were very friendly to us when they knew our purpose', Good recalled. In Sheffield, the trio secured weapons from a criminal gang.[207] Collins, however, was not impressed by their activities. He told Paddy Daly that it was 'a positive disgrac[e] that

205 BMHWS 933, Séamus Reader, p. 6
206 Patterson, 'Activities', pp. 44, 46
207 BMHWS 400, Richard Walsh, pp. 129–39; Good, *Enchanted*, pp. 183–85

such a man [i.e. Walsh] should be away from his own area doing work that local men over at your side could do'. GHQ decided to punish Walsh by confiscating the munitions he had procured in Britain. These included 19 revolvers, over 2,000 rounds of ammunition, bombs and rifle grenades. Collins believed that Walsh's gunrunning adventure in Britain had done 'a lot of harm evidently'.[208]

Walsh's visits to Britain led him to form a jaundiced opinion of GHQ's direction of gunrunning. The method adopted by headquarters for procuring munitions across the Irish Sea was 'faulty', he wrote. Some of the gunrunning agents were 'useless', as they lacked all initiative, preferring to wait for the weapons to come to them rather than seeking out sources of supply themselves. Walsh held that Dublin should have developed more comprehensive procedures for the procurement and importation of munitions. Noting that armaments were imported from continental Europe towards the end of the war, he believed that such missions should have been attempted earlier, especially given that 'millions and millions of firearms of every sort' were available for purchase in post-war Germany. If more weapons had been available to the IRA, more people would have joined the Volunteers, he held.[209]

Walsh's criticisms are corroborated to some extent. Jim Phelan, a peripatetic member of the IRA, remembered that Egdon Heath in Dorsetshire served as a virtual graveyard for thousands of British army tanks. If the IRA 'had *wanted* tanks', he wrote, 'a company of men could have driven away a machine each, across that heath, and in all probability no one would have noticed'.[210] Wyndham Childs, an assistant commissioner of the London Metropolitan Police (LMP) from late 1921 to 1928, claimed that 'thousands of rifles, machine guns, revolvers, Mills grenades, shells, etc., were lying about in dumps' at the end of the Great War. Due to army demobilization and the increased police workload, these munitions were 'absolutely unguarded'. He remembered one specific incident of lax security which the Volunteers could have exploited had their intelligence service learned of it. A lorry loaded with war surplus munitions was travelling from London to the Midlands when it broke down. The driver abandoned it at the side of the road in order to seek help. 'If the IRA organisation in England had known of the situation', Childs

208 Correspondence between Michael Collins and Paddy Daly, 9 May, 25 June, 5, 7, 8 July 1921 (RMP, P7/A/5–P7/A/6)

209 BMHWS 400, Richard Walsh, pp. 129, 166–68

210 Jim Phelan, *The Name's Phelan: The First Part of the Autobiography of Jim Phelan* (Belfast: Blackstaff, 1993), pp. 257–58; original emphasis

reflected, 'they might have secured enough ammunition to have kept their body on its legs for years.'[211]

At times, Dublin itself seems to have been dissatisfied with gunrunning operations in Britain. Seán McGrath states that Michael Collins attempted to revitalize the IRB in London in 1920 in the hope of increasing the amount of munitions procured and despatched. The Fenians proved unresponsive to the idea, however, leading McGrath to become suspicious of their commitment to the cause.[212]

Nevertheless, Peter Hart has argued that the IRB's 'old and well-tested smuggling routes', carrying a 'small but steady trickle of weapons from the black markets of England and Europe, and from the gun shops of America', proved much more reliable sources of munitions for the IRA in Ireland than did GHQ's grander gunrunning schemes, including that of importing hundreds of Thompson sub-machine guns directly from the United States.[213]

V

Once the munitions were acquired, they were usually hidden in dumps until an opportunity arose to despatch them to Ireland. Most dumps were located in private houses or business premises. In early 1921, when houses were no longer able to accommodate the accumulating materiel, the Manchester IRA hired a garage in a quiet suburban district.[214] In Glasgow, a sympathetic coal merchant from Derry allowed Joe Booker of the 1st Scottish Battalion to open an arms dump at his business premises. Booker remembered that handguns were brought to the dump in paper parcels and shopping bags, while the dismantled rifles were carried in sacks.[215]

In Liverpool, dumps were mainly located in the private houses of the Irish working class. 'They were the only people who would take a risk over there', commented Paddy Daly.[216] Such houses were sometimes located quite near the docks. The whereabouts of others, however, necessitated the carrying of munitions for long distances to and from the port.[217] In 1921, Daly decided

---

211 Sir Wyndham Childs, *Episodes and Reflections* (London: Cassell & Co., 1930), pp. 199, 203–04
212 Seán McGrath interview (EO'MN, P17b/100)
213 Hart, 'Thompson Submachine Gun', p. 183
214 BMHWS 847, Patrick O'Donoghue, pp. 6, 13
215 BMHWS 776, Joseph Booker, pp. 1–2
216 BMHWS 814, Patrick Daly, p. 4
217 BMHWS 814, Patrick Daly, p. 4

to move the dumps nearer to Nelson dock, the place where most Irish ships anchored. Indeed, the neighbourhood around these docks became 'a kind of headquarters' for the Merseyside gunrunners.[218] Hughie Morris, a member of the local Sinn Féin club, operated a corner shop in the area and Daly rented one of the rooms behind the premises. The set up was a good one, for the presence of the shop in the front provided an excuse for frequent visits; such calls, sometimes of strangers, to a private house might have aroused the suspicion of neighbours. Often, munitions were only moved to Morris's shop from smaller dumps when they were ready to be despatched to Ireland.[219] 'It is hard to believe', recollected Michael O'Leary,

> when I state that a lorry drove up to Morris's shop at 12 o'clock noon on a particular weekday, stopped, the tarpaulin was thrown back and there were delivered into this annexe six machine guns which he [i.e. Morris] took in himself, stored away and held in these stores until arrangements were made for shipment to Dublin.[220]

The Liverpool men were required to operate a large number of dumps because GHQ ordered them to receive and despatch munitions from other gunrunning centres in Britain. By the autumn of 1919, 'great difficulties in transport' were preventing the transfer of weapons from Glasgow to Ireland. As well as being worried about the security of the armaments accumulating on Clydeside, Joe Vize complained that the backlog was causing the Volunteers to become lackadaisical about procuring further supplies. By early February 1920, 80 .45 revolvers and 20 rifles were awaiting despatch and more were expected soon. When Vize suggested the opening of a new transport route to Ireland – to Dublin via Motherwell, Liverpool and Waterford – Michael Collins recommended that he send the munitions to Merseyside where 'Our communications … are extremely good and our men are extremely good'. On 3 March 1920, Paddy Clinton and Patrick Sullivan made the first journey, visiting Neil Kerr Senior's house in Bootle with a small batch of munitions. '[W]e will be able to keep them [i.e. the Liverpool men] going for sometime [sic]', boasted Vize.[221] Nine Volunteers

218 Paddy Daly interview (EO'MN, P17b/136)

219 BMHWS 814, Patrick Daly, pp. 30–31; BMHWS 797, Micheál Ó Laoghaire, p. 20

220 BMHWS 797, Micheál Ó Laoghaire, p. 21

221 Correspondence between Michael Collins and Joe Vize, 1 Oct., 16, 22 Nov. 1919, 7, 14, 15 Feb., 3, 14 Mar. 1920 (RMP, P7/A/11)

of 'A' Company were subsequently assigned the task of transporting the munitions belonging to the 2nd Scottish Battalion. 'They travelled by passenger train in turn from Motherwell to Liverpool', remembered James Byrne.

> This train left Motherwell at 11.30 each night and did not get into Liverpool until 6 in the morning. As it was very crowded the couriers had to remain in the corridor of the train all the night with their [suit] cases of material.

As time progressed, the Scottish men used road transport to carry the munitions to Merseyside. Just prior to the truce, they purchased a lorry for £585.[222] Liverpool and London gunrunners used cars for transportation.[223]

As we have seen, the Liverpool men took delivery of armaments from other gunrunning centres in addition to Glasgow. In the autumn of 1919, Manchester started to send some of its accumulated munitions to Merseyside. In January 1920, this despatch system was set on a new and more effective footing.[224] Weapons from Birmingham were transported to Liverpool by railway, sometimes in the luggage of the gunrunners themselves but mainly by carriage in crates disguised as pottery goods.[225]

On occasion, the Liverpool men made the journey to the other Irish centres to collect munitions for despatch. On 11 November 1920, for example, they drove their car to London. Two days later, the car began the return journey northward laden with 26 rifles, 31 automatics, 25 revolvers, 6,000 rounds of automatic ammunition, 900 rounds of .303 ammunition, 300 rounds of various calibres of ammunition, 200 sporting cartridges, two hand grenades and six ammunition magazines.[226]

Some of these munitions from London may have been hidden in the house of the Brown sisters. Arrested in the aftermath of the arson attacks on Merseyside in November 1920, Kathleen and Shelia Brown were charged with

---

222 BMHWS 828, James Byrne, pp. 3–4; Bernard McCabe's statement to the MSPB (EMP, 2/A/11); *MG*, 16 Mar. 1921

223 Seán McGrath to Michael Collins, 13, 16 Nov. 1920 (RMP, P7/A/8); Art O'Brien to Collins, 22 Dec. 1920 (DÉ, 2/326)

224 Correspondence between Collins, Liam McMahon, Séamus Barrett and Paddy O'Donoghue, 18 Sept. 1919, 31 Jan., 6 Feb. 1920 (RMP, P7/A/9)

225 BMHWS 922, James Cunningham, pp. 8–9

226 Neil Kerr to Michael Collins, 12 Nov.; Seán McGrath to Collins, 16 Nov. 1920 (RMP, P7/A/3, P7/A/8)

conspiracy to murder and to set fires.[227] In mid-January 1921, Paddy Daly told Michael Collins that the munitions hidden in the sisters' house were the last part of a backlog in Liverpool that remained to be despatched. As the likelihood was high of the sisters being acquitted of the charges against them, thus ending the police surveillance of their house, Daly thought it best to refrain from attempting to remove the munitions for now. Three weeks later, Daly was becoming impatient, hoping that at least one of the sisters would soon be acquitted so as to allow for the removal of the materiel. On 13 February, his prediction proved correct when all charges against the sisters were dropped. Five days later, he reported that the munitions hidden in the house had finally been removed. The batch contained armaments from Antwerp and London, including 224 lbs (101.6 kg) of explosives, seven rifles, four Owen guns, along with 1,102 rounds of assorted ammunition for automatic handguns and 20 rounds for the Owen.[228]

Glasgow was another frequent port of call for the Liverpool men. Paddy Daly experienced an eventful journey when Neil Kerr Senior asked him to travel to Clydeside to direct the gunrunner Henry Coyle to Liverpool with a munitions-laden lorry. Daly travelled to Glasgow by train and secured lodgings with a sympathizer. The lorry journey was postponed, however, due to the failure of an arms raid on a drill hall. After a short time, another cargo of munitions was accumulated and loaded into an Austin car. Coyle drove while Daly and another Glasgow Volunteer occupied the passenger seats. 'The back of the car was packed up to the level of the top of the front seat', remembered Daly.

> One of us was forced to recline on top of this load at the back and it was a most uncomfortable position, but we changed around [positions] as we proceeded on the journey.

When the car broke down about 32 kilometres into the journey, the trio were forced to wait for the arrival of a mechanic the next morning as they were ignorant of car maintenance. While attempting to fix the car, the mechanic drove it up and down the road as the trio looked on. Luckily for them, however, he never looked under the rug behind the driver's seat. The party proceeded on its journey but was forced to enlist another mechanic in Carlisle

---

227   *IT, TT,* 11 Dec. 1920

228   Paddy Daly to Michael Collins, 17 Jan., 10, 14 Feb., 18 Mar. 1921 (RMP, P7/A/4); *IT,* 14 Feb. 1921

in order to fix the gearbox from which smoke was emanating. Following a journey along dangerous mountain roads, the car's lights and horn failed in Preston. The trio purchased two bicycle lamps and a whistle. The passenger in the front seat held one lamp out the window to illuminate the road in front for the driver, while the man in the back held the other lamp in the rear window so as to alert cars behind to their presence. The whistle, meanwhile, was employed as a horn. They finally reached Liverpool about 24 hours after they had left Glasgow.[229]

VI

The smuggling of munitions to Ireland took a number of forms. Sometimes the gunrunners and their friends travelled to Ireland on passenger ships carrying the armaments on their persons or in their luggage. As we saw earlier, this seems to have been the favoured method of gunrunners in London and Glasgow in the period before and after the 1916 Rising. The London Volunteers continued to employ couriers during the war, though Michael Collins frowned on the use of women in this role.[230] In the early stages of gunrunning in Birmingham, the men there used the normal postal service as the most convenient method of despatch. The parcels were often addressed to Dublin drapery and department stores such as Arnotts, Todd Burns and Ferrier & Pollock. Volunteers employed in these workplaces would then take charge of the parcels, remove the weapons and carry them to a dump. With several parcels being sent every week, post offices throughout the Birmingham area were employed as the repeated use of one or two might have aroused the suspicions of the staff. The quantity of munitions despatched like this was small due to both a lack of money to fund large purchases and to the nature of the despatch system.[231]

The main method of smuggling was the hiding of armaments aboard trading vessels plying between Britain and Ireland. Many of the seafarers on these boats were Irishmen and some were willing to smuggle munitions. Ned Kavanagh and Billy Vernon were two such sailors and their ship, the SS *Blackrock*, became the virtual flagship of IRA gunrunning out of Liverpool. Other prominent Merseyside gunrunning seamen included Paddy Weafer on

229 BMHWS 814, Patrick Daly, pp. 15–16
230 BMHWS 945, Sorcha Nic Diarmada, p. 5; Michael Collins to Art O'Brien, 24 June 1920 (DÉ, 2/284)
231 BMHWS 922, James Cunningham, p. 2

board the SS *Wicklow*, Michael Byrne on the SS *Kildare*, Hughie Morris's son on the SS *Kirkcaldy*, Paddy Larkin on the SS *Bessbrook*, a ship owned by the Dundalk and Newry Steam Packet Company, Paddy McCarthy on the SS *Killiney* and Tom McGlew on the SS *Clarecastle*, a Guinness boat.[232] Paddy Nolan was the main seafarer used to carry munitions directly from Glasgow to Dublin in 1919–20. When Joe Vize criticized his slow work rate, Collins said Nolan was 'great old Brick' but conceded that he was 'not as young as he was'.[233]

The most detailed accounts of smuggling activities have been left by seafarers John Sherlock and William Nelson. In 1918, the success of the 40-year old Meath man Sherlock in smuggling a case of revolvers and ammunition from St Johns in Newfoundland to Dublin led to his being sworn into the Dublin IRA. Acting on instructions from Collins, he secured a job on a ship travelling between Dublin and London, the SS *Lady Emerald*. His first job involved delivering letters from Collins to the ISDL offices in London's Holborn district. About four days later, after meeting some of the capital's gunrunners, Sherlock returned to Ireland, having smuggled some arms aboard.[234]

He was then promoted to boatswain, a position which entailed responsibility for maintaining the ship and its equipment. He engineered the dismissal of the English crew members and had them replaced by Irishmen. Sherlock told the new crew men that in return for ensuring they got these jobs, the IRA expected them to help with the smuggling of munitions and correspondence. If they proved successful in these tasks, they would be enlisted in the Volunteers. Sherlock succeeded in placing similar recruits aboard other ships on the Dublin–London route.[235] The seafarers included Scottish Volunteer Eamonn Mooney, Thomas Byrne, Owen Lynch, Patrick Tyrrell, John Kelly, Thomas Ahern, Patrick Barrett and his son Patrick, Michael Heaney, Thomas Ellis and Liam Doyle.[236]

Onboard the ships, the munitions were hidden in the seafarers' bunks or private quarters.[237] In 1920, however, security at London port was increased,

232 BMHWS 814, Patrick Daly, pp. 6–7; BMHWS 797, Micheál Ó Laoghaire, p. 23; William Nelson's Story (NLI, MS 41,722), p. 1; William Nelson, '"Q" Company', *An tÓglach*, 2.2 (1966), p. 12

233 Correspondence between Joe Vize and Michael Collins, 6, 11 June 1919 (RMP, P7/A/11)

234 Sherlock Statement (NLI, MS 9,873), pp. 1–3

235 Sherlock Statement, pp. 3–4

236 Sherlock Statement, p. 5

237 Sherlock Statement, p. 6

with customs officials instituting closer inspections of ships and their cargo. This made the hiding of weapons in the seamen's quarters a risky proposition. Discussing the problem with Collins, Sherlock suggested that the munitions be secretly placed in such a position in the ship's hold that the regular cargo would obscure it from the view of the customs officials. Collins agreed and Sherlock instructed his contacts aboard the other Dublin–London boats to hide their consignments of materiel in a similar fashion.[238] Thus, after collecting a batch of munitions from a London gunrunner, the seaman, on returning to his ship, would 'take one of the Hatches opposite the Ladder':

> Descending to the hole [i.e. hold] the man in charge and one of the other [gunrunning] men would go down and place the war material underneath the cargo. The following day when the Hatches would be taken off the Customs [officials] would go into the hole of the Ship and the[y] would remain their [sic] untill [sic] the last Sling of the cargo went into the hole then the[y] would come up and wait there until the Hatches would be put on and covered with Tarpolins [i.e. tarpaulins] [.]

The procedure was a 'splendid' success, Sherlock claimed.[239] The munitions transported by Sherlock and his men included rifles, revolvers and ammunition, along with high explosives and such assorted equipment as wireless sets, range finders and field telephones.[240]

Sherlock operated out of London. From 1920 onwards, most munitions reaching Ireland from Britain were smuggled through Liverpool, Britain's major international port on the river Mersey. Many boats plied between Merseyside and Irish ports such as Dublin, Cork, Dundalk and Sligo, William Nelson's SS *Killiney* being only one.[241] The docks were over 11 kilometres long and occupied hundreds of acres of land. A high wall separated the dockland from the city. During working hours, entrance to the docks was gained through large gates. In the evening, however, these gates were closed, leaving narrow doorways guarded by policemen as the only means of entry.[242] 'Revolvers and ammunition were easy enough to handle', remembered Nelson, but carrying rifles in canvas bags required the use of newspapers and old rags

238 Sherlock Statement, pp. 6–8
239 Sherlock Statement, pp. 8, 11
240 Sherlock Statement, pp. 1, 14–16
241 Nelson's Story, p. 1; Nelson, '"Q" Company', p. 12
242 BMHWS 814, Patrick Daly, p. 3; Paddy Daly interview (EO'MN, P17b/136)

to disguise the weapons' characteristic shapes. '[M]any a little comedy was enacted in British docks', he continued.

> What could be more unsuspicious, for instance, than to see three sailors, half-drunk, trudging along the dock road, with sailor's [sic] bags on their backs? They would pause perhaps at the dock gates, one of them trying to persuade the others to go over for the last drink; but they would decide not to, then stagger through the gates with the Harbour Constable looking on.[243]

When ships arrived from New York, Hamburg and other places, the munitions were smuggled ashore, hidden in a dump and smuggled back into the port when a vessel bound for Ireland arrived. Later, however, it was decided to transfer the munitions directly from one ship to another so as to save time and avoid running the gauntlet of port security. Paddy Daly and Tim O'Sullivan would board the incoming ship early in the morning and, with the help of the crew, move the armaments to the Irish boat.[244]

Relations between the gunrunners and the seafarers were not always smooth. In February 1921, declaring that he did not like Paddy Daly's method of managing Merseyside gunrunning, Harry Shorte asked that Michael Collins deal with him directly. 'I have run into debt here since my own money vanished', he wrote '& very little they [i.e. the Liverpool men] bothered about me'.[245] Collins told Daly of the seafarer's complaint and asked him to assure the seaman that his contribution was valued.[246] Daly was surprised to hear of Shorte's complaint, stating that he had been well supplied with money. Indeed, Daly hinted that he himself was the one who had grounds for complaint against Shorte and not vice versa.[247] He stated that the seaman's demand to deal directly with Collins in gunrunning matters was 'in keeping with his own importance'. Daly argued that there had been no friction between himself and Shorte and that no acrimony would arise in the future if he continued to give his munitions to the Liverpool men for shipment to Ireland.[248] Shorte 'always means well', Collins

---

243 Nelson, '"Q" Company', p. 12
244 BMHWS 814, Patrick Daly, p. 14
245 Harry Shorte to Michael Collins, 23 Feb. 1921 (and not 1920 as it states) (RMP, P7/A/4)
246 Collins to Paddy Daly, 8 Mar. 1921 (RMP, P7/A/4)
247 Daly to Collins, 11 Mar. 1921 (RMP, P7/A/4)
248 Daly to Collins, 8 Apr. 1921 (RMP, P7/A/5)

replied, encouraging Daly to settle matters with him.[249] However, when the seafarer informed Dublin that the captain of the ship on which he was travelling had warned him that the police were watching his activities and had arranged for seamen to give evidence against him, Collins despaired of Shorte's 'knack of getting himself discovered'.[250]

Michael O'Leary later claimed that the security of the Liverpool gunrunning channels was such that '[n]ot even one round of ammunition was captured [by the police] or lost' by the Volunteers.[251] This is incorrect, for despite all the precautions taken gunrunners did indeed lose munitions and the British authorities did capture some armaments.

Paddy Daly remembered an incident which occurred while he and Volunteer James McCaughey were smuggling munitions on board the *Clarecastle*. On their third trip to the ship, carrying rifles, the two were stopped by a customs official who enquired after their business. Disbelieving their excuses, he placed his hand on their bag. 'There are rifles in that bag and I have to search it', he said. Daly refused to allow him to search the bag, insisting that only a senior customs official could do so. Daly, however, was merely buying time, for instead of going to the senior customs official who was in the stern of the ship, he and McCaughey proceeded to flee the scene. The customs official gave chase, accompanied by a policeman and some dockers, Daly noting later that a 'reference to Sinn Fein was sufficient to rally their support'. Eventually, Daly and McCaughey were forced to drop the bag in order to make good their escape and the police discovered it.[252]

On another occasion, James Creaney, one of Sherlock's seafarers, hid some munitions in his quarters on board his ship. The following morning, a group of customs officials boarded the vessel. One of them went into Creaney's room, sat down and proceeded to read his newspaper. Fearful that the batch of munitions might be discovered, Creaney left the room under the pretext of cooking his breakfast in the galley, fled the ship and contacted Denis Carr. Informed of the predicament when he arrived in the capital later that day, John Sherlock boarded the ship and retrieved Creaney's clothes, reasoning that if the seaman himself had returned he would have been detained as the munitions had likely been discovered. Creaney was then sent to Liverpool

249 Collins to Daly, 14 Apr. 1921 (RMP, P7/A/5)
250 Harry Shorte to Collins, 28 May; Collins to Daly, 9 June 1921 (RMP, P7/A/5)
251 BMHWS 797, Micheál Ó Laoghaire, p. 22
252 BMHWS 814, Patrick Daly, pp. 7–9; Paddy Daly interview (EO'MN, P17b/136)

where he went to ground for a while, before securing a job on a White Star ship sailing to New York.[253]

Those munitions that did reach Dublin safely were transferred from the ships onto ferry boats crossing the river Liffey. For a time, John Sherlock hid armaments in his own lodgings on the south side of the city, whence they were removed to dumps by members of the Dublin IRA.[254] However, the stationing of policemen in the Holyhead Hotel on the North Wall led Sherlock to warn Collins that ferrying the munitions across the Liffey would thenceforth be a risky enterprise. Collins, therefore, agreed to his suggestion that a dump be created on the south side of the city.[255]

Following incidents in which some gunrunning seamen were questioned and searched by the police in Dublin, the seafarers refused to unload the munitions. In response, QMG Seán McMahon summoned William Nelson and Archie Kennedy to a meeting. Kennedy was a docker; Nelson had taken up the same occupation following his failure to secure the officer's ticket necessary for him to continue working as a seaman. McMahon told them that munitions were accumulating in Liverpool and Glasgow due to the refusal of seamen to take them ashore in Dublin. He, therefore, ordered the establishment of a special unit to transport the armaments from the ships to the dumps. Nelson and Kennedy set about recruiting men to the unit. Eventually a group of between eight and 20 was formed. Later, in the backroom of a shop on Sir John Rogerson's Quay, Rory O'Connor administered the IRA oath of allegiance to the newly formed 'Q' Company of the Dublin Volunteers.[256]

The men usually operated in groups of four. They mostly worked during the day, but sometimes in the early hours of the morning as well. On occasion, the munitions were removed from the ships on cargo hoists. Mainly, however, they were moved by the men themselves, who then carried them – 'ammunition in their pockets, revolvers stuck in their belts around their waists' – to a dump located in the cellar of a house on Rogerson's Quay, wherefrom they were later removed to other stores.[257] In 1920, the police instituted close inspections of every ship that landed in Dublin. Although this led 'Q' Company to suspend their nocturnal work, their

---

253 Sherlock Statement, pp. 19–20; Martin Walsh to the MSPB, n.d. (EO'ML, P17a/154)
254 Sherlock Statement, p. 5
255 Sherlock Statement, pp. 5–6
256 Nelson's Story, p. 2
257 Nelson's Story, p. 3; Nelson, '"Q" Company', p. 12

activities were not adversely affected to any great extent, as they simply waited until the police had finished their inspections before boarding the ships and unloading the munitions.[258]

GHQ's method of distributing munitions to IRA units around Ireland was rather precarious, Richard Walsh remembered. Periodically, provincial brigades sent men to the capital to purchase some of the arsenal. It was then their responsibility to transport the munitions to their brigade area. The main method of transport was by rail, and many railway workers risked their lives by helping IRA men to smuggle munitions around the country. Another method involved placing munitions amongst the regular supplies being sent from Dublin to shopkeepers or merchants around the country. Once the box of supplies was delivered, the munitions would be removed by Volunteers in the businessmen's employ. Overall, Walsh described the distribution system as 'chancy'.[259]

VII

Gunrunning – the acquisition and smuggling of weapons to Ireland – was the most important activity of republicans in Britain. It was here that they most obviously served as 'auxiliaries' to the IRA in Ireland, for the lack of munitions was a perennial problem for the latter. In London, Liverpool and Glasgow, the IRB, under the direction of Michael Collins in Dublin, ran the clandestine operation. Elsewhere, in Birmingham, on Tyneside and in South Wales, IRA units acted on their own initiative in forwarding armaments to Ireland and only later came under the control of GHQ. Sometimes munitions were purchased from soldiers or black market traders. Otherwise they were stolen from collieries and army barracks. The machine guns, rifles, handguns, explosives and ammunition were then smuggled to Ireland by seafarers. In January 1921, Collins told Manchester's Paddy O'Donoghue that the supply of munitions would prove to be 'the main feature in overcoming the enemy'.[260] In the event the IRA in Ireland did not defeat the Crown forces. However, Volunteer attacks on police stations and army barracks, using munitions sourced in Ireland itself as well as in Britain, along with smaller quantities shipped from New York, Antwerp, Hamburg and elsewhere, disrupted British

---

258 Nelson's Story, p. 3
259 BMHWS 400, Richard Walsh, pp. 140–47; see also BMHWS 1692, John Feehan, pp. 15–29
260 Michael Collins to Paddy O'Donoghue, 5 Jan. 1921 (RMP, P7/A/10)

administration and led the British government to agree to a ceasefire in July 1921.

The contribution of the republican movement in Britain to the war was not limited to supplying munitions of war, however. In November 1920, the IRA began a campaign of violence, employing munitions acquired in its gunrunning activities. That is the subject of the next chapter.

CHAPTER 3

'We are doing what you are doing in Ireland': IRA Operations in Britain, January 1919–July 1921

I

Although the ambush at Soloheadbeg marked the beginning of the war, it was only the following year that the IRA's campaign against British rule in Ireland began in earnest. In November 1920, the theatre of operations was extended to Britain itself with the mounting of attacks in Liverpool. Over the subsequent seven-and-a-half months to the truce of July 1921, warehouses, farms and railway infrastructure suffered arson attacks, telegraph and telephone networks were sabotaged and Crown forces' relatives were terrorized. As one Volunteer declared while firing shots over the heads of staff members in a Manchester café as his comrade sprinkled the premises with paraffin: 'We are doing what you are doing in Ireland'.[1] This chapter examines such violence. Through the discussion of an operation in March 1921, section II provides a close insight into the mounting of attacks. Section III considers the motivation behind the violence. Sections IV and V examine the planning and execution of the operations and provide analysis thereof. Section VI focuses on the effects of the campaign and section VII concludes.

II

At a meeting of the Liverpool City IRA Company in February 1921, O/C Hugh Early announced that he had received an order to launch arson attacks on local farms in retaliation for farms being burned in Ireland by 'Black and Tan' RIC men. Early told his men, teamed up in small groups, to reconnoitre local farms and choose suitable targets for attack. Two Volunteers, John Pinkman and Charlie O'Gorman, discovered an 'ideal' objective, a farm on the outskirts

---

1 *The Observer*, 3 Apr. 1921

of Litherland with several large barns filled with hay and straw. They chose the property because its proximity to the town's back-alleys would facilitate an easy getaway once a fire had been started. However, at the subsequent meeting of the company on 9 March, Early informed his men that the plan had changed. Instead of attacking the farms they had each chosen, the Volunteers were now ordered to set fire to specific farms in the Little Crosby area. Two targets had been selected at opposite sides of a country lane: Whitehouse Farm and Hill Farm. Dissatisfied with the plan, that evening the group of eight Volunteers reluctantly travelled to Little Crosby by train and continued to the farms on foot.[2] 'We are having some farm-work to-night', Paddy Daly told Michael Collins that same day, 'just to keep the local co[mpan]y in practice.' The exercise culminated with 13 fires blazing in Liverpool and the surrounding area. Those within the city boundaries, such as the three in Birkenhead, were reported to be small in size, 'the damage being confined to barns and haystacks'. However, the other fires, especially that at Ormskirk, were more extensive. 60 tons of clover stacks were destroyed at Mill Farm in Lunt. A fireman tackling one of the blazes was killed when his engine overturned.[3]

Edward Brady had been placed in charge of orchestrating that night's operations in the Wallasey district. Agricultural areas were reconnoitred, rough maps were prepared and suitable targets were chosen. The Volunteers were divided into groups, each of which was allocated a number of farms. Petrol and paraffin were distributed, as were guns and ammunition. A timetable for the night's destruction was circulated too. The men met at Birkenhead's ferry-boat landing stage and set off towards their respective targets. At their first target, the constant barking of dogs and the presence of a number of people led to Brady's group cancelling the attack and moving on to their next one. In total, they started fires on four farms, including haystacks and buildings. It was an 'awesome-terrible spectacle', Brady later wrote, 'shooting flames into the inky sky'. He and his men then proceeded to make their escape across fields so as to avoid capture by the police on the roads. As they 'tramped wearily across the open country', they came across an isolated hay rick: Brady waded across a mucky river and set it alight too.[4]

The contribution of Pinkman and his accomplices to the night's operation

2 Pinkman, *Legion*, pp. 48–50
3 Paddy Daly to Michael Collins, 9 Mar. 1921 (RMP, P7/A/4); CC of Cheshire to the Under Secretary of State (USS), HO, 20 Oct.; ACC of Lancashire to the USS, HO, 27 Oct. 1922 (HO, 144/4645); *Liverpool Courier, TT*, 11 Mar. 1921
4 Brady, *Secret Service*, pp. 38–41

was not so impressive. When they reached the laneway, Pinkman asked if the farms they were about to attack were equidistant from the road, for if they were not the fire at the farm closer to the lane would illuminate the men on their way to the second farm, possibly alerting passers-by to their presence. He was assured that the farms were equidistant from the road. They then divided into two smaller groups and set off to burn down hay barns and any other targets they could find. As Pinkman's group neared their target, however, a Volunteer from the second group ran across their path. They then found themselves up against a fence when flames from a fire at the second farm illuminated the sky. Panicking, they ran about frantically trying to escape. As they hurried in the direction of the train station, they noticed people on the foot bridge; Pinkman's earlier concern about being seen had proved prescient. By now the two farms were on fire, sparks from the first having blown across the road and started a conflagration at the second. Convinced that they had been spotted, the men dived into a hollow in the ground beside a ditch. There they debated what to do. Unable to run across the electric railway lines, the four decided to rush their way across the bridge. Pinkman threw away his revolver, confident that his using it would result in him and his comrades being 'slaughtered'. With Pinkman in front, they made an attempt to dash across the bridge. 'I fought like a tiger', he remembered,

> – and so did the others – until I was finally pinned down by two men who nearly broke my arms as they twisted them behind my back. As they dragged me from the bridge towards the station platform, I could hear someone shouting, 'Throw him over! ... throw the bastard over!' Then I heard a train approaching and I prayed to God for the train to hurry and get into the station before they threw me onto the tracks. When we got to the platform I tried to dig my heels in, and struggled with every ounce of strength left in me to stop them from getting me to the edge of the platform. 'Throw him in!' – several people were shouting now – 'In with him! Throw the Sinn Féin bastard in!' But the train roared and shot past without even slowing down. It was an express. O Jesus, Mary and Joseph! I thanked God and began to relax. I had to: I was exhausted.[5]

'I hope our next move will have more effective results and come off very shortly', wrote Paddy Daly, reflecting on the arrest of six Volunteers, one of

---

5 Pinkman, *Legion*, pp. 48–54; ACC of Lancashire to the USS, HO, 27 Oct. 1922 (HO, 144/4645); *Liverpool Courier*, *TT*, 11 Mar. 1921

whom was shot by a sharp-eyed farmer.[6] Brady later said that the precautions which he and his men had taken in covering their tracks were lacking in Pinkman's case. Travelling to the targets in a body, he concluded, was 'tactically a mistake'.[7]

III

The main motive behind IRA violence in Britain was revenge. In the summer of 1920, GHQ staff and senior Volunteer commanders from around Ireland attended a meeting in Dublin. The country officers, remembered Ernie O'Malley, an IRA organizer, 'pressed for a campaign in England to counteract the destruction of creameries and houses by the military and police [in Ireland]'.[8] When George Fitzgerald, an I/O connected with GHQ, was sent to London to mount operations, he was told by Michael Collins that such attacks were 'by way of reprisals for burnings that were carried out at home by the Military and the Black and Tans'.[9]

The recruitment of 'Black and Tans' and Auxiliaries to the RIC in 1920 represented the British government's belated response to the rebellion in Ireland. By then, the Irish police force had shown itself completely unable to deal with the IRA insurgency. In 1919, Volunteer assaults on RIC barracks and patrols had caused the deaths of 15 members of the force. In the first nine months of 1920, fatalities had jumped to 95. In response, the police evacuated isolated rural barracks, retreating to and reinforcing stations in large towns and urban areas. Resignations and retirements due to the resultant low morale left the force undermanned, thus exacerbating its weakness. The British government was unwilling to mobilize its armed forces due to the cost it would entail but also because it was loath to admit that a war was taking place in Ireland. Instead of deploying the army, therefore, it responded by militarizing the police. An RIC recruitment drive was undertaken in Ireland and Britain, and between January 1920 and July 1921 over 8,500 men were recruited to the force. The Black and Tans, so called because of the mismatched clothing they wore, were former rank and file soldiers recruited to the RIC proper. The Auxiliaries, on the other hand, were former army officers recruited to a

6 Paddy Daly to Michael Collins, 11 Mar. 1921 (RMP, P7/A/4); *TT*, 10, 11 Mar. 1921; CC of Cheshire to the USS, HO, 20 Oct.; ACC of Lancashire to the USS, HO, 27 Oct. 1922 (HO, 144/4645)

7 Brady, *Secret Service*, p. 42

8 O'Malley, *Another Man's Wound*, p. 188

9 BMHWS 684, George Fitzgerald, p. 28

special auxiliary division of the police. Heavily armed and poorly trained, both groups soon acquired reputations for terrorism and looting in their attempts to combat the IRA's guerrilla warfare.[10] On 20 September 1920, in response to the shooting dead of Head Constable Burke in Balbriggan, County Dublin, Black and Tans and other policemen from the nearby Gormanstown Barracks descended on the village, where they shot dead two civilians and caused over £130,000 of damage to property.[11] The episode was repeated in Trim, County Meath, a few days later where, in response to an attack on the town's police barracks, a group of Black and Tans or Auxiliaries shot two young men and inflicted an estimated £50,000 of injury to property owned by Sinn Féin sympathizers.[12] Senior police officials and government politicians tacitly condoned such 'reprisals' as natural reactions to the criminality of the IRA.[13] Edward Brady later argued that it was the adverse publicity that such terrorism caused, rather than any enthusiasm for Sinn Féin or the IRA per se, that led to the majority of the Catholic population in Ireland supporting the republican movement.[14]

The proposal to launch a campaign of violence in Britain found its most forceful advocate in Cathal Brugha. As we saw earlier, in 1918 Brugha, the then C/S, led an IRA squad to Britain to assassinate members of the government in order to prevent conscription being imposed on Ireland.[15] According to Seán Ó Murthuile, a senior IRB man, 'the idea of carrying the war into England [in 1920] was not one that Dail Eireann wholeheartedly acquiesced in'. However, Brugha, 'adamant and stubborn', insisted on it and the Dáil Ministry finally granted its approval in early November.[16]

IRA men in Britain were very much in favour of opening a new front in the war. For Liverpool's Michael O'Leary, the sackings of Balbriggan and Trim called for revenge attacks 'of a similar nature' in England: 'we believed "an eye for an eye"'.[17] Trim also figured high in Edward Brady's justification

---

10 D.M. Leeson, *The Black and Tans: British Police and Auxiliaries in the Irish War of Independence, 1920–1921* (Oxford: Oxford University Press, 2011), pp. 9, 20–21, 24–26, 30–32, 68–82, 96–112, 157–82

11 *IT*, 22, 23, 28 Sept. 1920

12 *IT*, 28 Sept., 2 Oct. 1920

13 Leeson, *Black and Tans*, pp. 216–21

14 Brady, *Secret Service*, pp. 123–24

15 See Prologue

16 Seán Ó Murthuile manuscript, n.d., but *c.* mid 1920s–early 1930s, pp. 126–27 (RMP, P7a/209); minutes of meeting of the Dáil Ministry, 6 Nov. 1920 (DÉ, 1/3)

17 BMHWS 797, Micheál Ó Laoghaire, pp. 42–43

for the unleashing of what he admits was 'terrorism'.[18] Paddy O'Donoghue, O/C Manchester, agreed:

> Following the deliberate burnings by the Auxiliaries [in Ireland], the Army Executive [in Dublin] decided that the Volunteers in the English cities should adopt retaliatory measures in their areas ... It was felt that the people in England should be made conscious of what the people in Ireland were suffering as regards depredations carried out by the Crown Forces.

The overriding intention in launching attacks against property in Britain, therefore, was to avenge the violence of Crown forces in Ireland.

However, there also existed a related desire to force the British people to confront the bloodshed being perpetrated in their name across the Irish Sea. As O'Donoghue put it, the overall aim of the campaign was 'to bring home to the British people the sufferings and conditions to which the Irish people were being subjected by their police and soldiers'.[19] Michael Collins voiced similar sentiments. He disagreed with the comments of Barry Egan, the Sinn Féin deputy lord mayor of Cork city, that the Irish had no quarrel with the British people per se as opposed to the British government. Such talk was nonsensical, Collins argued, for the British people were indeed responsible, through their politicians, for the events in Ireland. 'It is not by getting them to avoid this point, but by getting them to understand it that any good will be done', he contended.[20] It was hoped, therefore, that the offensive would lead to a frightened and enlightened British public putting pressure on their public representatives to rethink the government's Irish policy.

The desire for revenge also motivated the other form of IRA violence in Britain, namely assassinations. There were a number of such plots which for one reason or another were not carried out. In September 1920, Patrick Murray, a member of the Cork Volunteers, led a three man team to London. Its mission was to assassinate a member of the British cabinet in the event of Terence MacSwiney, lord mayor of Cork and O/C of the county's 1st Brigade, dying on hunger strike in Brixton prison.[21] Later that year, when Crown forces

---

18 Brady, *Secret Service*, pp. 62–63
19 BMHWS 847, Patrick O'Donoghue, pp. 10–11
20 Michael Collins to Art O'Brien, 13 June 1921 (DÉ, 2/330)
21 Pa Murray to Florence O'Donoghue, 14, 26 Jan. 1959 (FO'DP, MS 31,296/1);

began using TDs as human shields in order to discourage attacks on their patrols in Dublin, Frank Thornton, George Fitzgerald and Dublin IRA man Seán Flood were sent to London to kidnap government MPs.[22] In March 1921, Thornton returned to London with Pa Murray and others to assassinate Major Percival, I/O of the Essex Regiment's 1st Battalion in County Cork, due to his penchant for torturing Volunteers.[23] Attempts on the lives of an RIC man and a British soldier were also mooted.[24]

Once the campaign of violence began in Britain in November 1920, the exigencies of war, including competition among rival units and the desire for prestige, began to motivate activities. 'Some of our people here are wondering why we don't carry out something similar to the operation of Nov[ember 1920]. here', Paddy Daly told Michael Collins in February 1921. As we have seen, just over a week later, on 9 March, an arson offensive against farms was duly executed, motivated less by any reprisals by Crown forces in Ireland than by a desire 'to keep the local co[mpan]y in practice', as well as a wish to imitate their comrades in Manchester.[25] In May, prestige motivated a revenge attack on a Liverpool farmer named John Rimmer. On 9 March, Volunteers attempting to set a fire were disturbed by the gun-wielding land-owner and Patrick Lowe was shot. Hearing that Rimmer was boasting of his exploit in the local press, the IRA decided to mount a revenge attack in order to preserve their *amour propre*.[26]

Most rank and file Volunteers and Cumann na mBan members appear to have supported attacks on property without demur. The sole exception seems to have been Charles Murphy, whose troubled conscience led him to confess to police his involvement in an arson operation in Manchester city centre on 2 April 1921.[27] The fact that attacks might have the effect of alienating the general population in Britain, including those of Irish descent, seems to have been of little concern to Volunteers, those born and raised in Britain included. According to the sources at our disposal, only one Volunteer expressed such qualms. Upon learning that some of his colleagues were planning to rescue a Sligo IRA man from police custody in May 1921, Glasgow's Séamus Reader

BMHWS 1584, Patrick Murray, pp. 17–20

22 BMHWS 615, Frank Thornton, p. 29

23 BMHWS 615, Frank Thornton, p. 47

24 Correspondence between Paddy Daly and Michael Collins, 16 Feb., 15 Mar. 1921 (RMP, P7/A/4)

25 Daly to Collins, 28 Feb., 9 Mar. 1921 (RMP, P7/A/4)

26 Brady, *Secret Service*, pp. 77–80; see pp. 164–65 below

27 See Chapter 1

expressed the fear that an attack on unarmed policemen might disgust the populace and cost the republican movement 'the support of the Scottish people'. His fellow Volunteers did not share his concern, however, and proceeded with the rescue attempt.[28] '[W]e did not consider such questions as danger, the logical conclusion of our efforts, or the consequences either to ourselves or to the community', Edward Brady wrote of his comrades in the Merseyside Volunteers. 'There was the great purpose always present in mind – the freeing of Ireland from English domination.'[29] Rather than fearing the consequences then, most Volunteers were excited to be involved in the campaign. On 27 November 1920, after setting fire to a timber yard on Liverpool's Grove Street, John Pinkman and Bernie Meehan returned home to watch their handiwork. They saw 'the flames from the timber yard getting higher and higher, and the smoke clouds rising in columns from various points near the docks'. The following day, they were impatient to read of their exploits in the newspapers, particularly the amount of damage that they had caused. 'We got a laugh reading the various estimates of the numbers of men involved in starting the fires', Pinkman wrote. '*The Times* said at least fifty were involved.'[30] Edward Brady also delighted in the media attention. He was 'highly amused' by press accounts of the farm fires mounted on Merseyside on 9 March which he had partly orchestrated.[31]

However, when he was initially called upon to participate in the opening operation in November 1920, Brady's scruples momentarily kicked in: 'my conscience seemed to rock – to waver on the right or the wrong of the action I was allotted to perform'. Yet, his qualms about the employment of violence were soon quieted by internalized military discipline: '[I] soon found myself ready to go on my mission, satisfied at any rate that I was not doing anything criminally wrong, or morally unlawful, as I considered that a state of war existed [between Ireland and England]'.[32]

A similar sense of discipline enabled Brady to participate in an ambiguous form of violence: the intimidation of people emigrating from Ireland. In July 1920, alarmed by the level of emigration, especially of men of military age, Dáil Éireann issued a decree prohibiting it without specific permission from the minister of home affairs. Emigration, argued *An t-Óglác*, was a 'cowardly

28   BMHWS 933, Séamus Reader, p. 10; see p. 147 below
29   Brady, *Secret Service*, p. 22
30   Pinkman, *Legion*, pp. 37–38
31   Brady, *Secret Service*, pp. 41–42
32   Brady, *Secret Service*, p. 29

desertion of the native land at a time when she is in the throes of a bloody struggle for freedom and her fate hangs in the balance'. The 'sternest measures' were necessary to counteract it.[33] In Britain – the main entrepôt for Irish emigrants – the IRA was authorized to use all means, including physical force, to tackle the problem. On 18 February 1921, armed Volunteers raided three lodging houses in Liverpool, confiscated the passports and travel tickets of 23 emigrants and warned them to return to Ireland.[34] Volunteers expressed mixed feelings about this particular operation. 'We never considered the illegal side of our mission', declared Edward Brady, writing in 1928, 'nor were we very concerned with the question of the "freedom of action" that is the basis of our Constitution, and the right of every man. The work was given to do – it was not our business to question the right or wrong of it.'[35] John Pinkman, however, felt differently. The emigrants he encountered stated that they wholeheartedly supported Sinn Féin and the Volunteers. Indeed, it was their patriotism that had forced their emigration, they said, for Black and Tans had destroyed their property and forced them to flee the country. Feeling sorry for the emigrants, Pinkman and his party returned their passports to them. Reflecting on the issue on his way home, he contended that many of his IRA comrades were as guilty of fleeing Ireland as any of the emigrants. 'Several of them had arrived in Liverpool since 1916 and had no family or other ties to keep them there', he thought. '*They* should have been back in Ireland where the fighting and dying was taking place.'[36]

Assassination assignments, the other main form of IRA violence in Britain, sometimes elicited from Volunteers less enthusiasm than strikes against property. When, in March 1921, Michael Collins requested that action be taken against a British army officer over-zealous in performing his duties in Cork and now residing in Liverpool, Paddy Daly replied that 'there are very few in the organisation here who would undertake any such work', indicating that most Merseyside Volunteers viewed assassination as a distasteful exercise. In the event, three men volunteered for the operation, but imperfect intelligence frustrated its successful execution.[37] A few months later, Edward Brady was given the task of executing an RIC Auxiliary officer recuperating

33 *An t-Óglác*, 15 Aug., 18 Sept. 1920

34 Brady, *Secret Service*, pp. 46–54; Pinkman, *Legion*, pp. 30–32; *Liverpool Courier*, 21 Feb. 1921

35 Brady, *Secret Service*, pp. 51–52

36 Pinkman, *Legion*, pp. 31–32; original emphasis

37 Correspondence between Michael Collins and Paddy Daly, 15, 18, 19, 21 Mar. 1921 (RMP, P7/A/4)

in a hotel in Blundellsands, near Liverpool. After some 'careful planning', Brady, masquerading as a commercial traveller, secured a room in the hotel on the same landing as that of his quarry. Not knowing the policeman by appearance, he decided to enter into conversation with his fellow guests. In the event, the first guest he approached proved to be his target, a fact which Brady verified by comparing the guest's signature in the hotel's visitors' book with that on a RIC report which he had received from GHQ. By shadowing the man, Brady learned his movements. With this information, he drew up a plan for kidnapping and executing him. At 11.45 p.m. on a specified night, two groups of Volunteers were to make their way to a meeting place near the hotel. One group was to travel by train. Travelling by taxi, the second group was to commandeer the vehicle, which would be used to transport the subsequently kidnapped policeman to a remote location where he would be executed. On the night, Brady and his accomplices reached the rendezvous location by train. However, the taxi carrying their associates never arrived. Frustrated, Brady contemplated raiding the hotel and executing the RIC man in his room. This, however, was a 'wild' idea. They, therefore, cancelled the operation and hailed a taxi for the journey back to Liverpool. Coincidently, the taxi proved to be the one which the second group of Volunteers had planned to commandeer. Brady later learned that his accomplices had travelled to Blundellsands in the car but the driver had driven away just as they were about to hijack the vehicle. The IRA men fired shots at the taxi but it did not stop. Brady was 'not sorry' that the operation had been scuppered.[38]

IV

In planning operations, IRA men in Britain were assisted by members of Rory O'Connor's staff visiting from Dublin. From the beginning, GHQ set down the parameters of the campaign. Firstly, O'Connor was instructed to confine operations to England: no attacks were to be mounted in Scotland or Wales. This was probably motivated by a romantic (if rather spurious) belief that the Scots and Welsh were fellow Celts suffering tyranny at the hands of the Anglo-Saxon/Norman English.[39] In fact, however, disregarding GHQ's ruling, the Volunteers in Scotland carried out at least 11 operations, one of which caused the death of a policeman. O'Connor was further ordered to make certain that in executing strikes every effort be made to

38 Brady, *Secret Service*, pp. 66–73
39 O/C Britain to C/S, 3 June 1921 (RMP, P7/A/19[16–20])

minimize civilian casualties. Moreover, he was charged with ensuring that unemployment amongst the Irish section of the population was avoided as much as possible. Therefore, attacks on large employers, such as factories, were effectively prohibited.[40]

Initially, GHQ played a dominant role in the selection of targets for attack. At a meeting in Dublin in August or September 1920, it was suggested that attacks in Manchester be launched against the Stuart Street electrical power station and the waterworks at Clayton Vale.[41] Meanwhile, GHQ sent John ('Jack') Plunkett – son of Count Plunkett and a senior member of the engineering department – to Merseyside 'to investigate the possibility of attacking the docks there and if possible crippling them'.[42] GHQ's involvement in planning continued the following year. In Liverpool, and presumably elsewhere, Dublin's approval was needed for the launching of attacks. In February 1921, Paddy Daly noted that some Volunteers were impatient to mount another operation similar to that of the previous November. 'Of course we cannot act on "our own" without the consent of GHQ', he concluded, perhaps an oblique way of asking for Dublin's permission.[43] By April, the role of headquarters in mounting operations on Merseyside was demonstrated by the arrival of a member of the O/C Britain's staff, charged with planning attacks in conjunction with the local IRA leadership.[44] In June, Dublin ordered a co-ordinated assault on communications infrastructure to take place in Liverpool, London, Manchester and Newcastle-upon-Tyne, among other places.[45] Mick McEvoy, another member of Rory O'Connor's staff, helped to plan operations on Tyneside.[46] O'Connor himself sometimes visited units to inspect plans and assess past operations. When Denis Brennan approached him with the idea of attacking London's Lots Road power station, the O/C Britain approved of the target but recommended that hammers rather than explosives be employed to destroy the turbo generators. He also enlisted the services of a trainee electrical engineer, asking him to assist Brennan by

40 O/C Britain to C/S, n.d. but *c.* Dec. 1920–Feb. 1921 (Parliamentary Archives House of Lords [PAHL], Andrew Bonar Law Papers [ABLP], 104/5/7)
41 BMHWS 847, Patrick O'Donoghue, p. 11
42 'Liverpool' in 'Account by Jack Plunkett of Events of 1914–21' (NLI, George Count Plunkett Papers [GCPP], MS 11,397); BMHWS 865, John Plunkett, p. 40
43 Paddy Daly to Michael Collins, 28 Feb. 1921 (RMP, P7/A/4)
44 Daly to Collins, 27 Apr. 1921 (RMP, P7/A/5)
45 BMHWS 1535, Hugh Early, pp. 8–9
46 BMHWS 773, Gilbert Barrington, p. 3

locating the station's underground cables. In the end, Brennan's failure to secure the architectural plans of the power station frustrated the mounting of an attack.[47]

As well as helping to plan strikes against property, GHQ assisted in the preparation of assaults on RIC men and their relatives. Through a number of means, GHQ ascertained their home addresses in Britain. A Volunteer working in Dublin's Richmond Hospital, for example, was able to access the medical records, which included the addresses, of Auxiliaries stationed in the nearby North Dublin Union.[48] And, in December 1920, a mail bag containing the correspondence of Auxiliaries stationed at Beggars' Bush Barracks was stolen by a group of Volunteers after an exchange of shots with police at the Shelbourne Road Post Office in Dublin.[49] GHQ also encouraged the mounting of assassination attempts in Britain. In 1920, it was involved in a plot to kill members of Lloyd George's government. Pa Murray, who volunteered to lead the mission to London, met Michael Collins in Dublin. 'He told me it was decided to shoot a member of the British cabinet, should Terry [MacSwiney] die', Murray recollected. Collins made arrangements for Sam Maguire and the capital's IRA to lend Murray and the other assassins all possible assistance in their mission. Ultimately, however, Collins aborted the operation. Murray, irritated by the unexpectedly protracted nature of MacSwiney's hunger strike, asked Collins for permission to mount the assassination regardless of the lord mayor's condition, for he had learned the movements of Arthur Balfour, the lord president of the council and former Conservative prime minister who had earned the moniker 'Bloody Balfour' during his tenure as Irish chief secretary in the 1880s. Collins refused. Murray was very annoyed, convinced that 'Collins was playing a game of bluff with us, pretending that he was eager [for assassinations] when he was not'.[50] However, Seán McGrath believed that Collins's grief at MacSwiney's death on 25 October steeled his nerve to launch operations in Britain in earnest the following month: 'It was the first time I saw Michael Collins really upset. he [sic] talked then about shooting in England'.[51]

In March 1921, GHQ ordered the assassination of a British soldier on leave in Liverpool. The soldier, named Donnerman, had been 'hunting down

47   Dennis Brennan interview (EO'MN, P17b/100)

48   'Account of Volunteer 'M'', in Uinseann MacEoin (ed.), *Survivors* (Dublin: Argenta, 1980), pp. 424–25

49   *TT,* 15 Dec. 1920

50   Pa Murray to Florence O'Donoghue, 14, 26 Jan. 1959 (FO'DP, MS 31,296/1); Pa Murray interview (EO'MN, P17b/88)

51   Seán McGrath interview (EO'MN, P17b/100); original emphasis

our people in Cork', Collins told Paddy Daly. 'Perhaps something can be done.'[52]

On occasion, GHQ's orders were ignored.[53] The most spectacular instance of such insubordination occurred in May 1921 when Frank Carty, an IRA man who operated in counties Derry and Sligo, was arrested in Glasgow. Motivated into action by Derry Volunteers who had arrived in the city to liberate their comrade, the Glasgow IRA proposed to mount a rescue of Carty. However, fearful that such an operation would precipitate police raids on Irish houses in the city and cause further disruption to the IRA's already disordered gunrunning network, Liam Mellows advised against it. D.P. Walsh supported the suggestion that the planned rescue be postponed until Carty was about to be transported to Ireland for trial. However, the Glasgow IRA ignored such concerns and mounted their attempt as originally planned, attacking a prison van containing Carty as it passed along Glasgow's High Street on 4 May 1921. Having anticipated a rescue attempt, some of the police escort were armed. As occurred in the rescue of two Fenians from a prison van in Manchester in 1867, a policeman was fatally injured in the incident. Unlike in the Manchester episode however, the Glasgow men failed to liberate their comrade. Mellows's concerns proved prophetic. In the aftermath of the incident, a large number of Volunteers were arrested and munitions dumps were uncovered, resulting in the 'complete collapse' of gunrunning activities for a period.[54]

Very little detail has been left regarding the detailed planning of the attacks. Following the meeting in Dublin in the autumn of 1920, Paddy O'Donoghue returned to Manchester in the company of a chemist named Cripps who, after a tour of Stuart Street power station, advised the IRA on the best means of disrupting the power supply.[55] Accompanied by Tom Kerr, Jack Plunkett spent a week inconspicuously touring every inch of Liverpool's dock system, 'every dock and dock gate, powerhouses, cranes, dock railways, piers, landing stages, etc., etc.', making notes as he went. Using Kerr's contacts, the duo were able to access areas normally prohibited to members of the public. Plunkett estimated that they walked 20 miles (32.2 kilometres) every day. He then returned to Dublin and submitted a comprehensive report to

52 Michael Collins to Paddy Daly, 15 Mar. 1921 (RMP, P7/A/4)

53 See p. 152 below

54 BMHWS 933, Séamus Reader, pp. 9–11; Seán (or Séamus) Mooney's statement on the 'Smashing of the Van' incident, n.d. (EMP, 5/36); extract from report by Lieut. M. Sheerin, Derry IRA, n.d. (MCP, A/0411, Group VIII, Item III); *Glasgow Herald*, 9 Aug. 1921

55 BMHWS 847, Patrick O'Donoghue, p. 11

Richard Mulcahy, detailing the most effective means of attacking the docks. Merseyside Volunteers had submitted plans of their own, but Plunkett judged most of them too grandiose to be realized. However, a plan submitted by Kerr, although slightly over-ambitious too, was judged a sound basis for action.[56] While planning the attack on Lots Road power station in London, Dennis Brennan 'spent an evening with a bloke who worked there and … was shown around the place', thus allowing him to reconnoitre the target, ascertaining its layout.[57] Sometime in early 1921, GHQ sent George Fitzgerald to London with the task of identifying properties for destruction. He was then to draw up plans for their demolition, although he himself was to refrain from involvement in the actual attacks. In the capital, he met Sam Maguire and Reginald Dunne. 'I outlined a scheme to them for the burning of a number of large wholesale houses in a very old part of London where the majority of warehouses were located', he recollected.

> We decided that the burning of certain [ware]houses would be attempted on a particular Saturday night at about 12 o'clock. The reason this time was selected was that the principal streets would be very crowded due to people coming from theatres and pictures houses etc. and we felt that this would provide the Volunteers with a good line of escape or get-away, by mingling with the crowd once clear of the warehouses area.

The means of setting the warehouses on fire was also discussed. The IRA men were to arm themselves with 'burning materials of an inflammable nature'. The *modus operandi* involved Volunteers breaking holes in the buildings' windows using diamond cutters, setting fire to the inflammable material and throwing it into the basements. Later, Fitzgerald also selected farms on the outskirts of the capital for attack.[58]

Edward Brady remembered the preparations undertaken for the operation against the relatives of policemen in Ireland. Having received from Dublin the addresses of 14 RIC families, the neighbourhoods in which their houses were located were carefully reconnoitred. 'The districts were examined for means of retreat, and every precaution taken to make the intended raid successful', he later wrote. For convenience, the paraffin and petrol to be used were stored nearby. A plan was then drawn up, which scheduled the attacks for 11.45 p.m.

---

56 'Liverpool' in 'Account by Jack Plunkett' (GCPP, MS 11,397)
57 Dennis Brennan interview (EO'MN, P17b/100)
58 BMHWS 684, George Fitzgerald, pp. 28–29

on a Saturday night, anticipating that at such a time the occupants of the houses would be retiring to bed.[59]

On another occasion, Brady was assigned the task of discovering the friends and relatives of an auxiliary who was reportedly about to be sent to Liverpool or some other part of England on a special mission. Ascertaining that there were three people of the same name as the auxiliary living in the Merseyside area, Brady and his accomplice set out on their mission. The first suspect ran a public house. The Volunteers got into a conversation with a barman in the establishment but after discussing war service in France and enquiring about old friends, Brady was satisfied that the proprietor had no connection with the Irish police. The next suspect sold ice-cream. Again, a conversation proved that Brady had not found his target. However, the retailer told the Volunteers of a restaurant proprietor on the same street who had a son serving with the Auxiliaries. The Volunteers went straight to the restaurant, where they drank some tea and 'made careful scrutiny of the lie of buildings, so that in the event of serious action being taken against this man, we would know where we stood'. In the event, the information gathered in this reconnaissance mission was never used, as the policeman's mission to Liverpool was shelved.[60]

As we have seen, on at least one occasion members of the Liverpool IRA were given the task of finding their own properties to attack from a specified category, namely farms. Presumably, the Volunteers then submitted their selections to the leadership for approval. Subsequently, however, the leadership decided to allocate targets of its own.[61] Planning for the first incendiary attacks in the Tyneside area was undertaken by the brigade staff. They chose as their objectives a bonded store, an oil refinery and a timber store. About a week before the operations were scheduled to be mounted, Rory O'Connor visited the area and approved the plans. The brigade staff, assisted by Mick McEvoy, then inspected the properties, decided on the best means of attacking them and selected Volunteers for the operation.[62] The following month, the brigade staff ordered the Tyneside companies to organize operations themselves. After choosing targets, companies submitted plans for their destruction to the brigade council. Members of the council then surveyed the targets in person and sanctioned or vetoed the arrangements. In May, the plans were put into effect with the mounting of farm fires and attacks on communications and

59 Brady, *Secret Service*, pp. 64–65

60 Brady, *Secret Service*, pp. 35–36

61 See pp. 135–36 above

62 Barrington, *Irish Independence Movement*, p. 14

the railway network.[63] Edward Brady states that in planning assaults on farms, the Liverpool IRA ensured that 'the ground was carefully surveyed, and rough maps made of the places selected for destruction'. The preparations involved for the sabotage of communications, he remembered, were demanding and wide-ranging, involving the careful study of ordnance survey maps.[64] In contrast, for at least one arson operation, in mid-March, the Manchester IRA did no such preparatory work. Perhaps this was an example of the 'happy-go-lucky air' that so annoyed Michael Collins.[65]

Some of the operations were planned to take place simultaneously across England. The November 1920 arson attacks, the inaugural event of the IRA's offensive, were planned to involve concurrent operations in Liverpool, Manchester and London. In March the following year, Volunteers in Liverpool and Manchester drew up plans for synchronized offensives in their respective city centres.[66] Three months later, a co-ordinated attack on communications was to take place in Liverpool, London, Manchester, Newcastle-upon-Tyne and St Helens, among other places.[67]

For various reasons, some of the plans which were drawn up were never implemented at all, some were tried but failed, while others were realized in a modified form. We have already seen some examples of the former, including Dennis Brennan's plan to attack the power station in London. In October 1920, Michael O'Kelly Simington, a member of the London Volunteers, was convicted of the unlawful possession of architectural plans of the Irish Office in Old Queen Street, stolen from the Office of Works, his former place of employment. Simington failed to explain his behaviour. Therefore, we can only speculate that he might have stolen the plans for use in preparing attacks in the Whitehall area. Interestingly, George Fitzgerald remembered taking Michael Collins for 'a good look at Scotland Yard and the principal Government offices in Whitehall' in the autumn of 1920. A precedent for strikes on such targets was set in the 1880s, when government buildings in Whitehall suffered at the hands of O'Donovan Rossa's 'Skirmishers'.[68] The

63   BMHWS 773, Gilbert Barrington, pp. 6–7

64   Brady, *Secret Service*, pp. 38, 82–83

65   John McGallogly to The Secretary, Military Service Pensions, 11 Oct. 1937, enclosing Patrick O'Donoghue's account of the Manchester IRA (MSPC, RO/608); see Chapter 1

66   Paddy Daly to Michael Collins, 31 Mar., 8, 14 Apr. 1921 (RMP, P7/A/5)

67   BMHWS 1535, Hugh Early, pp. 8–9

68   *TT*, 22 Oct., 23 Nov. 1920; BMHWS 684, George Fitzgerald, p. 11; Short, *Dynamite War*, pp. 105–06

mission to kidnap MPs in London in revenge for the employment of TDs as human shields by Crown forces in Dublin was called off before it could be executed. After monitoring the movements of government politicians, Frank Thornton, George Fitzgerald and Seán Flood identified 25 MPs 'who did a regular thing on the same night every week'. Premises were then arranged to accommodate the politicians once they had been kidnapped by members of the London IRA. Soon afterwards, however, Crown forces ceased to use TDs as hostages and the operation was cancelled. Though Thornton was confident that the mission would have been a 'huge success' if it had been implemented, he was relieved that it was abandoned as 'it would have been a very difficult job and, if we failed, the reputation of our whole department [i.e. IRA intelligence] was at stake'.[69] His next assignment in Britain, the mission to assassinate Major Percival, ended in failure. Having arrived in London in March 1921, Thornton – accompanied by Cork Volunteers Pa Murray, William ('Billy') Aherne and Tadhg Sullivan – met Sam Maguire and Reginald Dunne, and set about gathering intelligence on Percival's movements. Discovering that he was staying at a virtually impregnable military barracks in Dovercourt, Essex, they decided to postpone their attack until he was travelling back to Ireland. A few weeks later, learning that their quarry intended to journey by train to Liverpool, the party, supplemented by a few London Volunteers, positioned themselves in Liverpool Street train station and prepared to ambush the soldier. However, the operation was abruptly called off. Maguire had learned from a contact in Scotland Yard that the activities of Thornton and the others had been noticed by the authorities, who were now arranging to surround the station. The Volunteers fled the scene just a few minutes before the military cordoned it off. Upon returning to Cork, Sullivan was shot dead in a British army raid on a house under the orders of Percival.[70]

Another plan mooted but never implemented called for the destruction of the Crossley Motor Company's premises in Manchester, presumably motivated by the fact that Crown forces in Ireland used the company's vehicles.[71] A further plan proposed an attack on a house being occupied by a member of the royal family in London's St James's Square.[72] Rory O'Connor estimated

69 BMHWS 615, Frank Thornton, pp. 29–31

70 BMHWS 615, Frank Thornton, pp. 47–49; BMHWS 869, P.J. Murphy, p. 16

71 Correspondence between Michael Collins and Paddy Daly, 9, 11, 14 Apr. 1921 (RMP, P7/A/5); W.H. Kautt, *Ambushes and Armour: The Irish Rebellion 1919–1921* (Dublin: Irish Academic Press, 2010), pp. 63–65, 125

72 Martin Geraghty to MSPB, 20 May 1937 (EO'MP, P17a/154)

that the number of unsuccessful attacks carried out in the period up to the end of May 1921 constituted about ten per cent of the total attempted.[73]

In early November 1920, while on the trail of Richard Mulcahy, the police mounted a raid on a house in Dublin. The C/S escaped the dragnet but only at the cost of allowing some of his correspondence to fall into police hands. Jack Plunkett's plans for attacks in Manchester and Liverpool were among the correspondence and they were subsequently publicized by the Irish chief secretary, Sir Hamar Greenwood, in the House of Commons and published in the press.[74] On the back foot, the IRA nevertheless decided to proceed with its plans, though in a modified form. In Liverpool, for example, whereas the original plan called for the burning of warehouses and depots as a diversion to occupy the police and enable the attack on the docks to proceed unhindered, now the arson attacks were elevated to the main stage. In the end, however, it was only on Merseyside that attacks took place. Pinkman states that GHQ, realizing that the Volunteers in London and elsewhere were insufficiently organized, told the Liverpool men to cancel their plans. However, the Kerrs and Steve Lanigan made the argument for proceeding with their scheme regardless and Rory O'Connor eventually gave permission for them to do so.[75] Paddy O'Donoghue later blamed bad organization for his companies' failure to act that night.[76] On 2 April 1921, the roles were reversed: members of Manchester's renegade No. 2 Company launched arson attacks on hotels, warehouses and cafés in the city centre, despite their Liverpool comrades still awaiting permission from GHQ for a similar operation in what had been planned as a simultaneous strike. The Manchester attacks were 'a failure', claimed Paddy Daly.[77] The Liverpool men regained the initiative two months later with the GHQ-ordered synchronized sabotage of communications infrastructure in London, Manchester, Tyneside and Merseyside. Learning that many of the IRA units were ill-prepared for the operation, Dublin had ordered the Merseyside men to postpone the attack. However, frustrated by the repeated postponement of operations and with their lines of communication being too slow to prevent the assault going ahead anyway, the Liverpool Volunteers proceeded with their plan regardless.[78]

73 O/C Britain to C/S, 3 June 1921 (RMP, P7/A/19[16–20])

74 *Hansard 5* (*Commons*), cxxxv, cols 506–07 (24 Nov. 1920); *TT*, 25 Nov. 1920

75 Pinkman, *Legion*, pp. 35–36

76 Michael Collins to Neil Kerr, 27 Nov. 1920 (RMP, P7/A/3); BMHWS 847, Patrick O'Donoghue, p. 12

77 Paddy Daly to Collins, 8 Apr. 1921 (RMP, P7/A/5)

78 BMHWS 1535, Hugh Early, p. 8

Over the course of the IRA's seven-and-a-half month long campaign, attacks were mounted against warehouses, factories, farms and private houses, as well communications and the railway network. Why were such targets chosen? The contrast with the Fenian campaign of the 1880s is notable. The bombing offensive in London, Liverpool and Glasgow had targeted symbolic public buildings and infrastructure such as the House of Commons, the Tower of London, the Mansion House, Trafalgar Square, London Bridge and Liverpool Town Hall, along with the capital's underground railway system, railway stations, army barracks, gas works, the office of *The Times* newspaper, and government and police offices.[79] In contrast, the IRA seems to have been more interested in causing serious economic dislocation and annoyance. The power station and the water works were chosen for the planned attack in Manchester in November 1920 because of the city's dependence on them as sources of electric power. Stuart Street power station was a place of 'great importance' in connection with the powering of the city's trams and the local coal mines, Jack Plunkett noted. Meanwhile, with Clayton Vale waterworks supplying power to more than half of Manchester's factories, as well as its trams and mines, Plunkett contended that if the supply was disrupted the city would 'shut down'.[80] Targets in Liverpool also seem to have been picked with the aim of making an impression on the public. John Pinkman was 'overawed' by the inventiveness and destructiveness of Plunkett's initial plan for the November operation. In a 'devastating reprisal', the IRA was going 'to wreck the second largest dock system in the British empire'.[81] A plan submitted to Plunkett by Tom Kerr called for the destruction of the dock gates so as to cause ships to be swept into the river Mersey by the ensuing rush of water. According to Plunkett's revised version, the docks' inner gates, eight in number, were to be opened by means of the four pumps, all of which would subsequently be destroyed using gelignite. 'The object is to make it impossible to open or close the gates which are not destroyed, by hydraulic power, for a couple of tides', he asserted. This would probably lead to a situation where boats 'would lie down and be seriously damaged'.[82]

George Fitzgerald does not explain why warehouses were chosen as targets for attack in London. However, Rory O'Connor does. Although believing

79 Short, *Dynamite War*, pp. 50–51, 55, 64–65, 91, 104–06, 160–63, 176–77, 184–86, 200–01, 205–08, 259–60
80 Jack Plunkett to C/S, n.d., but *c*. Oct. 1920, reprinted in *TT*, 25 Nov. 1920
81 Pinkman, *Legion*, p. 33
82 Jack Plunkett to C/S, n.d., but *c*. Oct. 1920, reprinted in *TT*, 25 Nov. 1920

that 'large scale operations' in Britain were of 'paramount importance', he held that deficiencies in the training received by Volunteers made their realization unlikely. He concluded, therefore, that '[m]inor operations could well be carried on', including the destruction of buildings, ships, coal mines, blast furnaces, aqueducts and crops, along with the sabotage of railway and communications infrastructure.[83] When the Volunteers failed to set fire to the warehouses, Fitzgerald recommended that they turn their attention to burning farm crops. Suspecting that the fiasco was due to the men suffering from nervousness, he hoped that the relatively easy task of burning haystacks would help them to build up their confidence.[84] Farms were objects of attack in Ireland too, particularly in Connacht. In 1920, for example, there were 1,114 agrarian attacks. However, despite some IRA involvement, these were motivated more by land-hunger than by nationalism per se. Indeed, David Fitzpatrick argues that '"I.R.A. engagements" [in County Clare] were in many cases thinly disguised land seizures', a judgement which historian Fergus Campbell says applies equally to County Galway.[85] Attacks on farms in Britain were relatively safe to mount. As British police intelligence noted, 'nothing is easier [to do] than to fire a [hay] rick'.[86] O'Connor would have agreed. Three farms in the Liverpool area were apparently chosen as targets because the owners were related to an auxiliary who had ignored a threatening letter advising him to resign from the force.[87] The O/C Britain judged his men capable of mounting attacks on communications and the railway system as they did in Ireland. Paddy Daly made a similar argument, claiming that, with no recourse to 'technical or scientific laboratories', Volunteers were perforce restricted to arson attacks on farms and hotels. A critic might dismiss such operations as 'pin pricks', he conceded, yet, equipped as it was, the IRA 'could not have done more'.[88] John Pinkman and his fellow Liverpool inmates at Dartmoor numbered among the critics. From their prison cells, they condemned the cutting of telegraph wires as 'reckless and futile' and held Hugh Early responsible. Their animosity

83　O/C Britain to C/S, n.d. but *c.* Dec. 1920–Feb. 1921 (ABLP, 104/5/7)

84　BMHWS 684, George Fitzgerald, pp. 29–30

85　David Fitzpatrick, 'The Geography of Irish Nationalism 1910–1921', *Past & Present*, 78 (1978), p. 119; Fitzpatrick, *Politics*, pp. 62, 130–32, 146–47, 153–54, 193, 220; Campbell, *Land and Revolution*, pp. 246–55, 262, 264–68; Hart, 'Geography', p. 50

86　'RROUK', no. 94, 24 Feb. 1921 (CAB, 24/120)

87　*TT*, 12 Mar. 1921

88　Augusteijn, *Public Defiance*, p. 95; Paddy Daly interview (EO'MN, P17b/136)

towards Early was motivated by their having been captured during an arson operation which, as we have seen, he had planned incompetently. They did, however, approve of farm fires and attacks on the homes of Irish policemen and their relatives.[89]

The relative ease of the task and the high likelihood of the perpetrators escaping detection certainly figured high in the motives for launching a campaign of window-scratching in April 1921. By the end of June, thousands of windows had been scratched in Liverpool, London, Glasgow, Birmingham, Cardiff and elsewhere.[90] Edward Brady later maintained that the Volunteers had no involvement in the episode: 'It seemed to us maniacal'.[91] London's George Fitzgerald agreed, noting that the Volunteers presumed it to be the work of communists.[92] In fact, however, Rory O'Connor listed three window-scratching episodes as having been carried out by the IRA: the slashing of about 250 windows in London in April, 'all' windows in Chelmsford, Essex, slashed in May, and the destruction of eight plate glass windows in Middlesbrough's principle shops in June. He noted, however, that 'some other organisation or individuals' had decided to emulate the Volunteers' actions. Such copycat episodes were mounted in Leeds, Cambridge, Coventry, Nottingham and Sheffield, to name just a few places.[93]

Although the virtual simplicity of the task and the high probability of the architects avoiding discovery played a role in window-scratching and farm fires, they were not the only reasons. Overawing the British public seems to have been an important factor too. While planning operations for February, the Liverpool Volunteers aimed to enclose the city in 'a circle of fires'. This would probably have proven as impressive a spectacle as the destruction of the city's docks.[94] Intimidating the populace was also the aim of operations proposed by Rory O'Connor. If 'one train were wrecked it would have the effect of causing considerable alarm to the travelling public', the O/C Britain wrote in late 1920 or early 1921. By plunging towns into darkness through attacks on the gas supply, the IRA might also generate conditions conducive to the mounting of 'direct action' by communists, the unemployed and the 'mob'. Incidents such as these would cripple 'the daily life of enemy people'. He hoped that they would have an economic effect too. The targeting of trains

89 Pinkman, *Legion*, pp. 55, 66; see pp. 135–38 above
90 *TT*, 4, 21, 23, 25, 26 Apr., 15 June 1921
91 Brady, *Secret Service*, pp. 81–82
92 BMHWS 684, George Fitzgerald, p. 30
93 O/C Britain to C/S, 3 June 1921 (RMP, P7/A/19[16–20])
94 Pinkman, *Legion*, p. 48

might cause 'extra expense to the railway companies either in patrolling the railway lines or in employing pilot engines'.[95]

A similar motive seems to have driven a number of operations proposed by Liverpool's Paddy Daly. In March, he suggested that the Volunteers blow up five tanks of ship fuel. He imagined the destruction: '[t]he oil, being in a very thick state, would float on the surface of the water and on being ignited would burn the gates of many of the docks and would also damage many of the ships.'[96] A few weeks later, he advocated a bomb attack on the city. So as to maximize the devastation, it was proposed to disrupt the water supply in order to prevent the fire brigade from tackling the resulting fires. If this was achieved, 'whole streets would probably be demolished', he enthused.[97]

In the Tyneside area, local politics sometimes informed the choosing of targets. Miners' protests against bad working conditions at the Rising Sun colliery motivated the IRA, many of whom were miners themselves, to attack a farm owned by the company on 26 March. Class conflict may have played a role in the selection of other properties for attack in the area too.[98]

Therefore, the IRA's choice of properties to attack seems to have been informed by a number of factors, including the capabilities of the organization, the likelihood of being apprehended by the police, a desire to terrorize the British public, the hope of damaging the British economy and class conflict. In their attacks on warehouses, farms, timber yards, factories, communications and railway infrastructure, the IRA mainly chose arson as the best means of destruction. Why so? After all, Irish-American Fenians had established a precedent for the use of bombs in Britain in the 1880s. Their campaign did not succeed in its aim of forcing the British government to grant Irish independence. They had much exaggerated the likely effects of dynamite attacks. Moreover, the IRB, which had moral and political objections to the whole episode, prevailed upon their American cousins to call off the campaign for fear that its continuation would undermine the efforts of the IPP to secure limited autonomy for Ireland within the British Empire.[99] Still, O'Donovan Rossa, one of the leaders of the bombing campaign, was a revered figure amongst Irish nationalists. Why, then, was his

---

95 O/C Britain to C/S, n.d. but *c.* Dec. 1920–Feb. 1921 (ABLP, 104/5/7)

96 Paddy Daly to Michael Collins, 4 Mar. 1921 (RMP, P7/A/4)

97 Daly to Collins, 24 Mar. 1921 (RMP, P7/A/5)

98 Barrington, *Irish Independence Movement*, p. 10 n. 15; *Newcastle Daily Chronicle*, 28 Mar. 1921; CC of Northumberland to the USS, HO, 19 Oct. 1922 (HO, 144/4645)

99 Short, *Dynamite War*, pp. 225–28; Whelehan, *Dynamiters*, pp. 295–99

example not emulated? Moreover, sometime in the spring or early summer of 1921, a bomb-making factory was established in a garage in Greenwich, London.[100] Yet none of the incendiary bombs manufactured were used in operations. Why was arson preferred to the bomb as the means of carrying the war into Britain?

As Volunteers themselves have offered no explanations, we can only speculate as to why this was so. One factor may have been the lack of bomb-making expertise outside of London. Although their involvement in smuggling munitions to Ireland gave IRA men access to explosive material, they might have lacked the expertise necessary to construct bombs from it. This was certainly so in Liverpool.[101] GHQ might have taken the view that such know-how was more valuable to the organization in Ireland than it would be in Britain. Arson, in contrast, required little expertise, and indeed it was this very fact that led GHQ to order the burning of courthouses and abandoned police barracks in Ireland at Easter 1920.[102] Another factor determining the less frequent use of incendiary devices in Britain may have been the desire to avoid inflicting casualties on innocent civilians. Rory O'Connor had been ordered to ensure that in mounting operations every effort be made to avoid civilian casualties and that unemployment amongst the Irish be kept to a minimum. In late 1920 or early 1921, he unsuccessfully requested that such conditions be revoked in the name of military effectiveness.[103] Although fire could prove fatal, it was not as insidious a killer as an exploding bomb. A third factor may have been the relatively inexpensive nature of the materials required to mount arson attacks. Fuels such as paraffin oil and petrol were easy to acquire, as were the rags and paper which were soaked in the fuel, set alight with matches and then thrown on the hay stack or amongst the raw cotton in the warehouse.

V

As we saw earlier, Rory O'Connor believed that the IRA lacked the training necessary to launch major attacks in Britain. Yet, even with relation to the minor operations which the Volunteers did mount, no information exists regarding the training which they underwent in order to carry them out.

---

100 O/C Britain to C/S, n.d., but noted 28 Mar. 1921 (RMP, P7/A/19[91])
101 Paddy Daly to Michael Collins, 4 Mar. 1921 (RMP, P7/A/4)
102 Augusteijn, *Public Defiance*, p. 96
103 O/C Britain to C/S, n.d. but *c.* Dec. 1920–Feb. 1921 (ABLP, 104/5/7)

However, given that they carried weapons with them on such operations, the shooting practice they performed as part of their general training would have been of some benefit. In relation to the mounting of arson assaults, advice, if not training, was provided by an *An t-Óglác* article of July 1920 on the best means of ensuring the effective 'demolition of enemy works' by fire. It discussed the various types of fuels available, recommending turpentine over petrol and paraffin oil above all. Petrol was difficult to control due to its fluidity. Also, its propensity to evaporate quickly meant that setting fire to petrol often involved igniting petrol vapour in the air, potentially causing a dangerous back draft. Moreover, petrol tended to burn itself out very rapidly, leading to a situation where the object it coated might sustain only superficial damage. Paraffin, on the other hand, suffered none of these disadvantages. Though it was more difficult to ignite than petrol, paraffin burned for longer, hence increasing the chances of destroying the target. 'I[t] should be used with some solid substance', the article advised,

> such as wood shavings, straw or cotton waste which might be helped with small sticks, broken up furniture and the like, the whole being placed where it will get a good hold. In the case of a building the fire should be started at a staircase, or wooden partition or even a few planks placed near the rafters of the roof.
>
> The windows of the building should be opened to ensure a good stream of air and also to allow the heavy smoke of the burning oil to escape. This is most necessary for good results as the smoke, having no means of escape, may smother the flames and extinguish the fire.[104]

Assembling on the night chosen for launching an attack, paraffin oil in bottles was one of the tools which were dispensed to the Volunteers. Along with other arson paraphernalia such as matches and cotton waste, they received bolt-cutters for use in gaining access to warehouses and factories, along with saws, pliers and wire-cutters to cut telephone and telegraph poles and wires. They were also given weapons. In addition to such tools, Volunteers were assigned their specific tasks for that night's operations.[105]

Before embarking on the operation on 27 November 1920, Edward Brady took precautions to divest himself of incriminating documentation: 'I made a careful examination of all papers, letters, etc., in my possession,

104 *An t-Óglác*, 1 July 1920
105 Brady, *Secret Service*, pp. 38, 83; Barrington, *Irish Independence Movement*, p. 14

and destroyed anything I thought might be used in evidence against me in the event of arrest while carrying out the work allotted to me'.[106] 'Orders were to clear your house of all stuff and songs [i.e. munitions] etc. when going out', London Volunteer William Robinson noted, indicating that such precautions were urged on all units participating in operations.[107] Despite this, however, a significant number of men were arrested when the police, responding to attacks, found compromising evidence either on their persons or at their lodgings. Suspected of attempting to set fire to a timber warehouse in Finsbury, London, in November 1920, ISDL pamphlets and a membership form were found at Robinson's lodgings. Seven months later, police found bolt-cutters at the residence of Denis Tangley, one of Robinson's accomplices in a fire-fight with police in Kent on 17 June.[108] Similarly, a Sinn Féin membership card and a letter advocating the assassination of the British prime minister were found in the lodgings of Patrick Flynn, one of four men arrested on a charge of shooting at a policeman in Salford, Manchester, on 2 January 1921.[109] Later that month, when Wilfred Kenny was apprehended by police for drilling holes in barrels of oil in Wandsworth, London, incriminating papers were found on his person.[110] Some Volunteers, therefore, proved careless in taking precautions before embarking on operations.

Most Volunteers seem to have been armed while participating in attacks. Such weapons were acquired by the IRA as part of their gunrunning activities. In Liverpool and London at least, the weapons were distributed before the mounting of operations and then collected afterwards. For the warehouse fires in November 1920, for example, Edward Brady was supplied with a .45 Colt revolver and 20 rounds of ammunition.[111] 'I was armed and so were practically all the men except those who had to climb poles & carry saws etc.', London's Edward Roche remembered in relation to attacks on communications infrastructure. The 'safe return & custody of guns' was one of his responsibilities.[112] Paddy Daly proposed that the munitions be sold to

---

106 Brady, *Secret Service*, p. 29

107 William Robinson to unknown, n.d., but *c.* mid-1921, reproduced in appendix I of Cabinet Conclusions, 5 p.m. meeting, 22 June 1922 (CAB, 21/255)

108 Superintendent 'G' Division to Commissioner of LMP, 29 Nov. 1920 (Metropolitan Police Office File [MEPO], 3/466); Robinson to unknown, *c.* mid-1921 (CAB, 21/255)

109 *TT*, 2 Feb. 1921; see p. 163 below

110 *TT*, 17 Jan. 1921

111 Brady, *Secret Service*, p. 30

112 Edward Roche to MSPB, 4 Aug. 1937 (EO'MP, P17a/154)

the Merseyside Volunteers, either on an individual basis or collectively to their companies.[113]

Given that GHQ instructed the IRA to avoid fatalities in these operations, the main purpose of the weapons seems to have been to intimidate anyone who attempted to frustrate the setting of fires or the cutting of telegraph and telephone lines. 'I had the revolver to frighten anybody who came to arrest me', explained Thomas O'Sullivan, one of the men put on trial in connection with the incident at Wandsworth.[114] Night watchmen, railway signalmen, charwomen and others found themselves threatened with such weapons. At about 7.50 p.m. on 12 February 1921, as John Duffy – the night watchman at the Premier Rubber Works on Manchester's Bromley Street – entered his workplace, he exchanged pleasantries with two men. They pushed past him as he unlocked the door. 'What's the game?' Duffy asked. 'Come on and we'll let you see', said one of the men, producing a revolver and grabbing the night watchman by the collar. Pushed face first up against a wall with the barrel of the revolver at his neck, Duffy was warned that he would be shot if he turned around. 'I could hear the other man making a noise, and I knew that he was trying to set fire to the building', the night watchman remembered. 'There was a sudden glare, and I knew that he had succeeded in firing a lot of returned bags which were used to send out rubber heels.' The arsonists fled and, as soon as Duffy thought it was safe, he began tackling the fire.[115] That same month, Irish emigrants in Liverpool lodging houses were held at gunpoint while Volunteers divested them of their passports and travel tickets.[116] In April, charwomen in two Manchester warehouses found themselves looking down the barrels of guns while IRA men sprinkled paraffin oil on the cotton goods and set them alight. Elsewhere, a Volunteer fired shots over the heads of staff members in Lyons' Popular State café as his accomplice sprayed the premises with paraffin.[117] On 14 May, when the IRA raided the lodgings of RIC men and their relatives in London and Liverpool, some of the victims were held at gunpoint while Volunteers went about setting fire to the contents of their houses.[118] Maud Downer described the attack on the boarding house where she lived at

---

113　Correspondence between Paddy Daly and Michael Collins, 18, 26 May 1921 (RMP, P7/A/5)

114　*Pall Mall Gazette and Globe*, 18 Feb. 1921

115　*TT*, 14 Feb. 1921

116　Brady, *Secret Service*, pp. 48, 51

117　*The Observer*, 3 Apr.; *MG*, 28 Apr. 1921

118　The Commissioner of Police of the Metropolis to the USS, HO, 18 Nov. 1922 (MEPO, 3/462)

44 Coverton Road, Tooting. One of the other tenants, Walter Pratt, had a son in the RIC. Around 10 o'clock, while playing cards with her parents, sisters and a friend of the family, Downer heard a knock on the door:

> I went downstairs and opened the street door and saw 4 men standing against the door. The tallest of the men who stood on my right side said "Is Mr Pratt in?"[.] I said "I do not know but I will see"[.] I then went down the passage to Mr Pratt's kitchen which is on the ground floor at the rear, opened the door and saw that the room was in darkness. I then returned to the street door and said to the men who were standing on the door step "I'm sorry, he's not in"[.] The tall man said "Can we wait[?]" I then called out "Dad" in order that father could come down and see the men. I then went upstairs and passed Father who was coming down, on the stairs. I heard as soon as I got into the kitchen, a man's voice which I recognised as that of the tallest man who had spoken to me, say "Put your hands up. It is all right. Go upstairs." Dad then came into the kitchen followed by 2 men who were then wearing handkerchiefs which covered their faces, but I could see their eyes. The tallest man whose voice I again recognised then said "All put your hands up. We'll only keep you 5 minutes. It's quite all right." Both men pointed big black shiny revolvers at us. I then heard the noise of breaking glass and furniture being moved about in the front room. After about 3 minutes I heard someone go downstairs to the front door and then a man's voice said "It's all clear". The two men who were covering us with revolvers then backed out of the kitchen, closed the kitchen door, and left the house. I then rushed to the front room and saw that there was a huge flare in the middle of the room and I could smell spirits burning. Dad and [family friend] Mr Jermain then rushed in and tried to put out the flames. I then saw that there was a fire in the top back bedroom and shouted for help. A number of neighbours then arrived and helped to put out the flames. I also saw that the bedclothes in the back bedroom, which adjoins the kitchen, had been thrown back over the end of the bedstead and were soaked with spirits but had not been lighted.[119]

On a few occasions, as well as being held at gunpoint, night watchmen and signalmen were bound and gagged.[120]

---

119 Statement of Maud Downer, 15 May 1921 (MEPO, 3/489)
120 *TT*, 11 Apr., 18 June 1921

Figure 2: The home of S.R. Kerr, 16 Harewood Street, Liverpool. One of a number of houses attacked by the IRA on 14 May 1921 as part of its campaign against RIC men and their relatives. The fire-damaged contents have been thrown out onto the street. (© The British Library Board EW 1090)

In a number of cases, Volunteers discharged their weapons at policemen and civilians in order to escape from the scene of the crime or prevent the raising of the alarm. On 27 November 1920, a group of IRA men fleeing the scene of a warehouse fire on Liverpool's Jordan Street fired shots at a pursuing policeman. The bullets missed the constable but struck and killed a civilian, William Ward, who was trying to help in the capture of the arsonists.[121] That same night, Volunteer Tommy Moran was grabbed by two policemen as he was cutting the lock on a warehouse door. Michael O'Leary remembered what happened next:

> One of the detectives said, "There's another … ! Draw your gun and go for him!" I drew my .25 automatic and said, "No! I am going for you". I said very sternly, "Let that man go!" – I said it three times. I walked

121 *TT*, 29 Nov.; *IT*, 1 Dec. 1920

closer, discharged my revolver and wounded one of the detectives in the shoulder. He shouted, "My God! I am shot!" "Before I am finished," I said, "you will be worse. Face the wall!" They released Moran and I told him and the other Volunteer[s] to vamoose, which they did. The detectives were now against the wall. I pressed the automatic again, with no response, although there were 5 or 6 rounds in the magazine. It had jammed. So there was nothing left for me but to vamoose too. I cleared out of that street and was gone over 30 yards when they blew their whistles.[122]

On 2 January 1921, in Salford, Manchester, a policeman was shot through the wrist and in the chest when he attempted to bring two suspicious men to the police station for questioning.[123] Two weeks later, three policemen came under fire when they endeavoured to arrest a group of men acting suspiciously in the vicinity of an oil works in Wandsworth.[124] The same night that John Duffy was held at gunpoint, a second night watchman, at a tar and resin works in Holt town, was fired at as he attempted to escape from his captors.[125] The following week, a farmer on the Cheshire–Lancashire border was shot at when he interrupted an attempt to set fire to his barn.[126] On 18 March, four men were observed burning straw ricks in a field adjoining Morden Road, near Mitcham, London. Giving chase, two civilians came under gunfire. The police joined the pursuit and eventually one of the arsonists was apprehended.[127] In May, having failed to set fire to the house of an RIC man and being chased down the road by the householder's Airedale terrier, the raiders responded by shooting the dog.[128] Martin Geraghty and an accomplice used their guns to escape from police during a wire-cutting operation in London.[129] On 17 June, a group of Volunteers, apparently on a mission to sabotage communications, opened fire when policemen stopped the taxi in which they were travelling

122 BMHWS 797, Micheál Ó Laoghaire, pp. 44–45
123 CC of Salford to the USS, HO, 18 Oct. 1922 (HO, 144/4645); *TT*, 3, 4 Jan., 1 Feb. 1921
124 Superintendent of Wandsworth Division, LMP, to USS, HO, 27 Oct. 1922 (MEPO, 3/462)
125 *TT*, 14 Feb. 1921
126 *TT*, 21 Feb. 1921
127 *TT*, 19, 22 Mar. 1921; Commissioner of Police of the Metropolis to the USS, HO, 18 Nov. 1922 (MEPO, 3/462)
128 *TT*, 16 May 1921; Hugh Early interview (EO'MN, P17b/110)
129 Martin Geraghty to MSPB, 20 May 1937 (EO'MP, P17a/154)

in Bromley, Kent. One man was apprehended at the scene. The three others escaped but were arrested soon afterwards.[130]

In some other incidents, Volunteers acted seemingly with the deliberate intent of wounding if not killing people. This was particularly evident during some of the attacks on RIC men and their relatives. Four men called at 42 Bloenfontein Road, Shepherds Bush, London, and asked to see C. H. Corns, formerly of the police transport division. Horace MacNeill, the householder, responded that his nephew did not reside with him. 'There was pushing and shoving at the door', remembered Denis Brennan, 'and some one [sic] was a bit trigger happy and he [i.e. MacNeill] got shot.' He died in hospital the following week.[131] During a raid on a house in Catford, shots were fired, injuring an elderly couple.[132] In St Albans, a gang of four armed men entered the house of Lanclet Ashby, an Auxiliary. Ashby and his wife were shot in the head and beaten with revolver butts, while their landlady was bound and gagged. Amazingly, the Ashby's survived the attack as the bullets failed to penetrate their skulls.[133] That same month, the Liverpool IRA launched a revenge attack against John Rimmer. On 9 March, Rimmer, a prominent member of the local rural district council, had shot Volunteer Paddy Lowe while he was attempting to start a fire on his farm, and bragged about it. The IRA was unimpressed: 'we were not in the temper to take this kind of boasting lying down', Edward Brady remembered.

> To have ignored it would have been to admit fear, and the moral effect of such on other citizens in encouraging them to emulate this boasting fellow, might have had disastrous results – for us.

Thus, on 23 May, 14 armed and masked men descend on Rimmer's farm with the intention of 'roughing up' the braggart. There, they divided into two groups. Five men set fire to the outhouses and sheds, while the remaining nine proceeded to the dwelling house. Failing to gain admittance to the house, they proceeded to fire shots through the windows. A policeman quickly arrived on the scene and a fire-fight ensued. After a few minutes, the IRA men withdrew. Brady sympathized with the plight of the occupants, trapped in a house under siege, bullets smashing windows, flames from the burning outhouses spreading

---

130 *TT*, 18 June 1921
131 *TT*, 16, 23 May 1921; Denis Brennan interview (EO'MN, P17b/100)
132 *Evening News*, *TT*, 16 May 1921
133 *TT*, 16 May 1921

to the house itself. 'Yes! it was terrible', he conceded, 'but it was all part of the war in the struggle of a nation to free itself.'[134]

In another incident on 18 June, railway signal man, Edward Axon, was shot through the window of his signal box near Marple Station, Manchester. He was injured in the groin. Hearing a party of men approaching, he then threw a poker out the window and switched off the lights. The raiders entered the box and fired more shots, injuring Axon in the shoulder.[135]

Cumann na mBan members aided Volunteers in a number of operations. Shelia 'Cissie' Sheehan accompanied a London IRA man to the home of an RIC man's sister. She waited outside while he knocked at the door, went inside and instructed the woman to persuade her brother to resign from the police or be prepared to have her house attacked. 'My function was to act as a cover and make it appear that we were just a boy and girl out for a walk', remembered Sheehan, 'and if he were attacked to help in his escape by taking his gun.'[136] Women performed the same function during wire-cutting operations on Tyneside.[137]

Due to the nature of the sources at our disposal, it is difficult to state with complete precision the number of operations mounted by the IRA in the period November 1920–July 1921. The sources can be divided into three categories: police records, IRA correspondence and memoirs and press reports. None of these sources are definitive. Moreover, incidents appearing in one source are sometimes missing from the others. For example, Rory O'Connor claimed that a 'truck load [of] khaki clothing on route to Stirling' had been 'completely destroyed' in an operation mounted in London in April, but no reference to this event was found in police reports or the press.[138] Again, one newspaper claimed that police frustrated an attempt to set fire to a number of large petrol tanks in a railway yard near Liverpool's Edge Hill Station on 3 June, yet the incident does not appear in the police records or veterans' memoirs.[139] With this in mind, I opted to proceed cautiously, counting only those incidents for which IRA responsibility was certain or highly likely and excluding those for which it was debatable. As the police records are the most

134 Brady, *Secret Service*, pp. 77–80; *Liverpool Courier*, 11 Mar., 25 May 1921; *TT*, 25 May 1921

135 *MG, TT*, 20 June 1921; ACC of Lancashire to the USS, HO, 27 Oct. 1922; Scottish Office to Carew-Robinson, HO, 20 Nov. 1922 (HO, 144/4645)

136 BMHWS 924, Mary Cremin, pp. 6–7

137 BMHWS 773, Gilbert Barrington, pp. 7–8

138 O/C Britain to C/S, 3 June 1921 (RMP, P7/A/19[16–20])

139 Clipping from *Morning Post*, 6 June 1921 (HO, 144/4645)

authoritative and detailed of the three source types, I have relied mainly on these. In relation to a small number of incidents, however, I have depended on contemporaneous IRA sources, newspaper reports and veterans' accounts.[140]

The IRA was responsible for at least 239 operations or attempted operations in Britain between 27 November 1920 and 11 July 1921. Of these, Lancashire saw 103 (43.1 per cent of the total), the London Metropolitan area 44 (18.4 per cent), Durham 30 (12.6 per cent), Northumberland 18 (7.5 per cent), Cheshire 15 (6.3 per cent), Kent nine (3.8 per cent), Yorkshire North Riding six (2.5 per cent), Warwickshire, namely Birmingham, two (0.8 per cent), and Essex one (0.4 per cent). Scotland, meanwhile, witnessed 11 operations (4.6 per cent).[141] This demonstrates that parts of Britain saw more IRA operations than some areas of Ireland.[142] Outside of this time period, the police suspected Irish involvement in relation to a small number of incidents. The destruction by fire of the Manchester City football grounds in early

---

140   Returns to HO from 20 police units, the LMP and the Scottish Office, Oct.–Nov. 1922 (HO, 144/4645; MEPO, 3/462; NAI, Dept. of Finance file [FIN] 1/1589); O/C Britain to C/S, 3 June 1921 (RMP, P7/A/19[16–20]); *IT, MG, The Observer, TT*, Nov. 1920–July 1921; membership rolls of the Scottish Brigade IRA (EMP, 3/C/13); BMHWS. Note that due to the difficulties in dealing with the window-scratching phenomenon, namely the problems of attribution and quantification, I have excluded that whole episode from the following statistics. The figures here supersede those given in Gerard Noonan, 'Republican Terrorism in Britain, 1920–1923', in David Fitzpatrick (ed.), *Terror in Ireland 1916–1923* (Dublin: Lilliput Press, 2012), pp. 239–42.

141   I have grouped the police returns into their constabulary areas as set out in *Reports of His Majesty's Inspectors of Constabulary for the Year Ended the 29th September 1921* H.C. 1922 (5), pp. 18–27. Hence, Lancashire incorporates constabulary returns from Bootle, Lancashire County, Lancaster County, Liverpool City, Manchester City, Rochdale and Salford; Durham incorporates Durham and South Shields returns; Northumberland returns from Newcastle-upon-Tyne, Northumberland and Tynemouth; Cheshire returns from Cheshire and Stockport; Warwickshire consists of Birmingham; an 'incident' of violence is counted as such according to the property or person targeted. Hence, one fire on a farm is counted as one incident of terrorism, as are two fires on the same farm on the same night etc. All figures are rounded to the first decimal place. My figures differ greatly from those of Hart, 'Operations Abroad', tables 18 & 19, p. 165; this is partly due to the fact that he includes thefts of munitions in his figures, whereas I do not consider these violent incidents and therefore do not incorporate them here.

142   Hart, 'Geography', p. 39

November 1920 was the most spectacular. They were also suspected of four farm fires in the Birmingham area in September and December 1921. While the police may have been correct in suspecting IRA involvement in the latter incidents, it is unlikely that the Volunteers were responsible for the former. In 1925, faced with paying compensation for the attacks, the Irish government denied that the IRA was involved in any incidents which occurred outside the period 27 November 1920–11 July 1921.[143]

What explains the regional variation in the number of operations? The size of the Irish population may provide some explanation. According to the 1911 census, of the administrative units in England and Wales, Lancashire had the third highest Irish population as a proportion of its overall population. Cheshire had the fourth highest, Durham fifth, London sixth, Northumberland ninth and Kent tenth. These rankings do not strictly accord with those here, where Lancashire was the most violent area for six of the nine months. Also, Cumberland, the area with the second highest proportion, recorded no incidents at all. Yet, it would seem to be the case that, in general, those areas where the Irish population constituted a significant proportion of the population were more likely to experience incidents of violence than areas with fewer Irish inhabitants.[144]

Another factor which may explain the variation is the differing outlooks of the various IRA units themselves. We already saw that Michael O'Leary's sidelining of street-fighting in his lectures in favour of political topics led to his ousting as O/C of Liverpool City Company.[145] The rank and file, therefore, demonstrated a desire for military instruction. Such initiative was also evident in their pressing for the mounting of operations in February 1921.[146] Later that year, Rory O'Connor visited units throughout England and noted the 'military outlook' of the officers. He was particularly unimpressed by the officers in Birmingham, claiming that they lacked all initiative. His frustration was compounded by the fact that, being a great manufacturing

143 Secretary, Dept. of Defence, to Secretary, Dept. of Finance, 28 Jan. 1925 (FIN, 1/1589)

144 *Census of England and Wales 1911, ix, Birthplaces of Persons Enumerated in Administrative Counties, County Boroughs, etc, and Ages and Occupations of Foreigners* [Cd. 7017] H.C. 1913, table x, p. xiii; the unit with the highest proportion of Irish was Hampshire, a fact which the census report attributed in part to the stationing of naval and military personnel in the area, a significant amount of whom were Irish.

145 See Chapter 1

146 Paddy Daly to Michael Collins, 28 Feb. 1921 (RMP, P7/A/4)

centre, Birmingham would have been an 'excellent' place for the mounting of operations.[147] Hence, the fact that only two operations occurred in the Birmingham area during the war can be attributed to the cautious attitude of the local IRA leadership. Historians of the Volunteers in Ireland have emphasized the importance of local leadership in the willingness of companies to fight. Leadership was the 'decisive factor' in determining the level of IRA activity in County Limerick, for example. 'The units that did most of the fighting were, quite simply, the units that chose to create the opportunities to fight', argues John O'Callaghan.[148]

Of the 239 incidents, 46.9 per cent involved attacks on farms or crops, including the burning of hay, corn, barley etc., along with barns and machinery. Sabotage of communications and railway infrastructure, such as telephone and telegraph wires and poles, along with signal boxes, accounted for 17.6 per cent. Arson assaults on warehouses comprised another 16.3 per cent, factories and business premises 8 per cent, the homes of RIC men and their relatives 3.8 per cent and timber yards 2.5 per cent. The remaining miscellaneous targets amounted to 5 per cent of all incidents and consisted of the execution of the spy Fouvargue in London, the attack on the prison van in Glasgow, the burnings of a labour exchange in London, an observatory and some park chairs, a boat-house and three hotels in Manchester and an aerodrome in Newcastle-upon-Tyne, the smashing of windows at an art gallery in Manchester, the theft of money from a railway worker in Mount Vernon, Scotland, and the blowing-up of a water main in North Stockton, Durham. Farms were the most popular target. As we noted earlier, this was probably because of the relative ease of setting fire to a hay stack and making a successful getaway. As we saw previously, George Fitzgerald instructed London Volunteers to mount assaults on farms as a means of building up their self-confidence, important in light of their failure to torch a warehouse. Also, O'Connor described attacks against farms as one of a number of minor operations which the IRA in Britain could mount despite a lack of training. Sabotage of communications and railway infrastructure was viable for similar reasons.

The areas which saw the largest number of attacks mounted by the IRA also saw the largest variety in the targets assailed. Similarly, of the ten constabulary areas that witnessed attacks, those with the least number of operations exhibited the least amount of variety in their objectives. Lancashire,

---

147 O/C Britain to C/S, 15 Oct. 1921 (RMP, P7/A/29[264–73])

148 O'Callaghan, *Revolutionary Limerick*, pp. 212–13; see also Campbell, *Land and Revolution*, pp. 269–70, 274

Table 3: IRA Attacks in Britain by Constabulary Area, Nov. 1920–July 1921

Target of attacks / Constabulary area	Farms and crops	Communications and railway infrastructure	Warehouses	Factories, mills and retailers	Miscellaneous targets	Houses of RIC men and/or their relatives	Timber yards	Total
Lancashire	21	19	38	9	6	4	6	103
London Metropolitan Area	25	9	1	2	2	5	0	44
Durham	21	2	0	6	1	0	0	30
Northumberland	15	1	0	1	1	0	0	18
Cheshire	10	4	0	1	0	0	0	15
Kent	4	5	0	0	0	0	0	9
Yorkshire (North Riding)	6	0	0	0	0	0	0	6
Warwickshire	2	0	0	0	0	0	0	2
Essex County	0	1	0	0	0	0	0	1
Scotland	8	1	0	0	2	0	0	11
Total	112	42	39	19	12	9	6	239

Sources: Returns to HO from 20 police units, the LMP and the Scottish Office, Oct.–Nov. 1922 (HO, 144/4645; MEPO, 3/462; FIN, 1/1589); O/C Britain to C/S, 3 June 1921 (RMP, P7/A/19[16–20]); *IT, MG, The Observer, TT*, Nov. 1920–July 1921

Table 4: IRA Attacks in Britain by Month, Nov. 1920–July 1921

Targets of attack / Month	Farms and crops	Timber yards	Warehouses	Factories, mills and retailers	Communication and railway infrastructure	Houses of RIC men and/or their relatives	Miscellaneous targets	Total
November 1920	0	6	35	0	0	0	0	41
December	0	0	0	3	0	0	0	3
January 1921	1	0	2	2	0	0	1	6
February	12	0	0	6	0	0	0	18
March	58	0	0	1	0	0	3	62
April	19	0	2	0	3	0	5	29
May	21	0	0	7	1	9	2	40
June	0	0	0	0	38	0	1	39
July	1	0	0	0	0	0	0	1
Total	112	6	39	19	42	9	12	239

Sources: Returns to HO from 20 police units, the LMP and the Scottish Office, Oct.–Nov. 1922 (HO, 144/4645; MEPO, 3/462; FIN, 1/1589); O/C Britain to C/S, 3 June 1921 (RMP, P7/A/19[16–20]); *IT, MG, The Observer, TT,* Nov. 1920–July 1921

Graph 4: Number of Attacks per Month, Nov. 1920–July 1921

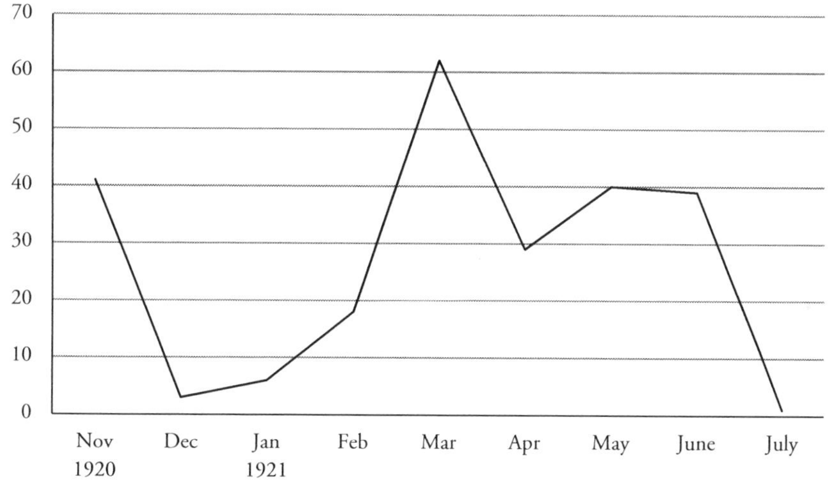

Sources: Returns to HO from 20 police units, the LMP and the Scottish Office, Oct.–Nov. 1922 (HO, 144/4645; MEPO, 3/462; FIN, 1/1589); O/C Britain to C/S, 3 June 1921 (RMP, P7/A/19[16–20]); *IT, MG, The Observer, TT*, Nov. 1920–July 1921

the area in Britain which boasted the largest number of incidents, witnessed attacks on farms, communications, the railway network, warehouses, factories, timber yards and the homes of RIC men and their relatives, along with miscellaneous targets such as hotels. Essex, on the other hand, which saw the least number of incidents of the ten areas, saw only one operation, against communications and railway infrastructure.

Why such a pattern? The argument that London and Lancashire boasted a variety of targets which the other areas lacked may have some currency when compared to Yorkshire North Riding. This, after all, was a rural area, lacking in the type of warehouses and factories which existed in the cities. Hence the preponderance of farms as objects for incendiarism. However, that explanation does not apply to Durham, Northumberland and Warwickshire. These areas possessed conurbations in which a variety of properties were available. Why, then, were more attacks not mounted? Again, deficiencies in leadership may be partially to blame. As we have seen, O'Connor believed that the leadership of the IRA in Birmingham, Warwickshire, lacked 'the slightest military outlook'. The O/C, Patrick O'Neill, refused to countenance any operation 'on even a moderate large scale' lest his men suffer arrest. Yet a lack of initiative does not seem to account for the relative absence of variety in the targets attacked by the Tyneside IRA in Durham and Northumberland, for O'Connor found the officers there to be 'intelligent' and 'hard working'.[149]

March 1921 was the month which saw the largest number of incidents, 62. There were 41 incidents in November 1920, 40 in May 1921 and 39 the following month. The variation in the number of operations mounted per month can be attributed mainly to the reaction of the police. In Merseyside for example, the arson attacks of November 1920 precipitated a major response from the Merseyside police. A number of Volunteers, including Tom Kerr and his successor Peter Roland, were arrested. Without leadership and under close police surveillance, the Liverpool IRA spent the subsequent few months lying 'quiet, very quiet'.[150] When the IRA mounted an assault on property in Manchester city centre on 2 April 1921, the police reacted by arresting a significant number of men, and this caused some Volunteers who had escaped the dragnet to flee the city.[151] Only a few operations were mounted in the Manchester area subsequent to this. Another factor was the type of target chosen for attack. As the campaign proceeded, operations against warehouses and timber yards declined, while those against farms, telephone and telegraph lines and railway infrastructure increased significantly. These latter types of property were easier to attack, requiring less planning and preparation. Success in mounting assaults on such targets seems to have contributed to an increase in such operations.

The number of farm fires increased from one in January 1921 to 12 in February and 58 the following month. They constituted over 92 per cent of all operations mounted in March. Attacks on communications and railway infrastructure increased from one in May to 38 in June, comprising over 97 per cent of all incidents that occurred in the latter month. Thus, it would seem that as the objects chosen for attack changed from warehouses to farms and infrastructure, Volunteers became practiced in mounting such operations, which in turn led to an increase in their frequency.

According to the police, the IRA campaign caused damage to the value of £668,501 5s. 1d.[152] Incidents in Lancashire accounted for the

---

149 O/C Britain to C/S, 15 Oct. 1921 (RMP, P7/A/29[264–73])

150 Pinkman, *Legion*, p. 47

151 BMHWS 274, Liam McMahon, pp. 19–20; BMHWS 1678, William O'Keeffe, pp. 12–13

152 The monetary damage was calculated using figures for insurance compensation paid to the victim or, where such compensation was not paid, by using the assessors', owners' or police estimates of damage caused or the replacement

overwhelming majority of this amount, 86.2 per cent in fact. Durham was responsible for 5.9 per cent, Northumberland 3.3 per cent, London 1.9 per cent, Cheshire 1.5 per cent and the remaining areas less than 0.5 per cent each. The disparity is accounted for by the type of targets attacked in each area. Warehouses constituted a far higher proportion of properties torched in Lancashire than they did elsewhere in Britain. Indeed, 38 of the 39 attacks on warehouses took place in Lancashire, resulting in a loss of £536,576 15*s.* 11*d.* (It should be noted that in four of these operations, the only damage inflicted was the breaking of the padlocks.) For example, on 27 November 1920, in one warehouse on Atlantic Road, Bootle, damage was caused to 500 bales of cotton, 97 boxes of tin, 500 bags of algarrobilla seed, 53 bales of quillai bark, two bales of horse hair, 326 bags of haricot beans, about 600 bags of timothy seed, 100 bags of millet seed, 23 cases of artificial silk hose, 40 casks of preserved peas, one bag of extract, 1,923 cases of match blocks, 114 bags of sugar, 37 barrels of soda and three bags of cotton cake; insurance compensation came to £12,897 12*s.* 5*d.*[153] (The only attack on a warehouse to take place outside of Lancashire occurred in London that same night but it was interrupted by police before the fire could be started.[154]) All of the six assaults on timber yards that took place were mounted in Lancashire, inflicting £13,917 16*s.* 5*d.* of destruction. Lancashire also accounted for nine of the 19 attacks on factories and wholesalers, causing £10,083 9*s.* 9*d.* of the £39,170 12*s.* 6*d.* inflicted. On the other hand, Lancashire witnessed only 21 of the 112 operations against farms and farm produce which, in total, caused £67,345 13*s.* 10*d.* of damage. Attacks on warehouses, therefore, with their valuable contents, caused the greatest destruction per attack in monetary terms, followed in descending order by assaults on timber yards, factories, miscellaneous targets, farms, communications and railway infrastructure, and the homes of RIC men and their families. The overwhelming majority of attacks on warehouses took place early in the offensive. Indeed, the assaults on 34 warehouses in Liverpool city and Bootle in November 1920, the IRA's first offensive in

cost. It should be noted that in 32 incidents either no figure or an incomplete figure was given for the damage inflicted. These comprised 22 attacks on communications and railway infrastructure, four on miscellaneous targets, two on factories, two on the homes of RIC men and their families, one on a warehouse and one on a farm.

153   CC of Bootle to the USS, HO, 27 Oct. 1922 (HO, 144/4645)
154   Report of Superintendent of 'G' Division, LMP, 29 Nov. 1920 (MEPO 3/466); *Pall Mall Gazette*, 17 Jan. 1921

Britain, caused devastation to the value of £507,686 5s. 11d., 75.9 per cent of the total damage caused during the whole campaign.

In 1925, the Irish government agreed to pay compensation of £500,000 'on account of damage done by Irish agency in Great Britain' between November 1920 and July 1921.[155]

VI

What was the effect of all this violence? The most immediate effect, of course, was the actual devastation inflicted. Four people were killed: William Ward in November 1920, Vincent Fouvargue in April 1921, Horace MacNeill and policeman Robert Johnston the following month. In addition, a number of others were injured. C.H. Cornes, MacNeill's son-in-law, described the trauma of losing a loved one. 'It is hard enough to think that this poor man's untimely death was practically because I was then in the Royal Irish Constabulary', he wrote. His worries were compounded by the effect the death was having on MacNeill's widow. Her health was 'being undermined through having to continue living in the same house, and having to pass daily the door where it [i.e. the shooting] happened[:] the scene naturally all comes back to her especially at night time it is most terrifying for her to go near the door'.[156] Other victims of IRA violence endured similar emotional suffering. John Duffy, the night watchman at the Manchester Premier Rubber Works attacked by the IRA on 12 February, committed suicide. His wife told the corner's court that Duffy had complained of his nerves since the attack, when he was held at gunpoint. The incident led Duffy to arm himself with a revolver, and it was with this weapon that he shot himself on 25 June.[157] A similar such indirect death was that of the fireman who was killed when a fire-engine toppled over on top of him while tackling a Volunteer arson attack on a farm in Lancashire in March.[158]

The IRA itself suffered one fatality as a result of its campaign. The death of Seán Morgan occurred on 2 April 1921, when a shoot-out took place at the Irish Club in Hulme, Manchester, between Volunteers and police investigating the arson attacks committed earlier that day.[159]

---

155   'Extract from Agreement Between the British Government and the Irish Free State Government', 21 July 1925 (FIN, 1/1589)

156   C.H. Cornes to the Home Secretary, 25 Nov. 1921 (HO, 144/22333)

157   *MG*, 28 June 1921

158   See p. 136 above

159   *TT*, 4 Apr. 1921; see p. 152 above

As well as emotional suffering, the death of spouses and relatives also gave rise to financial problems. Despite the support of her two working sons, Mrs MacNeill, raising two other children, found it difficult to pay her husband's funeral expenses of £150. In addition, the local council threatened legal action due to her failure to pay the half-yearly rates of £40. Claiming that she was unable to find a smaller house, she also had to pay the upkeep of the family's large abode: 'I am left destitute', she lamented.[160] Though the British government compensated RIC personnel who suffered at the hands of the IRA in Ireland, for financial reasons it refused to include in the scheme those who experienced similar attacks in Britain. The Irish Office did persuade the Treasury to grant MacNeill an ex gratia payment of £100, along with £300 from the Royal Bounty Fund. This money, however, was consumed by doctors' fees, living expenses and funeral costs. If not for the intervention of the Southern Irish Loyalist Relief Association, who provided additional financial aid and clothing, MacNeill believed that she would have lost her home.[161]

Those who suffered attacks on their property also sometimes encountered financial difficulties. Finding that their insurance companies refused to compensate them for the loss they suffered, some businesses had to bear the cost themselves. Indeed, in the aftermath of the events of 27 November 1920, some insurance companies introduced a specific policy covering 'malicious damage by Sinn Fein or other evilly disposed persons', implying that previous policies would not cover such an eventuality.[162] RIC man S.R. Kerr spent over £400 replacing the uninsured furniture which was burned when his Liverpool house was attacked. As in the case of Horace MacNeill, the government refused his request for help.[163] The attacks provoked vigilance on the part of property owners. 'Extra watchmen were engaged to guard premises containing inflammable material', noted one newspaper, 'reinforced police lurked in the dark doorways of the warehouse quarter of the city [of Manchester], and farmers patrolled their stackyards with a trustworthy dog at heel and a shotgun at the ready.'[164] The sabotage of communications had the effect of disrupting intercourse. Such attacks in Lancashire in early June, for example,

160 C.H. Cornes to the Home Secretary, 25 Nov. 1921; A.M. MacNeill to Lady Astor, 8 May 1922 (HO, 144/22333)

161 H.R. Boyd, HO, to Harry Varney, Buckingham Palace, 21 July, 3 Nov. 1922; MacNeill to The Queen, 9 Oct. 1926 (HO, 144/22333)

162 Art O'Brien to Michael Collins, 18 Dec. 1920 (DÉ, 2/326)

163 Damage to 16 Harewood Street, Liverpool, n.d.; Whiskard to Troup, 18 Jan. 1922; S.R. Kerr to Andrew Bonar Law, 7 May 1923 (HO, 144/4645)

164 *MG*, 16 July 1921

caused significant interruption to telegraphic and telephonic communications between Liverpool and the north of England for up to three days.[165]

An indirect victim of the campaign was the IRA in Ireland, for operations precipitated a police response which in turn sometimes affected the operation of gun-smuggling to Ireland. In the aftermath of the Liverpool arson attacks on 27 November 1920, the police raided the houses of a large number of well-known Irish nationalists. With the arrest of Neil Kerr Senior, his son Tom and Steve Lanigan, the Merseyside gunrunning organization was decapitated and, much to the irritation of Michael Collins, activity was perforce suspended, thus depriving the Volunteers across the Irish Sea of much-needed armaments. Within little over a week, however, Paddy Daly had stepped into Neil Kerr's shoes and munitions-smuggling was resumed.[166] Increased police vigilance also led to the arrest of Henry Coyle and Charles McGinn, two senior Scottish munitions-smugglers, in Alloa. This contributed to the confusion which engulfed gunrunning operations north of the border in late 1920 and early 1921. The police reaction to the shooting of Inspector Johnston during the attempted rescue of Frank Carty from a prison van in Glasgow five months later compounded the mess.[167] Despite this, however, there is no evidence that Collins, QMG Seán McMahon or their associates in IRA GHQ argued against violence in Britain on the grounds that it was undermining gunrunning activities. Evidently, a reduction in the amount of munitions arriving in Ireland was tolerated for the sake of extending the war to Britain.

How does IRA violence in Britain compare with that in Ireland? The war in Ireland can be divided into four stages. The first stage, from January 1919 to early 1920, saw Volunteer units continue to raid for arms, an activity they had been engaged in since 1917. During the second stage, from January to the summer of 1920, units began attacking RIC barracks. The robust reaction of the authorities precipitated the third stage, involving the IRA's creation of ASUs or flying columns. With the disbandment of the flying columns in the winter of 1920, the fourth and final stage saw Volunteer units return to harassing Crown forces by disrupting communications and roads.[168] In 1919,

165 Clipping from *Morning Post*, 4 June (HO, 144/4645); *TT*, 9 June 1921

166 'G' to Michael Collins, n.d., but date-stamped 1 Dec.; Collins, 'Memo to Liverpool', 4 Dec.; Paddy Daly to Collins, n.d. but *c.* 5 Dec. 1920 (RMP, P7/A/3); Pinkman, *Legion*, p. 47

167 *MG*, 16 Mar. 1921; BMHWS 933, Séamus Reader, pp. 9–11; see Chapter 2

168 Charles Townshend, 'The Irish Republican Army and the Development of Guerrilla Warfare, 1916–1921', *English Historical Review*, 114.321 (1979), pp. 324–25, 329–31; Augusteijn, *Public Defiance*, pp. 183–84

17 RIC men were killed by the IRA. In the first six months of 1920, the figure had more than doubled to 41 fatalities. By 31 March 1921, just over three months before the truce, a total of 270 policemen and 98 soldiers had been killed.[169] We can see, therefore, that a large increase in police fatalities coincided with the creation and operation of the flying columns. Joost Augusteijn argues that two factors were critical in enabling the Volunteers in Ireland to wage bloody guerrilla warfare. The first was the alienation of the Volunteers' community from the forces of law and order, while the second was the separation of IRA men from the restraining authority of that community. By removing Volunteers from the influence of neighbours and friends, the flying columns enabled them to overcome the social and psychological barriers which normally prohibited the killing of policemen and soldiers.[170]

While the IRA in Ireland had the support of a large alienated populace and established flying columns, their comrades in Britain had a much smaller support base and lacked flying columns. As they did not record their opinions on the matter, it is impossible to gauge the attitude of the politically-inactive Irish in Britain towards the IRA campaign in Britain. The attitude of the Irish actively involved in republican politics was ambiguous. In November 1920, nationalists in Manchester expressed incredulity at the publication in the press of Jack Plunkett's report detailing plans for attacks in the city. They contended that the document had been forged by the British authorities.[171] No mention of the seven-and-a-half month long offensive appeared in the ISDL's newspaper, the *Irish Exile*. Neither did the publication cover the IRA's campaign in Ireland. Perhaps it believed that the mass of the league's membership did not support violence. This may explain why the newspaper's coverage of bloodshed in Ireland focused exclusively on reprisals carried out by Crown forces. On the other hand, large and sympathetic crowds sometimes packed the galleries in support of Volunteers on trial for violent offences.[172]

The IRA in Britain failed to emulate its colleagues in Ireland in the establishment of ASUs. The night before the Liverpool attack in November

---

169 *Return Showing by Monthly Periods the Number of Murders of Members of the Royal Irish Constabulary and of the Dublin Metropolitan Police … from the 1st Day of January, 1919, to the 30th April, 1920* [Cmd. 709] (1920), p. 2; *Return Showing by Monthly Periods the Number of Murders of Members of the Royal Irish Constabulary and of the Dublin Metropolitan Police … for May and June 1920* [Cmd. 859] (1920), p. 2; *Hansard 5 (Commons)*, cxl, cols 463–64 (7 Apr. 1921)

170 Augusteijn, *Public Defiance*, pp. 342–48

171 *Irish Independent (II)*, 27 Nov. 1920

172 E.g. *MG*, 15 July, *Glasgow Herald*, 22 Aug. 1921

1920, Michael O'Leary, anticipating a police crackdown, suggested that a flying column be created so as to facilitate further operations, but Rory O'Connor disagreed.[173] According to Séan Mooney, by mid-1921 the Scottish Brigade's 1st Battalion had formed a flying column. It was composed of between 20 and 30 men specially selected from the companies in the battalion. The column's (undisclosed) activities were mainly in the west of Scotland, though they sometimes ranged as far east as Edinburgh and Leith. However, as the members seem to have been living at home throughout, this flying column was not comparable to those in Ireland.[174]

Does the absence of flying columns in Britain account for the IRA's failure to fight a campaign there similar to that of their colleagues in Ireland? In other words, did the communities in which they resided constrain the Volunteers in the type and intensity of operations they could mount? While this was certainly the case in Ireland, where operations were sometimes modified so as to avoid discommoding the populace for example, it does not appear to be true of Britain.[175] The sources at our disposal do not indicate any attempts by the friends or neighbours of IRA men or by organizations such as the ISDL and Sinn Féin to influence the Volunteers' offensive there. Rather, the only constraints imposed were those set down by GHQ. In contrast to the IRA in Ireland, therefore, the Volunteers in Britain seem to have operated free from communal constraints. That this did not lead to the IRA in Britain matching or exceeding their comrades in Ireland in the quantity and character of operations mounted must be ascribed to the fact that the *raison d'être* of the two were different. For the Volunteers in Ireland, attacking policemen and soldiers, the personification of foreign rule, was an end in itself. The Volunteers in Britain, meanwhile – living in a hostile environment and deficient in comparison with their comrades across the Irish Sea in both membership and in the level of support they received from the general populace – existed only to assist the IRA in Ireland. For them to have engaged in similar attacks on policemen and soldiers in Britain would have been foolhardy, for the response by an outraged government would probably have led to the collapse of the republican movement through mass arrests. This, in turn, might have precipitated a complete breakdown in gunrunning, the most important activity of republicans in Britain.

173 BMHWS 797, Micheál Ó Laoghaire, pp. 43–44

174 Seán (or Séamus) Mooney's statement on the 'Smashing of the Van' incident, n.d. (EMP, 5/36)

175 Augusteijn, *Public Defiance*, pp. 313, 317–19, 324, 327–28

The press gave considerable coverage to the IRA's campaign of violence. Some Volunteers held that such publicity had a good consequence. 'It had a very good effect as it got great publicity in the [illegible] Papers', remembered London's Dennis Kelleher, referring to the attacks on RIC men and their relatives.[176] His comrade Dennis Brennan claimed that as a result of the Volunteers' sabotage of communications, '[t]he man in the street knew there was something going on. The papers played up our little acts tremendously'. Indeed, the nature of the operations led the press to believe that the IRA had a 'tremendous organisation' in the capital and was very well equipped, thus exaggerating its strength and arsenal.[177] The Manchester IRA was also heartened by media coverage of its activities. John McGallogly was unimpressed with the efforts of a party of Volunteers under his command to set fire to a cotton print works, but 'the papers gave it a better write up' than he expected.[178]

As well as sometimes encouraging the Volunteers themselves, however, press coverage of their activities also influenced the British reading public. 'People were very suspicious of the Irish then', Dennis Brennan recollected:

> They [i.e. the English] think it is the [Irish] bloke they know themselves [who is committing the attacks] … At my digs I w[as] sure they were suspicious for I came home often at 3/[i.e. or]4 o clock [in the morning] and I wasn't used to late hours and always something happened in the papers when I was in late.[179]

Fear and anger, as well as suspicion, were aroused by the violence. Indignation at the fires in the Manchester area in February and March 1921 led to declarations that unless the violence ceased, 'Englishmen and loyal Irishmen will refuse to work with men known to have Sinn Fein sympathies'. Moreover, the police learned of threats to burn clubs and other Irish institutions by way of retaliation. 'In outlying districts where fires have occurred the temper of the people is such that it would hardly go with anyone caught redhanded', one reporter concluded.[180] We saw earlier that members of the public tried to throw John Pinkman, labelled a 'Sinn Fein bastard', into the path of the on-coming train as he and his accomplices attempted to flee the scene of

---

176 Dennis Kelleher interview (EO'MN, P17b/107)

177 Dennis Brennan interview (EO'MN, P17b/100); original emphasis

178 BMHWS 244, John McGallogly, p. 19

179 Dennis Brennan interview (EO'MN, P17b/100)

180 Clipping from *Daily Telegraph*, 4 Mar. 1921 (HO, 144/4645)

some farm fires on Merseyside.[181] Anger at IRA activities led members of the public in Cheshire and Manchester to volunteer to work as special constables to help the police prevent further outrages.[182]

Unsurprisingly, the press was overwhelmingly hostile to the IRA's campaign. The *Liverpool Courier* condemned the 'outbreak of incendiarism and crime' on Merseyside in November 1920. Their authors were 'men with a Nihilistic faith in violence alone'. Such violence would retard Ireland's demand for justice, the newspaper continued, for it would 'only have the effect of uniting good citizens and patriots of all parties in a solid determination to crush the conspiracy and extirpate the criminals'.[183] The London *Evening News* agreed. The arsonists were 'savage and gloomy fanatics' who wanted not peace but war between the people of Ireland and Britain. If such violence were to continue, it would 'only mean the postponement of Irish hopes for many a long year to come'.[184] The *Courier* claimed that the attacks on farms on 9 March had 'a close parallel to the German method of waging war'.[185] Noting the conviction of six men in relation to that night's events, the *Newcastle Daily Chronicle* opined:

> To say that, because Sir Hamar Greenwood's policy in Ireland is wrong the hard-won crops of some obscure Lancashire farmer must be destroyed, may be good enough logic for the Sim Tappertits of Ireland. But it is not good enough logic for the British people, without whom there can be no settlement.[186]

The following month, the *Pall Mall and Globe* questioned the logic of the 'criminal theory' behind the operations. Reprisals 'are presumed to check the original offence', it noted, but 'it would surely be doing the wit of the Sinn Fein leaders an injustice to suppose that they believe the people of this country can be intimidated in such a way'. Rather, the likely effect of the violence was to make the English people 'irreconcilable' to Irish demands.[187] Reacting to

---

181   See p. 137 above
182   CC of Cheshire to J.N. Brickland, HO, 5 Mar. 1921; clipping from *TT*, 8 Mar. 1921 (HO, 144/4645)
183   *Liverpool Courier*, 29 Nov. 1920 (Editorial)
184   *Evening News*, 29 Nov. 1920 (Editorial)
185   *Liverpool Courier*, 10 Mar. 1921 (Editorial)
186   *Newcastle Daily Chronicle*, 11 Apr. 1921 (Editorial); in the Charles Dickens novel *Barnaby Rudge* (1841), Simon ('Sim') Tappertit was a leader in the Gordon Riots of 1780.
187   *Pall Mall and Globe*, 5 Apr. 1921 (Editorial)

the shooting dead of Inspector Robert Johnston on 4 May, the *Glasgow Herald* wanted it to 'be known the world over that Glasgow, the real Glasgow, abhors these crimes, perpetrated by alien criminals'.[188] *Forward*, a socialist newspaper, also lamented the episode, though for more pragmatic reasons. Not only had the shooting precipitated the 'immediate irruption again of that cursed anti-Irish, or rather anti-Catholic prejudice, which has for a hundred years kept the working class split into sections, and which only in the last decade have we got partially smothered', the incident had also undermined 'the growing sympathies of the Protestant and other non-Catholic workers for the Irish people, under the vicious Greenwood-George terror'. The episode was a boon to the prime minister as it diverted public attention from 'the horrible reprisals and creamery burnings and Black and Tan atrocities' taking place across the Irish Sea. 'The remedy for Ireland's wrongs is to persuade the people of this country to lift the Georgian ban upon Irish freedom', the editorial concluded, but incidents such as the shooting of policemen made such persuasion 'more difficult'.[189] 'These murderous attacks upon the parents of men who stepped into the breach in Ireland at the call of the Government, when Ireland was given over to the domination of terror, will be bitterly resented', declared the *Daily Telegraph*, referring to the targeting of RIC men and their relatives in London and Liverpool in May. Moreover, they would isolate those MPs and religious leaders who had criticized the behaviour of Crown forces in Ireland. The government's only response to 'arson and assassination' could be a policy of 'determined resistance and repression'.[190] The *Liverpool Courier* compared the attacks to the Phoenix Park murders of 1882. Just as the killing of Irish chief secretary Lord Frederick Cavendish and under secretary Thomas Burke in Dublin by the Irish National Invincibles, an IRB splinter group, had prevented conciliation between the government and the Fenians, 'so now irresponsible, though organised, ruffianism has clouded the hope of settlement' raised by the recent meeting between Eamon de Valera and Northern Ireland premier Sir James Craig. The incidents were acts of 'insane hooliganism' carried out by 'depraved elements of a wide political party whose hope was always for personal opportunity for gain and plunder, and never, as was that of their leaders, for national happiness and prosperity'.[191]

In his reflections on the campaign up to the end of May 1921, Rory

---

188   *Glasgow Herald*, 5 May 1921 (Editorial)
189   *Forward*, 14 May 1921 (Editorial)
190   *Daily Telegraph*, 17 May 1921 (Editorial)
191   *Liverpool Courier*, 16 May 1921 (Editorial)

O'Connor pronounced the offensive to have been 'fairly successful'. Operations enjoyed a 90 per cent success rate, he said. Moreover, figures quoted in the press indicated that almost £1,400,000 of damage had been inflicted. The O/C Britain, however, was 'satisfied' that the real overall total amounted to at least £5,000,000. There were some notes of disappointment, however. Thoughts of linking up with British radicals had proved fruitless. 'The hope that the Miners would take a lead from our activities is not so far justified', he noted. 40 coal pits had been completely flooded due to striking miners refusing to allow the water pumps to be worked. Also, miners had apparently caused £40,000 of damage in an arson attack. Overall, however, the strike had been disheartening. Meanwhile, communists in Newcastle-upon-Tyne had proven 'useless'. O'Connor noted that some IRA activities had been imitated by copycats, but he bewailed the fact that such emulation tended to take the form of window-slashing, 'the line of least resistance'. Chief amongst the disappointments, however, was that the Volunteers' lack of battle-hardened experience had prevented the mounting of large scale operations.[192]

This was noted by a LMP official writing in the aftermath of operations targeting the railway network in mid-June 1921, and he drew an unfavourable comparison: 'What strikes me mainly is the [illegible] ineffectiveness of these attacks. They [i.e. the Volunteers] don't even succeed in doing any substantial damage. The suffragettes were far better at their job.'[193] In 1909, frustrated by the government's unwillingness to grant voting rights to women, the Women's Social and Political Union (WSPU), led by the Pankhursts, had begun a campaign of violence. Windows were smashed with stones, politicians were assaulted and acid and other substances were poured into post office pillar boxes, destroying thousands of letters. In early 1913, the violence escalated with arson and bomb attacks on property. Emmeline Pankhurst stated that 'if it was necessary to win the vote they were going to do as much damage to property as they could'. Houses, hotels, haystacks, farm buildings, sports pavilions, boathouses, churches, railway stations, goods yards, post offices and timber yards were attacked, among other types of property. Between February 1913 and August 1914, when the campaign was suspended upon the outbreak of the Great War, 337 attacks caused an estimated £750,000 of damage, some of it to property in Ireland.[194]

192   O/C Britain to C/S, 3 June 1921 (RMP, P7/A/19[16–20]); see *Hansard 5* (*Commons*), cxl, col. 711, Secretary for Mines Bridgeman (11 Apr. 1921)

193   Minute, 20 June 1921 (MEPO, 3/489)

194   Andrew Rosen, *Rise Up Women!: The Militant Campaign of the Women's Social*

In terms of devastation inflicted, therefore, the suffragettes were more effective than the Volunteers, though over a longer period of time. However, unlike that of the WSPU, the IRA's campaign of violence in Britain was merely an auxiliary to that being carried out by comrades in Ireland. Some newspapers grasped this. In an editorial in early March 1921, the *Manchester Guardian* condemned as 'despicable criminals' those responsible for farm fires which had occurred in Manchester earlier that week. Yet, the newspaper proceeded to place the episode in the context of events occurring in Ireland. The recent arson attacks were part of the 'horrible game of felony, counter-felony and counter-felony yet again that is carried on between the lawless extremists of Sinn Fein and the lawless element in the irregular police now in Ireland'. In response to the burning of a police barracks by the IRA, Auxiliaries burned creameries owned by people unconnected with the Volunteers. In turn, the IRA in Britain attacked the property of farmers unrelated to the offending Auxiliaries. 'At every step', the editorial lamented, 'there is the same abomination of cruelty, injustice, and unreason.' In order to break the cycle of destruction, the newspaper proposed a two-pronged solution. The preservation of law and order required both that the perpetrators of such violence be brought to justice and that similar crimes be prevented in the future through the watchfulness of special constables and soldiers. It also warned against vigilantism, the 'mobbing of inoffensive Irishmen or wrecking their property', for such attacks would themselves precipitate reprisals. The spiral of violence would then lead to a situation where 'decent Englishmen and decent Irishmen' were 'outnumbered' by perpetrators of violence and the two countries would 'sink to the level of a criminal lunatic asylum with the keepers away'.[195]

This second approach hinted at a political rather than military solution to the Irish question. In the end, this was the avenue which the British government chose to explore. With Ulster Unionists' objections to all-Ireland home rule having been addressed by the granting of limited autonomy to the Protestant-dominated six north-eastern counties of Ireland in late 1920, the British government was faced with the prospect of resorting to martial law and 'crown colony government' in order to suppress the IRA's rebellion in the south. Reluctant to take such a step without exhausting all available avenues

and Political Union 1903–1914 (London: Routledge & Kegan Paul, 1974), pp. 107, 119, 122–23, 129, 143, 154, 157–58, 170, 183–84, 188, 190, 192, 197, 201–02, 217, 221–22, 229, 231, 238, 242; C. J. Bearman, 'An Examination of Suffragette Violence', *English Historical Review*, 120.486 (2005), pp. 368–69, 372, 378

195 *MG*, 4 Mar. 1921 (Editorial)

beforehand, the government agreed to a truce beginning on 11 July and began to explore the possibility of a negotiated settlement.[196]

VII

In November 1920, with the burning of warehouses and timber yards on Merseyside, the IRA began a campaign of violence in Britain. It was primarily motivated by outrage at the activities of the RIC in Ireland, and aimed to force the British government to change its Irish policy. Over the course of the subsequent seven-and-a-half months, Volunteers mounted at least 239 operations, mainly taking the form of burning property. Targets included farms, factories, warehouses, communications and railway infrastructure situated in and around the cities of Liverpool, London, Manchester, Newcastle-upon-Tyne and Glasgow. RIC men and their relatives were also attacked and a number of attempts were made to assassinate and kidnap politicians, soldiers and policemen. The offensive terminated with the truce of 11 July 1921 and Rory O'Connor judged it to have been quite successful. Its role in motivating the British government to embark on peace negotiations is almost impossible to ascertain. Michael Collins later told Reginald Dunne, Sam Maguire and Denis Kelleher that Lloyd George confessed to him at the opening of the treaty negotiations in October 1921 that 'The destructive work of your London Unit caused my Government greater concern than that of your whole organisation in Ireland'.[197] However, this seems unlikely. Seán Ó Murthuile believed that the campaign 'had the effect of concentrating the average Englishman's attention of [i.e. on] what was being done in Ireland in his name'. He was doubtful, however, if Englishmen, thus enlightened, actually influenced the government's thinking on the Irish problem.[198] Yet, the fact that the activities of the 'murder gang', as the British prime minister called it, precipitated the provision of increased security for senior politicians surely brought home to legislators, at the most personal level, the implications of their Irish policy.[199] At the very least, the campaign was 'a thorn in the side of the authorities'.[200] Charles Townshend has written that, 'on the British side,

---

196   Ronan Fanning, *Fatal Path: British Government and Irish Revolution, 1910–1922* (London: Faber & Faber, 2013), pp. 247–62

197   Seán Dillon to The Secretary, Office of the Referee, 6 Oct. 1936, enclosing 'London Battalion I.R.A.' (MSPC, RO/605)

198   Ó Murthuile manuscript, pp. 126–27 (RMP, P7a/209)

199   See Chapter 6

200   Paddy Daly interview (EO'MN, P17b/136)

some form of military struggle was inevitable before Irish demands would be taken seriously'.[201] Taking the war to Britain, therefore, served as an auxiliary to IRA violence in Ireland.

In the next chapter, we will look at the activities of republicans in Britain during the period of the truce and afterwards.

201 Charles Townshend, *The British Campaign in Ireland 1919–1921: The Development of Political and Military Policies* (London: Oxford University Press, 1975), p. 206

CHAPTER 4

Truce, Treaty and Dissension,
July 1921–June 1922

I

The truce began at noon on 11 July. With Sinn Féin demanding British recognition of the Irish republic and Lloyd George's government refusing to countenance Ireland's withdrawal from the empire, the likelihood of a peace agreement seemed remote. Many Volunteers, therefore, saw the truce as brief respite before the inevitable resumption of hostilities. 'I wonder if it would be possible to have a run down home for a few hours during this truce', Offaly man Paddy Daly asked Michael Collins. Promising that he would be back at his post in Liverpool 'within three or four days', he too believed that the ceasefire was only temporary.[1] Volunteers and Fenians in Britain, therefore, continued gun-smuggling and made arrangements for the recommencement of attacks. Consequently, it came as some surprise when Dublin and London reached an agreement in December. The 'Articles of Agreement for a Treaty' (known popularly as 'the treaty') divided the republican movement in Ireland and Britain and precipitated the outbreak of civil war in June 1922. This chapter, then, deals with republicanism when the pinnacle of its success precipitated its disaster. Sections II, III and IV deal with the truce period, discussing the problems experienced by the republican movement in Britain, along with gunrunning and the planning of attacks. Section V tackles the treaty, noting the arguments for and against of those closely associated with republicanism in Britain. Sections VI, VII and VIII address the period from January–June 1922, tracing the division among republicans regarding the merits of the treaty, continued gunrunning and the role the assassination of a Conservative MP played in the outbreak of the civil war. Section IX concludes.

1 Paddy Daly to Michael Collins, 11 July 1921 (RMP, P7/A/6)

II

In September and October 1921, Rory O'Connor toured IRA units in England, visiting London, Birmingham, Nottingham, Sheffield, Newcastle-upon-Tyne, Manchester and Liverpool. Membership of republican organizations seems to have peaked around this time. As we saw earlier, there were 682 Volunteers in 31 companies in England.[2] Meanwhile, the Scottish Brigade comprised 49 companies with a combined membership of around 2,000.[3] The total membership in Britain, therefore, in the autumn of 1921 was about 2,700. In addition, new companies were being organized in Tyneside, Leeds, Wolverhampton, Walsall and Swansea.[4] Recruitment to the Scottish Volunteers ceased in 1921, though accounts disagree as to the precise date, with one claiming 11 July, the day the truce came into operation, and the other 7 December, the day after the signing of a peace agreement between Sinn Féin and the British government.[5] With IRA membership having increased fivefold over the previous year and the organization enjoying a greater geographical spread, O'Connor advised that a divisional structure be created to effectively manage the force. He also recommended the establishment of 'an English General Head Quarters, somewhat similar to G.H.Q. Ireland'.[6]

The Cumann na mBan boasted at least 29 branches in Britain in October 1921, though the membership figures are not recorded. The London Cumann na mBan experienced significant growth during the truce period. Six delegates from Britain attended the organization's annual convention in October 1921. 'Don't think it is going to be peace', Countess Markievicz told the gathering. 'Go out and work as if the war was going to break out [again] next week.'[7] (Membership figures for the IRB and Na Fianna Éireann are not available for this period.)

2 O/C Britain to C/S, 9 Sept. 1921 (RMP, P7/A/24[63–65]); see Chapter 1
3 John Carney to C/S, 22 Feb. 1922 (SO'MP, MS 24,474); S. Fullerton to Minister for Defence, 31 Aug., 6 Sept. 1922 (MCP, A/06181)
4 O/C Britain to C/S, 9 Sept., 15 Oct. 1921 (RMP, P7/A/24[63–65], P7/A/29[264–73])
5 S. Fullerton to Minister for Defence, 31 Aug., 6 Sept. 1922 (MCP, A/06181); John Carney to C/S, 7 Dec. 1921 (SO'MP, MS 24,474)
6 O/C Britain to C/S, 9 Sept., 15 Oct. 1921 (RMP, P7/A/24[63–65], P7/A/29[264–73])
7 Report of Cumann na mBan Annual Convention, 22–23 Oct. 1921; 'List of those who have paid affiliation fees', Nov. 1920–Oct. 1921 (SHP, P106/1131[1–25], P106/1132[1–16]); BMHWS 945, Sorcha Nic Diarmada, pp. 6–7; see Chapter 1

Unemployment amongst the Volunteers in Britain was a major concern during the 11½ month period between the end of the war and the beginning of the civil war. On 20 July, Art O'Brien told Michael Collins that 38 London Volunteers had been out of work for some time and were consequently in need of assistance.[8] 'It is coming up against us now on all sides', he warned the following month, instancing cases in London, Manchester, Newcastle-upon-Tyne and other areas, 'and [it] is going to create a great deal of mischief, annoyance and unpleasantness, unless we deal with it now in a definite manner.'[9]

Though it was a problem for Volunteers throughout England (and presumably Wales and Scotland too), unemployment seems to have been particularly acute in London. The situation was one of 'continual risk and menace', O'Brien asserted in August, and, with the number of cases of distress increasing, it was getting 'more serious as each day goes by'.[10] Two months later, Rory O'Connor confirmed the extent of the problem in Newcastle-upon-Tyne and Sheffield. However, it was London that concerned him most. Noting that financial troubles were forcing some of the men to sleep on the streets and another to eat for only four days a week, he feared for the continued existence of Volunteer units in the capital.[11]

Seán Golden provided specific details on 16 Volunteers in need of assistance in London. All had joined before the truce. Other Volunteers who had joined after 11 July were also experiencing distress, he noted, but as their commanders had not yet 'proved the worth of these men', they had been omitted from the list. Of the 16, six had lost their jobs due to their employers believing them to have been involved in the IRA's campaign of violence. In the North London Company, for example, J. Walsh and J. Woodrofe, a cooper and a motor mechanic respectively, had both lost their jobs due to being suspected of participation in IRA activities. Of the remaining ten people, six had become unemployed due to the economic turndown, while the other four had been unable to find work. The men's respective commanders recommended that each receive financial assistance of between £1 10s. and £3 10s. per week. The total sum for the 16 Volunteers was £37 per week.[12] Two months later, in February 1922, the situation had only worsened. M. O'Higgins, for example, a squad

8 Art O'Brien to Michael Collins, 20 July 1921 (AÓBP, MS 8430/18)

9 O'Brien to Collins, 22 Aug. 1921 (DÉ, 2/331)

10 O'Brien to Collins, 10 Aug. 1921 (AÓBP, MS 8430/19)

11 O/C Britain to C/S, 15 Oct. 1921 (RMP, P7/A/29[264–73])

12 London Battalion QM to Art O'Brien, n.d., but *c.* 3 Dec. 1921 (AÓBP, MS 8424/13)

leader in 'A' Company who had worked in a post office, was '[t]hrown out of work owing to arrest and internment'.[13]

Initial attempts to address the plight of the London men highlighted problems within republican ranks in the capital. The first concerned the personality of Reginald Dunne. 'He is, as you know, an excellent young fellow, and I have the greatest regard for him', O'Brien told Collins, '[but] unfortunately, he is young, and he has no experience, and is very sensitive, evidently, to guidance from anybody else.'[14] Believing that the unemployment problem should be handled by republicans in London, Dunne had refused to bring the issue to the attention of GHQ in Dublin. He was also very reluctant to supply O'Brien with a clear statement on the issue. Dunne thought that each of the 38 unemployed Volunteers should receive £2 per week. With the IRA lacking the funds necessary to supply such assistance, he believed that he was entitled to demand the money from Irish organizations in London. Having first been alerted to the whole issue by a member of the ISDL informing him that an IRA officer had demanded £100 from him, O'Brien disagreed with Dunne's approach. As bodies such as the ISDL and the Irish National Aid and Central Distress Fund (INACDF) were subject to public audit, their donating large sums of money to the IRA could not be countenanced, he argued. Moreover, the ISDL did not have such funds in any case, and the INACDF was not established to cater for such needs. That, however, did not stop Dunne instructing his officers to approach treasurers of local ISDL branches for money. O'Brien said the treasurers were being threatened by the IRA men, while Dunne preferred to describe their approaches as 'demands'.[15] Rory O'Connor supported Dunne. Despite the existence of various Irish societies in the capital, money had been lacking to allow a comprehensive tackling of the unemployment problem, he complained. Concerts had raised a small amount of money, but the situation was such that Seán Golden had been forced to 'practically extract money from members of the G.A.A.'.[16]

The role to be played by the Cumann na mBan in any solution was also a subject of controversy. O'Brien maintained that the women's auxiliary should mount collections for funds, 'and if they cannot do this essential work, it is difficult to see what justifies their existence over here'. However,

13 O'Brien to Richard Mulcahy, 16 Feb. 1922, enclosing list by Reginald Dunne (AÓBP, MS 8424/13)

14 O'Brien to Michael Collins, 20 July 1921 (AÓBP, MS 8430/18)

15 O'Brien to Collins, 20 July 1921 (AÓBP, MS 8430/18)

16 O/C Britain to C/S, 15 Oct. 1921 (RMP, P7/A/29[264–73])

relations between the IRA and the Cumann na mBan in the capital had always been tense.[17] This situation was compounded by the latter recently experiencing a split. As we saw earlier, so as to avoid unwanted attention, the Cumann na mBan in London had gone under the name of the Irish Ladies Distress Committee during the war.[18] However, with the advent of the truce, a number of members wearied of the subterfuge. 'They wanted us to do what the Cumann na mBan did here [in Ireland] openly such as marching in uniforms openly in military formation', remembered Sorcha McDermott. 'It was ridiculous in a foreign country.' As a result, Grace Lally and a group of about 12 women formed a rival outfit in West London openly calling itself the Cumann na mBan. The organization's executive in Dublin refused to recognize Lally's group.[19] However, believing that Lally's outfit contained the 'best material' and that McDermott's unit was 'not only useless, but dangerous', Dunne recognized the former and called on the executive to reverse its decision. McDermott's group retaliated by questioning the prudence of allowing a former British army soldier to occupy the leadership of the IRA in the capital. The row affected the distressed Volunteers. When Dunne asked the Cumann na mBan to help raise funds to pay for an IRA man's hospital treatment, McDermott's group agreed to do so only if the O/C London told them the name of the hospital in which he was staying. Dunne refused.[20] Describing the resultant situation as 'hopeless', O'Brien tried to impress upon the O/C London that he had no authority in the affairs of the women's auxiliary, but Dunne insisted otherwise. Overall, O'Brien described Dunne as stubborn and lacking perspective and of having 'muddled notions'. Collins agreed.[21] However, Rory O'Connor placed the blame on the Cumann na mBan. Meeting a representative of the executive in London, he demanded that Dublin order McDermott's branch to cease interfering with and criticizing Dunne and his Volunteers. Moreover, while advising the O/C London to recognize both sections of the women's auxiliary, he counselled him to keep them at arm's length.[22]

In place of Dunne's and Golden's alarmingly direct approach, Collins and O'Brien proposed that funds be raised from the various Irish organizations in

17 Art O'Brien to Michael Collins, 20 July 1921 (AÓBP, MS 8430/18)

18 See Chapter 1

19 BMHWS 945, Sorcha Nic Diarmada, pp. 6–7

20 O/C Britain to C/S, 15 Oct. 1921 (RMP, P7/A/29[264–73])

21 Correspondence between Art O'Brien and Michael Collins, 20, 23 July 1921 (AÓBP, MS 8430/18)

22 O/C Britain to C/S, 15 Oct. 1921 (RMP, P7/A/29[264–73])

a consensual manner. The distribution of the money would then be entrusted to the INACDF, an organization which had been created in early 1921 by combining the various fund-raising groups, including the INAVDF, that had been established in Britain in support of the republican movement. Before this, the INACDF had used its money to defend suspects arrested in Britain and to maintain the families of men tried and convicted in Britain as well as the dependents of men from Ireland incarcerated in British prisons.[23] Collins and O'Brien's scheme was put in place. In January 1922, however, O'Brien complained that the 'wretched truce' was frustrating the administration of relief.[24] In response, Dunne suggested that a 'combined civil & military board of inquiry' be established to investigate the situation. Each Volunteer experiencing hardship would be interviewed by the board, which would be composed of two INACDF officials, two IRA officers and a chairman.[25] Taking the recommendation on board, a joint committee of the INACDF began hearing cases and dispensing relief in the form of weekly grants of between 10s. and £4. On 22 February, for example, the committee approved a weekly grant to 12 men: two were to receive 10s., one 15s., four £1, three £1 10s. and two £2.[26] In March 1922, O'Brien estimated that the organization had received over 100 applications for aid, along with numerous requests for 'special grants'.[27] Such grants often gave applicants the funds necessary to move to Ireland. A Volunteer named Creaghan, for example, injured in an explosion in a munitions factory in Greenwich in July 1921, was in receipt of a weekly payment of £2 and had it exchanged for a lump sum of £5 to finance his return to Ireland.[28]

However, the decisions of the joint committee soon became the subject of controversy. Patrick Kerrigan, a member of Tyneside's 'A' Company, complained of having received no assistance. He and two others had been on trial for setting fire to hay stacks on a farm in Durham in late March 1921. Set free when the jury failed to agree a verdict in his case, Kerrigan lost his job as a result of the press publicity. Living with his parents and his five younger

---

23 Correspondence between Michael Collins and Art O'Brien, 8, 10 Nov. 1921 (DÉ, 2/451)

24 O'Brien to Reginald Dunne, 17 Jan. 1922 (AÓBP, MS 8424/16)

25 Dunne to O'Brien, 4 Feb. 1922 (AÓBP, MS 8424/13)

26 Minutes of Joint Committee of Irish National Aid Committee, held at 182 Shaftesbury Avenue, 22 Feb. 1922 (AÓBP, MS 8432/9)

27 Art O'Brien to James Lawless, 9 Mar. 1922 (AÓBP, MS 8429/21)

28 Correspondence between Seán McGrath and O'Brien, 17, 18 May 1922 (AÓBP, MS 8432/9); see p. 206 below

brothers, he was in straitened circumstances as his father did not work and he himself was unable to find employment. Meanwhile, the men who were on trial with him, Patrick Coyne and Michael Wynne, having been released from prison under the general amnesty in February 1922, were receiving £1 10s. per week. Kerrigan felt he was entitled to the same relief, describing it as 'a down wright [sic] shame leaving one man out of a Bunch'.[29] At a meeting of his local ISDL branch, he was offered £5 relief. However, outraged to learn that some of his Tyneside comrades were being given larger sums, up to £15 10s., he refused the offer. 'The least I expected from the I.N.A. [i.e. INACDF] was to get my board and lodgings paid', he complained. Demanding that his case be revisited, he stated that if he did not receive proper treatment, he would reveal all the details to his fellow ISDL members and then resign from the league and 'A' Company. 'I am treated since I came out of jail [i.e. acquitted of the charge] as if I was a Black & Tan', he protested. 'If I was a one [sic] I would be working to-day, not parading the streets.' His comrades were receiving kudos and financial rewards for their involvement in IRA operations but Kerrigan, who had, despite his acquittal, partaken in the arson operation, was receiving nothing.[30]

However, the most serious complaint came from William Robinson, the London IRA man who, following his acquittal on a charge of attempting to set fire to a warehouse in London on 27 November 1920, had been sentenced to 12 years for shooting at policemen in Bromley seven months later. 'I am merely an unemployed & invalid ex-convict living on the charity of my parents, in receipt of no assistance whatever', he complained in April 1922. Had he not sacrificed his 'health', 'piece of mind [sic]', 'pocket-money', 'time' and 'liberty' for Ireland, he would now be working in a professional job, he claimed.[31] Robinson failed to mention that he and his brother Charles had been expelled from the London IRA for 'certain military offences'. Dunne believed that recent events pointed to the brothers, whom he condemned as 'pests', having informed the police of the identities of certain Volunteers.[32] Robinson also never acknowledged that he and his family had already received £124 from the INACDF over the previous five months: £30 was granted to his father to fund his passage to India, his mother received £30

---

29 Patrick Kerrigan to O'Brien, 5 Mar. 1922 (AÓBP, MS 8432/21); Barrington, *Irish Independence Movement*, p. 16; *MG*, 11 July 1921
30 Kerrigan to O'Brien, 11 Mar. 1922 (AÓBP, MS 8432/21)
31 William Robinson to O'Brien, 25 Apr. 1922 (AÓBP, MS 8432/21)
32 Reginald Dunne to O'Brien, 24 Apr. 1922 (AÓBP, MS 8432/21)

to complete the purchase of a motor bicycle, £52 10s. was paid for two operations on Robinson's nose, £6 10s. covered dental charges and £5 was given to Robinson's mother to enable her to visit him in Parkhurst prison.[33] Unsurprisingly perhaps, the INACDF declined Robinson's request for further financial assistance.[34]

O'Brien worried, however, that Robinson's case was attracting 'notoriety' due to the allegations he was making against the INACDF. In particular, Robinson alleged that assistance was being granted to dozens of men 'who have not lost one penny piece for Ireland' and who had little connection with any Irish organization prior to the truce. In addition, he stated that he knew of cases where men had deliberately left their jobs so as to claim assistance from the fund. Moreover, he claimed that he had proof that 'blackguards of the convert type' were also in receipt of funds.[35] O'Brien wrote to Robinson demanding that he substantiate these allegations, which were doing 'much harm'.[36] In particular, such charges of corruption were frustrating INACDF collections amongst the Irish population in London. Indeed, by May 1922 O'Brien feared that in the absence of 'a considerable revival of support from our people', the organization would soon have to cease operation. One woman, for example, declined O'Brien's invitation to an entertainments evening. Due to the 'misappropriation of these funds by headquarters in London', she felt unable to contribute to an event some of whose proceeds were going to the INACDF. She added that she would attend the event if the money was sent to Ireland instead.[37]

Five weeks later, Robinson detailed his accusations against the INACDF. He levelled charges of corruption, obtaining money by false pretences and misappropriation of funds against five people, including Reginald Dunne. He charged that in late 1921 and early 1922 two of the 'soi-distant "men's representatives"' on the INACDF's joint civil and military board had conspired to raise funds for 'corrupt purposes'. He then made the vague contention that the representatives had used their position of power to 'bribe, or to attempt to bribe certain men, in order that they should do what they, the

33 Correspondence between Séan McGrath and O'Brien, 29 Apr. 1922 (AÓBP, MS 8432/21)

34 McGrath to William Robinson, 26 Apr. 1922 (AÓBP, MS 8432/21)

35 Art O'Brien to McGrath, 29 Apr.; Robinson to O'Brien, 25 Apr. 1922 (AÓBP, MS 8432/21)

36 O'Brien to Robinson, 28 Apr. 1922 (AÓBP, MS 8432/21)

37 Connie Creaghan to O'Brien, 19 Apr.; O'Brien to D.H. Evans, 1 May; O'Brien to Seán Golden, 18 May 1922 (AÓBP, MS 8432/21)

said certain men, believed to be wrong'. Thirdly, he alleged that one of the representatives had misappropriated a sum of money voted by the board. Finally, he contended that the representatives had managed the affairs of the board 'in a most tyrannical, autocratic and impudent manner'.[38] He had already aired some of these allegations at a meeting of the Lewisham branch of the ISDL. It was 'pretty evident that Robinson is out to make mischief', O'Brien commented when a report of the meeting appeared in the London *Catholic Herald*.[39] Robinson also hinted at an allegation of embezzlement against O'Brien himself. It concerned a complicated series of payments and re-payments involving O'Brien, Robinson's mother and the INACDF in relation to the purchase or sale of two motorbikes by the London IRA.[40] Robinson further brought to O'Brien's attention the fact that members of the capital's Volunteers had yet to return two bicycles which they had borrowed from their owners in late 1921.[41]

In the end, however, despite his litany of complaints and allegations, Robinson proved amicable. He met the INACDF committee on 17 June. The organization decided to help him to pay his remaining bills and he professed himself satisfied that he had 'secured justice'. He now believed that the INACDF had 'done their best for me, having regard to their lack of funds'.[42]

The unemployment problem in London highlighted difficulties of personality and organization in the ranks of the capital's republican movement. Reginald Dunne's abrasive character caused another problem in October 1921, when he unilaterally prohibited his men from attending Gaelic League classes. His motivation was apparently concern that their presence would bring unwelcome attention on the Volunteers. 'The war is not over; and I shall not cancel this order until peace is declared', he wrote. He assured O'Brien that he was not hostile to the Gaelic League itself, though he held that many of its London members were 'deserving of contempt'.[43] Exasperated, O'Brien

---

38 William Robinson to Joint Honorary Secretary of the INACDF, 4 June 1922 (AÓBP, MS 8432/21)

39 Art O'Brien to Séan McGrath, 20 May 1922 (AÓBP, MS 8432/21)

40 Correspondence between O'Brien and James Mooney, 13, 17, 18 May; correspondence between O'Brien and Séan Golden, 18 May, 7 June 1922 (AÓBP, MS 8432/21)

41 William Robinson to O'Brien, 10 June 1922 (AÓBP, MS 8424/13)

42 Robinson to O'Brien, 22, 23 July 1922 (AÓBP, MS 8432/21)

43 Correspondence between O'Brien and Reginald Dunne, 15, n.d., but *c.* 16–24 Oct. 1921 (AÓBP, MS 8424/16)

reproached Dunne for having failed to consult him before he issued the order. 'Without really generous co-operation from you, it will almost be impossible to prevent misunderstandings taking place amongst all the different organisations here', he explained.[44]

Another problem afflicting the London IRA was the tension that existed amongst the rank and file Volunteers, some Irish-born, others born and reared in Britain. 'The men from each [Irish] county hang together like Freemasons', Dunne complained. 'Cork men think that their men of their city & county have won the war; Kerry men imagine they are the salt of the earth – & so on.' This rivalry was exacerbated by the men from Ireland scorning those born in London. Many of the latter were quite sensitive about their accents and mannerisms.[45]

However, it was the Scottish Brigade that exhibited the most serious problems. John Carney, Brigade O/C, convened a meeting for 13 November in Uddingston in order to review the outfit's finances. Officers of the 2nd Battalion, however, failed to attend. Instead, they sent Carney a letter stating that they refused to allow their QMs to attend any meeting until they were satisfied that he had authority from GHQ to convene such meetings. Carney claimed that the officers of the 2nd Battalion knew full well that Dublin had so empowered him, noting that they had obeyed his command to hand over their funds to him when he last did so, six months before. Carney, therefore, had 'no alternative but to bring a charge of mutiny against each and all of the Officers of the 2nd Battalion'. 'What makes these charges more serious', he noted, 'is that our country is at war at the present time.' He then travelled to Dublin to submit a report on the incident to GHQ.[46]

Subsequently, Joe Vize arrived in Scotland and told Carney that he would assume command of the brigade, a position he had held up to July 1920. Carney, however, found Vize's attitude 'most irregular'. Thinking, moreover, that Vize intended treachery towards him, due to his reminding the Wexford man 'of the several Officers of the S[cottish].B[rigade]. whom he [i.e. Vize] had let down', Carney offered to resign if it was felt that he had acted incorrectly. Vize refused the offer, but offered him an honourable discharge if he wished to leave the organization. Vize then decided to postpone the proposed court-martial in order to give himself time to enquire into the matter. Noting in February 1922 that the investigation had yet to be held,

44 O'Brien to Dunne, 24 Oct. 1921 (AÓBP, MS 8424/16)

45 O/C London to O/C Britain, 24 Oct. 1921 (RMP, P7/A/27[49–50])

46 John Carney to C/S, n.d. but *c.* 7 Dec. 1921, 22 Feb. 1922 (SO'MP, MS 24,474)

Carney complained that Vize had effectively encouraged disobedience of orders, so creating an unenviable situation for whoever was to succeed him as brigadier, Carney himself having resigned. 'My impression now', he wrote, 'is that he [i.e. Vize] never intended to hold any Enquiry, this being only a subterfuge in order to shield his friends in the 2nd Battalion'.[47]

This tense situation was then compounded by the police capturing 13 Volunteers, including the O/C 1st Battalion, while they were packing munitions into boxes in a hall attached to St Joseph's Church, near Tullcross, Glasgow, on 23 December. Carney blamed Vize for the fiasco, claiming that if he had arrived sooner on Clydeside from Dublin, instead of travelling to Motherwell for underhand purposes, the issue of backlogged munitions could have been dealt with sooner and the arrests avoided. Vize, however, blamed the O/C 1st Battalion for the debacle. Carney was outraged: 'I never thought Commandant Vize could be so unscrupulous, and dishonourable, in order to take the blame from his own shoulders for the loss of the material at Tullcross, and to save his friends at Motherwell.' He also stated that Vize had started organizing a new brigade in Scotland without informing him, thus throwing the existing brigade into confusion. In late February 1922, Carney travelled to Dublin to discuss the situation with the new C/S, Eoin O'Duffy having succeeded Richard Mulcahy. Unfortunately, the upshot of that meeting and subsequent developments in regard to the whole situation are not known.[48]

III

'[F]or us in England there was no Truce; in fact if anything our activities were intensified', recollected the Birmingham gunrunner James Cunningham.[49] Michael Collins encouraged the continuation of gun-smuggling during the ceasefire. The opening of new sources 'may be very much more important in the future', he wrote in September 1921, 'and we might [i.e. must] be prepared for absolutely all eventualities', hinting at the possible collapse of the peace talks and the resumption of war.[50]

Gunrunning continued under the direction of the same figures as during the closing stages of the war: Paddy Daly in Liverpool, Cunningham

---

47 Carney to C/S, n.d. but *c.* 7 Dec. 1921, 22 Feb. 1922 (SO'MP, MS 24,474)
48 Carney to C/S, 22 Feb. 1922 (SO'MP, MS 24,474); *MG*, 27 Dec. 1921
49 BMHWS 922, James Cunningham, p. 14
50 Michael Collins to Paddy Daly, 19 Sept. 1921 (RMP, P7/A/7)

in Birmingham, Denis Kelleher and Seán Golden in London, Gilbert Barrington in Newcastle-upon-Tyne. In August, D.P. Walsh, John Carney and 11 others were acquitted of the murder of Inspector Johnston in Glasgow on 4 May. However, Walsh was immediately re-arrested on a charge of having escaped from Strangeways Prison in October 1919.[51] GHQ does not seem to have appointed anyone to succeed him in directing gun-smuggling activities in Scotland during the truce. When Barrington was arrested in October 1921, David Fitzgerald, adjutant of the Tyneside Battalion, stepped into the breach.[52]

Munitions were acquired using the same means employed during the war. Between 11 July and 6 December, the Scottish police suspected the IRA of responsibility for eight thefts from collieries. For example, on 26 August, 30 lbs (13.6 kg) of gelignite was stolen from Gorehill Colliery, near the Lanarkshire village of Longriggend, while between 30 September and 8 October, 1,350 detonators and 25 coils of fuse were taken from an explosives store in High Bonnybridge. In total, the property stolen in the eight incidents was estimated at £40 6s.[53]

In late September, a drill hall was raided in Birmingham. Volunteers in Liverpool and Birmingham had begun making preparations for the operation months earlier. In May, Paddy Daly said that he expected the raid to net 100 rifles, two machine guns and a large quantity of ammunition 'without any difficulty'.[54] Two weeks later, one of the Birmingham men, probably James Cunningham, told him that the hall also contained 15 cwt (762 kg) of explosive cordite.[55] The summer passed, however, without the raid being mounted. Perhaps in an attempt to motivate Daly, on 21 September Collins reminded him that ammunition 'is one of our greatest wants, so that no opportunity should be lost of obtaining it'.[56] The following day, Daly reported that the raid had taken place. Four Lee Enfield rifles and just under 3,500 rounds of .303 ammunition had been secured but, perhaps comparing it with his high expectations, he pronounced the episode 'a dismal failure'.[57] Fearful that the use of a motor car might have attracted the attention of the police

51 *Glasgow Herald*, 22 Aug. 1921
52 David Fitzgerald to D/P, 4 Jan. 1922, reprinted in Barrington, *Irish Independence Movement*, pp. 28–29
53 Scottish Office to Carew-Robinson, HO, 20 Nov. 1922 (HO, 144/4645)
54 Paddy Daly to Michael Collins, 23 May 1921 (RMP, P7/A/5)
55 Daly to Collins, 6 June 1921 (RMP, P7/A/5)
56 Collins to Daly, 21 Sept. 1921 (RMP, P7/A/7)
57 Daly to Collins, 22 Sept. 1921 (RMP, P7/A/7)

and consequently precipitated a political controversy regarding the breaking of the truce agreement, the Volunteers were forced to carry the booty on their persons, thus limiting the amount of rifles they were able to remove. Daly thought it might be possible to mount another raid but only after the truce had collapsed, as a second operation without the use of a motor car was not worth effecting.[58] Collins, however, disagreed with Daly's view that the raid was a failure. 'If the Cork no. 3 [Brigade] had had it [i.e. the 3,500 rounds of ammunition] at one period in last February, they would have smashed up 650 of the enemy', he enthused.[59]

IRA gunrunners in Wales also mounted raids. Operations were headed by J.P. Connolly, who worked under Liam Mellows. Connolly's day job was that of an ISDL organizer and he used the league as a recruiting ground for agents. Among those who aided his clandestine activities were Michael Donoghue, David Evans and his wife Kate, Maurice O'Toole and Thomas Tierney. 'I am working Bargoed [,] Penjam [sic] & Blackwood myself', Connolly told David Evans in October 1921, referring to towns in South Wales, 'don't cover that ground please.'[60] The types of weapons acquired by the gunrunners included Lee Enfield rifles, handguns, ammunition, detonators and fuse, though the quantities are not recorded.[61] Once procured, the munitions seem to have followed a circuitous route to Ireland, travelling via Cardiff, Newcastle-upon-Tyne, Connolly's old stomping ground, and Liverpool.[62]

Sometime in August, Connolly told Mellows that, although misfortune had dogged his activities up until now, he trusted that things would soon improve. He was making arrangements in connection with an army barracks in Hampshire and hoped for 'big things'.[63] On 29 August, 19 short .303 rifles, valued at £133, were duly stolen from Aliwal Barracks in Tidworth.[64] Buoyed by this successful operation, Evans suggested that a number of army magazines in his area could be raided and Connolly asked Mellows for authorization.[65] The D/P evidently granted permission, for on the night of 10–11 October

58 Daly to Collins, 24 Sept. 1921 (RMP, P7/A/7)
59 Collins to Daly, 26 Sept. 1921 (RMP, P7/A/7)
60 J.P. Connolly to D. Evans, n.d., but postmarked 12 Oct. 1921 (AÓBP, MS 8442/5)
61 List of munitions purchased, n.d. (AÓBP, MS 8442/5)
62 Gilbert Barrington to J.P. Connolly, 21 Sept. 1921 (AÓBP, MS 8442/5)
63 Connolly to Liam Mellows, n.d., but *c*. Aug. 1921 (AÓBP, MS 8442/5)
64 CC of Hants to the ASS, HO, 13 Oct. 1922 (HO, 144/4645)
65 J.P. Connolly to Liam Mellows, 21 Sept. 1921 (AÓBP, MS 8442/5)

almost 5,300 detonators and 100 gelignite cartridges were taken from the powder magazine at the Thomas Merthyr Colliery in Waunwyllt. Two nights later, 500 fuses and a 50 lb (22.7 kg) box of compressed powder were stolen from the central magazine at the same colliery.[66] A few hours after the first theft was discovered, however, a policeman had noticed David and Kate Evans carrying an attaché case and a parcel at Merthyr Tydfil railway station. When the theft at the central magazine was uncovered two days later, the police again found the husband and wife on the train bound for Cardiff with two attaché cases. Detained at the police station, they and their luggage were searched. The cases were found to contain 1,000 detonators, another five boxes of detonators and 100 gelignite cartridges, part of the batch stolen on 10–11 October. Also, a handbook containing gunrunning accounts was found on David Evans, as was a key to the central magazine and a letter-card from Connolly in Cardiff. Connolly was arrested at his lodgings in possession of 'a large quantity of firearms, Explosives etc'.[67] Incriminating documents found in his possession allowed the police to smash his gun-smuggling network. In Cardiff, Michael Donoghue and Thomas Tierney were quickly arrested and gelignite was seized.[68] In Liverpool, John Fitzgerald, an old Fenian who allowed the IRA to operate an arms dump in his house, was taken into custody. The munitions seized by the police at Fitzgerald's house were obsolete, Paddy Daly told Michael Collins, but the loss of a good dump was a setback.[69] Meanwhile, in Newcastle-upon-Tyne, a large quantity of explosives was found in the house of Arnold Margetts, 'an Englishman who had been of occasional use [to the Volunteers] in getting arms'. The munitions had been stolen earlier that month from Bebside Colliery by men from 'E' Company. Richard Purcell and Gilbert Barrington were arrested soon afterwards. Connolly, Donoghue, the Evans and Tierney were found guilty of contravening the Explosive Substances Act 1883. All were sentenced to seven years' imprisonment, except Connolly who received a 14-year sentence. Meanwhile, Purcell, Barrington and Margetts were found guilty of possessing high explosives with intent to endanger life and of conspiring with Connolly and others to contravene the Act. The IRA men were sentenced to three years

66 Deposition of William Price, 10 Nov. 1921 (TNA, Director of Public Prosecutions File [DPP], 1/64)

67 CC of Merthyr Tydfil to the DPP, 14 Oct.; James Abbs to the Attorney General, 24 Oct.; deposition of Charles Hunter, 10 Nov. 1921 (DPP, 1/64)

68 *TT,* 15 Oct. 1921

69 Paddy Daly to Michael Collins, 18 Oct. 1921 (RMP, P7/A/7); BMHWS 814, Patrick Daly, pp. 10–11

in prison, while Margetts received one year with hard labour.[70] Fitzgerald, meanwhile, got a ten-year sentence.[71]

The British government considered Connolly's activities and those of a gunrunner captured in Hamburg to be of the 'gravest character', Lloyd George told the Irish delegates at the peace conference on 21 October, for it proved that the truce was being used 'to accumulate destructive stores for the purpose of manufacturing bombs and arming your forces'. (He was correct. As we saw earlier, in March or April 1921 the IRA's arsenal consisted of 2,035 firearms. By the end of October, it had increased to 61 machine guns, 3,295 rifles, 15,260 shotguns, 5,197 handguns, 327,812 rounds of ammunition for rifles, handguns and shotguns, 8,423 grenades and 5,303 kg of explosives.[72]) Michael Collins replied that the importation of weapons was not in violation of the terms of the ceasefire. However, in the interests of pursuing peace, 'they would agree to import no arms into Ireland'.[73] The concession angered Cathal Brugha, partly because he had not been consulted beforehand. Grudgingly, however, he agreed to abide by the commitment, except in relation to consignments for which he had already paid.[74]

In fact, however, gunrunning continued as normal. In November, John Creana, Henry Collins and Herbert Friday attempted to entice soldiers in Chatham Barracks near London to supply them with munitions. 'We want a quantity of ammunition, and will pay spot cash', Friday told one of the soldiers, with Creana later offering to pay £10 per 1,000 rounds of .303 or .455 ammunition, along with £100 for the soldier's help. The soldier, however, informed his superior officer of the approach and the trio were arrested, tried and convicted.[75]

The capital saw a second such episode end with equally disastrous results. As noted earlier, sometime towards the end of the war, Denis Kelleher had made contact with Sergeant Michael Roche, a Kilkenny man in the Irish

70 *Newcastle Daily Chronicle*, 21, 25 Oct., 11 Nov. 1921; *IT*, 18 Nov. 1921; CC of Northumberland to the USS, HO, 19 Oct. 1922 (HO, 144/4645); BMHWS 773, Gilbert Barrington, p. 13

71 List of prisoners in custody for offences connected with the Sinn Fein movement who were convicted in England and Wales, n.d. (HO, 144/4645)

72 QMG, 'Statement of Munitions – October, 1921' (EO'ML, P17a/2); see Chapter 2

73 Thomas Jones, *Whitehall Diary, iii: Ireland 1918–1925*, ed. Keith Middlemas (London: Oxford University Press, 1971), pp. 138, 145

74 BMHWS 410, Mrs Austin Stack, p. 48; C/S to all O/Cs, 17 Nov. 1921 (MCP, A/0772/XII)

75 *IT*, 23 Dec. 1921; list of prisoners amnestied on 1 Apr. 1922 (HO, 144/4645)

Guards based in Chelsea Barracks. On a number of occasions, Roche smuggled small amounts of weapons out of the barracks to the gunrunners' car parked nearby. In November 1921, a group of IRA men from Ireland arrived in Britain on a mission. Having received £1,000 from Cathal Brugha, Clare's Michael Brennan had sent the men, led by Michael Hogan, to London to buy some materiel. Learning of Roche, the Clare men decided to mount a raid on a barracks. Kelleher thought the plan impossible and refused to introduce them to Roche or allow them use of the car. However, Hogan eventually got in touch with Roche, now working in Windsor Barracks, and after plying him with alcohol and promising him money, they agreed a deal. On 19 November, Roche, Hogan and a third man drove into Chelsea Barracks in a taxi. From the store room they surreptitiously removed two Lewis machine guns and two rifles, placed them in the taxi and left the scene. Two nights later, the gang targeted Windsor Barracks, where they stole four Vickers machine guns and 18 rifles. However, the police evidently had Roche under surveillance, for they found him on the Euston train for Dublin the following day and asked him to accompany them to Scotland Yard. On him was found a card with an address on Edgware Road. Visiting the address, the police found Hogan and two other men. On them they found notebooks detailing the purchase of munitions, the manufacture of explosives and shipping routes, along with a key to the lecture room at Windsor Barracks from where the machine guns had been taken. The six machine guns and 20 rifles were recovered in a yard in Shepherd's Bush. Questions were raised about the episode in the House of Commons. Lieut. Col. Croft, MP for Bournemouth, implied that members of the Irish delegation at the peace talks may have been involved in planning the raids. '[W]ere the delegates of Sinn Fein at the Conference exploring the avenues to Windsor and Chelsea barracks at the very moment that they were also exploring the avenues to allegiance at the Conference with His Majesty's Ministers?' he asked. Having promised the cessation of gunrunning the previous month, Michael Collins managed to convince the British government that the operations were unauthorized. Pleading guilty to conspiracy and turning king's evidence, Roche was sentenced to six months' imprisonment, while Hogan and John Cooley each received 12 months'. Hogan declared that just as the British government continued to manufacture arms and ammunition in spite of the truce so was the IRA entitled to build up its arsenal.[76]

76　See Chapter 2; Dennis Kelleher interview (EO'MN, P17b/107); Brennan, *War in Clare*, pp. 107–08; *TT*, 24 Nov., 3 Dec. 1921, 18, 19 Jan. 1922; *Hansard 5* (*Commons*), cxlix, cols. 244, 248 (15 Dec. 1921)

Liverpool also suffered mishaps. On 29 November, ten Thompson submachine guns, 14 handguns, a rifle and some ammunition were lost to eagle-eyed customs officials. Paddy Daly offered to 'take all responsibility for breach of truce agreement', but the incident does not seem to have caused a political controversy.[77] Just over a month later, another batch of munitions, including eight Thompsons, suffered the same fate.[78]

Liverpool continued to be the main centre for the despatch of munitions to Ireland. As is the case for the war, however, the nature of the sources at our disposal prevents the arrival at an accurate figure in regard to the total amount of armaments sent across the Irish Sea during the truce. According to the detailed extant records, dating from 11 July to 4 October, 20 machine guns, 45 rifles, 94 handguns and 11,501 rounds of ammunition were smuggled, along with 96.4 kg of explosives. There were six despatches in July, eight in August, 15 in September and one in October.[79] It was later stated that the three months from November 1921 to January 1922 saw Liverpool transmit two rifles, eight handguns, 4,200 rounds of ammunition and 232 empty Mills grenades. However, as the dates of despatch of specific items are not recorded, it is impossible to say what portion of this arsenal was sent before 6 December, the day the treaty was signed.[80] Only a small amount of the armoury transmitted up to 4 October was procured by the Liverpool gunrunners themselves. The vast majority was obtained by men elsewhere in Britain or abroad, such as the 17 Thompson machine guns which arrived from New York.[81] Birmingham sent the largest number of consignments to Merseyside: eight between 22 August and 28 September, and they included nine rifles, 14 handguns, 3,303 rounds of ammunition of various calibres and a ¼ lb (0.1 kg) box of gunpowder.[82] Over the same period, three loads were received from Tyneside, containing three German machine guns and nine rifles, along with 11 handguns, 425 rounds of ammunition of various calibres and 1 st (6.4 kg) of explosives.[83] (The Tyneside men claimed to

77 Paddy Daly to Michael Collins, 1, 5 Dec. 1921 (RMP, P7/A/7)

78 'RROUK', no. 139, 19 Jan. 1922 (CAB, 24/132)

79 Correspondence between Michael Collins and Paddy Daly, 11 July–4 Oct. 1921 (RMP, P7/A/6–P7/A/7)

80 Letter 30: 'UD' to 'P.L./Liverpool', 4 Apr. 1922 (ASSI, 13/52/2)

81 Paddy Daly to Michael Collins, 23 Aug., 6, 20 Sept., 6 Oct. 1921 (RMP, P7/A/7)

82 Daly to Collins, 22 Aug., 3, 10, 12, 19, n.d. but *c.*19/20, 27, 28 Sept. 1921 (RMP, P7/A/7)

83 Daly to Collins, 22 Aug., 27 Sept. 1921 (RMP, P7/A/7)

have delivered an additional nine handguns, 39 rounds of ammunition, five grenades, 3.2 kg of explosives and various other accoutrements unaccounted for in the Liverpool records.[84]) Manchester too sent three consignments, in July and August, including seven rifles, seven handguns and 11 bayonets.[85] Two batches arrived from Glasgow, amounting to five rifles and five bayonets, 14 handguns, 416 rounds of ammunition and 22 ordinary detonators.[86] London sent just one consignment, in August, consisting of eight handguns, 303 rounds of ammunition and a bayonet.[87] In early to mid-August, the newly founded Volunteers in Nottingham sent their first batch of munitions to Liverpool. On 19 August, Paddy Daly wrote to Michael Collins as follows:

Goods forwarded [to Ireland on] Aug.18th.21

Ex N-O-T [i.e. received from Nottingham]

11	Web[ley]. Rev[olver]s .45	94	r[oun]ds [of] 303 [ammunition]
2	Colt " "	40	" .45 Rev Amm.
1	Mauser Auto[matic] (P[eter the]. Painter)	120	" Morris Tube Amm
2	Auto.32	40	Sport Cart[ridge]s
1	Parab[ellum]. (long)	3	Coils [of] fuse
1	Auto.38 (Web & Scot)	75	yds. [of] cable
5	Batteries.	1	st[one]. Pot[assium]. Chlor[ate]
500	2oz stick [of] G[elignite].	75	rds [of].25 Auto Am.
142	Fuse Det[onator]s		
50	Elect[ric]. Dets[88]		

If gunrunners in London, Birmingham, Nottingham, Manchester, Newcastle-upon-Tyne and Glasgow despatched weapons and equipment directly to Ireland during the truce, it has not been recorded in any surviving sources.

It is likely, however, that much more munitions than those counted above were sourced and despatched from Britain. Between 11 July and 17 December, GHQ imported 51 machine guns, 313 rifles, 637 handguns and 98,481 rounds of ammunition for rifles, handguns and shotguns.[89] Many if not most

---

84 Note entitled 'By Car 24th September '21 – (Sat.)', reprinted in Barrington, *Irish Independence Movement*, pp. 26–27

85 Paddy Daly to Michael Collins, 25, 26 July, 17 Aug. 1921 (RMP, P7/A/7)

86 Daly to Collins, 17 Aug., 27 Sept. 1921 (RMP, P7/A/7)

87 Daly to Collins, 30 Aug. 1921 (RMP, P7/A/7)

88 Daly to Collins, 19 Aug. 1921 (RMP, P7/A/7)

89 QMG, 'Report on Activities of Department', 19 Dec. 1921 (EO'ML, P17a/2)

of these are likely to have passed through the hands of James Cunningham, Paddy Daly, Dennis Brennan and their gun-smuggling comrades.

IV

In September 1921, Cathal Brugha instructed Rory O'Connor to travel to Britain to organize and evaluate plans for an active offensive in the event of the peace negotiations breaking down. The O/C Britain doubted the ability of the Volunteers to launch anything on a 'large scale' similar to the Merseyside operation of 27 November 1920. Yet two developments gave him pause for thought. The fact that IRA units now covered a large part of England inspired optimism that 'operations on a wide area' were possible. Also, recent riots by the unemployed led him to believe that the jobless would prove more troublesome to the government from now on than they had to date, thus raising the possibility of their being used for republican purposes.[90]

Travelling about Britain, O'Connor sought to evaluate the 'military outlook' of officers. All those in London had a 'good' attitude, in that plans were now 'well advanced' for the execution of operations there. The officers in Newcastle-upon-Tyne, 'the best area in Britain', were intelligent and hard-working. The O/C Sheffield, a former officer in the British army, was 'the best man we have in Britain', according to an enthusiastic O'Connor: 'if this man could spend a month in Ireland he would be easily ranked with the best of our Brigade Commandants, he has big ideas on operations and personally, would, I believe be fearless in action'. He described the junior officers there as being impressive as well, displaying eagerness and diligence. However, the officers in other areas were not so imposing. He judged that those in Birmingham lacked 'the slightest military outlook'.[91] Meanwhile, in Manchester the leadership structure was confusing. O'Mara, O/C of No. 1 Company, was also in charge of No. 2 Company and the Rochdale Volunteers. Yet, Matt Lawless commanded the same companies although he did not have any rank. O'Connor judged O'Mara 'too timid' and Lawless – though a brilliant soldier – unfit for leadership. The only officer to display initiative by contemplating future operations was Adjutant Wallace, a former Royal Air Force officer who had recently transferred from the London IRA. The O/C Britain recommended that Wallace be promoted to the leadership of the Manchester Volunteers, for he was 'the only man amongst all other officers

90 O/C Britain to C/S, 9 Sept. 1921 (RMP, P7/A/24[63–65])
91 See Chapter 3

whom I met who is any use'. O'Connor was not impressed by the Liverpool officers either, finding them 'slow' and 'lacking initiative'. He noted that the city's IRA had experienced a high rate of turnover in its membership. All the officers had joined within the previous six months while about half the rank and file had left the organization since November 1920. Such high turnover was due to men leaving the city in search of employment. O'Connor considered this a serious problem, contending that 'men who are asked to operate in the city will do so with greater confidence if they are familiar with it'.[92]

The London Volunteers proposed to mount attacks on the following list of targets in the event of the peace talks failing:

Individuals
Goods, Sheds,
B[lack]&T[an] houses
Large Bus. Garage.
Ministry of Pensions, Regent Park
Sub. Stations of tube.
Maypole Dairy Factory.
Water main [in] Plaistow,
Tar & Rope Works, on River,
Railway Rolling Stock,
Certain points on Railways,
[Irish Police Advisor Major-General] Tudor['s] House (Bury St Edmond)[93]

The residences of Irish policemen and their relatives were the most popular targets for operations in the plans submitted by the various units. Interestingly, given how prevalent they were during the war, attacks on farms were only proposed by one unit, Birmingham. Manufacturing was to be hit too, with targets such as an oil factory, a rope works, a joiner's shop and a paper mill as well as power stations and infrastructure of all kinds – communications, road, rail, canal and lighting. Ambitiously, the Sheffield men planned to derail troop trains and flood the lower part of the city by bursting a dam. The London Volunteers also asked for permission to raid banks and post offices and to hold up pay-clerks. By mid-October, plans for 90 per cent of the operations had already been completed. O'Connor believed that 'good results' would be obtained from Newcastle-upon-Tyne,

92 O/C Britain to C/S, 15 Oct. 1921 (RMP, P7/A/29[264–73])
93 O/C Britain to C/S, 15 Oct. 1921 (RMP, P7/A/29[264–73])

London and Sheffield, Liverpool and Manchester 'may do something', but Birmingham 'cannot be relied upon'.[94]

A number of these operations required the use of explosives. Republicans in the capital had been experimenting in bomb-making for a number of months and one officer had perfected the design of an incendiary bomb, the manufacture of which did not require the employment of machinery. However, on 28 July, calamity struck: three explosions and a large fire engulfed their Greenwich bomb factory. A Volunteer named Michael McInerney later died of his injuries in hospital. 'It appears that the mixing pan had developed a leak', the IRA's director of chemicals reported, 'and as the incorporation was being done over a naked flame, the result was disastrous.' The repeated warnings of a trained chemist in the Volunteers as to the dangers inherent in using the same premises as a bomb factory, incendiary dump, garage and petrol store had been ignored.[95] The episode, however, did not stop the experimentation. Three months later, having witnessed the testing of an incendiary device and finding it 'satisfactory', Rory O'Connor made arrangements for three men to be assigned full-time to its manufacture. Contending that 400 such bombs could be produced per week, he argued that they could be supplied to Volunteer units through England, the cost of materials and labour being charged of course. Alternatively, London could send the explosives formula to those units equipped with a chemist, thus enabling them to begin manufacturing bombs themselves.[96]

During the war, the political leadership of republicanism had never publicly defended the actions of the IRA in Britain. This caused tension in some units. British-born Volunteers were risking their prosperity by involving themselves in Volunteer activities, Reginald Dunne argued. With 'very little to interest them materially in our cause' and sometimes encountering hostility from their parents, such men fought 'because of the blood that's in them'. Contending that such tensions probably existed in units in other parts of Britain as well, the O/C London argued that an address from GHQ, in the style of an exhortatory *An t-Óglác* article, would soothe them.[97] O'Connor took this argument on board. In the event of the truce breaking down, he recommended that the IRA in Britain be 'placed on a

---

94 O/C Britain to C/S, 15 Oct. 1921 (RMP, P7/A/29[264–73])

95 O/C Britain to C/S, n.d., but noted 28 Mar.; Director of Chemicals to C/S, 1 Aug. 1921 (RMP, P7/A/19[91], P7/A/23[219–20]); *MG*, 30 July, 2 Aug.; clipping from *Kentish Mercury*, 5 Aug. 1921 (MEPO, 3/489)

96 O/C Britain to C/S, 15 Oct. 1921 (RMP, P7/A/29[264–73])

97 O/C London to O/C Britain, 24 Oct. 1921 (RMP, P7/A/27[49–50])

proper footing', either by a declaration of the resumption of 'hostilities in England, as well as in Ireland, or by an official statement in An t-Oglac'. He also advised that Volunteers be instructed that, in the event of their being arrested and put on trial, they should declare their position to be 'soldiers acting under orders'.[98]

In an attempt to enlist British workers and the unemployed in a renewed campaign of violence, Cathal Brugha had discussions with Irish labour leaders and Willie Gallacher of the Communist Party of Great Britain (CPGB).[99] At the same time, British intelligence agents reported that republicans and Indian communists, meeting in Berlin in September 1921, had agreed to establish a 'United Committee of Action'. Its chief aim, alongside sourcing munitions with the help of the Comintern and the German Communist Party, was 'to simultaneously set fire to [such targets in England as] Government buildings, docks, jettys [sic], English warehouses and Police stations, and to destroy Railway lines, and bridges and telegraph wires and to loot Post-offices and treasuries, and to paralyse the Government in every possible way'. Irishmen and Indians were to unite to mount these attacks in London, attacking the India Office or removing 'undesirables', for example. In addition, Irish revolutionaries were to travel to Egypt and India to train their revolutionary brethren in these methods, presumably so that similar attacks could be mounted there.[100]

V

In July, Eamon de Valera, recently elected president of the Irish Republic, travelled to London for peace talks with Lloyd George, but they proved fruitless. Three months later, however, a peace conference began in London. The Irish delegation was led by Arthur Griffith, minister for foreign affairs, and included Michael Collins. Members of the London IRA, some of them unemployed, guarded the delegates' rented accommodation in South Kensington.[101] On 6 December, the Irish and British negotiators signed the treaty to end the war in Ireland. According to its terms, 26 of Ireland's 32 counties were to become the 'Irish Free State', enjoying dominion status within

98 O/C Britain to C/S, 15 Oct. 1921 (RMP, P7/A/29[264–73])

99 William O'Brien, *Forth the Banners Go: Reminiscences of William O'Brien as Told to Edward MacLysaght* (Dublin: Three Candles, 1969), p. 158

100 Intelligence reports on 'Irish Communist Party and Comintern', n.d., and 'United Committee of Action', n.d. (HO, 317/59)

101 Dennis Kelleher interview (EO'MN, P17b/107)

the British Commonwealth. The remaining six counties, in the north-east of the island, constituted Northern Ireland, a unionist-dominated statelet that had been created by Westminster in December 1920. Acknowledging strenuous nationalist opposition to the very existence of Northern Ireland, the treaty stated that, in the event of the statelet refusing to join the new Free State, a Boundary Commission would be established to decide on the border between the two polities. Other provisos set out that members of the new parliament in Dublin would be required to swear an oath of fidelity to the British monarch.[102]

Art O'Brien was unimpressed. A few months previously, he had dismissed dominion status as worthless. 'Ireland seeks, and has always sought, complete independence', he told a Spanish journalist, 'and when she speaks of a Republic she means "an Independent and Sovereign State".'[103] On 8 December, two days after the treaty was signed, he reiterated the position. 'Be not mislead into rejoicing and thanksgiving without cause or reason', he warned the readership of the *Irish Exile*.

> The claim of the people of Ireland is, and always has been, the recognition of the complete independence of their country. That is a claim no nation can forgo, and until it is met in their case the Irish race cannot rejoice.

The Irish delegation, he intimated, had been forced to agree to the terms under the threat of renewed war by the British. While the agreement constituted a 'milestone' on the road to achieving Ireland's freedom, it did not represent the attainment of freedom itself. Should Dáil Éireann vote to accept the terms, the Irish in Britain would 'bow their heads in resignation and take the road once again'.[104]

When Seán McGrath, released from Ballykinlar internment camp in County Down, told Michael Collins that he too disagreed with the settlement, the Cork man pointed to the problems the IRA was experiencing in Ireland: 'You know the difficulty we had in trying to get arms, he said. We hadn't enough arms to carry out a decent ambush, and if I had enough arms I wouldn't have signed the Treaty and you know that.'[105]

102 *Articles of Agreement for a Treaty Between Great Britain and Ireland* [Cmd. 1560] (1921)

103 Art O'Brien to Salvador de Madariaga, 8 Aug. 1921 (AÓBP, MS 8427/46)

104 *Irish Exile*, Dec. 1921

105 Seán McGrath interview (EO'MN, P17b/100); original emphasis

Dáil Éireann spent 13 days debating the treaty in December 1921 and January 1922. A number of speeches were made by people who had been associated with republicanism in Britain. Michael Collins presented the major defence of the agreement. 'In my opinion it gives us freedom, not the ultimate freedom that all nations desire and develop to, but the freedom to achieve it', he argued. The Irish negotiators 'were not in the position of conquerors dictating terms of peace to a vanquished foe', he reminded TDs. After all, the IRA 'had not beaten the enemy out of our country by force of arms'. Therefore, some compromise on the 'absolutely rigid line of the isolated Irish Republic' was inevitable. By ensuring the withdrawal of British military strength from Ireland, the treaty demonstrated that 'our national liberties are established'. He denied having signed the agreement under the threat of war from the British. However, he maintained that if the Dáil rejected the treaty, it would constitute 'a declaration of war until you have beaten the British Empire'.[106]

Cathal Brugha argued that acceptance of the agreement would be 'national suicide', as it would break the 'national tradition' of resistance to British rule that had been passed down from one generation to the next for centuries. 'We would be doing for the first time a thing that no generation ever thought of doing before', he declared, namely 'wilfully, voluntarily admitting ourselves to be British subjects, and taking the oath of allegiance voluntarily to the English King.' Ireland was currently in a strong position, while England was weak and beset with enemies. Therefore, Ireland should press its advantage.[107]

Liam Mellows disagreed with the contention from Collins that entering into negotiations inevitably entailed a compromise. The Irish delegates were sent to London, he argued, 'to make, if they could, a treaty of settlement – personally I doubt if it could be done – but they were not sent to bring about what I can only call a surrender.' The treaty was not a step towards the Irish Republic, for the republic already existed and had the mandate of the Irish people in successive elections. 'To my mind the Republic does exist', he declared. 'It is a living tangible thing, something for which men gave their lives, for which men were hanged, for which men are in jail, for which the people suffered, and for which men are still prepared to give their lives.' The agreement offered the Irish material rewards, he noted, but only at the

106 *Dáil Éireann Debates*, vol. 3, cols 30–36 (19 Dec. 1921), accessed at http:// historical-debates.oireachtas.ie/D/DT/D.T.192112190002.html on 24 Apr. 2012
107 *Dáil Éireann Debates*, vol. 3, cols 325–34 (7 Jan. 1922), accessed at http:// historical-debates.oireachtas.ie/D/DT/D.T.192201070002.html on 24 Apr. 2012

expense of their honour, and '[t]his fight has been for something more than the fleshpots of Empire.'[108]

Séamus Robinson, veteran of the Glasgow Volunteers and O/C 3rd Tipperary Brigade during the war, opposed the treaty because of its imperialistic aspects. 'I wish to state emphatically that no people have the right to go into any empire, much less an Empire that is based on a big section of downtrodden humanity', he declared. 'They have no right because it would mean slavery of some type; and no form of slavery is a fit state for free-willed human beings'. Instead, he advocated the resumption of war, not just in Ireland but in England too – targeting factories and shipyards – and in trouble spots throughout the British Empire. 'We could fight the English for three years – the English themselves could not fight us for longer than six months, especially if we took the fight up seriously in England as well as in Ireland and India and Egypt.'[109]

At one stage, Arthur Griffith referred to Collins as 'the man who won the war', and as the debate became acrimonious, the Cork man was the subject of a lot of personal criticism.[110] Mary MacSwiney, whose brother Terence died on hunger-strike in London in October 1920, complained that many people accepted the treaty simply because Collins agreed to it. 'What is good enough for Michael Collins is good enough for me' was the refrain, she despaired.[111] Contrasting the legendary Michael Collins of press reports with the 'weak' man who put his signature to the agreement, Séamus Robinson demanded answers to a number of questions:

(*a*) What positions exactly did Michael Collins hold in the army?
(*b*) Did he ever take part in any armed conflict in which he fought by shooting; the number of such battles or fights; in fact, is there any authoritative record of his having ever fired a shot for Ireland at an enemy of Ireland?

108 *Dáil Éireann Debates*, vol. 3, cols 227–34 (4 Jan. 1922), accessed at http://historical-debates.oireachtas.ie/D/DT/D.T.192201040002.html on 24 Apr. 2012
109 *Dáil Éireann Debates*, vol. T, no. 5, col. 239 (17 Dec. 1921), vol. 3, cols 288–92 (6 Jan. 1922), accessed at http://debates.oireachtas.ie/dail/1921/12/17/00002.asp and http://historical-debates.oireachtas.ie/D/DT/D.T.192201060002.html on 1 May 2012
110 *Dáil Éireann Debates*, vol. 3, col. 20 (19 Dec. 1921), accessed at http://historical-debates.oireachtas.ie/D/DT/D.T.192112190002.html on 24 Apr. 2012
111 *Dáil Éireann Debates*, vol. 3, col. 114 (21 Dec. 1921), accessed at http://www.oireachtas-debates.gov.ie/D/DT/D.T.192112210002.html on 24 Apr. 2021

He concluded that there was 'a prima facie case ... for the charge of treason' against Collins and Griffith.[112] Brugha, who as we have seen harboured long-standing animosity towards Collins because of arguments over the IRB, gunrunning finances and other matters, complained of the 'notoriety' that had attached to the Cork man: such celebrity was completely unwarranted, he declared, as Collins was 'merely a subordinate in the Department of Defence'.[113]

On 7 January 1922, the Dáil voted by 64 votes to 57 to accept the treaty. In what proved to be a prescient remark, on 8 December Art O'Brien had told Collins that he could not foresee the parliament accepting or rejecting the terms by the margin necessary to secure general consent in Ireland. Such indecision would have the effect of dividing the country and retarding the 'national movement' for 'a hundred years'.[114] On 10 January, de Valera led his supporters out of the Dáil in protest at the acceptance of the agreement. Soon the republican movement became divided between those who supported the treaty and those who rejected it. Rory O'Connor emerged as the leader of hard-line opponents of the agreement. The Provisional Government established by the treaty and headed by Collins announced its intention to hold a general election, effectively giving the people an opportunity to pass judgement on the agreement. Opponents of the treaty, however, feared that they would be beaten at the polls. At a press conference on 22 March, therefore, the O/C Britain indicated that anti-treatyites in the IRA – whom he claimed constituted 80 per cent of the army – would forcibly prevent the election from taking place. Asked if there would consequently be a military dictatorship in Ireland, he replied 'You can take it that way if you like'.[115] In late March, at a convention in Dublin, anti-treatyite Volunteers repudiated the authority of the Dáil and established their own executive.[116] On 13 April, members of Dublin IRA, acting on the orders of the executive's army council, occupied a number of buildings in Dublin city centre. The Four Courts became the executive's headquarters and O'Connor took up residence there.[117] Despite this provocative development, however, neither side seriously

112 *Dáil Éireann Debates*, vol. 3, cols 291–92 (6 Jan. 1922), accessed at http://historical-debates.oireachtas.ie/D/DT/D.T.192201060002.html on 1 May 2012

113 *Dáil Éireann Debates*, vol. 3, col. 326 (7 Jan. 1922), accessed at http://historical-debates.oireachtas.ie/D/DT/D.T.192201070002.html on 24 Apr. 2012

114 Art O'Brien to Michael Collins, 8 Dec. 1921 (AÓBP, MS 8429/5)

115 Michael Hopkinson, *Green against Green: The Irish Civil War* (Dublin: Gill & Macmillan, 2004), p. 67

116 Hopkinson, *Green*, pp. 67–68

117 Hopkinson, *Green*, p. 72

contemplated civil war. As the British army evacuated barracks throughout the country as per the terms of the treaty, agreements between the leaders of the IRA and the Provisional Government's newly founded National Army prevented violent confrontations between their forces on the ground.[118] In addition, strenuous efforts were made to achieve re-unification in Irish ranks. As part of an election pact agreed with de Valera in May, Collins promised anti-treatyites that the constitution of the Free State would be essentially republican, regardless of the fact that the polity was to be a dominion of the British Commonwealth.[119] Intensive talks were held in the hope of re-uniting the IRA. That some common ground remained between the two sides was demonstrated by the fact that pro- and anti-treaty IRA units participated in operations designed to undermine the existence of Northern Ireland, including an invasion of the territory in May.[120]

VI

In February 1922, as part of a general amnesty, 55 republicans found guilty of committing offences in England prior to the truce were released from prison. Soon afterwards, the men arrested in possession of munitions in Tullcross, Glasgow, were released.[121] In early April, the pardon was extended to a further 14 men convicted of offences committed during the truce period.[122] (Those interned in Ireland had begun to be released two months previously.[123]) The Jarrow branch of the ISDL held a reception for James Conroy and other members of the Tyneside IRA who had been found guilty of perpetrating arson attacks in March and May the previous year. Councillor Terence O'Connor raised the toast to 'our heroes of the I.R.A. on Tyneside'. The league's district president argued that the IRA had succeeded where O'Connell, Parnell and Redmond had failed: 'Only force on our part had brought England to realize that Ireland was in earnest at last'. Father Brennan, one of a number of Catholic priests present, contrasted the plight of the Volunteers who fought in Ireland with those in England. Whereas the former had the support of

118 Hopkinson, *Green*, pp. 62–66, 75

119 Hopkinson, *Green*, pp. 97–98

120 Hopkinson, *Green*, pp. 79–81, 83–86; Lynch, *Northern IRA*, pp. 99–105, 130–67

121 S. Duggan to Art O'Brien, 26 Feb. 1922 (AOBP, MS 8445/16)

122 *TT*, 13 Jan. 1922; lists of prisoners amnestied in Feb. and Apr. 1922 (HO, 144/4645); on the Volunteers' experiences in prison, see Chapter 6

123 *Irish Exile*, Jan. 1922

the populace, the latter experienced 'scorn and indignity', even at the hands of those of Irish descent. Nevertheless, they 'took it willingly for the sake of Ireland', they 'had come thro' [sic] & were going to gain their reward'. After the Volunteers fell into military formation, Conroy 'very proudly called the roll', each man 'stepping forward in a soldierly manner as his name was called'. On behalf of the Volunteers, Conroy thanked the attendees for their good wishes but emphasized that 'other men had also done their duty and done it well'. The evening ended with the singing of the 'The Soldiers' Song', a popular Volunteer marching song.[124] Prisoners were also freed in Scotland. Jubilant crowds greeted those released from Peterhead prison on 13 February. Henry Coyle and Bernard McCabe were 'carried shoulder high through the crowd to the cab rank while there was continuous cheering and the "Soldiers' Song" was sung'.[125]

For the *Glasgow Observer and Catholic Herald*, an Irish newspaper, the release of republican prisoners in Britain was the work of Michael Collins and Arthur Griffith. It represented 'one more proof of the sincerity of the British Government … and one more step taken in the work of conciliation and goodwill between England and Ireland'.[126] Others, however, took a different view, as the dissention in republican ranks in Ireland – due to the differing opinions on the merits of the treaty – also became apparent in Britain. Liverpool's John Pinkman supported the agreement because Collins had championed it. Pinkman was in two minds regarding the actual terms of the treaty. On the one hand, he thought the agreement 'unjust', believing that the British government had negotiated treacherously and that the Dáil had only ratified it out of fear of renewed war. On the other hand, he followed Collins in believing that the treaty was 'at least a stepping stone to the Republic we all eventually wanted'. Above all, however, there was loyalty to Collins himself. Pinkman and others like him 'were prepared to follow him in whatever course he decided to take. Such was our faith in Mick Collins.'[127]

Pinkman's comrade Paddy Daly took the opposite view. In early February, Collins had placed him in charge of an operation to kill two English hangmen

124 Jarrow ISDL Minute Book, 'Report of Reception given to Returned Prisoners', 24 Feb. 1922 (Patrick Brennan Papers), accessed at http://www.donmouth. co.uk/local_history/ira/conroy_reception.html on 25 Apr. 2012; *Irish Exile*, Mar. 1922; in 1926, 'The Soldiers' Song' became the national anthem of the Free State.

125 *Glasgow Observer and Catholic Herald*, 18 Feb. 1922

126 *Glasgow Observer and Catholic Herald*, 18 Feb. 1922 (Editorial)

127 Pinkman, *Legion*, pp. 93–95

who were scheduled to execute three prisoners in Derry for the murder of two policemen during an unsuccessful escape attempt from the city prison on 2 December 1921; the mission was aborted when the men's sentences were commuted to periods of imprisonment.[128] Soon afterwards, however, Daly broke with the Corkman. Acknowledging that in signing the treaty Collins had acted in what he considered to be Ireland's best interests, he nevertheless stood firm with the Volunteers: 'I am in sympathy with the majority of the IRA; I would wish them to continue now and finish the fight; I want to help them to do so'. To lay down arms now, with full independence yet to be achieved, only to begin the struggle again years in the future would be illogical, he continued. The interests of the 'big businessmen' and 'politicians', ensconced in the Free State in the interim, would work to prevent such a 'renewal of war'.[129]

The IRA in England sent six delegates to the anti-treaty Army Convention in Dublin in March and April, while the organization in Scotland sent two representatives.[130]

On the same day that the IRA occupied buildings in Dublin, Rory O'Connor wrote a letter to the O/C Liverpool. With the letter he included a long statement on the 'recent Army crisis', detailing events from the Dáil's acceptance of the treaty to the Provisional Government's attempt to proclaim the Army Convention. The implementation of the terms of the treaty would involve the 'disestablishment of the Existing Republic', the statement noted. The Volunteer oath of allegiance was one not of loyalty to the Dáil but rather 'to the Irish Republic itself'. Therefore,

> The Republican section of the Army intends still to stand by the Irish Republic holding that the Dail (having ratified the establishment of the Republic) and acted as the Government thereof had no moral right to approve of a Treaty subverting the Republic and bringing Ireland within the British Empire.

The IRA's opposition to the treaty did not amount to 'interference in politics' but was rather 'a fulfilment of the object for which they voluntarily banded themselves together [,] surrendered their personal liberty, and offered their

---

128 BMHWS 824, Patrick Daly, pp. 37–38; BMHWS 922, James Cunningham, p. 15; *MG*, 3 Dec. 1921, 13 Jan., 8 Feb. 1922; *II*, 7, 8 Dec. 1921
129 Paddy Daly to Michael Collins, 3 Apr. 1922 (RMP, P7/A/7)
130 O'Donoghue, *No Other Law*, p. 335

lives'. O'Connor ordered the O/C to read out the statement at a parade of Volunteers: 'Every man must decide then whether he will continue to work in the Republican Army or not.'[131]

The executive sent Michael Cremin to London to recruit the city's Volunteers to the republican side. He attended a meeting of the battalion and put forward the case against the treaty. Reginald Dunne told Cremin that he was concerned to prevent the split in the IRA in Ireland spreading to London. For that reason, he was in communication with both the executive and the National Army command.[132] In late April, 'acting under orders from the I.R.A. Executive', Liam McMahon and others called a meeting of the officers and men of the Volunteers in the Manchester area, encompassing the two companies in Manchester city, as well as those in Rochdale, Bolton, Stockport and Salford.[133] Although the outcome of the meeting is not known, it indicates that at least some of the Manchester leadership took the anti-treaty side.

Fearful that the Volunteers in Scotland might support the anti-treaty IRA, either by joining its ranks or by supplying it with armaments, Joe Vize, re-appointed to his old position of O/C Scotland for the pro-treatyities, arranged for the full-time officers previously involved in purchasing munitions there to receive a regular wage from Dublin. Starting in April 1922, Michael Burke, James Byrne, Séamus and William Fullerton, Michael O'Callaghan and Seán Adair were paid £20 each per month 'to hold their Brigade in the interests of G.H.Q. and to prevent Scotland becoming a stronghold for the Irregulars [i.e. the anti-treaty IRA]'. (William Fullerton was one of the four people convicted alongside O'Callaghan for attempting to smuggle munitions to Belfast in 1918.[134]) Séamus Fullerton later claimed that their efforts made it 'practically impossible for the irregulars to obtain arms and ammunition from Scotland'.[135]

In May or June 1922, divisions in the republican movement in Britain were made starkly clear when anti-treaty Volunteers held John Pinkman and

131 Exhibit no. 37: O/C Britain to O/C No. 1 Area Britain, 13 Apr. 1922 (AÓBP, MS 8419/10)
132 BMHWS 903, Michael Cremen, p. 1
133 Exhibit 70: L. McMahon et al to the Manchester IRA, 24 Apr. 1922 (ASSI, 13/52/2)
134 See Prologue
135 S. Fullerton to Minister for Defence, 31 Aug., 6 Sept.; Diarmuid O'Hegarty to Minister for Defence, 27 Oct. 1922 (MCP, A/06181)

Neil Kerr Senior at gunpoint in Liverpool in an unsuccessful attempt to acquire weapons.[136]

An unknown number of Volunteers decided to travel to Ireland. 'Now that Ireland was independent', Pinkman recalled thinking at the time, 'we [Merseyside Volunteers] wanted to live and work there.' The fact that IRA men faced 'considerable hostility' in Britain was also a factor. Praising the activities of the Liverpool IRA, Countess Markievicz promised to help get jobs for the men. Pinkman duly secured employment as a fitter in a railway workshop in Dublin. Soon afterwards, however, one of the ex-Volunteers suggested that they all enlist in the nascent National Army. 'We agreed that since Ireland was building a real army of its own we who had been Volunteers should be among the first to join', Pinkman recalled. Although the group broke up before they could enlist together, Pinkman joined the army anyway.[137] By way of contrast, when the London gunrunner Joe Carr returned to Ireland in January 1922, he joined the IRA's 2nd Western Division, which became anti-treaty.[138]

Dissension also affected political organizations in Britain. According to police intelligence, a meeting of Scottish Sinn Féin's comhairle ceanntair (area council) on 17 December 1921 re-affirmed the organization's adherence to the 'proclamation of the Irish Republic made in Easter week, 1916' and voted 99 to 16 in favour of de Valera's opposition to the treaty.[139] Soon afterwards, and without consulting the Scottish Sinn Féin leadership, Dublin authorized the establishment of Republican clubs in Scotland. 'This caused great confusion of thought and dissension', one member later wrote: 'many [people] then imagined that SINN FEIN stood for the Free State.'[140]

Meanwhile, the ISDL's central executive council regretted that the Dáil had 'felt itself compelled to agree to a settlement which is less than the complete claim of Ireland to absolute independence'. Nonetheless, it pledged to support the government of the Free State 'if and when established'. However, it also called upon 'the Irish people of Great Britain to help their compatriots at home in every way' until complete independence was 'finally

---

136 Pinkman, *Legion*, pp. 104–12; National Army intelligence report, 'Charges Against Irregulars Living in England', 12 Jan. 1923 (EO'ML, P17a/182)

137 Pinkman, *Legion*, pp. 82–84

138 Joe Carr to Art O'Brien, 31 May 1938 (AÓBP, MS 8461/25)

139 'RROUK', no. 136, 22 Dec. 1921; 'RROUK', no. 137, 5 Jan. 1922 (CAB, 24/131)

140 Joseph Browne to unknown, 'Organiser's Report on Irish Republican Organisation in Scotland', 20 Sept. 1923 (MTP, P69/44[373–74]); original emphasis

achieved'.[141] Two months later, after a heated debate at the annual conference, delegates voted 103 to 48 to support a motion declaring that the league should wait until the general election had been held in Ireland before deciding on its future policy.[142]

The Provisional Government viewed the anti-treaty section of the ISDL with displeasure. In a letter published in the *Catholic Herald* in February, Michael Collins claimed that Art O'Brien was 'using all our old machinery as a Propaganda Department against us'.[143] O'Brien and Seán McGrath took issue with the comment and requested that Collins issue a retraction, but he refused.[144] In late March, Diarmuid Fawsitt, an IRB man, visited London to investigate the situation. 'Unquestionably it is beyond dispute that the general attitude of officials in A.O'B's [i.e. Art O'Brien's] department, and also in the offices of the I.S.D.L. is inimicable [i.e. inimical] to the Treaty', he reported to Collins. Anti-treaty propaganda was being disseminated with the aim of 'securing moral and material support from our people in Great Britain for the Anti-Treaty (Republican) party in Ireland'. Speakers at ISDL rallies had complained that Dublin was not working hard enough to secure the speedy release of Irish prisoners in English jails. Moreover, McGrath was suspected of diverting for 'republican party purposes' monies raised by local ISDL branches for 'charitable and other organisations' in Ireland.[145] On 17 April, the *Irish Independent* published a letter from O'Brien which criticized the failure of the Provisional Government to secure the release of a number of republican prisoners from British jails, including at least 12 incarcerated in Scotland. Dublin reacted by dismissing O'Brien from his position as Dáil envoy to Britain.[146]

Dissension was not the only problem afflicting the ISDL. In May, O'Brien admitted that 'signs of apathy and indifference' had become 'very apparent' since the signing of the treaty. 'Many branches have ceased to function', he continued, 'membership has markedly dropped, and the financial revenue has decreased very considerably.'[147] Discussing the decline in donations

---

141 *Irish Exile*, Feb. 1922
142 *Irish Exile*, Apr. 1922
143 Clipping from the *Catholic Herald*, 25 Feb. 1922 (D/T, S1605)
144 Correspondence between Art O'Brien, Séan McGrath and Michael Collins, 27, 28 Feb., 2, 6, 9 Mar. 1922 (D/T, S1605)
145 Diarmuid Fawsitt to Collins, 25 Mar. 1922 (D/T, S1605)
146 *II*, 17 Apr. 1922; extract from minutes of Dáil Cabinet meeting, 21 Apr. 1922 (D/T, S1605)
147 *Irish Exile*, May 1922

to the INACDF, he lamented that 'many of our people think that everything is over'.[148]

VII

On 4 January 1922, David Fitzgerald asked Liam Mellows if he would issue some 'special instructions' regarding gunrunning in light of the 'peculiar situation' created by the treaty.[149] Whether the D/P acceded to the request is not known, but if he did his response may have been similar to that received by the Birmingham men when they raised the same question: 'You are enrolled as members of the Irish Republican Army and until you get orders to the contrary you are to carry on your work of training, organisation etc, as heretofore.'[150] And so gun-smuggling continued in Britain.

Detailed accounts relate only to gunrunning by the anti-treaty IRA. In Liverpool, Paddy Daly and Tim O'Sullivan remained in charge, as did David Fitzgerald on Tyneside. Fitzgerald complained that it was proving 'damn hard' to procure armaments and that 'the only hope [for weapons] is from the sea [i.e. abroad]'. 'I feel ashamed to take money from the D/P when I am returning so little', he confessed.[151] Operations in Manchester appear to have been under the direction of Liam McMahon and a man named Joseph Scanlon. Scanlon was a particularly active gunrunner, visiting Sheffield, Liverpool, Glasgow, Birmingham and Bradford on business.[152] In early 1922, Glasgow's Joe Robinson was released from prison after serving four years of a ten-year sentence for munitions smuggling. With tensions mounting in Ireland, Rory O'Connor provided him with funds and told him that weapons should be bought regardless of the cost and smuggled across the Irish Sea as quickly as possible. Prior to 28 June, Glasgow also received £330 from the D/P 'for purchases and balance of Bicycle', while £75 was sent to Edinburgh.[153] Patrick O'Neill and James Cunningham organized matters

148   Art O'Brien to James Lawless, 9 Mar. 1922 (AÓBP, MS 8429/21)

149   David Fitzgerald to D/P, 4 Jan. 1922, reprinted in Barrington, *Irish Independence Movement*, pp. 28–29

150   Exhibit 98: 'T.M.' to O/C No. 5 Area, 28 Feb. 1922 (ASSI, 13/52/2)

151   Exhibit 20: David Fitzgerald to 'P.A.', n.d. but prior to 5 May 1922 when he was arrested (ASSI, 13/52/2)

152   Exhibit 76: J. Scanlon's diary, entries for 22 Feb., 11, 13, 18 Mar., 13, 24, 25 Apr. 1922; exhibit 24: Scanlon to Paddy Daly, dated 'Thursday', probably 27 Apr. 1922 (ASSI, 13/52/2)

153   O/C Scotland to O/C Britain, 27 Feb. 1923 (HO, 144/3746); D/P to QMG,

in Birmingham, and between March and May they received £318 from Mellows.[154] He also sent £690 to London.[155] Here, gunrunning continued under Martin Geraghty and others.[156]

Whether pro-treatyites were engaged in procuring munitions in Britain during this period is difficult to say. Joe Scanlon worried that a man named 'Joe' intend to source munitions in Wales for the National Army. He hoped that J.P. Connolly, the chief gunrunner in Wales, would prevent Joe from 'doing too much'. Soon afterwards, however, rumours circulated that Connolly himself had 'joined the F[ree].S[tate]. Army'.[157] The details of Joe's and Connolly's gunrunning activities for the National Army, if indeed that is what they were doing, are not known.

In relation to the anti-treaty IRA, little information exists as to the sources tapped for munitions during this period. Presumably, however, the gunrunners used such proven sources as soldiers and the black market. Neither did they lose their appetite for large operations. On 29 April, Birmingham and Liverpool Volunteers combined to launch a raid on the Premier Aluminium Casting Company, a factory that was breaking down surplus war materiel. During the truce, Birmingham's Dan O'Malley had made contact with a man working in the factory and soon he was receiving between 800 and 1,000 rounds of ammunition from him every week. However, in early 1922, the prospect of 'trouble at home over Belfast', where sectarian clashes had broken out, and the fact that the factory contained 'hundreds of millions of rounds' of ammunition prompted the Volunteers to contemplate a raid on the facility. The plan for the operation called for the mobilization of 16 men. Divided into four parties, they were each to take turns on lookout duty while the others filled two cars with as much ammunition as possible.[158] The police, however, had learned of the operation and, lying in wait in the factory, they arrested

5 Apr. 1923, enclosing receipts marked 'Glas[gow]', n.d. but *c.* 28 June, and 'Edinburgh', 20 June 1922 (NAI, Dept. of Justice File [JUS], 93/3/4)

154 D/P to QMG, 5 Apr. 1923, enclosing receipts marked 'Bham', 18 Mar., 18, 20 Apr., 16 May 1922 (JUS, 93/3/4)

155 D/P to QMG, 5 Apr. 1923, enclosing receipts marked 'London', 1, 5, 19, 26 June 1922 (JUS, 93/3/4)

156 Martin Geraghty to the MSPB, 20 May 1937 (EO'ML, P17a/154)

157 Exhibit 24: Joe Scanlon to Paddy Daly, 'Thursday', probably 27 Apr. 1922; exhibit 76: Scanlon's diary, entries for 24, 25 Apr. 1922; exhibit 40: David Fitzgerald to Daly, n.d. (ASSI, 13/52/2)

158 BMHWS 922, James Cunningham, pp. 14–16; exhibit 95: Notes for operation, n.d. (ASSI, 13/52/2)

a number of Volunteers, including O'Neill and Cunningham. Merseyside's Paddy Daly barely escaped the dragnet. '[T]hings may not be as bad as they look now but it is doubtful', Joe Scanlon told Tim O'Sullivan. In fact, things got worse, for documents found in the prisoners' lodgings soon led to the arrest of Scanlon, O'Sullivan, David Fitzgerald and others.[159] Art O'Brien asked the Provisional Government to help pay the men's legal fees, stating that they had been involved in 'illegal ammunition traffic apparently for national purposes'. Michael Collins dismissed the appeal, telling a fellow Provisional Government minister: "The "national purposes" of course are supplying our opponents here in order that these may be in a position to shoot down their fellow country-men'.[160] Charged with conspiracy to overthrow the Provisional Government, 11 men were put on trial. However, when they were granted bail they absconded to Ireland.[161]

The Birmingham debacle did not dissuade the Liverpool IRA from launching further raids, however. On 3 June, large quantities of explosives and gunpowder and thousands of detonators were taken from eight collieries in south-west Lancashire.[162]

If the sources for gunrunning during the war and truce periods make it difficult to estimate with any precision the quantity of munitions sent to Ireland from Britain, the paucity of extant records and the confusing nature of some of those that do survive mean that it is impossible to reach an approximation of the amount of armaments despatched in the post-treaty and civil war periods. The following figures, therefore, constitute the *minimum* amount of armaments despatched between 6 December 1921 and 28 June 1922, the day the civil war broke out. In January and February 1922, Manchester sent 11 handguns, 550 rounds of ammunition, two flare pistols, three lbs (1.4 kg) of gelignite, 36 sticks of gelignite and 4,375 detonators directly to Ireland.[163] In the first two months of 1922, the Tyneside men despatched six machine guns, 49 handguns, 950 rounds of ammunition, 262 detonators and 80 ft (24.4 m) of fuse wire. In March, they sent 50 handguns to Merseyside.

159 Police statements, May 1922; exhibit 78: Joe Scanlon to Tim O'Sullivan, 5 May 1922 (ASSI, 13/52/2); BMHWS 922, James Cunningham, pp. 16–17; BMHWS 824, Patrick Daly, pp. 40–42

160 Michael Collins to George Gavan Duffy, 4 May 1922 (DÉ, 2/410)

161 *MG*, 11 May 1922; Art O'Brien to Pa Murray, 28 Jan. 1923 (AÓBP, MS 8424/4); BMHWS 922, James Cunningham, p. 18

162 *MG*, *TT*, 5, 6 June 1922

163 Exhibit 75: Note by 'J.T.S.', 18 Dec. 1921; note by 'J.S.', 20 Jan. 1922 (ASSI, 13/52/2)

These were presumably forwarded to Ireland, for the only explicit record of munitions being sent from Liverpool during this period relates to 800 rounds of .303 ammunition despatched to Sligo.[164] Between 22 December 1921 and 28 April 1922, Birmingham sent Liverpool 26 rifles, one handgun, 7,000 rounds of buckshot, 1,050 rounds of .303 ammunition and 150 lbs (68 kg) of gunpowder, as well as a case of unspecified munitions for the Donegal IRA.[165] These too were probably sent to Ireland.

In total therefore, the six-and-a-half month period following the signing of the treaty saw at least six machine guns, 26 rifles, 111 handguns, 3,350 rounds of ammunition, a quantity of gelignite, 150 lbs of gunpowder and almost 4,400 detonators despatched by gunrunners in Britain.

VIII

At around 2.30 p.m. on 22 June 1922, Conservative MP Sir Henry Wilson, having unveiled a war memorial at a railway station in London city centre, alighted from a taxi outside his house at 36 Eaton Square, Belgravia. Reginald Dunne and Volunteer Joseph O'Sullivan had been awaiting his arrival for almost half an hour. As Wilson crossed the road to his house, the two followed him, O'Sullivan going straight after Wilson and Dunne endeavouring to intercept him before he reached the front door. Within about four yards of Wilson, O'Sullivan aimed his gun and fired two shots, but the bullets appear to have missed their target. As Wilson was about to turn round, however, Dunne, from about seven or eight feet, 'fired three shots rapidly, the last from the hip'. Staggering on the footpath, Wilson was struck once more by a bullet from O'Sullivan's gun. Hit in the arm, leg and torso, he collapsed on the footpath and died. Dunne and O'Sullivan, both of whom had leg injuries sustained in the Great War, fled the scene. However, policemen and members of the public gave chase and they were captured.[166]

Dunne later defended his and O'Sullivan's actions by referencing the fact that as soldiers in the British army during the First World War, they had

---

164 Exhibit 13: 'ÚS' to 'D.F./"T"', 4 Apr.; exhibit 22: Paddy Daly to General Pilkington or Divisional Q.M., 26 Apr. 1922 (ASSI, 13/52/2); 'Material Sent to P. 15th March 1922', reprinted in Barrington, *Irish Independence Movement*, p. 30

165 Correspondence between James Cunningham and Daly, 'T.O.B.', C. Gildea and unknown, 22, 23 Dec. 1921, 30 Jan., 8 Feb., 28 April 1922 (ASSI, 13/52/2)

166 *TT*, 23 June 1922; Reginald Dunne to new O/C London, n.d., but *c.* 9 Aug. 1922 (BMHCD 188/6/2, Frank Thornton)

taken human life in the name of self-determination and freedom for small nations. He held that Britain, in its relations with Ireland, had hypocritically refused to abide by these principles. Instead, it had divided Ireland in two, and in Northern Ireland 'outrages were being perpetrated that are a disgrace to civilisation'. Such incidents had caused the deaths of around 500 people and the wounding of nearly 2,000 others, the expulsion of 23,000 from their homes and 9,000 from their employment. Wilson, he continued, was responsible for this 'Orange Terror' and 'was at the time of his death the Military Adviser to what is colloquially called the Ulster Government, and as Military Adviser he raised and organized a body of men known as the Ulster Special Constables, who are the principal agents in this campaign of terrorism.' With Ulster Catholics suffering so, Dunne declared that his and O'Sullivan's assassination of Wilson was motivated by the 'same principles for which we shed our blood on the Battle Field of Europe'.[167]

Dunne also seems to have hoped that the assassination would provoke the British into revoking the treaty and renewing its war against the IRA. The Irish, divided over the merits of the agreement, would then re-unite in the face of the common enemy. As we saw earlier, Dunne feared that the bitter divisions caused by the treaty would spread to London. Members of the capital's Cumann na mBan were outraged by the agreement. 'None of us was willing to accept the Treaty as a settlement of our claims', remembered Sorcha McDermott.[168] Subsequently, the majority of the women's auxiliary went 'violently republican' and refused to co-operate with the Volunteers out of suspicion of their attitude towards the peace agreement. The day before the assassination, Dunne beseeched the Cumann na mBan to have patience, stating that there would soon be some 'activities'.[169]

Historians estimate that in the north of Ireland in the period January 1920–October 1922, 400–500 people were killed, 1,000–2,000 were injured, over 10,000 were forcibly expelled from their workplaces and over 23,000 were compelled to flee their homes.[170] Dunne's figures, therefore, are largely correct. However, his claim that all the victims of violence were 'men, women, and children of my race', implying that they were Catholic

---

167 Dunne Statement (BMHCD 188/6/3, Frank Thornton, reprinted from *II*, 21 July 1922)

168 BMHWS 945, Sorcha Nic Diarmada, p. 9

169 BMHWS 903, Michael Cremen, p. 3; BMHWS 924, Mary Cremin, pp. 9–10

170 Peter Hart, 'Ethnic Conflict and Minority Responses', in Hart, *IRA at War*, p. 248; Alan Parkinson, *Belfast's Unholy War: The Troubles of the 1920s* (Dublin: Four Courts Press, 2004), pp. 12–13

nationalists, is incorrect. In fact, over a third of those killed in Belfast, the cockpit of violence in the area, were Protestants and presumably loyalists. While Catholics did indeed suffer a disproportionate amount of violence, they also perpetrated the same. What happened, therefore, was not 'Orange Terror' or a pogrom against Catholics, but rather 'a communal and sectarian war'. Belfast had experienced outbreaks of such violence from the mid-nineteenth century onwards, especially at times of political tension. What made the episode in 1920–22 so deadly was the unprecedented nature of nationalists' opposition to British rule in Ireland, embodied in the IRA's campaign of violence.[171] Moreover, Dunne was mistaken about Sir Henry Wilson's role in Northern Ireland affairs. Undoubtedly, he did not share nationalists' desire for an independent Ireland. As Chief of the Imperial General Staff, the highest professional office in the British army, up to his retirement in February 1922, the County Longford-born Wilson had consistently urged the government to crush the IRA, and he vehemently opposed the treaty. However, when asked to advise Sir James Craig's government on the security situation in March 1922, his recommendation was that the Ulster Special Constabulary – a force of part-time police established in October 1920 which, contrary to Dunne's statement, Wilson had no role in founding – should become non-sectarian. Moreover, fearful that the force might emulate the Black and Tans, he emphasized the importance of military discipline, recommending that a senior army officer be given the post of military adviser (contra Dunne, Wilson himself did not occupy the position) with command of the entire police force in Northern Ireland. Craig, however, ignored this advice.[172] Nevertheless, nationalist propaganda alleged that Wilson and Craig were working hand in glove. The month he was killed, for example, the *Irish Exile* stated that Wilson and the Northern Ireland leader had ensured that 'every little breach of the law in Southern Ireland' was noticed by the British press but that the facts in relation to the 'pre-arranged campaign for the extermination of Irish Nationalists in Belfast' were ignored.[173]

Wilson's assassination was, *The Times* declared, a deed that 'must rank among the foulest in the foul category of Irish political crimes', an outrage whose 'horror' called to mind the murders of Cavendish and Burke in 1882.

171 Hart, 'Ethnic Conflict', pp. 248–51
172 Keith Jeffery, *Field Marshal Sir Henry Wilson: A Political Soldier* (Oxford: Oxford University Press, 2006), chapter 13 generally, esp. pp. 273–74, 279–80
173 *Irish Exile*, June 1922

An angry country, it continued, would wreak revenge not only against those who perpetrated the act but also against those others 'who have tolerated the system of political murder of which this crime is an outcome'. The following day, the newspaper demanded that responsible Irishmen take to task 'the militant sections of Irish opinion'.[174] While denouncing Dunne and O'Sullivan as 'misguided or ignorant criminals', the *Glasgow Observer and Catholic Herald* nevertheless found that their actions were understandable, given that Wilson was the 'boasted organiser' of the 'murderous campaign against the Catholics of Ulster'.[175]

The British cabinet met six times in the 72 hours following Wilson's assassination. The killing was just the latest in a number of incidents since the signing of the treaty six months previously that had strained London's patience with Dublin. Foremost amongst them was the residence in the Four Courts of Rory O'Connor's group of heavily armed IRA men. Lloyd George told Michael Collins that Scotland Yard had received intelligence indicating that 'active preparations are on foot among the irregular elements of the IRA to resume attacks upon the lives and property of British subjects both in England and in Ulster'. Therefore, noting that the pro-treatyites had won the general election held earlier that month, he demanded that Collins take military action against the IRA and offered to loan the National Army the military equipment to do so. Failure to act would constitute a breach of the treaty, he warned.[176] The cabinet rejected Collins's request that it share the intelligence with him on the grounds that to do so would endanger the lives of the people who supplied it. Later, it was admitted: 'There was no proof as yet of any connection between the IRA or at any rate between the Four Courts and the murder [of Wilson]'. Still, it was thought 'by no means improbable' that the assassination had been 'instigated' by the Four Courts, 'that focus of seditious activity'.[177] Collins's procrastination so annoyed the cabinet that on 24 June it ordered a British army assault on the Four Courts for the

---

174 *TT*, 23, 24 June 1922 (Editorials); the last assassination of a political nature to have occurred in Britain happened in July 1909 when Madan Lal Dhingra, an Indian nationalist, shot dead Sir William Hutt Curzon Wyllie, an official in the government of the raj (BMHWS 839, P.S O'Hegarty, pp. 21–22). The last politician to be assassinated in Britain was Prime Minister Spencer Percival in 1812.

175 *Glasgow Observer and Catholic Herald*, 1 July 1922

176 Cabinet Conclusions, 5 p.m. meeting, 22 June; David Lloyd George to Michael Collins, 22 June 1922 (CAB, 21/255)

177 Cabinet Conclusions, 11 a.m. meeting, 24 June 1922 (CAB, 21/255)

following day.[178] However, General Macready, the commander of British forces in Ireland, refused to carry it out. His representative later explained to the cabinet that such an attack would have been counter-productive. It would have had the effect of exposing British troops in other parts of Ireland to attack at the hands of the outraged populace. He also believed that it would 'draw the two wings of the IRA together' in opposition to the British, which indeed had been one of Dunne's aims. Therefore, with the army leadership opposing an offensive, the cabinet resolved to dispense with a British military solution to the problem and instead pressurize the Provisional Government to deal with the issue forthwith.[179]

The cabinet did not have to wait long. 'It appears that it was on 26 June that the Provisional Government cabinet virtually decided to make a definite move', the historian Michael Hopkinson observes. The following day forces loyal to the government surrounded the Four Courts. At 4.15 a.m. on 28 June, after the expiry of an ultimatum to evacuate the building, the National Army opened fire on it using British weapons.[180] The civil war had begun.

The assassination of Wilson was the trigger for the civil war. However, the political scientist Bill Kissane contends that this was merely the immediate cause, for 'some military conflict between the more radical IRA men and the Provisional government was inevitable once the Treaty was signed', especially given the political vacuum that existed in Ireland for months afterwards. This was because the agreement revealed a fault line among republicans, one that divided pragmatists from doctrinaires, democrats from self-determinationists.[181] In other words, while the spark that exploded the Irish powder keg was indeed lit in London, a conflagration was inevitable irrespective of events in Britain.

Nevertheless, the killing later became a topic of controversy. Michael Collins was suspected of having played an underhanded role in the episode, namely that he ordered the assassination but refused to admit responsibility for it, thus allowing the British government to believe that the IRA executive was the guilty party, and that he then bowed to British pressure to attack the Four Courts. This was despite the fact that Dunne's statements on the incident did not make any mention of Collins or of his having acted under

178 Cabinet Conclusions, 5.30 p.m. meeting, 24 June 1922 (CAB, 21/255)
179 Cabinet Conclusions, 11.30 a.m. meeting, 25 June 1922 (CAB, 21/255)
180 Hopkinson, *Green*, pp. 116–17
181 Bill Kissane, *The Politics of the Irish Civil War* (Oxford: Oxford University Press, 2005), pp. 10, 234

orders from Dublin. The attempts of historians to reach definite conclusions regarding responsibility for the killing have been stymied by the contradictory accounts left by veterans. Thus on the one hand, Michael Hopkinson argues that the evidence pointed to Collins having ordered the assassination, motivated by outrage at events in Northern Ireland and a desire to re-unite Irish ranks by removing a common enemy.[182] On the other hand, Peter Hart has tentatively concluded that Dunne and O'Sullivan acted without explicit orders, that Collins may have ordered the assassination in the autumn of 1921 in the event of the peace talks breaking down, but that in killing the field marshal in June 1922, Dunne and O'Sullivan may have resurrected a plan that had been shelved by the signing of the treaty.[183]

Memoirs of veterans that have become public in recent years overwhelmingly support the contention that the IRA men were acting under orders. 'I know for a fact that the orders for this execution, as well as two others, were given by the late General M. Collins <u>prior</u> to the Treaty split', Seán McGrath wrote in 1953, implying that the orders were never cancelled.[184] Sorcha McDermott concurred. She heard that 'long before the Treaty', Collins had ordered Dunne to assassinate Wilson 'when he could', and the command was 'apparently never rescinded'. Billy Aherne, who later succeeded to Dunne's position of O/C London, agreed.[185] Hence, Wilson was probably one of the unnamed 'individuals' marked down for attack by the London IRA in the event of the truce collapsing.[186] Also, the operation was not planned to be as virtually suicidal as it appeared. Apparently, a third man driving a car was to have provided a means of escape from the scene of the crime. However, when the sound of gunfire attracted a crowd, 'the man with the motor car got the wind up and his nerve failed him at the last moment and instead of driving up a little bit nearer [to collect Dunne and O'Sullivan] he drove away'.[187] Collins sent Joe Dolan, a former member of his assassination squad and now an officer in the National Army, to London to investigate the possibility of rescuing Dunne and O'Sullivan from prison and a probable death sentence.

182 Hopkinson, *Green*, pp. 112–14
183 Peter Hart, 'Michael Collins and the Assassination of Sir Henry Wilson', in Hart, *IRA at War*, pp. 194–220
184 Seán McGrath statement, 14 Oct. 1953 (BMHCD 247, Frank Lee); original emphasis
185 BMHWS 945, Sorcha Nic Diarmada, p. 7
186 See p. 205 above
187 BMHWS 902, Mary McGeehin, p. 7; see also Frank Lee to Joseph Dolan, 29 Sept. 1953, reprinted in BMHWS 900, Joseph Dolan, appendix b

Dolan himself believed that Collins had ordered the assassination, speculating that the shooting occurred when it did because it was only then that cast-iron proof of Wilson's involvement in organizing the 'Belfast pogrom' was ascertained.[188] (In the event, neither the rescue planned by Dolan nor that contemplated by the IRA's Michael Cremin were mounted. Found guilty of Wilson's assassination, Dunne and O'Sullivan were sentenced to death and executed at Wandsworth prison on 10 August.[189])

The evidence currently available does not allow us to reach a definitive conclusion as to the involvement of Collins. Did outrage at events in Northern Ireland lead him to order Wilson's death, thereby potentially placing the treaty settlement at risk? Although perilous, it cannot be ruled out. As Hopkinson observes, Collins's behaviour in early 1922 indicated that he signed the treaty 'for tactical reasons' and that he was not totally committed to it. His collusion with anti-treaty IRA units in mounting an unsuccessful invasion of Northern Ireland the month before Wilson's death suggests that Collins 'remained a physical-force nationalist' at heart, one 'who placed an especial emphasis on attacking partition'.[190] On the other hand, Dunne, agonising over the treaty, irritated by taunts from hard-line republicans in the Cumann na mBan and outraged by the deaths of Catholics in Belfast, may have acted on his own initiative, deciding to kill Wilson so as to re-unite the republican movement. Whichever is closer to the truth, the assassination of Sir Henry Wilson had an unmistakeable consequence: it hastened the outbreak of civil war in Ireland.

IX

The period July 1921–June 1922 witnessed the triumph and tragedy of the republican movement. Basking in the prestige of having forced the British to the negotiating table, the IRA in Britain, like that in Ireland, experienced a surge in membership during the truce, gunrunning continued and plans were put in place for the resumption of hostilities. The treaty's concession of dominion status to the majority of Ireland represented a considerable advancement on previous attempts by British governments to solve the 'Irish question'. Undoubtedly, it was the IRA that compelled Lloyd George into

188 BMHWS 900, Joseph Dolan, pp. 2, 5
189 BMHWS 900, Joseph Dolan, pp. 2–5, 8; BMHWS 903, Michael Cremen, pp. 2–3; *TT*, 11 Aug. 1922
190 Michael Hopkinson, 'From Treaty to Civil War, 1921–2', in J.R. Hill (ed.), *NHI, Vol. VII: Ireland, 1921–1984* (Oxford: Oxford University Press, 2003), p. 8

that compromise, as did the prime minister's fear of international disapproval should his government adopt the harsh measures necessary to defeat the Irish rebellion. The insurgency of the Volunteers in Ireland, aided and abetted by IRA gunrunning and violence in Britain, brought home to the prime minister the cost of retaining the Union. Then, however, tragedy struck. The treaty satisfied some republicans but angered just as many. As tensions mounted, comrades-in-arms found themselves on opposing sides. Those such as Michael Collins and John Pinkman pragmatically accepted the agreement as a means to eventually achieve complete independence, while others like Rory O'Connor and Paddy Daly considered it a dishonourable compromise. Although neither side actively prepared for nor sought civil war, its outbreak was virtually inevitable with or without the assassination of Sir Henry Wilson in London in June 1922 by Reginald Dunne and Joe O'Sullivan. The next chapter will trace the course of the civil war.

CHAPTER 5

The Civil War, June 1922–May 1923

I

The civil war was 'the greatest tragedy of Irish history', Liam Daly, veteran of the London Volunteers, declared in 1950.[1] With former comrades now fighting each other, the achievements of the 1919–21 war were tarnished and overlaid with bitterness and sadness. While some Volunteers remained in Britain, others travelled to Ireland and fought in the ranks of the National Army or the IRA there. Consequently, this chapter treats the civil war period on both sides of the Irish Sea. Section II traces the course of the war in Ireland through the eyes of the fighters from Britain. Section III deals with rival republican and Free State organizations in Britain, from the Volunteers to the ISDL, while the following section covers the gunrunning activities of the IRA. Section V discusses the plans laid down for the resumption of hostilities in Britain and the reason why they were not realized, namely the mass arrest of republicans in March 1923. Section VI concludes.

II

Men and women who served in the Volunteers in Britain from 1914 onwards fought on both sides during the civil war in Ireland. In a census conducted in November 1922, 267 soldiers in the National Army listed their home addresses as being in Britain. Scotland accounted for 183 of these, 80 in Glasgow alone. Another 81 soldiers came from England: 20 from Liverpool, 17 from London, ten from Manchester, four from Birmingham, two from Newcastle-upon-Tyne and 28 from elsewhere. The remaining three soldiers came from Wales. An additional 113 soldiers who gave home addresses in Ireland listed their

---

1 BMHWS 425, Liam Daly, p. 4

next-of-kin addresses as being in Britain. England accounted for 77 of these: London 25, Liverpool 14, Manchester nine, Birmingham one, Newcastle-upon-Tyne one and the remainder of the country 27. 34 were in Scotland, including 24 in Glasgow, while the remaining two were in Wales. As the majority of next-of-kin were close relations, such as parents, wives and siblings, it is fair to surmise that these soldiers were from Britain too. Therefore, at least 380 soldiers in the National Army were from Britain. As total army strength at this time was around 35,000, this constituted almost 1.1 per cent of recruits. Of the 380, 57 had sworn the oath of loyalty before the outbreak of war on 28 June, and 306 did so afterwards. (In the remaining 17 cases, the dates of attestation are either not stated or are illegible.)[2]

However, this figure of 380 is an underestimate. Some Volunteers who joined the army, such as John Pinkman, are missing from the census. In addition, others had been killed in action by the time it was conducted, as we shall see presently. One source lists at least 35 Scottish Volunteers who joined the army but are missing from the census.[3] Therefore, it seems safe to conclude that in excess of 400 men from Britain fought in the ranks of the National Army during the civil war.

How many of these were members of the IRA in Britain during the war of independence and the truce periods? This is very difficult to say. It was claimed that around 250 men from the Scottish Brigade enlisted. (If this is correct, a number are missing from the census where only 217 soldiers gave their own address or that of the next-of-kin as being in Scotland.)[4] Seemingly, no similar record was kept in relation to former Volunteers from England and Wales.

Veterans of the 1919–21 war in Britain who joined the army included Joe Vize, a commandant-general who became director of purchases. Seán Golden and Séamus Fullerton worked under Vize with the respective ranks of lieutenant-general and staff captain. Meanwhile, Joe Good became a 1st lieutenant on the command staff of the 2nd Eastern Division.[5]

Fullerton pressed for the employment of Scottish Volunteers in the army, stating they had given 'good service' in the IRA and were now finding their nationality a handicap in securing employment in Scotland.[6] In late

2 National Army Census, 12–13 Nov. 1922 (MAI); Hopkinson, *Green*, p. 136

3 Membership rolls of Scottish Brigade IRA (EMP, 3/C/13)

4 S. Fullerton to Minister for Defence, 31 Aug., 6 Sept. 1922 (MCP, A/06181)

5 National Army Census, 12–13 Nov. 1922 (MAI)

6 Diarmuid O'Hegarty to Commander-in-Chief, 2 Nov. 1922 (MCP, A/06181)

September 1922, however, an incident arose indicating the complications of allegiance and identity in a time of civil war. A group of 86 Volunteers from the Coatbridge Company, 'pillars of the Sinn Féin Movement in the west of Scotland' according to their O/C, Patrick Fleming, arrived in Dublin to enlist. At their initial reception, they were told to 'consider themselves Soldiers of the I.R.A.'. At the Curragh military camp, however, they were asked to sign the oath of loyalty to the Provisional Government. This they refused to do as they considered themselves 'a unit of the Irish Regular Army [i.e. IRA]'. They were therefore forced to return to Coatbridge. This was not an isolated incident. Joining up prior to the outbreak of the civil war, recruits from Britain were not always aware of the distinction between the National Army and the Volunteers. 'To us it was still the I.R.A.', remembered John McPeak, one of the Glasgow Volunteers arrested with munitions near Tullcross in December 1921. 'We didn't know there was any difference at that time between them and the Free Staters. All we had been told was that they wanted soldiers.'[7] Interestingly, the National Army referred to itself as 'Óglaigh na hÉireann', the official Irish language title of the IRA.[8] Fleming complained that many of his men had resigned from good jobs in order to enlist. Unable to find work, they were now 'walking the streets, Idle [sic]'. He feared that news of the men's treatment would have an adverse effect on the movement in Scotland. Loath to 'see our flag pulled down', he wrote to Richard Mulcahy, the National Army's then commander-in-chief, to demand an investigation. Enquiring into the matter, Diarmuid O'Hegarty, the director of organization, attributed the incident to concerns about money. A previous batch of recruits from Scotland had experienced difficulties in receiving pay and dependents' allowance, he reported. Despite reassurances from Fullerton, the former O/C 1st Battalion, Scottish Brigade IRA, that they would not suffer similar problems, the Coatbridge men's fears were not allayed. 'It is quite beyond my comprehension how they could have been a regular unit of the Army in Scotland', declared O'Hegarty reflecting on the men's conduct. Indeed, he doubted that IRA units had ever really existed outside of Ireland. Therefore, the decision to decline the men's service because of their refusal to take the oath was upheld.[9]

The IRA kept no records of its civil war membership comparable to the National Army census. Therefore, any attempt to estimate the number of

7 *II*, 18 May 1971
8 Hopkinson, 'Treaty', p. 13
9 Patrick Fleming to Richard Mulcahy, 8 Oct.; Diarmuid O'Hegarty to Commander-in-Chief, 2 Nov.; Mulcahy to Fleming, 13 Nov. 1922 (MCP, A/06181)

Volunteers from Britain that fought in its ranks is dependent on fragmentary sources. At least 46 IRA men imprisoned by the National Army had addresses in Britain or were former members of the Volunteers there. Of the 41 who gave addresses in Britain, 24 came from England: ten from Liverpool, six from London, four from Manchester, two from Birmingham and two from elsewhere. 17 came from Scotland, 15 of them from Glasgow. Of the five who gave Irish addresses, four originally came from Glasgow and one from Newcastle-upon-Tyne.[10] According to another source, at least a further 25 men from Scotland fought in the Volunteers.[11] Glasgow and Liverpool each boasted of having sent an 'I.R.A. Expeditionary Force' to Ireland.[12]

Veterans of the struggle in Britain who fought in the IRA in Ireland included Tom Kerr, Gilbert Barrington, James Cunningham, Séamus Robinson, Margaret Skinnider, the Volunteers' Paymaster General, and Séan Mooney.[13]

The progress of the civil war can be followed through the activities of Seán Mooney, John Pinkman and others. The war can be divided into three stages. The first, from 28 June until mid-August, saw fighting in Dublin city, the midlands and County Limerick. The IRA boasted more experienced leaders than the National Army, but this advantage was dissipated by its failure to go on the offensive. Instead, C/S Liam Lynch, perhaps hoping that National troops would refuse to attack their former comrades, insisted on waging a defensive war, or what Séamus Robinson dismissively referred to as 'the policy of each Unit staying home in its own area and having a "bump off of them"'. Volunteers simply attempted to hold their positions in the face of enemy onslaughts.

---

10 National Army Prisoner Location Books [NAPLB] (MAI, CW/P/01/01, CW/P/02/02/21, CW/P/02/02/29, CW/P/02/02/32–33, CW/P/03/01**Fergus, CW/P/03/05, CW/P/03/06, CW/P/05/01, CW/P/08/11, CW/P/08/13–14, CW/P/10/15–16, CW/P/13/01, T3/359[5], CW Ledger Cross Reference B2, BB, 4, 26, 28–29); membership rolls of Scottish Brigade IRA (EMP, 3/C/13)
11 Membership rolls of Scottish Brigade IRA (EMP, 3/C/13)
12 *Poblacht na hÉireann* (Scottish edition), 23, 30 Dec. 1922
13 Col. Tomás MacAosa to the Director of Intelligence, 15 June 1923 (EO'ML, P17a/182); NAPLB (CW/P/01/01, CW/P/08/11, CW/P/08/13–14, CW/P/03/01**Fergus, CW/P/03/05, CW Ledger Cross Reference B2, 4); Liam Ferris's Military Service Pension Application, 14 May 1935, 3 July 1938 (Patrick Brennan Papers); BMHWS 1721, Séamus Robinson, pp. 76–78; anonymous memoir, 1972–73 (ECP, P61/4[67–69]); Lawrence William White, 'Skinnider, Margaret (Ní Scineadóra, Máighréad)', in *DIB*, downloaded from http://dib.cambridge.org on 1 Dec. 2009

Once overwhelmed, or caught unawares by such operations as the landing of National troops from the sea outside Cork city, IRA men's reluctance to fight led many to simply abandon the field. By the middle of August, the National Army controlled all the cities and most of the major towns.[14]

Initially, John Pinkman, who had participated in skirmishes with the IRA in Kilkenny city the month previous to the outbreak of fighting, helped to supply ammunition to the National troops attacking the Four Courts. Subsequently, he was involved in an operation to clear IRA snipers from a block of buildings at the intersection of Parnell Street and Sackville Street. Passing from one building into another by demolishing the walls, he was involved in fire-fights with some Volunteers and a Cumann na mBan member. Following this, he was part of a contingent of the elite Dublin Guard sent to Limerick city. IRA forces had retreated to the towns and villages of Bruff, Bruree and Kilmallock, and National troops set off to engage them. On 2 August, the army's positions in Bruree were attacked by Volunteers. The house where Pinkman was billeted was besieged. 'At first, Irregular snipers tried unsuccessfully to pick us off by firing through the windows', he recounts. 'Then they fired grenades at the house. But it wasn't until we were attacked by motor bombs that we became really worried.' The soldiers, however, put up a stout resistance, preventing the IRA men from getting within range of actually hitting the house with the grenades and mortars. The siege lasted for two days before news of the imminent arrival of reinforcements of National troops from Kilmallock led the IRA to retreat. The soldiers then continued their pursuit of the Volunteers into County Cork, soon reaching Mallow. When intelligence was received indicating that Eamon de Valera might be meeting Volunteer leaders at an abandoned railway station near the town on a certain night, Pinkman took part in an operation to kill the former president of the republic. He had 'no qualms about shooting Dev' as he believed that he was 'so largely responsible not only for the outbreak of the Civil War, but also for its prolongation'. However, no one was seen at the station. A few nights later, more reliable intelligence enabled Pinkman and his comrades to arrest three senior leaders of the North Cork IRA.[15]

Paddy Lowe had joined the army too and was killed during the fighting in Dublin.[16] On 13 July, Seán Adair was killed in an ambush. One of the

14 Hopkinson, *Green*, pp. 123–26, 142–71; BMHWS 1721, Séamus Robinson, p. 76

15 Pinkman, *Legion*, pp. 96–100, 114–74

16 Pinkman, *Legion*, p. 116

Glasgow Volunteers who had attempted to rescue Frank Carty from the prison van in May 1921, Adair had joined a convoy of National troops while returning to Athlone after paying his mother a visit in Lisburn. Symbolising the divisions that had rent Irish nationalism, the fleet ran into an ambush laid by IRA men under the command of Carty. A long fire-fight ensued and Adair was one of four National soldiers killed. Sergeant Louis O'Carroll, a comrade of his from the Scottish Brigade's 'A' Company, 1st Battalion, was wounded in the incident.[17]

During the opening battle of the war, 20 Volunteers from Glasgow fought in IRA ranks. Following the fall of Dublin, they were passed from one unit to another and all the while Joe Robinson's outfit paid their expenses, including the cost of lodgings. In August, however, they were arrested by National forces.[18] Seán Mooney was probably among this group, for he fought under Cathal Brugha, who was killed in fighting on 5 July.[19] Rory O'Connor and Liam Mellows were imprisoned after surrendering at the Four Courts.

The second stage of the conflict, from mid-August to late 1922, saw the IRA revert to the guerrilla tactics it had used in the war against the British. This enabled Volunteers to mount effective resistance to enemy 'mopping up' operations, especially in counties Cork, Kerry and Mayo. Irritated by its failure to crush the resistance, the Provisional Government reacted by instituting the execution of republican prisoners, the first being carried out on 17 November.[20]

The most famous event of this stage was the death of Michael Collins. On 20 August, the commander-in-chief of the National Army left Dublin for Cork. Officially, he was on an inspection tour of his forces. Unofficially, he seems to have hoped to meet with IRA leaders in order to discuss ways of ending the fighting. As dusk fell on 22 August, Collins's convoy entered the Béal na mBláth valley on its way to Cork city. Encountering an obstruction, a wagon blocking the road, Collins ordered a halt. Coming under gunfire from a nearby hill, the National soldiers, including Collins, scrambled from their vehicles and took up positions to return fire. A long fire-fight ensued. Collins sustained a bullet wound to the back of his head and died soon afterwards.

17 *Glasgow Observer and Catholic Herald*, 29 July 1922; membership roll of 'A' Company, 1st Battalion, Scottish Brigade IRA (EMP, 3/C/13); Michael Farry, *The Aftermath of Revolution: Sligo 1921–23* (Dublin: University College Dublin Press, 2000), p. 77

18 O/C Scotland to O/C Britain, 27 Feb. 1923 (HO, 144/3746)

19 *Poblacht na hÉireann* (Scottish edition), 14 Oct. 1922

20 Hopkinson, *Green*, pp. 172–79, 189–92, 201–20

John 'Jock' McPeak was the machine-gunner in the convoy's armoured car, the *Slievenamon*. His failure to use the machine gun effectively and the fact that he absconded to the IRA with the car four months later are only two of many suspicious aspects to Collins's death that have fuelled debates on it ever since. McPeak later denied that he was an IRA agent. His desertion from the National Army was due to revulsion at the mistreatment of prisoners in army custody, he stated. Approaching the IRA, he asked for safe passage to Scotland and they agreed to arrange it in return for the *Slievemamon*, which they then used in a number of operations. (After spending over six months on the run in counties Cork and Kerry, McPeak was eventually smuggled to Glasgow by the Volunteers. However, arrested by police, he was returned to Ireland and put on trial for the theft of the armoured car. Convicted, he was sentenced to six years in prison.) In explanation of his failure to keep up sustained firing during the ambush, he pointed to the fact that he had no assistant to load the loose ammunition into the belts. An officer tried to help but he did it improperly. 'From then on there was nothing but stoppages, continuous stoppages', McPeak complained. 'You had to clear the gun, you had to take the round out again. This meant very desultory fire.' In any event, even if the machine gun had worked properly, 'it would not have made a whole deal of difference': the ambushers were concealing themselves so well that McPeak 'didn't have a real target' at which to fire. The Glaswegian inclined to the belief that Collins was killed by a bullet that ricocheted off the armoured car. 'It was silly to stand and fight', he reflected. 'The convoy could easily have gone round the cart that had been drawn hurriedly across the road ... I will never understand why we had to halt.'[21]

For John Pinkman in Mallow, the death of Collins was 'catastrophic'. He compared it to the death in 1603, reputedly by poisoning, of Red Hugh O'Donnell, the king of modern day County Donegal who led a rebellion against English rule: 'With lesser men unable to assume the splendour of their leadership, Ireland sank into periods of despondency and internecine strife after their assassinations'. Remaining steadfast to the treaty and Collins's ideals, the Liverpudlian spent the second stage of the war on countryside patrols hunting for 'fugitive Irregulars reportedly foraging among the wild, rain-soaked hills'.[22]

Three National soldiers from Britain died during this period. On 29 August, Hugh Thornton, one of the Frongoch internees and now a captain,

21 *II*, 18, 19, 20, 21 May 1971
22 Pinkman, *Legion*, pp. 177–78, 182

was killed by gunfire while travelling through the town of Clonakilty, County Cork.[23] On 2 September, one soldier was killed and 15 were wounded by machine gun fire while on parade in Cork city. One of the maimed, Glasgow's James McCann, died of his injuries almost two weeks later.[24] Finally, on 17 September, a group of about 18 soldiers were ambushed on their way to mass at Boher Church in County Tipperary, and John Lynn, another Glaswegian, was killed.[25]

The activities of former Tyneside Volunteer Liam Ferris afford us an insight into IRA operations during this period. He had joined 'C' or Newcastle-upon-Tyne Company in December 1920 or January 1921 and was involved in gunrunning and arson operations. In September 1922, he transferred to the ASU of the 5th (or Mullingar) Brigade, 1st Eastern Division. James Cunningham, one of the 13 men who absconded while on bail in connection with the raid on the Birmingham ammunition factory in April 1922, was the Brigade O/C, while his fellow defendant David Fitzgerald was an officer in the ASU. Ferris's role was that of an engineer and he saw active service in County Westmeath. In October, he helped to block roads and sabotage telephone communications near Castlepollard and participated in a raid on Multyfarnham railway station during which the bridge was blown up. The following month, the ASU mounted an unsuccessful ambush of National troops near Delvin, fought at Fore and Collinstown and blocked roads near Drumcree. In December, they attacked Killucan railway station, destroying the signal cabin, and blew up Neill's bridge near Mullingar.[26]

The final stage of the war, from late 1922 to the end of May 1923, witnessed the disintegration of the IRA. Despite attacks on railway infrastructure and the houses of prominent Unionists, the morale of Volunteers was undermined by desertions and executions. The death of Liam Lynch, following a skirmish with National soldiers in County Tipperary on 10 April, removed the major obstacle to the IRA ending its increasingly futile struggle. Finally, on 24 May, Volunteers were ordered to 'dump arms'.[27]

This stage of the conflict was characterized by brutality. John Pinkman was one of three NCOs placed in charge of a prison in Tralee, County Kerry. The facility had earned 'a bad reputation for the treatment of its prisoners',

---

23 *IT*, 30 Aug. 1922
24 *IT*, 18 Sept. 1922
25 *IT*, 20 Sept. 1922
26 Liam Ferris's Military Service Pension Application, 14 May 1935, 3 July 1938 (Patrick Brennan Papers)
27 Hopkinson, *Green*, pp. 228–47, 256–58

he noted.[28] One National soldier from Britain was killed during this period. While on guard near Dublin's Mountjoy Prison on 14 March, Corporal Donald McGuinness of Port Glasgow was shot dead.[29]

Brutality was not confined to this stage. In late September 1922, Seán Mooney was in the custody of the Criminal Investigation Department (CID), a plain-clothes police outfit originally formed by Michael Collins during the truce. He was taken to Dun Laoghaire Naval Base and interrogated. Frustrated by his refusal to divulge information, the policemen stood him up against a wall and fired four or five shots at him. Unruffled, Mooney merely reproached the men for their bad marksmanship. He was then transferred to Wellington Barracks.[30] Arrested in Dublin, Glasgow Cumann na mBan members, including 'Pidge' Duggan, were interrogated as to whereabouts of Joe Robinson, Duggan's fiancée. When the women refused to answer, they were taken by lorry into the Dublin Mountains. They remained adamant in refusing to divulge the O/C Scotland's location: 'Three times they [i.e. the National troops] stopped the lorry, got their guns, made the girls kneel, [and] asked them to say their prayers as they would shoot them when they would count up to number ten'. In the event, however, they were not shot but incarcerated in Kilmainham Jail.[31]

Nevertheless, the introduction of capital punishment in late 1922 precipitated a noticeable increase in the level of wanton violence. On 8 December, Rory O'Connor, Liam Mellows and two other IRA leaders – untried and unconvicted of any crime – were executed in Mountjoy Prison in response to the Volunteers' assassination of a pro-treaty TD.[32] James O'Malley and Seán O'Connor were also executed. As a Liverpool Volunteer, O'Malley had been sentenced to ten years' imprisonment for involvement in the arson attack of 9 March 1921. Following his release from Dartmoor in February 1922, he returned to his native County Galway and joined the anti-treaty 2nd Western Brigade. In early 1923, he took part in an attack on Headford Barracks, during which two National soldiers were killed. Captured with five others on 21 February, O'Malley was interned in Galway Jail, where he was involved in an unsuccessful escape attempt. On 11 April, he was one

28 Pinkman, *Legion*, p. 192

29 *IT*, 17 Mar. 1923

30 *Poblacht na hÉireann* (Scottish edition), 14 Oct. 1922; Eunan O'Halpin, *Defending Ireland: The Irish State and Its Enemies Since 1922* (Oxford: Oxford University Press, 1999), pp. 11–15

31 Anonymous memoir, 1972–73 (ECP, P61/4[67–69])

32 *IT*, 9 Dec. 1922

of six men executed at Tuam Barracks after being found guilty of illegal possession of munitions.[33] Seán ('Jack') O'Connor worked on a boat plying between Merseyside, Limerick and Kerry. During the war of independence, he served as I/O in the 1st Cork Brigade. He had then transferred to the 3rd Brigade before going on the run to Liverpool. On 5 March 1923, suspected of smuggling weapons for the IRA, he was arrested in Fenit, County Kerry. The following day, he was one of eight prisoners killed by the explosion of a mine at Ballyseedy Cross. Republicans claimed that National soldiers under the command of Dubliner Paddy Daly had deliberately set off the mine and later fired shots into the dead bodies. The army denied this, stating that the IRA-laid mine had exploded while the prisoners were clearing an obstruction.[34] Few, however, believed this explanation. Even Pinkman noted that Daly's men were the 'cruellest swine in all Ireland'.[35] Meanwhile, George King, another Frongoch internee, died from injuries sustained on 5 February during an attempt to disarm National troops in Rathmines, County Dublin.[36]

III

Much to Liam Lynch's annoyance, at least three months elapsed from the time of Rory O'Connor's arrest on 30 June to the new O/C Britain, Pa Murray, taking up his position.[37] Murray had experience in Britain. In 1920, he participated in the plot to assassinate a cabinet minister in retaliation for Terence MacSwiney's death, while the following year he took part in the attempt on Major Percival's life.[38] An adjutant in Tom Barry's flying column in the 1st Southern Division, Murray was unenthusiastic about his new role. GHQ's request that he 'take charge of London [i.e. Britain]' was rather vague, he complained. He asked for more definite details before he would agree to assume the position: 'what do you propose to do there? Burn houses – shoot people – what is expected?' Believing that 'very little was done in England' during the 1919–21 war, he wondered what could be achieved there now given that the IRA enjoyed much less support. Still, he said that he would take up

33 Connemara Brigade roll of honour (MTP, P69/165(48–49, 51–54)]; *TT*, 11 Apr. 1921; *IT*, 12 Apr. 1923; see Chapter 3

34 'C.J.C.' to Maurice Twomey, 6 May 1927 (MTP, P69/162[2]); *Éire: The Irish Nation*, 14 Apr. 1923; Hopkinson, *Green*, p. 241

35 Pinkman, *Legion*, pp. 193–94

36 *IT*, 10, 17 Feb. 1923

37 Patrick Murray interview (EO'MN, P17b/88)

38 See Chapter 3

the position if a detailed plan of operation was drawn up by men familiar with the situation in Britain.[39]

The arrest of O/C London Reginald Dunne for assassinating Sir Henry Wilson had the effect of 'shaking the confidence of the entire organisation' in the capital, remembered the gunrunner Martin Walsh. Acting O/C Denis Kelleher seems to have demobilized the IRA in the aftermath of the incident. Liam Lynch complained that Kelleher and most of the rank and file 'were outwardly on our side [but] they were actively working for the F[ree]. State'. He then dismissed them from the IRA. A new Volunteer unit was founded under the leadership of Billy Aherne, a Cork man who had also partaken in the Percival mission in 1921.[40] Meanwhile, in Liverpool Denis Fleming was O/C and on Tyneside Anthony Mularkey was in charge.[41] Intelligence gathered by Free State agents in Britain indicates that J. Walsh was O/C Manchester and P. O'Brien was his counterpart in Birmingham.[42] The O/C Scotland was Joe Robinson and his officers consisted of Séamus Reader as vice-commandant, Charles Diamond adjutant and James McCafferty I/O and QM.[43]

These men remained in charge of the IRA in Britain until mid-March 1923, when 110 republicans were arrested by the police and deported to Ireland, where they were interned. In addition, a small number were arrested over the subsequent two months and some of them were deported too. Those caught in the dragnet included the O/Cs of Birmingham, Liverpool, Tyneside and Scotland, along with members of their staffs.[44] Liam Horan apparently succeeded Denis Fleming as O/C on Merseyside only to be arrested himself two months later, while Séamus Reader stepped into Joe Robinson's shoes.[45] The IRA was 'pretty hardly hit' by the arrests, Liam Lynch noted, but he hoped that the replacement of those captured would prevent a collapse

39 Pa Murray to Divisional Adjutant, 22 Sept. 1922 (EO'ML, P17a/51)

40 Martin Walsh to MSPB, n.d. (EO'ML, P17a/154); C/S to QM 1st Cork Brigade, 7 Aug. 1922; O/C Britain to C/S, 2 Nov. 1923 (MTP, P69/24[18], P69/120[40–41]); C/S to O/C 1st Southern Division, 3 Sept. 1922 (EO'ML, P17a/17); C/S to Assistant C/S, 12 Sept. 1922 (HO, 144/3746); see Chapter 3

41 O/C Liverpool to O/C Britain, 7 Feb. 1923; O/C Newcastle to O/C Britain, 2 Mar. 1923 (HO, 144/3746); BMHWS 824, Patrick Daly, pp. 43–44

42 List of active republicans in Manchester, *c.* Jan. 1923; list of active republicans in Birmingham, *c.* Jan. 1923 (MCP, A/0913)

43 Col. MacAosa to Director of Intelligence, 15 June 1923 (EO'ML, P17a/182)

44 *TT*, 13 Mar. 1923; O/C Britain to C/S, 30 Mar. 1923 (RMP, P7/B/92[18]])

45 'RROUK', no. 206, 17 May 1923 (CAB, 24/160); O/C Britain to C/S, 29 Sept. 1923 (MTP, P69/37[190–94])

of the organization.[46] Pa Murray proffered his resignation as O/C Britain in response to the police's capture of so many men and correspondence. Describing the offer as 'shameful', Lynch refused to accept it at such a 'critical moment'. He was confident that victory was imminent as long as republicans remained united.[47]

Along with Lynch, those at IRA GHQ who took particular interest in activities in Britain were Maurice 'Moss' Twomey, deputy C/S from January 1923, and Michael Cremin, the D/P. In January 1923, with the civil war in its seventh month, Lynch placed the strength of the Volunteers in England at a minimum of 289. In London, membership numbered only 20. When the unit under Billy Aherne was being formed the previous September, Lynch had insisted on recruitment being confined to 'reliable men', despite the fact that this would perforce limit the membership; 'no risks' could be taken, he said. Still, the Volunteers there were 'well organised', largely due to it being the headquarters of the O/C Britain. In the north of England, Newcastle-upon-Tyne had 29 Volunteers, Bedlington 40 and Barrow 25. Chester-le-Street, Middlesbrough, Consett, Thornley and Wallsend all had 'small numbers'. Commenting on the north-east as a whole, the C/S was content that 'a fairly good Organisation' existed there, one which was improving week on week. Liverpool had 25 men and St Helens 15, and he judged these members 'fairly reliable'. Listing Manchester, Birmingham, Sheffield, Cardiff, Bristol, Newport and Plymouth, Lynch stated that 'very few' Volunteers were enrolled in any of these places. Still, organizational work had begun, albeit only recently in some, and he was confident that membership could be built up, perhaps to levels that were enjoyed during the war of independence. In Scotland, the Glasgow Brigade had a membership of 140, but only 40 were deemed reliable. Lanarkshire boasted 70 men, while Stirlingshire had 50. These three parts of Scotland were 'fairly well organised', he commented, due largely to enthusiastic efforts over the previous few weeks. Finally, in Wales, 15 'good men' constituted the Swansea Volunteers.[48]

Little information exists on the state of organization of the Cumann na mBan at this time. According to Sorcha McDermott, the outfit's monthly meetings in London ceased after the assassination of Sir Henry

46 C/S to O/C Britain, 4 Apr. 1923 (EO'ML, P17a/51)

47 C/S to Deputy C/S, 9 Apr.; C/S to O/C Britain, 9 Apr. 1923 (EdeVP, P150/1749)

48 C/S to President de Valera and Ministers, 30 Jan. 1923 (EdeVP, P150/1749); C/S to O/C 1st Southern Division, 3 Sept. 1922 (EO'ML, P17a/17)

Wilson.[49] However, Free State agents believed that the organization in the capital continued its activities under the leadership of Shelia Sheehan, and they thought likewise of the Liverpool section.[50] The women's auxiliary was active in Glasgow too.[51] Unfortunately, no membership figures are available. In March 1923, Cumann na mBan members were among those arrested and deported to Dublin. In Liverpool, Mary Finan, Catherine 'Kitty' Furlong, Mary Leonard and Maura Lively were detained. In London, Grace Lally and Cissie Sheehan were taken into custody, while in Glasgow, Elizabeth 'Lizzie' Moran was arrested.[52]

Even less information exists as to the activities of Na Fianna Éireann during the civil war. In April 1923, Denis Breslin, described by the police as being 'in command of the Fianna, or Boy's Scouts' Section of the Irish Republican Army', was arrested in Glasgow. However, another source states that Breslin ceased being a Fianna organizer in 1922 and gives no information on the existence of the organization during the civil war.[53]

As during the war of independence and the truce, therefore, republicans in Britain boasted units of the IRA, Cumann na mBan and perhaps the Fianna. However, they lacked IRB circles. The Fenians was the one organization that did not split into pro- and anti-treaty sections. The body's Supreme Council had taken an ambiguous position on the treaty. On the one hand, it endorsed the agreement, yet, on the other, it allowed individual IRB men who happened to be members of the Dáil to vote with their consciences on the issue.[54] Due to Michael Collins being Fenian President, republicans (erroneously) viewed the organization as having been instrumental in securing the Dáil's ratification of the treaty. As Mary MacSwiney later argued, 'It was the IRB that had ruined us in getting the Treaty passed'.[55] Disgusted, they

49 BMHWS 945, Sorcha Nic Diarmada, p. 7
50 Col. Carter to H.R. Scott, 3 Apr. 1923, enclosing intelligence report on Shelia Sheehan, n.d. (HO, 144/2894); Diarmuid O'Hegarty to Carter, 10 Apr. 1923, enclosing intelligence reports (HO, 144/2865); intelligence reports on Mary Finan, n.d. (HO, 144/2866); O'Hegarty to Carter, 1 May 1923 (HO, 144/2904)
51 O/C Scotland to O/C Britain, 17 Feb. 1923 (HO, 144/3746)
52 *TT*, 13 Mar. 1923
53 'RROUK', no. 201, 12 Apr. 1923 (CAB, 24/259); membership roll of 'A' Company, 1st Battalion, Scottish Brigade IRA (EMP, 3/C/13)
54 IRB Circular, 'The Organisation and the New Political Situation in Ireland', 12 Dec. 1921 (AÓBP, MS 8428/13)
55 Mary MacSwiney to C/S, 25 June 1923 (EdeVP, P150/1752); Hopkinson, 'Treaty', p. 11

left the Fenian organization to the pro-treatyites. By the outbreak of the civil war, the IRB was effectively dead.[56]

The IRA had the support of some public organizations. On 29 July, representatives of 43 of the ISDL's 217 branches met in London and reaffirmed the body's objectives as being 'the application of the principle of self-determination for Ireland and the recognition of the Irish Republic proclaimed in Dublin in Easter, 1916'. Anticipating such an outcome, President P.J. Kelly had refused to attend the conference, complaining that it was unrepresentative of the views of the Irish in Britain, 90 per cent of whom were in favour of offering the Provisional Government 'every opportunity and support in giving effect to their policy'. Therefore, Art O'Brien was elected president in Kelly's place, Gilbert Barrington became one of the vice-presidents, while Liam McMahon was re-elected as one of the honorary treasurers. Seán McGrath remained as general secretary.[57]

The activities of the ISDL were hampered somewhat by O'Brien's arrest soon afterwards in Dublin while attending the funeral of McGrath's mother. Disputing the right of the Provisional Government to dismiss him from his position as the Dáil's representative in London, he had refused to comply with its request that he hand over funds connected with the office. Still, he hoped to settle the matter amicably. However, released after three weeks imprisonment, he was served with a writ indicating that Michael Collins was instituting legal proceedings to secure the monies. Offering his services to de Valera, O'Brien was instructed to return to London 'and carry on there in the most effective manner possible'.[58] At the end of the year, de Valera, by now president of the notional Republican government, conditionally renewed O'Brien's position as 'Representative from the Government of the Republic to ENGLAND' and instructed him to surrender the funds only on the orders of his government.[59] Another factor frustrating the ISDL was, McGrath complained, the apathy of the Irish in Britain. By the end of November, the number of affiliated branches had dropped from 59 to 45.

---

56 Curran, 'IRB', p. 22

57 Report of the Second Session of the Third Annual Conference of the ISDL, 29 July; P.J. Kelly to the Secretaries of the ISDL, 26 July 1922 (AÓBP, MS 8432/1)

58 Art O'Brien to Eamon de Valera, 6 Oct. 1922; O'Brien to the Secretary, Dept. of Finance, 3 May 1932 (AÓBP, MS 8423/13, 8460/19)

59 De Valera and Austin Stack to O'Brien, 22 Nov.; de Valera to O'Brien, 1, 20 Dec. 1922 (AÓBP, MS 8423/13, 8461/3); original emphasis

Of these, only 20 were functioning, in London, Tyneside, Birmingham, Earlestown and elsewhere. The total membership was merely 1,952.[60]

Consequently, it was not until late 1922 that the league began to make its presence felt. On 25 October, it held a meeting, attended by over 1,000 people, to mark the second anniversary of Terence MacSwiney's death.[61] On 6 December, meetings were organized in London and Birmingham to protest the establishment of the Free State, one year after the signing of the treaty. The agreement, declared O'Brien, was to be condemned because it surrendered 'two things which no generation in a nation can give away – Sovereignty and Unity'. The meeting repudiated the treaty and denounced 'the sustained efforts of England to impose on Ireland, by armed might, her Imperial domination for her own material interests'.[62] On 21 and 22 January 1923, 'to celebrate the Declaration of Independence and the re-affirmation of the Establishment of the Irish Republic by Dail Eireann made on the 21st January, 1919', meetings occurred in London, Manchester, Tyneside and Derby. At the London meeting, O'Brien was reported as saying: 'The Irish Republican Government incorporated and had attracted to it an army, so that in giving financial assistance to it they [i.e. the audience] were giving support to something which was real, not mythical'.[63] O'Brien and McGrath were among those arrested in March 1923.[64]

In September 1922, the Republican Clubs in Scotland came together to found Poblacht na h-Éireann in Albain, or the Irish Republican Organization in Scotland. Membership was open to those who rejected the treaty and refused 'allegiance to any person or persons prepared even for a moment to subvert the Republic, or to compromise in any way the claim of the Irish people for full and unfettered moral, material, political and economic freedom'. Joe Robinson was involved in the organization. 'Of all the children of Irish race in foreign lands, none have been more faithful than you in SCOTLAND', de Valera declared in a message sent to the body's inaugural convention in

60 Report of General Secretary to Standing Committee meeting, 2 Dec.; report by General Secretary on each existing branch, 16 Dec. 1922 (AÓBP, MS 8432/1)

61 'RROUK', no. 179, 2 Nov. 1922 (CAB, 24/139)

62 *Poblacht na hÉireann* (Scottish edition), 30 Dec. 1922; 'RROUK', no. 185, 14 Dec. 1922 (CAB, 24/140)

63 *Éire: The Irish Nation*, 3 Feb. 1923; Frank McDonagh to Desmond FitzGerald, 22 Jan. 1923, enclosing transcription of speeches (UCDA, Desmond & Mabel FitzGerald Papers [DMFP], P80/331[33/1])

64 *TT*, 13 Mar. 1923

November 1922.[65] Like the ISDL, Poblacht na h-Eireann in Albain organized a meeting on 6 December to condemn the signing of the treaty. The civil war raging in Ireland was the result of 'dictation' by 'Churchill & Co. in the British Parliament', who demanded that the Provisional Government turn 'English guns on the faithful army of the Republic', declared one speaker.[66] Further meetings were held in January and February 1923, some addressed by Countess Markievicz, still president of the Cumann na mBan, who subsequently visited London and other parts of England.[67] The establishment of Poblacht na h-Éireann in Albain eased the 'chaos' that had reigned in Irish circles in Scotland since Dublin's abrupt formation of the Republican Clubs earlier in the year, one member reflected. However, dissension was caused by members of the first Republican Club attempting to use the organization to propagate communist politics.[68] Meanwhile, difficulties in securing printing facilities in Ireland led republican newspapers *Poblacht na hÉireann* (Scottish edition) and its successor *Éire: The Irish Nation* to base themselves in Glasgow, where IRA men such as Eamonn Mooney and Cumann na mBan members helped in their production.[69] The 'kidnapping of Irish Republicans in Scotland and England is a political persecution', *Éire* declared in reaction to the mass arrest and deportation of 11 March. By encroaching on much-vaunted English constitutional liberties, the British government had demonstrated to the world that there was no civil war in Ireland but rather a British war 'against Irish Freedom'.[70]

Meanwhile, the IRA's pro-treaty enemies maintained a presence in Britain too. It was claimed that around 2,000 members of the Scottish Brigade remained loyal to the Provisional Government.[71] Complaining that his men had no work to do, Coatbridge's Patrick Fleming threatened to disband his

---

65 *Poblacht na hÉireann* (Scottish edition), 7 Oct., 18 Nov., 16 Dec. 1922 (original emphasis); 'RROUK', no. 181, 16 Nov. 1922 (CAB 24/140)

66 *Poblacht na hÉireann* (Scottish edition), 16 Dec. 1922

67 *Éire: The Irish Nation*, 27 Jan., 3, 24 Feb. 1923; 'RROUK', no. 194, 22 Feb.; 'RROUK', no. 195, 1 Mar.; 'RROUK', no. 196, 8 Mar.; 'RROUK', no. 198, 22 Mar.; 'RROUK', no. 199, 28 Mar. 1923 (CAB, 24/159)

68 Joseph Browne to unknown, 'Organiser's Report on Irish Republican Organisation in Scotland', 20 Sept. 1923 (MTP, P69/44[373–74])

69 'A.A.C.S' to Joe Robinson, 15 Sept. 1922 (MAI, Captured Documents Collection, A/1016, lot 28); list of active republicans in Scotland, n.d. but *c.* Jan. 1923 (MCP, A/0913); anonymous memoirs, 1972–73 (ECP, P61/4[65–69])

70 *Éire: The Irish Nation*, 14 Apr. 1923 (Editorial)

71 S. Fullerton to Minister for Defence, 31 Aug., 6 Sept. 1922 (MCP, A/06181)

unit unless Dublin clarified its function.[72] An 'active organisation' loyal to Dublin also existed in London, which Liam Lynch complained was frustrating the work of the IRA in the capital.[73] However, its membership is not known, and neither is the existence of pro-treaty Volunteers elsewhere in England and Wales. The pro-treatyites also established rivals to the republican ISDL and Poblacht na h-Eireann in Albain. Following his refusal to attend the London conference on 29 July, P.J. Kelly and others, including former Tyneside Battalion officers Richard Purcell and J.P. Connolly, attempted to organize pro-treaty ISDL branches into a coherent body.[74] (In the general election in November 1922, Purcell, Connolly and a number of other pro-treaty organizers canvassed Irish voters in Birmingham and Dundee to vote for Austen Chamberlain and Winston Churchill, the most prominent signatories to the treaty standing for re-election, as the Provisional Government feared that the agreement might be endangered if moderates such as these were defeated by die-hard Conservatives opponents. Chamberlain was returned to parliament but Churchill lost his seat.[75]) Their apparent lack of success may have motivated the establishment of the Irish Exiles' League of Great Britain.[76] Scotland, meanwhile, boasted 72 pro-treaty Sinn Féin branches.[77] 'All the Irish in Britain are strongly in favour of the Treaty', claimed a pro-treaty newspaper, 'except a small minority of irresponsible people, most of whom never saw Ireland, and have fallen under the influence of Communism in Britain.'[78]

During the truce, Rory O'Connor had recommended the establishment of 'an English General Head Quarters'.[79] By January 1923, a GHQ had indeed been founded, in London. Unlike O'Connor, therefore, who travelled back and forth across the Irish Sea, Pa Murray, his successor, lived full-time in Britain. He was assisted by a staff consisting of a chemist, an engineer, an adjutant and an I/O; these positions were filled by fellow Cork men.[80]

72 Patrick Fleming to Richard Mulcahy, 8 Oct. 1922 (MCP, A/06181)

73 C/S to O/C 1st Southern Division, 3 Sept. 1922 (EO'ML, P17a/17)

74 Clipping from *Young Ireland*, 14 Oct.; report of General Secretary to Standing Committee meeting, 2 Dec. 1922 (AÓBP, MS 8432/1)

75 Correspondence between Alfred Cope, Desmond FitzGerald and Richard Purcell, Nov. 1922 (DMFP, P80/391[1–7])

76 Frank McDonagh to Desmond FitzGerald, 22 Dec. 1922 (DMFP, P80/331[28])

77 Clipping from *Young Ireland*, 14 Oct. 1922 (AÓBP, MS 8432/1)

78 Clipping from *Young Ireland*, 14 Oct. 1922 (AÓBP, MS 8432/1)

79 See Chapter 4

80 C/S to President de Valera & Ministers, 30 Jan. 1923 (EdeVP, P150/1749); Patrick Murray interview (EO'MN, P17b/88); C/S to O/C 1st Southern

Upon his appointment in August 1920, O'Connor's mandate was 'to organise and carry out operations in Enemy Territory'. In contrast, his successor had five responsibilities, four of which related to gunrunning. One, however, concerned the IRA in Britain in general: the O/C had responsibility for 'all men working for [the] organisation, [in the] purchases [section] or otherwise'.[81] Murray remained in close contact with GHQ in Ireland and carried out its orders, supplying it with maps detailing Volunteer units in Britain, organizing a clandestine communications system with republicans in America and undertaking organizational work.[82]

Murray believed that the IRA leadership in Ireland did not fully appreciate how divisions caused by the treaty created difficulties in operating in Britain.[83] Such dissension was evident at a gala organized by the pro-treaty mid-Durham branch of the ISDL on 7 August 1922. Republicans attempted to disrupt the event, held in Wharton Park. When one of the gatecrashers 'exclaimed something [complementary] about De Valera', Richard Purcell engaged him in a fight and a general melee ensued. The violence eventually ended and the speeches began. However, the speakers, including Seán Milroy, a pro-treaty TD, were greeted with whistles, screams and catcalls of 'traitor' and a smoke bomb was thrown at the platform. More violence arose when the stewards attempted to remove the hecklers.[84] Other Irish organizations adopted a neutral position. In February 1923, *Éire* criticized the London GAA for failing to support its cause. In the past, the sporting body had associated itself with every movement that sought to achieve Irish freedom, it was claimed. 'If the London GAA cannot supply recruits for the Irish Republican Army it certainly can and should supply funds to maintain the Republic', the newspaper declared. It would not suffice for young Irishmen in the capital to continue playing football and hurling while the republic was in a life-or-death struggle with the 'Imperial Slave Staters': 'Irish games not wedded to Irish Nationality are of no more service to the Irish Republic than the playing of ping-pong'.[85] The London Gaelic League was also criticized for its detachment. Art O'Brien later stated that the treaty-split and civil war gave rise to 'disruptive elements' in the

Division, 10 Sept.; O/C Britain to Divisional Adjutant, 22 Sept.; Divisional Adjutant to C/S, 4 Dec. 1922 (EO'ML, P17a/17, P17a/51)

81 QMG to O/C Britain, 5 Jan. 1923 (HO, 144/3746)

82 Patrick Murray interview (EO'MN, P17b/88)

83 Patrick Murray interview (EO'MN, P17b/88)

84 *Newcastle Daily Chronicle, North Mail*, 8 Aug. 1922

85 *Éire: The Irish Nation*, 24 Feb. 1923

organization.[86] In Britain as in Ireland, the Catholic Church was hostile to republicans. In Glasgow, priests prohibited the sale of republican newspapers at church doors. According to British police intelligence, the priest in St Roch's parish 'used physical force to remove two Republicans who were distributing bills outside his church' in mid-April. When two Cumann na mBan members arrived the following week to defiantly dispense leaflets, 'a stormy scene ensued'. A crowd of about 50 'infuriated' women attacked the two republicans, throwing them to the ground and almost tearing their clothes off. The duo had to be rescued by the police.[87]

The finances of the Glasgow IRA posed a problem during the closing stages of the civil war. In January 1923, reading a report sent to him by Pa Murray, Liam Lynch judged the outfit's financial position as 'very unsatisfactory', perhaps due to the fact that 90 per cent of the Volunteers there were unemployed and therefore could not afford to pay the normal subscriptions.[88] The following month, the Cumann na mBan's Glasgow council agreed that units attached to Volunteer companies would assist the latter 'in every way possible especially regarding finance'. Soon, however, a dispute arose regarding the women's auxiliary despatching funds to their GHQ in Dublin and their refusal to lend financial aid to the IRA. Pa Murray assured the council that their right to send money to Dublin had never been questioned and he hoped the matter could be clarified. However, if the Cumann na mBan members persisted in their obstinacy, he would order the IRA to cut all links with them.[89] Whether this dispute was resolved is not known. However, accusations of misuse of Scottish Brigade funds led to the court-martial of Séamus Reader, O/C Scotland, and Tim Healy, Brigade QM, in the autumn of 1923. They were charged with misappropriating funds between 29 April and 30 June. At that time, Reader and Healy were the only active members of the brigade staff in Scotland, their colleagues having been arrested and deported to Ireland the previous March. The money in question, amounting to £102 11s. 6d., had been received by Healy from the brigade battalions, the O/C Britain, the Cumann na mBan and Countess Markievicz. At the court-martial, Healy pleaded guilty to misappropriating £43 11s. 6d. His account of the remaining £59 was vague. Reader denied any knowledge of the money or its misappropriation, but

86 *Éire: The Irish Nation*, 7 July 1923; Ó Bríain, 'Gaedhil thar sáile', pp. 122–23

87 *Poblacht na hÉireann* (Scottish edition), 2 Sept. 1922; 'RROUK', no. 203, 26 Apr. 1923 (CAB, 24/160)

88 C/S to O/C Britain, 30 Jan. 1923 (HO, 144/3746)

89 O/C Scotland to O/C Britain, 17 Feb.; O/C Britain to Mrs Moran, 7 Mar. 1923 (HO, 144/3746)

admitted that his failure to check Healy's accounts was a derogation of duty. In his evidence, the O/C 1st Battalion stated that the battalion council, dissatisfied with Reader's management of brigade funds, had recommended that he, the O/C 1st Battalion, sit on the brigade council. Refusing to discuss the matter, Reader had suspended the council and the entire 1st Battalion. Reader stated that he had acted so because of the battalion's indiscipline and insubordination. He had refused to answer questions regarding the brigade's finances because some of the money had been expended in sensitive areas, particularly £7 'given for information'. The court ruled that both Reader and Healy were guilty of deliberate misappropriation of funds and 'sentenced them to be dismissed with ignominy from the army'. The punishment was lenient, the court explained, because the fact that the defendants were unemployed made the recovery of the money impossible. Also, 'the peculiarities of our position in Britain make any other capital punishment impossible'. Holding, however, that it had not been proven that Reader had misused the money, the C/S subsequently ruled that while both men should indeed be dismissed, only Healy should be discharged with ignominy.[90]

IV

Four of the O/C Britain's five responsibilities were related to gunrunning. These involved the purchase of munitions in Britain; the packing and transport of these weapons to Ireland; the receipt of armaments from America and their despatch across the Irish Sea; and similar duties in relation to munitions from Germany.[91]

For details on those involved in gunrunning in Britain, we are mainly dependent on intelligence gathered by Free State agents. In London, Billy Aherne was assisted by Martin Donovan, Pat Flood, D. O'Grady, W. Newman, J. Woods and others. According to British police intelligence, Seán McGrath was 'acting as a go-between or introducer for the Republican arms agents', this despite rumours questioning his commitment to the republican cause. On at least two occasions, Michael Cremin used Art O'Brien to send funds to Aherne.[92] In Birmingham, the men of importance were Jack Byrne, T. Woods

90 Correspondence between O/C Britain and C/S, 29 Sept., 8 Oct. 1923 (MTP, P69/37[188–94])

91 QMG to O/C Britain, 5 Jan. 1923 (HO, 144/3746)

92 List of active republicans in London, n.d. (EO'ML, P17a/182); list of active republicans in Birmingham, n.d. but *c*. Jan. 1923 (MCP, A/0913); 'RROUK', no. 180, 9 Nov. 1922 (CAB, 24/140); exhibit 11: O'Brien to R. Purcell, 13

and W.J. Feely.[93] On Merseyside, Paddy Daly worked alongside Pat Fleming, Mick Brennan and P. Walsh.[94] The Manchester operation involved war veterans Liam McMahon, Matt Lawless and Séamus Barrett, along with P. Lee, J. Leahy and ISDL man George Clancy.[95] Thomas Flynn was QM of the Tyneside IRA.[96] The Sheffield Volunteers engaged in weapons-smuggling too, though their identities are not known. Meanwhile, in Scotland, the major players were Joe Robinson, Séamus Reader, William Clark, William Doherty, Frank Jordan and James Griffin.[97]

Free State intelligence believed that Cumann na mBan members aided the IRA in gunrunning matters. Cissie Sheehan, leader of the organization in London, purportedly made 'several journeys to the Continent in search of arms and material for the manufacture of explosives'.[98] Liverpool's Kitty Furlong, a cousin of Matt Fowler, one of the men convicted of involvement in the arson attacks of 27 November 1920, allegedly worked as a 'clerk to the Gun-running Section' of the local Volunteers.[99] Her comrade Mary Finan supposedly stored munitions in her house.[100] Meanwhile, Margaret Leonard was alleged to have been 'very active … in connection with the arms traffic in Liverpool', namely in assisting 'personally in the transfer of arms and ammunition from one place to another in the city'. She was also accused of hiding munitions in her house.[101] The three Liverpool women later denied any involvement in gunrunning activities.

Feb. 1923 (AÓBP, MS 8419/2); D/P to QMG, 5 Apr. 1923, enclosing receipts marked 'London', 29 July, 25 Oct. 1922 (JUS, 93/3/4)

93 List of active republicans in Birmingham, n.d. but *c.* Jan. 1923 (MCP, A/0913)

94 List of active republicans in Liverpool, n.d. but *c.* Jan. 1923 (MCP, A/0913); 'P.W.' to unknown, 16 Nov. 1922 (JUS, 93/3/4)

95 List of active republicans in Manchester, n.d. but *c.* Jan. 1923 (MCP, A/0913)

96 Col. Carter to H.R. Scott, 1 May 1923; T.G. Flynn to Tilla Cregan, 13 Jan. 1924 (HO, 144/3748)

97 List of active republicans in Scotland, n.d. but *c.* Jan. 1923 (MCP, A/0913); Director of Intelligence to Seán Golden, 16 Dec. 1922 (EO'ML, P17a/182)

98 Col. Carter to H.R. Scott, 3 Apr. 1923, enclosing intelligence report on Shelia 'Cissie' Sheehan, n.d. (HO, 144/2894)

99 Diarmuid O'Hegarty to Carter, 10 Apr., enclosing intelligence reports; Catherine Furlong's hearing before the Advisory Committee, 16 Apr. 1923 (HO, 144/2865)

100 Mary Finan's hearing before the Advisory Committee, 16 Apr. 1923 (HO, 144/2866)

101 Diarmuid O'Hegarty to Col. Carter, 1 May; Margaret Leonard's hearing before the Advisory Committee, 4 May 1923 (HO, 144/2904)

In mid-March 1923, gun-smugglers were among those arrested by police and deported to Ireland, including Liam McMahon, Séamus Barrett, Thomas Flynn, T. Woods, J.J. King, James McCafferty, William Clark, Frank Jordan, Joseph Brown and James Griffin. The Cumann na mBan's Sheehan, Furlong, Finan and Leonard were arrested too.[102] Unbelievably, Pa Murray told the C/S that the arrests had little adverse effect on gunrunning activities.[103] A number of Glasgow men had already been arrested in January.[104] P. Walsh and two others had been convicted of illegal possession of munitions in a Liverpool house that same month, while February had seen the capture of a gunrunner named Michael O'Donoghue in the city.[105] Further arrests occurred in late March, April and May. Denis Breslin, John Gallagher and Fred Farrell were detained in connection with a raid on a brick factory in Glasgow. Having escaped the dragnet on 11 March, Breslin and Gallagher were deported.[106] Meanwhile, Liam Horan and another man were arrested at an arms dump and convicted of illegal possession of munitions.[107]

As they had during the war of independence, the IRA employed agents from outside its ranks to help source munitions. In January 1923, however, Liam Lynch argued that a lot of money had been wasted on paying agents who had proven to be of 'no use'. He, therefore, recommended exclusive reliance on Volunteers.[108]

The O/C Britain received requests for weapons from IRA units in the field and GHQ, though, in contrast to the situation during the war against the British, the IRA's difficulties often arose not from a lack of munitions but from a shortage of men to use the armaments on hand and the unwillingness of units to share weapons.[109] Nevertheless, in January 1923 the Cork Volunteers asked for 2.5 or 3 inch mountain guns, .45 revolvers and automatics, .303 and .45 revolver ammunition and .45 automatic ammunition, explosives and 4.5- or 9-volt batteries. The QMG commented that the conflict in Ireland would be brought to a rapid conclusion if the IRA had a few mountain

---

102 *TT*, 13 Mar. 1923

103 C/S to O/C Britain, 5 Apr. 1923 (RMP, P7/B/92[14])

104 *II*, 13 Jan.; *MG*, 13, 18 Jan. 1923

105 'RROUK', no. 188, 11 Jan.; 'RROUK', no. 189, 18 Jan.; 'RROUK', no. 195, 1 Mar. 1923 (CAB, 24/158–24/159); *MG*, 26 Feb., 19 Mar., 13 Apr. 1923

106 'RROUK', no. 201, 12 Apr. 1923 (CAB, 24/159); *Hansard 5* (*Commons*), clxii, col. 2249: Capt. Elliot (19 Apr. 1923)

107 'RROUK', no. 206, 17 May 1923 (CAB, 24/160); *TT*, 19 June 1923

108 QMG to O/C Britain, 5 Jan. 1923 (HO, 144/3746)

109 Hopkinson, *Green*, pp. 127, 239

guns.[110] The following week, Liam Lynch recommended that Murray purchase some Stokes guns, a type of trench mortar. 'You realise that one of these, with sufficient shells, would finish the war here very quickly', he wrote.[111]

The Provisional Government worked to prevent IRA gunrunners from exploiting sources, facilities and personnel used during the 1919–21 war. Therefore, republicans were forced to undertake the time-consuming task of developing new sources, making arrangements in relation to new arms dumps and finding reliable seafarers to smuggle the munitions to Ireland.[112] In February 1923, the O/C Liverpool explained the delay in placing sympathetic seafarers on coal ships plying between Dublin and Garston: '[I]t would be necessary for the men who would go in the ships to be down at the Docks at every tide & then it might be two or three weeks before they get on.'[113]

Pa Murray tried to source mountain guns at the British army's base in Aldershot, but failed. Explosives were relatively easy to procure, he remembered.[114] In 1922, a lieutenant in the Tyneside IRA who later supported the Provisional Government stated that his anti-treaty comrades were being instructed to acquire as many weapons as possible. However, due to a shortage of money resulting from having paid too much for munitions during the war and the truce (£3 to £4 for revolvers), they were told to ensure value for money.[115] On 4 October, four Volunteers were arrested while attempting to steal arms from a drill hall in Edinburgh.[116] In early March 1923, the O/C Newcastle stated that fuse detonators could easily be obtained by raiding colliery magazines but that electric detonators were proving difficult to acquire.[117] The Glasgow IRA mounted a raid on Knightswood Brickworks, near Anniesland, early the following month and left with between 8 and 50 lbs (3.6–22.7 kg) of gelignite and 50 detonators. Three days later, however, Joe Robinson's men suffered a setback when the police discovered 112 lbs (50.8 kg) of gelignite cartridges and 27 yards (24.7m) of fuse hidden in the Balgray railway tunnel.[118]

110 QMG to O/C Britain, 17 Jan. 1923 (HO, 144/3746)
111 C/S to O/C Britain, 26 Jan. 1923 (HO, 144/3746)
112 Patrick Murray interview (EO'MN, P17b/88)
113 O/C Liverpool to O/C Britain, 7 Feb. 1923 (HO, 144/3746)
114 Patrick Murray interview (EO'MN, P17b/88)
115 Col. Carter to H.R. Scott, 1 May 1923, enclosing 'Instructions regarding I.R.A. movements in Tyneside Area', n.d. (HO, 144/3748)
116 *IT*, 6 Oct. 1922; 'RROUK', no. 176, 12 Oct. 1922 (CAB, 24/139)
117 O/C Newcastle to O/C Britain, 2 Mar. 1923 (HO, 144/3746)
118 *TT*, 9, 10 Apr. 1923; 'RROUK', no. 201, 12 Apr. 1923 (CAB, 24/159)

There was a 'regular consistent flow' of munitions from continental Europe and America, according to Pa Murray.[119] Bob Briscoe, the IRA's arms agent in Germany during the war of independence, had continued his gunrunning activities there during the truce and the treaty-split. In August 1922, D/P Michael Cremin ordered him to America and Seán MacBride took up the position in Germany.[120] He sent Mauser handguns from Hamburg to Glasgow.[121] Free State intelligence suspected Londoners John McCann and Ted Brown of importing guns from Germany for the IRA, and the former was arrested in late March 1923.[122]

As mentioned in the previous chapter, the dearth of extant sources and the confusing nature of some of those that do survive make it impossible to be precise as to the amount of munitions acquired by gunrunners in Britain during the civil war. Between 30 June 1922 and 11 February 1923, Liverpool men spent £823 12s. The overwhelming majority of this money was used to pay the gunrunners' wages and cover various expenses. Strikingly, the only munitions recorded as having been purchased by them are three handguns and 32 rounds of ammunition, along with 4 tons 16 cwt (4,877 kg) of potassium chlorate.[123] Due perhaps to the paucity of munitions acquired by the Merseyside men, Pa Murray later declared that Liverpool was 'no good'.[124]

Between June and December 1922, the London gunrunners spent £883. Of this, £330 14s. 6d. was spent on purchasing 15 .45 revolvers and 18,200 rounds of ammunition, along with such explosives paraphernalia as 14 cwt (711.2 kg) of dinitrotoluene, two tons (2,032 kg) of potassium chlorate and small quantities of peroxide and ballistite. The remaining money was expended on various expenses, including the cost of transporting the munitions to Merseyside.[125] According to another account, the London men

119 Patrick Murray interview (EO'MN, P17b/88)
120 Robert Briscoe, with Alden Hatch, *For the Life of Me* (London: Longmans, 1958), pp. 183–84
121 Patrick Murray interview (EO'MN, P17b/88)
122 Intelligence report on John McCann, n.d. (HO, 144/2897)
123 'A/C of expenditure from June 30th', marked 'Lpool', n.d.; D/P to QMG, 3 Apr. 1923, enclosing account marked 'POD "A"', 10 July 1922; D/P to QMG, 5 Apr. 1923, enclosing receipts marked 'Lpool', 6 Nov. 1922; 'P.W.' to unknown, 16 Nov. 1922; Liverpool purchases account, 30 Jan.–17 Feb. 1923, n.d. (JUS, 93/3/4)
124 Patrick Murray interview (EO'MN, P17b/88)
125 O/C London to C/S, 8 Dec. 1922; C/S to O/C Britain, 30 Jan. 1923 (HO, 144/3746)

also purchased one .38 revolver, 10,000 percussion caps and three mine exploders.[126]

Eight Volunteer companies were involved in gunrunning on Tyneside. At one stage they had in various dumps three guns, 194 lbs 13 oz (88.6 kg) of high explosives and 174 detonators. In July and October 1922, they sent three batches of munitions to Liverpool. The two in July included nine handguns, 648 rounds of ammunition and 2 lbs (0.9 kg) of high explosives. The consignment sent on 14 October contained 52 lbs (23.6 kg) of high explosives and 250 rounds of ammunition.[127]

In late 1922 or early 1923, the QMG recorded having received 17 handguns and 209 rounds of .32 automatic ammunition from Glasgow. In addition at least three machine guns, 20 rifles, ten shotguns and 3,400 rounds of ammunition were shipped to Ireland from Clydeside.[128] Still, Pa Murray found Glasgow 'hard'.[129] Between June and September 1922, the Sheffield IRA used £100 to purchase 19 handguns, one rifle and 120 rounds of .303 ammunition.[130] The only record relating to Birmingham refers to the acquisition of, among other things, one Lee Enfield rifle, one .45 Colt revolver, 158 rounds of assorted ammunition and a quantity of potassium chlorate.[131]

The D/P supplied small amounts of money to Southampton and Manchester as well, though the type and quantity of munitions purchased in these areas is not recorded.[132] Munitions continued to be sourced in New York too. Between 23 May and 8 November, 31 handguns and 25,664 rounds of ammunition were received in Liverpool from there.[133]

Therefore, a minimum of three machine guns, 22 rifles, ten shotguns, 99 handguns, 48,681 rounds of ammunition, over 6,909 kg of potassium

126 'Statement of a/c from 1.6.22 to 31.12.22 as per attached sheets', marked 'London', 31 Dec. 1922 (JUS, 93/3/4)

127 Col. Carter to H.R. Scott, 1 May 1923, enclosing list of 'Stuff', n.d., and despatches dated 2, 6 July and 14 Oct. 1922 (HO, 144/3748)

128 'Ammunition Purchases and Inwards' n.d.; 'Arms Purchases and Inwards', n.d. (JUS, 93/3/4); *TT*, 7 Oct. 1922

129 Patrick Murray interview (EO'MN, P17b/88)

130 D/P to QMG, 3 Apr. 1923, enclosing account marked "B", n.d. but *c.* Nov. 1922 (JUS, 93/3/4)

131 'By orders of D. Fleming O.C. Lpool', 8 Aug. 1922 (JUS, 93/3/4)

132 D/P to QMG, 5 Apr. 1923, enclosing receipts marked 'So[u]'t[hampt]on', 1 July, 21 Nov., and receipt marked 'M[an]'chester', 18 July 1922 (JUS, 93/3/4)

133 'P.W.' to unknown, 16 Nov. 1922 (JUS, 93/3/4)

chlorate, 14 cwt (711.2 kg) of dinitrotoluene, 248 lbs 13 oz (112.9 kg) of high explosives and small quantities of peroxide and ballistite, along with 174 detonators, 10,000 percussion caps and three mine exploders were acquired or handled by the gunrunners in Britain during the civil war.

Liverpool remained the main port for the despatch of munitions to Ireland. In February 1923, the adjutant general enquired about the possibility of using whaling vessels to smuggle munitions from continental Europe and Britain into ports on Ireland's western seaboard.[134] However, Cumann na mBan members in Glasgow smuggled munitions directly to Ireland. Lizzie Moran, Pidge Duggan, Molly Duffy, Mary Nelson and Julia Foy made 'numerous trips' to Dublin. In January 1923, Cathal Brugha's wife Caitlín covered the travel expenses involved in their smuggling armaments to the South Dublin Brigade.[135]

Munitions despatched from Liverpool were landed in Dublin, Belfast, Cork, Limerick, Sligo and Drogheda.[136] Joe Robinson sent munitions to Dundalk as well as Dublin.[137] In March 1923, the QMG recommended that more munitions be sent to ports outside of the capital. 'It is almost impossible to remove stuff from here [i.e. Dublin] to Southern or Western Divisions', he wrote.[138]

Some of the arsenal acquired by the gunrunners in Britain never reached the Volunteers in Ireland as it was intercepted by the British and Irish authorities. On 6 October, National troops in Sligo Bay found three machine guns, 20 rifles, ten shotguns and 3,400 rounds of ammunition on a steamer arrived from Glasgow.[139] Two months later, Liverpool port officials discovered 12,000 rounds of rifle and revolver ammunition and 12 casks of explosives and chemicals aboard a steamer about to leave for Ireland. 'I am at a loss to understand how the goods were suspected', Billy Aherne confessed,

> for the D.N.T. [i.e. dinitrotoluene] and the pot. chloride [i.e. potassium chlorate], were packed in barrels with thick layers of soda on top and

134 Adjutant General to O/C Western Command, 2 Feb. 1923 (EO'ML, P17a/23)
135 Anonymous memoir, 1972–73 (ECP, P61/4[67–69]); O/C Scotland to O/C Britain, 27 Feb. 1923 (HO, 144/3746)
136 O/C London to C/S, 8 Dec. 1922; QMG to O/C Britain, 17 Jan.; O/C Liverpool to O/C Britain, 7 Feb.; QMG to O/C Britain, 3 Mar. 1923 (HO, 144/3746); Patrick Murray interview (EO'MN, P17b/88)
137 O/C Scotland to O/C Britain, 27 Feb. 1923 (HO, 144/3746)
138 QMG to O/C Britain, 3 Mar. 1923 (HO, 144/3746)
139 *TT*, 7 Oct. 1922

bottom, while the ammunition was placed in the centre of drums of putty.[140]

The National Army sourced munitions in Britain too though, unlike their IRA enemies, they had official British government channels at their disposal. In the five months prior to the outbreak of the civil war, the army had received 79 Lewis machine guns, 11,900 rifles, 4,200 revolvers and 3,504 grenades.[141] The two 18-pounder guns which were used to attack the Four Courts on 28 June were supplied by the British too.[142] 'I hope you may be successful with your own forces aided by any equipment and supplies we can give you', Colonial Secretary Winston Churchill told Michael Collins later that day.[143] By noon on 2 July, the British had reinforced the National troops with five armoured cars, ten Lancia trucks, 100 Lewis machine guns, 2,000 rifles, 500 revolvers with ammunition, 800 grenades and 1,500 rounds of 18-pounder ammunition.[144] On 20 July, the Provisional Government received another 1,000 rifles it had requested to equip its troops for combat in Munster.[145] On 30 August, it received a further delivery of 500 rifles and 25 Lewis guns.[146]

The necessity of responding to the upsurge in sectarian violence in Northern Ireland in early 1922 led the Provisional Government to exploit more dubious sources in Britain. Frank FitzGerald, a London businessman and brother of Provisional Government minister Desmond FitzGerald, was asked to procure munitions in the English capital so as to arm the Northern IRA for a campaign against the unionist state-let. During the war of independence, FitzGerald and Joseph White, a fellow Irish businessman, had apparently been involved in smuggling munitions for the IRA. In December 1921, FitzGerald was arrested in connection with the Clare IRA men's raids on Windsor and Chelsea Barracks, but the charges against him

140 *TT*, 6 Dec. 1922; O/C London to C/S, 8 Dec. 1922 (HO, 144/3746)

141 Hopkinson, *Green*, p. 127

142 Telegram, Alfred Cope to Lionel Curtis, 7.34 a.m., 28 June 1922 (CO, 906/21)

143 Telegram, Winston Churchill to Cope, 12.30 p.m., 28 June 1922 (CO, 906/21)

144 Telegram, GHQ Ireland to WO, 4.35 a.m., 2 July; telegram, Cope to Churchill, 10.31 a.m., 2 July 1922 (CO, 906/21)

145 Telegram, Cope to Churchill, 10.53 p.m.; telegram, Mark Sturgis to Cope, 11.06 p.m., 29 July 1922 (CO, 906/21)

146 Telegram, Loughnane to Sturgis, 2.04 p.m.; telegram, Freeston to Loughnane, 3.50 p.m., 30 Aug. 1922 (CO, 906/21)

were dropped.[147] After making enquiries, FitzGerald learned that munitions could be acquired from the British army's disposal board, with Horace Soley & Company acting as an intermediary; the company had seemingly supplied munitions to the IRA prior to the treaty. In June 1922, Seán MacMahon, the National Army's QMG, authorized the payment of £10,000 to FitzGerald for the purchase of Hotchkiss machine guns, rifles and revolvers. In August, FitzGerald and White paid Horace Soley a deposit of £2,250 for 10,000 rifles. That same month, they received five Hotchkiss guns. However, Scotland Yard had learned of the men's activities and seized the weapons.[148] In the autumn and winter of 1922–23, FitzGerald continued to acquire munitions, mainly revolvers and chemicals for explosives. However, his activities soon ran into further controversy when Horace Soley threatened him with legal action due to unpaid bills. It later transpired that FitzGerald had earned a large profit by charging the army significantly higher prices for the munitions than he himself had paid. Moreover, the quantity of munitions that the army had actually received was less than that for which it had paid.[149]

The uncovering of Frank FitzGerald's clandestine activities led the British government to demand that the Irish authorities cease attempting to acquire munitions in such a manner. Churchill proposed that the Provisional Government should, in the first instance, apply to him for any munitions it required. He would then ascertain whether his government was in a position to fulfil the request. If so, the munitions would then be supplied on credit, with payment to occur at a later date. If the British government was unable to meet the request, the Provisional Government would be free to source their munitions elsewhere. However, the colonial secretary requested that he be kept informed of any orders placed with other parties. The British were 'endeavouring through our intelligence service to keep track of all attempts on the part of the irregulars to purchase munitions in this country or abroad', he explained.

147 *TT*, 24, 25 Nov., 10 Dec. 1921, 19 Jan. 1922; see Chapter 4
148 Lionel Curtis to Winston Churchill, 25 Aug. 1922 (CO, 739/6); Michael Farrell, 'Frank FitzGerald and the Arms Crisis of 1922', *Magill*, 6.6 (1983), pp. 31–35
149 Farrell, 'Frank FitzGerald', pp. 31–35; *Epitome of the Reports from the Committee of Public Accounts on the Appropriation Accounts for the years 1922–23 to 1933–34, Inclusive, and of the Minutes of the Minister for Finance Thereon* (Dublin: Stationary Office, 1937), pp. 160–65

You will readily see that efforts of our agents are stultified, unless I am fully informed of all transactions for which the Provisional Government is responsible. We cannot tell which is which. We track an irregular order and find it backed by the Free State.[150]

The Provisional Government agreed to the new procedures, and throughout the autumn and winter of 1922 the National Army continued to receive supplies of munitions from the British.[151] In total, it took delivery of 29 artillery guns, 603 machine guns, almost 42,000 rifles, 8,200 revolvers and over 8.8 million rounds of ammunition, among other armaments.[152]

V

In June 1922, at the outbreak of the civil war, orders were issued by the Four Courts garrison to begin attacks in England. However, the 'disorganisation' of the IRA there prevented these orders from being implemented.[153] Liam Lynch was impatient for action in Britain and, following the arrest of Rory O'Connor, pressed for someone to assume the vacant position of O/C Britain and begin planning operations as soon as possible. 'We are letting precious time pass by, and should have things going there already', he complained in September 1922, appealing to the O/C 1st Southern Division to allow two of his men to take up vacancies in Britain. In the event of the British 'going to war with us', the C/S believed that it would be in England that 'we will deliver our hardest blows against her'. He speculated that 'action' would take the form of 'a war on Political-leaders, and their leading Soldiers'. He also contemplated 'the carrying out of destructive operations in Cities'.[154] The following month, a meeting of the IRA executive discussed the subject of 'action, if and when, in Britain' and reiterated that 'organisation' was the most important issue there at the moment.[155] In January 1923, Lynch informed Pa Murray that GHQ was contemplating the mounting of 'active hostilities in England owing to the advanced development of [the] situation' in Ireland.

150 Winston Churchill to William Cosgrave, 26 Sept. 1922 (CO, 739/11)
151 Cosgrave to Churchill, 18 Oct. 1922 (CO, 739/11); Cabinet Conclusions, 22 Nov. 1922 (CAB, 23/39)
152 'Statement of War Material Received from the British Government', 30 June 1923 (MAI, Military Secretary File, 203)
153 C/S to President de Valera and Ministers, 30 Jan. 1923 (EdeVP, P150/1749)
154 C/S to O/C 1st Southern Division, 3, 10 Sept. 1922 (EO'ML, P17a/17)
155 Minutes of IRA Executive meeting, 16–17 Oct. 1922 (EO'ML, P17a/12)

Noting that such hostilities would take the form of an 'active destruction policy', he asked Murray to supply information on the ability of the IRA to mount such operations.[156] A few weeks later, James O'Donovan, the director of chemicals and munitions, pressed the C/S to initiate 'incendiary and destructive operations in England'. Lynch agreed. The IRA was now organized satisfactorily and its leadership efficient, so 'the situation there will be made the most of in the immediate future'.[157]

Soon afterwards, Lynch put the case for a campaign of violence in Britain before de Valera. 'As the Republican Government has repudiated the Treaty', the C/S observed,

> I can see no reason to be put forward against active hostilities against the common enemy [i.e. England], even in his own country. He is waging war against us – if anything, more desperate than before. All his resources are at the disposal of the Free State Army including finance, experience, artillery, general supplies, etc.

England was to be the target of IRA wrath as it was 'directly responsible' for the fratricidal warfare in Ireland. Lynch's reference to England as the 'common enemy' may indicate that he hoped that attacks there would lead the British government to attempt a re-conquest of Ireland, thus reuniting republicans and Free Staters in the face of the invader. The attacks should be confined to England, he continued. Although republican forces were strongest in Scotland, he recommended refraining from launching attacks there, as the Scots, and presumably the Welsh too, were 'more or less Gaelic'. Lynch acknowledged the existence of large obstacles to the effective waging of war in Britain, especially the fact that the Free State intelligence service was co-operating closely with the British secret service to stymie the IRA's activities there. The unemployment situation could also pose problems, he noted cryptically, perhaps indicating his fear that a backlash against attacks might see Irishmen thrown out of work. Overall, however, the C/S felt that while the Volunteers would face risks operating in Britain, they were prepared to suffer the same dangers as their comrades fighting in Ireland.[158] De Valera approved of the launching of attacks in England, opining that 'the first blow

156 C/S to O/C Britain, 9 Jan. 1923 (HO, 144/3746)
157 Correspondence between Director of Chemicals & Munitions and C/S, 27, 31 Jan. 1923 (NLI, James O'Donovan Papers, MS 22,306)
158 C/S to President de Valera and Ministers, 30 Jan. 1923 (EdeVP, P150/1749)

should be concerted BIG, followed quickly by a number in succession of other blows'. He agreed that attacks in Scotland were to be avoided 'for the present'.[159]

The following day, Lynch issued instructions for the planning of attacks.[160] Unfortunately, little information exists as to the targets chosen. Pa Murray later stated that the C/S wanted 'bridges etc blown up'.[161] Given that the truce period had seen the IRA making plans for the destruction of bridges, among other targets, in the event of the peace talks collapsing, the Volunteers may simply have adopted those plans.[162] In 1922, the pro-treaty lieutenant in the Tyneside IRA stated that anti-treaty Volunteers were about to begin reconnaissance work on prominent buildings and bridges, along with manufacturing and railway infrastructure. A campaign of violence was to be launched in the event of the British army reoccupying Southern Ireland. In comparison to the situation in 1920–21, IRA men involved in this mooted campaign were authorized to kill when necessary.[163] In the aftermath of Sir Henry Wilson's assassination, a search of the lodgings of one Herbert Wrigley, a republican according to Free State intelligence, uncovered notes on a petrol station, a gas factory and underground power stations in the London area. As documents mentioning the IRA were also uncovered, such notes may have been part of the reconnaissance for choosing targets for attack.[164] Documents belonging to the London IRA captured by police in March 1923 included the addresses and movements of 'a well-known ex-Cabinet Minister' and prominent police officials, suggesting perhaps that the Volunteers were contemplating assassinations.[165] Meanwhile, the press claimed that the London IRA planned to blow up Buckingham Palace and bridges over the Thames, while also setting fire to railway stations and jewellery shops.[166]

Lynch contended that mines manufactured from petrol tins, which had been used effectively in Dublin, could be employed in the attacks in Britain. The skill to make them was not lacking, for he contended that

---

159 De Valera to C/S, 2 Feb. 1923 (EdeVP, P150/1749); original emphasis

160 C/S to de Valera, 3 Feb. 1923 (EdeVP, P150/1749)

161 Patrick Murray interview (EO'MN, P17b/88)

162 See Chapter 4

163 Col. Carter to H.R. Scott, 1 May 1923, enclosing 'Instructions regarding I.R.A. movements in Tyneside Area', n.d. (HO, 144/3748)

164 *TT*, 27 July 1922; 'Active Sinn Feiners in London', n.d. (EO'ML, P17a/182); see Chapter 6

165 *TT*, 16 Apr. 1923

166 *Liverpool Echo*, 20 June 1923

the O/C Britain's adjutant was as good an engineer as any in the IRA in Ireland. He also advocated the establishment of a munitions factory to manufacture incendiary grenades.[167] Anticipating opposition to the campaign from pro-treaty Volunteers in London, the C/S had already instructed Billy Aherne to 'take such action against them as will be necessary'.[168]

Pa Murray thought that many of the proposed operations were unachievable given the limited resources at the disposal of the IRA. He blamed Moss Twomey for these 'ridiculous' plans: the deputy C/S had 'no sense of reality'.[169]

At the end of February, the C/S ruled that 'activities in England' were to commence once certain munitions (perhaps the sought-after mountain guns) had been despatched from there to Ireland; he may have feared that the weapons would be discovered by the police in the crackdown that the attacks were likely to precipitate. '[D]ays count now in this matter', he wrote.[170] On 7 March, having learned that the armaments had not been secured, GHQ sent Pa Murray an order 'to have operations carried out at once'.[171] Four days later, however, the mass arrest and deportation of republicans took place. 'You knew the possibilities of Operations before – Judge for yourself the possibilities now', a despondent Murray wrote to Lynch on 30 March.[172] A few days later, Twomey judged the likelihood of attacks in Britain 'negligible if not altogether impossible'.[173]

The IRA's plans for an offensive in Britain, therefore, were not realized. However, a number of minor incidents did occur for which Volunteers were responsible. In February 1922, an attempted robbery occurred at a post office in Brentford. One of the men convicted stated that the object was not to steal money but rather to intercept a letter.[174] On 14 April, £32 was stolen from a post office in Glasgow.[175] The following July, a four-man team stole £244 from a bank in Prestwick, Manchester. Bartley Iago and John Foley were arrested soon afterwards and upon conviction received ten-year sentences each. However, their accomplices, Francis Breen and Patrick Gavin,

167 C/S to President de Valera and Ministers, 30 Jan. 1923 (EdeVP, P150/1749)
168 C/S to O/C 1st Southern Division, 3 Sept. 1922 (EO'ML, P17a/17)
169 Patrick Murray interview (EO'MN, P17b/88)
170 C/S to Assistant C/S, 29 Feb. 1923 (HO, 144/3746)
171 C/S to O/C Britain, 7 Mar. 1923 (HO, 144/3746)
172 O/C Britain to C/S, 30 Mar. 1923 (RMP, P7/B/92[18])
173 Maurice Twomey to C/S, 5 Apr. 1923 (EO'ML, P17a/51)
174 *TT*, 22 Apr. 1922
175 *IT*, 17 Apr., 28 Dec. 1922

fled to Ireland. In 1921, Breen had been sentenced to five years in prison for gunrunning offences. In Dublin, he quickly resumed IRA activities. He later admitted to involvement in 'several attacks' on National troops and confessed to 'complicity' in the fatal shooting of Assistant Inspector Matthew Daly of CID on 23 December. According to Gavin, Breen also participated in an attempted raid on a shop during which James Tierney, a member of the family with whom the two lodged, was killed. In addition, he claimed that Breen engaged in gunrunning activities. Apprehended in April or early May 1923, Breen was sent to Britain to stand trial for the bank robbery and received a life sentence. Gavin received the same sentence two years later, despite claiming that he had only participated in the robbery under duress.[176] On 3 November 1922, a fire occurred at the Victory Casino in South Shields. The police suspected that the incident was an arson attack mounted by the IRA so as to prevent Sir Hamar Greenwood, the former Irish chief secretary, from delivering an electoral address at the venue.[177] In June 1923, Jim Phelan and an accomplice named Seán McAteer raided a post office in Liverpool, apparently in order to acquire money for the dependents of their imprisoned IRA comrades in Ireland. A clerk named Thomas Lovelady was shot dead. Phelan was arrested near the scene. Found guilty of Lovelady's murder, he was sentenced to death but this was later commuted to life imprisonment. (McAteer, a communist, escaped to Russia, where he was executed in Stalin's purges in 1937.)[178]

In May 1923, Art O'Brien won a court case questioning the legality of the deportation.[179] The deportees were released from internment in Ireland and returned to Britain. By then, however, Liam Lynch had died. Following him to the grave was the willingness to resort to drastic measures, including operations in Britain, as a means of shoring up the republican position. With the exhaustion of the republicans, the civil war in Ireland concluded. In a

176 CC of Lancashire to the USS, HO, 4 May 1925, enclosing Patrick Gavin statement, n.d.; Francis Breen's petition to the Home Secretary, 12 May 1923 (HO, 144/20092); list of prisoners amnestied on 11 Feb. 1922 (HO, 144/4645); Patrick Finn, 'C.I.D. MAN SHOT AT QUEEN'S STREET BRIDGE', 23 Dec. 1922 (JUS, H169/34); *IT*, 21 Apr. 1923; *TT*, 16 July 1921, 30 Nov. 1922; *MG*, 4 July 1923; see Chapter 6

177 Col. Carter to H.R. Scott, 1 May 1923 (HO 144/3748)

178 *MG*, 16, 19, 23 June, 3, 4, 10, 11, 28 July, 11 Aug. 1923; Phelan, *The Name's Phelan*, pp. 280–82; Barry McLoughlin, *Left to the Wolves: Irish Victims of Stalinist Terror* (Dublin: Irish Academic Press, 2007), pp. 219–84

179 See Chapter 6

communication to local commanders throughout Britain, Pa Murray tried to soothe the pain of defeat with a call to perseverance:

> The objects for which the IRA was formed still await achievement. The lesson of the past is that patient and thorough organisation is the sure means to success. Discouragement and difficulties do not alter the determination of men like you who so far have persevered. The Ideal for which you worked in conjunction with your comrades in Ireland is yet before you. Its final realisation depends on the earnestness with which you face the new situation and the assistance which you will be in a position to give when again necessary.[180]

A number of senior republicans were not in any position to assist the Volunteers, in the short-term at least. In July, Art O'Brien, Seán McGrath, Anthony Mularkey, Denis Fleming, Thomas Flynn and Londoner Michael Galvin were found guilty of aiding the IRA in its conspiracy to overthrow the Irish government. O'Brien and McGrath were each sentenced to two years' imprisonment, while the others each received one-year sentences.[181]

VI

The civil war saw men and women who had seen action in the republican movement in Britain during the war of independence serve on both sides, in Britain and in Ireland. The IRA, the Cumann na mBan and others in Britain attempted to hinder the nascent Free State. However, due to a decline in membership and organizational problems, they were never able match the vitality they possessed before the treaty. Yet the mass arrest and deportation of March 1923 demonstrated the seriousness with which the Free State government viewed anti-treaty activity in Britain. It also paralysed the movement. In particular, it prevented the mounting of violent attacks, though, given the state of the IRA in Ireland at the time, their efficacy at that stage of the conflict even if they had been realized is doubtful. By the time the deportation was declared illegal and the internees released, the civil war had virtually ended. In the penultimate chapter, we will discuss the reaction of the authorities to the republican threat in Britain.

180 O/C Britain to O/Cs 'All Areas', 13 June 1923 (MTP, P69/37[240])
181 *TT*, 28, 30 June, 3, 5 July 1923

CHAPTER 6

Combating the 'Sinn Fein Movement' in Britain: The Response of the Authorities, 1919–1923

I

'We have murder by the throat', Lloyd George declared in early November 1920, promising the imminent defeat of the Volunteers in Ireland.[1] By the end of the month, however, Crown forces there had suffered a number of deadly attacks and the IRA had extended its campaign of violence to Britain itself. 'The Sinn Fein movement, in its Irish Republican Army stage, is spreading to this country [i.e. England]', Sir Hamar Greenwood was forced to warn the House of Commons. 'It has its own areas, its own commandants, its own soldiers in this country.'[2] This chapter studies the reaction of the authorities to the threat posed by Irish republicanism in Britain. Section II discusses the political situation in post-war Britain and the British Empire, the context which coloured the government's view of the republican movement. Sections III and IV examine the means by which politicians and the police attempted to thwart IRA gunrunning and violence, noting the similarities and differences between these and the instruments used in wrestling with the Fenians in the 1860s and 1880s. Sections V and VI focus on republicans' experiences of the criminal justice system in Britain, namely the courts and the prisons. Section VII discusses the authorities' approach during the post-treaty and civil war periods. Section VIII concludes.

II

Britain emerged from the First World War as a victor. Its main rival for worldwide naval supremacy, Germany, was defeated. Moreover, as a result

---

1 *TT*, 10 Nov. 1920
2 *Hansard 5* (*Commons*), cxxxv, cols 505–07 (24 Nov. 1920)

of the Paris Peace Conference, the British Empire expanded in Africa and the Middle East. Yet, the war also unleashed powerful forces of disorder. The period 1919–22 saw a 'crisis of empire' as rebellions of varying intensity broke out in Afghanistan, Egypt, India and Iraq, as well as in Ireland.[3] Nationalism was the main force in these rebellions. Some members of the British establishment, however, discerned the involvement of a more sinister force, that of communism.

In the revolution of October 1917, the Bolsheviks under Lenin overthrew the Provisional Government and declared Russia the world's first communist state. Hoping for the outbreak of similar revolutions in other parts of Europe, the Russians quickly established the Communist International (Comintern) as a vehicle to foster such revolts. The Comintern's statutes of 1920 stated that 'the dictatorship of the proletariat' was 'the only means for the liberation of humanity from the horrors of capitalism'.[4] That same year, Grigory Zinoviev, chairman of the Comintern, declared that communist revolutions were imminent worldwide. The 'twilight of the gods of capitalism has set in', he announced. Once the workers had revolted, a new world would be constructed 'on the basis of the Communist principles of brotherhood'.[5] A number of communist rebellions did indeed occur in Europe. In January 1919, the Spartacus League mounted a revolt in Berlin. Three months later, a soviet republic was established in Bavaria, while in Hungary a similar regime existed under Béla Kun. All, however, proved transient. The Spartacist uprising was crushed by demobilized soldiers, while Kun's regime, after indulging in a reign of terror, was unseated by an invading Romanian army.[6] Basil Thomson, an assistant commissioner of the LMP from 1913 to 1921, spoke for many establishment figures throughout Europe when he later noted the view, one with which he agreed, that Bolshevism was 'an infectious disease rather than

---

3 John Gallagher, 'Nationalisms and the Crisis of Empire, 1919–1922', *Modern Asian Studies*, 15.3 (1981), pp. 355–68; John Darwin, *After Tamerlane: The Rise and Fall of Global Empires, 1400–2000* (London: Allen Lane, 2007), pp. 368–94

4 'Statutes of the Communist International, 4 August 1920', in Rex A. Wade (ed.), *Documents of Soviet History, ii, Triumph and Retreat 1920–1922* (Gulf Breeze, Fl.: Academic International Press, 1993), pp. 109–13

5 'Zinoviev on the World Revolution: Opening Address to the Second Congress of the Comintern, 19 July 1920' in Wade (ed.), *Documents of Soviet History, ii*, pp. 96–101

6 Zara Steiner, *The Lights that Failed: European International History 1913–1933* (Oxford: Oxford University Press, 2005), p. 10

a political creed – a disease which spreads like a cancer, eating away the tissue of society until the whole mass disintegrates and falls into corruption'.[7] Fear of communist revolution was one factor at play in the ferocious right-wing paramilitary violence that ravaged central and eastern Europe in the aftermath of the Great War.[8] To a certain extent, it also motivated Western intervention in the Russian civil war of 1917–22.[9]

As well as inspiring rebellions, the Bolshevik revolution partly stimulated the wave of industrial unrest that swept Europe following the end of the World War. In 1915, the three largest trade unions in Britain, those of transport workers, railwaymen and miners, formed a 'triple alliance'. Due to its ability to call a general strike, the alliance was viewed with suspicion by the government. Following the armistice, this distrust was only increased by the burgeoning unions' demands that workers be rewarded for their wartime sacrifices and that wages be increased to compensate for price inflation. In the event, a general strike was never called. Britain, nevertheless, did experience a large number of strikes, including those of railwaymen, policemen and miners. 35,000,000 working days were lost through disputes in 1919. The following year, it declined to 27,000,000. In 1921, however, it jumped to 86,000,000, while the following year saw 20,000,000. In 1923, with the end of the post-war economic boom and a large increase in unemployment, the figure had declined to 10,600,000.[10] Basil Thomson believed that the industrial unrest of early 1919 was the most revolutionary situation in Britain in almost 90 years.[11] Ireland also saw an upsurge in strikes, by farm labourers in particular.[12]

In all this upheaval, some commentators saw a deadly communist-inspired

---

7 Basil Thomson, *My Experiences at Scotland Yard* (New York: Doubleday, Page & Co., 1923), p. 328

8 Robert Gerwarth, 'The Central European Counter-Revolution: Paramilitary Violence in Germany, Austria and Hungary after the Great War', *Past & Present*, 200 (2008), p. 182

9 Steiner, *Lights*, pp. 131–52; Clifford Kinvig, *Churchill's Crusade: The British Invasion of Russia, 1918–1920* (London: Continuum, 2006)

10 Keith Jeffery and Peter Hennessey, *States of Emergency: British Governments and Strikebreaking Since 1919* (London: Routledge & Kegan Paul, 1983), pp. 1–75; Peter Clarke, *Hope and Glory: Britain 1900–2000* (London: Penguin, 2004), p. 107

11 Thomson, *Scotland Yard*, p. 309

12 Emmet O'Connor, *Syndicalism in Ireland 1917–1923* (Cork: Cork University Press, 1988)

threat to order and civilization. To some degree, this perceived menace coloured the British government's view of republicanism in Ireland and Britain. With relation to Ireland, for example, police intelligence claimed in January 1920 that Sinn Féin was 'inclined to become Bolshevist in tone' in order to attract support in British labour circles.[13] In March, land agitation in County Galway was condemned as 'purely Bolshevist'.[14] The following month, the industrial situation in Ireland was said to be tending towards Bolshevism.[15] In July 1919, the cabinet was informed that ICA members in Glasgow might use their positions in other labour bodies to foment industrial unrest for the purpose of aiding Ireland.[16] The most 'awkward feature' of the activities of John Maclean, the Scottish Marxist, was held to be his 'association with the Sinn Fein movement'. A leaflet of his, entitled 'Proposed Irish Massacre', called upon Scottish workers serving as soldiers in the British army in Ireland to refuse to 'murder the Irish race' and instead begin a general strike with their Irish and American brethren so as to cause the overthrow of capitalism in the United States.[17]

Allegations that Irish republicanism was in league with (or was a manifestation of) menacing hidden forces, such as communism and Freemasonry, all of whom were involved in a worldwide plot to destroy civilization, were nothing new.[18] There was some evidence of a relationship between Fenianism and communism going back to the 1870s, when IRB men or lapsed members formed a significant part of the rank and file of Marx's International Workingmen's Association in Ireland and Britain.[19] Concerns regarding republican links with

13 'RROUK', no. 36, 9 Jan. 1920 (CAB, 24/96)

14 'RROUK', no. 47, 25 Mar. 1920 (CAB, 24/101)

15 'RROUK', no. 49, 8 Apr. 1920 (CAB, 24/103)

16 'RROUK', no. 11, 10 July 1919 (CAB, 24/83)

17 Report by Deputy Prosecutor Fiscal of Glasgow on hostile propaganda, 20 Aug.; Under Secretary for Ireland to Under Secretary for Scotland, 30 July 1920, enclosing Maclean's leaflet, n.d. (FWWF, HH31/34/20); John McHugh, 'Maclean, John (1879–1923)', in *ODNB*, online edn, May 2006, accessed at http://www.oxforddnb.com/view/article/37721, on 13 Oct. 2010

18 Máirtín Ó Catháin, "The Black Hand of Irish Republicanism'?: Transcontinental Fenianism and Theories of Global Terror', in Fearghal McGarry and James McConnel (eds), *The Black Hand of Republicanism: Fenianism in Modern Ireland* (Dublin: Irish Academic Press, 2009), pp. 135–46

19 Cormac O Grada, 'Fenianism and Socialism: The Career of Joseph Patrick McDonnell', *Saothar: Journal of the Irish Labour History Society*, 1.1 (1975), pp. 35–36

communism closer to the present day were not entirely misplaced either, for they did indeed have some contact with radical leftists. During the war of independence, for example, the ICA performed a number of support services for the IRA in Ireland, including supplying and hiding weapons.[20] More seriously, in 1920 Ireland and Russia drafted a treaty of mutual recognition, and the former loaned the latter US$20,000.[21] In Moscow the following year, Patrick McCartan, envoy of the IRB, asked the Soviets to supply the Volunteers with weapons. The Tipperary IRA made a similar request on another occasion. Although both requests were turned down, Moscow was interested in events in Ireland. At its second congress, in mid-1920, the Comintern discerned communist potential in anti-colonial struggles such as that in Ireland. Roddy Connolly, son of James Connolly and leader of the small Socialist Party of Ireland (SPI), attended the congress and promised to support the IRA in its liberation struggle. The following year, at the third congress, Connolly informed Lenin that the IRA's rank and file could be converted to communism.[22]

Republicans in Britain also had some contact with communists, radical socialists and anti-colonial nationalists. As mentioned earlier, among Art O'Brien's acquaintances were Burmese and Egyptian nationalists in London and the communist Shapurji Saklatvala, and he was in indirect contact with people associated with the Russian delegation too.[23] According to David Neligan, a detective who secretly worked for the IRA in Dublin during the war, Michael Collins sought to liaise with the police trade union, which was agitating for a strike in Britain, in the hope of smashing the RIC in Ireland.[24] In 1919, IRA GHQ sent Dublin Volunteer Seán McLoughlin to Britain to uncover possible sources of munitions, recruit people for the mounting of 'sabotage work' and 'to attend at public gatherings to produce a favourable atmosphere for the Irish cause' in labour circles. McLoughlin addressed a number of meetings of the 'Hands off Ireland' campaign. Like the 'Hands off Russia' movement that British labour launched in 1919 in an attempt to frustrate Western intervention in the Russian civil war, the Irish campaign

---

20 Hanley, 'Irish Citizen Army', pp. 37–39

21 *Intercourse between Bolshevism and Sinn Féin* [Cmd. 1326], H.C. 1921

22 Emmet O'Connor, *Reds and the Green: Ireland, Russia and the Communist Internationals, 1919–43* (Dublin: University College Dublin Press, 2004), pp. 42–49

23 See Chapter 1

24 Kenneth Griffiths and Timothy E. O'Grady, *Curious Journey: An Oral History of Ireland's Unfinished Revolution* (London: Hutchinson, 1982), pp. 163–65; A.V. Sellwood, *Police Strike–1919* (London: W.H. Allen, 1978)

endeavoured to mobilize British public opinion against its government's policies in Ireland.[25] However, McLoughlin went beyond merely denouncing the behaviour of Crown forces across the Irish Sea. As a political theorist, he believed that events in Ireland had the potential to precipitate social revolution throughout the British Isles. 'We have made up our minds that the time is come when we must bring about a workers' republic, not only in Ireland, but in Great Britain [too]', he declared in Glasgow in January 1920.

> It is the duty of every Irishman to get into every revolutionary movement in Great Britain to bring about the overthrow of the capitalist system. The British workers must wake up to the fight if they are ever to be free and it must be through the Irish people.[26]

Therefore, as well as gunrunning for the IRA, McLoughlin sought to arm radicals for a socialist revolution in Britain.[27]

The internment without trial of almost 200 Irishmen from Ireland in London's Wormwood Scrubs in 1920 proved a rallying point for republicans and radicals. In March, disgusted with the Labour Party's pusillanimous Irish policy, Irish electors in Stockport – many of them members of the socialist Independent Labour Party – nominated trade unionist William O'Brien, one of over 170 Irishmen hunger-striking in protest at their internment, as a candidate in the town's by-election. Standing as a 'Workers' Republican', O'Brien insisted on 'the right of the people of Ireland to sovereign independence, their right to choose the Republic' and 'the right of the workers to the control of industry, and to the exercise of the right in their own form of government: the workers' Republic'. He finished last of seven candidates.[28] Then, from 28 April to 3 May, a strike occurred on Merseyside in protest at the internments. At its height, around 20,000 workers were involved, including dockers, coal-heavers and warehousemen, mainly Irish or of Irish extraction. 'The

25 'RROUK', no. 32, 4 Dec. 1919; 'RROUK', no. 36, 9 Jan.; 'RROUK', no. 52, 29 Apr.; 'RROUK', no. 61, 1 July; 'RROUK', no. 65, 29 July; 'RROUK', no. 66, 5 Aug. 1920 (CAB, 24/94–24/110); L.J. MacFarlane, 'Hands off Russia: British Labour and the Russo-Polish War, 1920', *Past & Present*, 38 (1967), pp. 126–52

26 'RROUK', no. 36, 9 Jan. 1920 (CAB, 24/96)

27 BMHWS 290, Seán McLoughlin, pp. 46–47; Charlie McGuire, *Sean McLoughlin: Ireland's Forgotten Revolutionary* (Pontypool: Merlin Press, 2011), p. 86

28 *Freeman's Journal*, 22, 23 Mar., 12 Apr. 1920

dock labourers and the crews of the cross-Channel boats – B[ritish] & I[rish], Cork, Limerick, Dundalk and Newry – came out to a man', Michael O'Leary recollected, 'and several of the Transatlantic ships, if not actually tied up, had their personnel very much reduced.' The ISDL's P.J. Kelly declared that the work stoppage aimed not only to secure the release or trial of the internees but also 'the emancipation of British labour from the rule of British capital'. T.P. O'Connor, IPP MP for Liverpool's Scotland division, warned that, with the Irish betraying 'a feeling of blind resentment against the Government' and the passions of the Great War having generated 'a dangerous feeling of unrest' among certain groups, a potentially explosive situation existed in Britain.[29]

The activities of the RIC Auxiliaries and Black and Tans also outraged British radicals. These forces constituted the 'British edition of a White Guard', one MP claimed, a force that conservative elements in Britain might unleash in the event of a radical Labour government coming to power.[30] A speaker at the Labour Party's special conference on Ireland, held in December 1920, declared that the Auxiliary Division was 'a class weapon forged in Ireland which could be used in England also'.[31] Indeed, rumours existed that 'many of the ex-Black and Tans, who had got their training in Ireland, were being recruited as special police and sent to Central and West Fife' to contend with strikes, remembered one Scottish miner.[32]

Communists on Tyneside helped the IRA to acquire a small number of machine guns.[33] Moreover, as we have seen, Rory O'Connor hoped that IRA operations would facilitate 'direct action' by communists, among others, though he was disappointed by the outcome.[34] And, during the truce, Cathal Brugha and others attempted to enlist the support of the CPGB and Indian communists for a renewal of the Volunteers' campaign of violence in the event of the peace talks collapsing.[35]

29 *Freeman's Journal*, 29 Apr., 4 May 1920; BMHWS 797, Micheál Ó Laoghaire, p. 29; *Hansard 5 (Commons)*, cxxviii, cols 1337–43 (28 Apr. 1920)

30 *Hansard 5 (Commons)*, cxxxv, col. 572: Joseph Kenworthy (24 Nov. 1920)

31 *Report of the Labour Commission to Ireland* (London: Caledonian Press, 1921), p. 107

32 John McArthur, 'The Recollections of John McArthur', in Ian MacDougall (ed.), *Militant Miners: Recollections of John McArthur, Buckhaven; and Letters, 1924–26, of David Proudfoot, Methil, to G. Allen Hutt* (Edinburgh: Polygon Books, 1981), p. 110

33 Barrington, *Irish Independence Movement*, p. 20

34 See Chapter 3

35 See Chapter 4

Given all these contacts, therefore, it is not surprising that the British authorities took the view, enunciated by the prime minister's former private secretary, that Irish revolutionaries had 'linked up with Indians, Egyptians, Bolshies, & all the haters of England in France, Germany etc' in the hope of 'smashing the British Empire'.[36] It was against such a background that the British reacted to republican activity in their midst.

III

Despite receiving intelligence reports on the matter, the highest echelons of the British government did not evince much concern regarding IRA gunrunning prior to the Volunteers' arson attack on Merseyside in November 1920. Indeed, thereafter, tackling violence was their primary concern. This echoed the government's tardy response to the IRA's campaign in Ireland.[37] Nevertheless, some attempts were made to frustrate the Volunteers' access to munitions. On 12 April 1921, upon being warned that Irishmen were joining the armed forces with the intention of 'deserting with their arms', the cabinet resolved that the attention of all army commands and recruiting stations be brought to the problem.[38] The following day, it was noted that recruiting officers had no means of identifying 'Sinn Feiners or Communists' among new recruits. However, a careful watch was being kept and men in the ranks were reporting on suspect soldiers. The cabinet decided that army commanders should liaise with the police so as to gather information on recruits.[39]

Republican gunrunning did not occasion any specific legislative response from the government. This was in contrast to the Fenian bombing campaign of 1881–86 to which the government of the day reacted with the Explosive Substances Act 1883.[40] However, the Firearms Act 1920, although passed more out of fear of Bolshevist than Irish activities, was of course applied to republican gun-smugglers too.[41]

36 Philip Kerr to David Lloyd George, 14 Sept. 1921 (PAHL, David Lloyd George Papers [DLGP], LG/F/34/2/7)

37 Kenneth O. Morgan, *Consensus and Disunity: The Lloyd George Coalition Government, 1918–1922* (Oxford: Clarendon Press, 1979), pp. 126–28

38 Cabinet Conclusions, 12 Apr. 1921, 7 p.m. meeting (CAB, 23/25)

39 Cabinet Conclusions, 13 Apr. 1921, 6 p.m. meeting (CAB, 23/38)

40 Short, *Dynamite War*, pp. 141–44; see Chapter 2

41 Joyce Lee Malcolm, *Guns and Violence: The English Experience* (Cambridge, Mass.: Harvard University Press, 2002), pp. 141–42; see Chapter 2

Intelligence gathering was part of the mix as well. Domestic spying was a somewhat controversial subject in Britain, a country that boasted about its liberalism and respect for individual freedom. (Ireland was a different matter.) In December 1867, in response to Fenian gunrunning and violence, a special investigative unit was set up in the Home Office to gather and sort intelligence on IRB men. However, when it is was realized that the Clerkenwell explosion was not the opening salvo of a Fenian bombing campaign, the unit was reduced to a one-man operation.[42] Fifteen years later, the activities of O'Donovan Rossa's Skirmishers caused the resurrection of domestic surveillance. In March 1883, after the bombing of the local government offices in Whitehall, 'section b', known colloquially as the 'Irish Brigade', was established in the LMP's Criminal Investigation Department. Indeed, the organization's office in Great Scotland Yard was the target of a bomb attack in May the following year. In addition, a 'secret service' unit was established in the Home Office under Edward Jenkinson, a Dublin Castle expert on Irish republicanism. Moreover, two Irish resident magistrates were charged with travelling around northern England and Scotland collecting intelligence. When this latest Fenian threat subsided in 1886, section b continued to exist though on a reduced scale, and by the turn of the century it had been amalgamated with other sections founded to counter the dynamite menace to form what soon became known as the Special Branch. The 'secret service' continued on a much smaller scale too.[43] Some twenty years later, German spy mania and the outbreak of the Great War led to a large expansion in the scope of domestic surveillance.[44]

In late April 1919, the government established a directorate of intelligence under Basil Thomson, who continued in his job as head of the Special Branch. He was charged with collecting intelligence relating to 'seditious meetings and conspiracies, threatened disturbances and revolutionary movements', along with 'labour unrest', both in Britain itself and abroad. Such intelligence was

---

42 Jenkins, *Fenian Problem*, pp. 148, 168–72, 215; Padraic C. Kennedy, 'The Secret Service Department: A British Intelligence Bureau in Mid-Victorian London, September 1867 to April 1868', *Intelligence and National Security*, 18.3 (2003), pp. 100–127

43 Short, *Dynamite War*, pp. 5–6, 105–06, 110–12, 144–46, 184–87; Lindsay Clutterbuck, 'Countering Irish Republican Terrorism in Britain: Its Origin as a Police Function', *Terrorism and Political Violence*, 18.1 (2006), pp. 101–03, 107, 111–12

44 Christopher Andrew, *The Defence of the Realm: The Authorized History of MI5* (London: Allen Lane, 2009), chs. 1–3

then to be supplied to the cabinet in regular reports.[45] On 30 April 1919, the cabinet received its first 'Report on Revolutionary Organisations in the United Kingdom' from the directorate. One of the sections in this report was entitled 'SINN FEIN IN WALES', in which it was stated that a branch of Count Plunkett's Liberty League at Merthyr had now joined the Sinn Féin organization.[46] Such reports would continue to be produced into 1924, even after the abolition of the directorate following Thomson's controversial dismissal by Lloyd George in November 1921.[47] The activities of Irish republicans became a mainstay of the reports, the information they contained being gathered by means of the local police, interception of suspects' postal correspondence and informers.

As in the 1860s, the police tended to take a mainly reactive approach to tackling republican gunrunning. Action on their part was precipitated either by an actual theft of munitions or by their receiving information regarding a gun-smuggling operation. Such action then took the form of shadowing suspects, raiding their homes in the hope of uncovering compromising evidence and chasing leads.[48]

The directorate of intelligence's first mention of gunrunning was in July 1919, when the smuggling activities of a man named Jack Tanner and the ICA in Scotland were detailed. The latter reportedly had a scheme for the running of explosives from coal mines to Ireland via Wigtonshire. 'As it is impossible to check the amount of explosives actually used in the mines', the report noted, 'considerable quantities may have been stolen.'[49] Thereafter, accounts of gunrunning became regular. By January 1920, there was 'a steady stream' of munitions being remitted to Ireland. The following month, Art O'Brien was identified as being involved in weapons-smuggling in the capital.[50] In March, it was reported that munitions were being run via Holyhead in passengers' luggage and by fishing trawler.[51] Four months later, £500 of the £3,000 subscribed to the Dáil loan in Glasgow had allegedly been used to purchase munitions for IRA men who intended to travel to

45 Edward Troupe, USS, HO, to Chief Constables, 22 Apr.; Troupe to Basil Thomson, 17 Apr. 1919 (HO, 144/1590/380368)
46 'RROUK', no. 1, 30 Apr. 1919 (CAB, 24/78)
47 Andrew, *Defence of the Realm*, pp. 119–20
48 Jenkins, *Fenian Problem*, p. 111 etc
49 'RROUK', no. 10, 3 July; 'RROUK', no. 11, 10 July 1919 (CAB, 24/83)
50 'RROUK', no. 37, 15 Jan.; 'RROUK', no. 43, 26 Feb. 1920 (CAB, 24/96, 24/99)
51 'RROUK', no. 47, 25 Mar. 1920 (CAB, 24/101)

Ireland during the forthcoming Glasgow Fair holidays. Around 500 rifles were reported to be on hand, along with ample supplies of ammunition.[52] In September, the directorate warned that Volunteers had made a 'secret survey' of several Territorial Army drill halls in Glasgow, so as to draw up plans to raid for weapons in the event of Terence MacSwiney dying on hunger-strike. Arms raids on Maryhill and Hamilton military barracks were also considered possible.[53]

Information provided to the police by informers could prove valuable and sometimes led to successful prosecutions. In the 1880s, Jenkinson's secret service organization employed a large number of agent provocateurs in Fenian ranks, leading to the arrest and conviction of some would-be bombers but also embarrassing accusations of complicity in violence.[54] The use of informers and agent provocateurs was one way of penetrating the secretive IRA organization. As we saw earlier, in 1921 Charles Murphy was accused of being an agent provocateur, a charge he denied.[55] His giving King's evidence against his former comrades was reminiscent of the behaviour of William Lynch (alias E.R. Norman), a would-be bomber who testified against his co-conspirators in 1883.[56] We have already seen the case of John Byrnes, the spy employed by military intelligence who infiltrated the Volunteers in London in an attempt to entrap Michael Collins.[57] Republicans themselves suspected others of being informers. In June 1921, Art O'Brien claimed that a number of female members of Irish organizations in London were 'in the pay of the enemy'.[58] Also, as we saw, Reginald Dunne believed that the Robinson brothers betrayed fellow members of the capital's IRA.[59]

In late 1918, the police learned that Seán McGrath was purchasing munitions without a permit. On 11 January the following year, two policemen observed him boarding a train at Euston Station. They boarded too and alighted at Rugby after McGrath did so. There, they saw him meet a man named William Burrows. After McGrath produced an envelope, Burrows gave him two packages. The police then intervened and arrested both men

52 'RROUK', no. 63, 15 July 1920 (CAB, 24/109)

53 'RROUK', no. 73, 23 Sept.; 'RROUK', no. 77, 21 Oct. 1920 (CAB, 24/111–24/112)

54 Whelehan, *Dynamiters*, pp. 122–37

55 See Chapter 1

56 Short, *Dynamite War*, pp. 148–49

57 See Chapter 2

58 Art O'Brien to Michael Collins, 30 June 1921 (AÓBP, MS 8430/17)

59 See Chapter 4

under the wartime Defence of the Realm Regulations (DORR). Upon examination, the packages were found to contain 12 revolvers of .32 and .38 calibres, along with 1,000 rounds of ammunition for each and 30 lbs (13.6 kg) of gunpowder. Two revolvers, a munitions price list, a list of expenses and a Sinn Féin membership card were found on McGrath. The envelope contained £84 13*s.* 6*d.* Meanwhile, police in London raided the two men's homes and found correspondence referring to munitions deals. Pursuing a reference in one of the documents uncovered, the police also raided the house of John Murphy in Bootle and found about 7,000 empty cartridge cases. The following month, both McGrath and Burrows were found guilty of contravening DORR and sentenced to six months' imprisonment each.[60]

Two years later, a tip-off also led to the apprehension of some Manchester Volunteers at one of their munitions dumps. On 2 April 1921, a number of men were arrested in connection with arson attacks in the city centre. Charles Murphy had gone to the police station to confess his participation in the attacks.[61] A photograph of one of the arrested Volunteers, O/C Manchester Paddy O'Donoghue, then appeared in the newspapers. O'Donoghue had rented a garage from a woman and she, recognizing him, alerted the police. They visited the garage and found a large amount of materiel. They then decided set a trap and lay in wait until the owners came to collect their armaments. On 25 May, Volunteers John McGallogly and Francis Breen were arrested while stock-taking at the garage. They, along with some comrades, were later imprisoned after being convicted of various explosives and firearms offences.[62]

On other occasions, successful prosecutions for gunrunning involved the police being at the scene when the crime was being committed. In June 1920, a policeman on the premises of the Linthorpe Ironworks came face-to-face with four members of the Middlesbrough IRA, including Michael McCann, who were raiding for explosives. He was shot in the ear by McCann. Fleeing the scene, the Volunteer left a travel bag full of munitions but was quickly apprehended. Subsequently, the police traced the bag to William Whelan. At York Assizes, Whelan and McCann pleaded guilty to illegal possession of gelignite and were each sentenced to five years' imprisonment.[63] On 28

60 *TT,* 29 Jan., 9 Feb. 1919
61 See Chapters 1 and 3
62 BMHWS 244, John McGallogly, p. 20; BMHWS 847, Patrick O'Donoghue, pp. 13–14; *TT,* 27 May, 16 July; *MG,* 7 June, 9 July 1921
63 BMHWS 369, William Whelan, pp. 9–12; *TT,* 13 July 1921

October later that year, a policeman interrupted an arms raid on a Territorial Army drill hall in Bothwell, Scotland, and was beaten and shot. Four months later, seven men were charged with attempting to murder him. Four were found guilty and sentenced to between eight and ten years' imprisonment.[64]

In a departure from policing tradition, the threat posed by armed IRA men, epitomized by the Bothwell incident, led to ordinary policemen being issued with arms. In July 1920, despite reports of Volunteers drilling in public and possessing weapons, the chief constable of Dunbartonshire stated that he did 'not take a very serious view' of the IRA's activities.[65] Glasgow's prosecutor fiscal expressed similar sentiments the following month. Hitherto, 'no outbreak of disorder' had taken place in Glasgow and he believed that this would remain so as long as the IRA was not 'interfered with'.[66] However, outraged by the Bothwell episode two months later, the chief constable of Lanarkshire argued that the police in the area needed to be armed in order to be able to defend themselves. Although realizing the momentous nature of the suggestion, the joint standing committee of Lanark County Council agreed and asked the secretary for Scotland to approve the measure.[67] A precedent existed for this request. In the aftermath of the Clerkenwell explosion in 1867, some 35 local police forces were issued with handguns on a temporary basis and the LMP was trained in the use of the cutlass.[68] Permission was duly granted for the Lanarkshire police to be armed for a six-month period. In May 1921, requesting that the arrangement be extended, the chief constable asked that, in a departure from instructions received, detective constables be allowed carry the weapons in their pockets and take them home with them. The current regulations necessitated that the detectives collect their munitions at the station before coming on duty and return them when they went off duty. Such rules were onerous, he argued, especially in county districts where police stations were few and detectives did not work fixed hours of

64 Scottish Office to Carew-Robinson, HO, 20 Nov. 1922 (HO, 144/4645); BMHWS 828, James Byrne, p. 5; BMHWS 777, Patrick Mills, pp. 4–5; *MG*, 8, 9, 10 Feb. 1921

65 CC of Dunbartonshire to the USS for Scotland, 5 July 1920 (FWWF, HH31/34/19)

66 Report by Deputy Prosecutor Fiscal of Glasgow on hostile propaganda, 20 Aug. 1920 (FWWF, HH31/34/20)

67 County Clerk, County Council of Lanark, to Under-Secretary for Scotland, 8 Nov. 1920, enclosing CC's report and newspaper clipping (NAS, Police Services General File [PSGF], HH55/465)

68 Jenkins, *Fenian Problem*, pp. 166, 333

duty. Allowing policemen to carry their weapons in their pockets and home with them was 'absolutely necessary', he explained, 'as the Detectives in this Constabulary are almost daily engaged in dangerous duty in making inquiries and apprehensions in connection with Sinn Fein activities'. It was 'most hazardous work'.[69]

The records of the Felling-on-Tyne police division in Durham afford us an insight into the measures taken on the ground to combat the IRA. To frustrate Volunteer gunrunning, colliery owners in the area were encouraged to ensure the security of their explosive supplies.[70] In May 1921, the explosives and detonators belonging to the majority of the collieries and magazines were hidden in the mines or safely secured elsewhere. In the case of two other businesses that made use of explosives in their work, the police took possession of the keys to where the munitions were stored and arrangements were made for a sergeant to distribute the explosives when necessary.[71] Police also monitored retailers of chemicals with a view to uncovering orders by people from Ireland.[72] Following the detection of J.P. Connolly's gunrunning network in nearby Newcastle-upon-Tyne in October, 'diligent and discreet' inquiries were made in an effort to uncover any associates in the area. Postmasters were asked to check their records to see if any communications had passed through their hands on the subject of gun-smuggling or munitions.[73]

The police were aided by customs officials at ports in Britain and Ireland. In the 1880s, detectives working for the specially established section c of the Criminal Investigation Department and local police forces had been despatched to ports in Britain and continental Europe to intercept bombers and their explosives.[74] In April 1921, upon learning that the port authorities on Merseyside had established a new force to search ships for contraband, Michael Collins predicted that it would prove ineffective. 'One of the old "G" crowd would be worth twenty of them', he argued, referring to the Dublin

69 CC of Lanarkshire to USS for Scotland, 5, 11 May 1921 (PSGF, HH55/465)

70 Superintendent of Felling-on-Tyne to CC of Durham, 12, 27 Apr. 1921 (Tyne and Wear Archives, Police Records [PR], T148/5[256, 301])

71 Superintendent of Felling-on-Tyne to CC of Durham, 18, 21 May, 9 Nov. 1921 (PR, T148/5[378, 385, 796, 798])

72 Superintendent of Felling-on-Tyne to CC of Durham, 2 Dec. 1921 (PR, T148/5[840])

73 Superintendent of Felling-on-Tyne to CC of Durham, 18 Oct. 1921 (PR, T148/5[762])

74 Clutterbuck, 'Countering', p. 102; Short, *Dynamite War*, pp. 178–79

Metropolitan Police's plain-clothes detective division.[75] Yet, we have already noted incidents in which such officials succeeded in discovering munitions.[76]

In 1867, concern that Fenian gunrunners might acquire weapons belonging to the Volunteer Rifle Corps had led to the removal of the munitions to secure locations.[77] In April 1921, fearful of the IRA purloining armaments from barracks, the British army instituted counter-measures. The commanders of the Durham brigade group ordered that a close watch be kept on new recruits. Anyone whose behaviour aroused suspicion was to be discharged immediately and the police notified.[78] The following day, a list of 'SINN FEIN RUSES' was drawn up in order to put soldiers on their guard against attempts by republicans to illicitly gain entry to army barracks. 'All efforts or approaches by anyone should be looked upon with suspicion, whether dressed in uniform (Naval or Military) or plain clothes', the circular stated, for 'Sinn Feiners are first class masqueraders.' IRA men might assume a number of disguises, soldiers were warned, including those of an army officer, soldier, policeman, postman, telegraph messenger, civilian or military doctor, clergyman, Red Cross nurse or someone delivering provisions. Soldiers were also cautioned to be wary of people wearing soft hats, trench coats, 'anyone wearing a gilt ring about the size of a 6d. piece in their button holes, or a combination of the colours green, white and yellow', along with anyone who had their hands in their pockets. They were enjoined to refuse all refreshments and food offered by persons unknown to them. Vehicles were to be approached with caution, as they could be used as sniping positions.[79]

IV

Of all the IRA's activities in Britain, it was its campaign of violence that most alarmed the British government. On 29 November, two days after the Merseyside arson attack, the cabinet met to discuss the protection of government buildings. The incident underlined the importance of the issue, for they demonstrated that 'the Sinn Feiners had definitely decided to carry

---

75 Correspondence between Paddy Daly and Michael Collins, 27, 30 Apr. 1921 (RMP, P7/A/5)

76 See Chapters 2 and 4

77 Jenkins, *Fenian Problem*, p. 93

78 Circular by Lieut. Col. A.T. Brooke, 14 Apr. 1921 (Durham County Record Office, Durham Light Infantry Papers [DLIP], D/DLI2/6/549[8])

79 'SINN FEIN RUSES', 15 Apr. 1921 (DLIP, D/DLI2/6/551)

their war of outrage into England'. The cabinet was told that Irishmen in Britain were manufacturing bombs and that 30,000 detonators had been stolen from mines in Scotland during the recent miners' strike.[80] On 6 December, it was resolved that special precautions were necessary to protect the principal government offices and the House of Commons. A committee under the Home Secretary was therefore appointed to make arrangements for such security measures as well as for the protection of ministers and of officials 'threatened by the present menacing attitude of the Sinn Feiners'.[81] In the meantime, the cabinet contemplated offering 'large rewards' for information from the public on 'Sinn Fein emissaries and activities' in Britain. It was felt that such information was 'more likely to be forthcoming now than after the Sinn Feiners might have established some degree of terror among timid people'.[82]

Prior to this, the government had received periodic warnings of the likelihood of violence from the directorate of intelligence. As early as June 1919, a report cautioned that arson attacks 'after the manner of militant suffragettes' were being planned by the Gaelic League.[83] In December, certain Irishmen were reportedly contemplating a campaign of 'armed outrage'.[84] 'It is thought that the Sinn Feiners in England may have resource to outrage before long', the directorate reiterated in January 1920.[85] The following month, the organization's Glasgow correspondent considered 'outrages' likely in the event of violence increasing in Ireland or a general strike being called in Britain, for republicans in the city were in a 'dangerous' mood.[86] In March, however, the prospect of a 'Sinn Fein rising' in Britain was thought unlikely as little would be gained by it.[87] Violence in Liverpool was also considered improbable due to the large number of Orangemen in the area.[88] Yet, in early November, it was reported that 'reprisals' were being threatened in revenge for the government allowing MacSwiney to die on hunger-strike.[89] Two weeks later, the directorate argued that the seizure of IRA documents in Dublin

---

80 Cabinet Conclusions, 29 Nov. 1920, 12 noon meeting (CAB, 23/38)
81 Cabinet Conclusions, 6 Dec. 1920, 5 p.m. meeting (CAB, 23/23)
82 Cabinet Conclusions, 1 Dec. 1920, 11.30 a.m. meeting (CAB, 23/23)
83 'RROUK', no. 9, 26 June 1919 (CAB, 24/82)
84 'RROUK', no. 32, 4 Dec. 1919 (CAB, 24/94)
85 'RROUK', no. 36, 9 Jan. 1920 (CAB, 24/96)
86 'RROUK', no. 40, 5 Feb. 1920 (CAB, 24/97)
87 'RROUK', no. 47, 25 Mar. 1920 (CAB, 24/101)
88 'RROUK', no. 50, 15 Apr. 1920 (CAB, 24/103)
89 'RROUK', no. 79, 6 Nov. 1920 (CAB, 24/114)

detailing plans to attack the docks in Liverpool along with a power station and waterworks in Manchester 'may prove to be the death blow to the murder gang in Ireland'.[90] Three days later, however, Volunteers set alight warehouses and timber yards on Merseyside and attempted to do the same in London, leading police intelligence to note glumly: 'The week-end saw the beginning of what is apparently an attempt to carry out the Sinn Fein campaign of arson and murder in this country'.[91]

The government's main innovatory policy response to the threat of violence was to deport suspect individuals to Ireland for internment without trial. This stood in marked contrast to the reaction to Fenian violence in the 1860s when the suspension of *habeas corpus* was rejected as an unacceptably extreme move, while its infringement does not even seem to have been considered in the face of the dynamite campaign almost two decades later.[92] The change in mindset was partly due to the First World War when, with the acquiescence of the mass of civil society, the government assumed previously unimaginable powers to restrict individual liberty. Moreover, unlike the previous episodes of Irish republican activity in Britain, the campaign of 1919–21 was accompanied by a level of violence in Ireland that represented an unprecedented threat to British rule of the island. On 30 November 1920, fearful that Glasgow might soon experience an attack akin to that which occurred on Merseyside a few days earlier, the city's prosecutor fiscal bemoaned the fact that although the police had 'authentic information' on Irish revolutionary activity, it was not of a standard sufficient to satisfy a court. Therefore, 'other means' would have to be found to deal with the threat. He proposed that the government follow the lead of Dublin Castle in arresting and interning Irish rebels. Such 'Sinn Féiners' in Britain, 'equally with their Irish associates, are levying war against this country, and against the Executive Government of Ireland', he noted.

> They are instigating the disorders in Ireland, supporting the Irish Republican Army with money, arms and ammunition, and I apprehend even supplying them with men. It is beyond all question that Republican troops are in this city with the avowed object of taking part in hostile operations, both in Ireland and here.

90 'RROUK', no. 81, 18 Nov. 1920 (CAB, 24/115)
91 'RROUK', not numbered, 28 Nov.; 'RROUK', no. 83, 2 Dec. 1920 (CAB, 24/115–24/116)
92 Jenkins, *Fenian Problem*, p. 168; Short, *Dynamite War, passim*

The 'most active Sinn Feiners' in Glasgow, therefore, should be arrested, deported to Ireland and detained there, he suggested. A similar policy was recommended for Liverpool, London and Manchester. Such arrests would cow rank and file republicans and render harmless the whole outfit.[93] Basil Thomson agreed, stating that arrests on the basis of suspicion were justified in circumstances where definite evidence linking Irishmen with violent incidents was absent. He noted that the police already possessed the names and addresses of all the leading members of the ISDL, a body 'which has now definitely thrown in its lot with the extreme Sinn Fein movement'.[94]

The first such deportations occurred a few weeks later, in mid-December, when a number of people were arrested on Merseyside in connection with the previous month's arson attack. While police intelligence was certain that the arrested men were responsible for the incident, 'there is not sufficient evidence to convince a Court'; therefore, 'As in the [world] war, internment appears to be the only solution'. Seven or eight people, including Tom Kerr and Michael O'Leary, were deported to Ireland and interned, a development which reportedly had 'a very sobering effect' upon republicans in Britain.[95] In February 1921, Seán McGrath suffered similar treatment. The directorate of intelligence had 'no doubt' that, with McGrath's approval or involvement, a section of the ISDL was communicating with the IRA in Ireland and mounting attacks in England. It later claimed that McGrath's internment also had the effect of disconcerting Irish agitators in Britain.[96] More arrests and deportations occurred on Merseyside the following month.[97] In April, Fintan Murphy, Art O'Brien's office manager, was deported. In May, he was followed into internment by C.B. Dutton, his replacement, along with six others, including the Carr brothers.[98] Around the same time, Edward Brady was interned in Dublin's Mountjoy prison.[99] On 7 July, the directorate claimed to have received information that the IRA had planned attacks to

93   Report of the Prosecutor Fiscal of Glasgow, 'Operations of Sinn Fein Organisation within the City', 30 Nov. 1920 (PSGF, HH55/69)

94   Director of Intelligence to the Home Secretary, 2 Dec. 1920 (HO, 317/48)

95   'RROUK', no. 83, 2 Dec. 1920; 'RROUK', no. 88, 13 Jan. 1921 (CAB, 24/116, 24/118); BMHWS 797, Micheál Ó Laoghaire, pp. 47–48

96   'RROUK', no. 90, 27 Jan.; 'RROUK', no. 94, 24 Feb.; 'RROUK', no. 96, 10 Mar. 1921 (CAB, 24/118, 24/120)

97   Brady, *Secret Service*, p. 43

98   Art O'Brien to Michael Collins, 7 Apr., 19, 26 May 1921 (DÉ, 2/329–2/330); 'RROUK', no. 106, 19 May 1921 (CAB, 24/123); *Irish Exile*, July 1921

99   Brady, *Secret Service*, pp. 122–23

take place that week but was forced to cancel them because of the number of deportations taking place. Overall, such internments had 'a very marked effect' on Volunteer violence in England, police intelligence claimed.[100]

As in their reaction to IRA gunrunning, in dealing with the Volunteers' seven-and-a-half-month long campaign of violence, the police took an approach that had both proactive and reactive elements.

On 5 December 1920, a week after Merseyside attacks, the superintendent of Felling-on-Tyne informed the chief constable of Durham of the arrangements he had taken to deal with the 'SINN FEIN MOVEMENT'. He had alerted his inspectors and sergeants to the possible threat. He ordered that they instruct the men under their command to take note of strangers in the area. Where unknown, the strangers' nationalities were to be ascertained and if they acted suspiciously they were to be shadowed. The superintendent was to be informed of the discovery of anything unusual. 'I have given instructions for strict attention to [be] paid, [sic] to all public buildings, warehouses & factories', he noted, 'and most especially to Motor Cars containing strangers who might be seen on their [i.e. the policemen's] respective beats.' Sergeants were to report daily to the superintendent on the issue.[101] The police were already monitoring labour unrest and radical political agitation, recording instances of 'seditious speech' and 'revolutionary propaganda'.[102] Their reaction to the threat posed by Irish republicans, therefore, was on a par with their response to subversion in general. Along with strangers, local residents of Irish nationality – who numbered around 3,500 – were also kept under observation.[103] In mounting such operations, 'care, discretion, and tact' were enjoined on the rank and file policemen.[104] On occasion, investigations were established into the movements of specific individuals, usually people associated with the ISDL.[105] In late May 1921, it was resolved to draw up a list of Sinn Fein suspects. The homes of such people were to be put

100 'RROUK', no. 113, 7 July 1921 (CAB, 24/126)
101 Superintendent of Felling-on-Tyne Division to CC of Durham, 5 Dec. 1920 (PR, T148/4[922]); original emphasis
102 Superintendent of Felling-on-Tyne Division to CC of Durham, 15, 29 May 1921, 13 Mar. 1922 (PR, T148/5[367, 413, 1000])
103 Superintendent of Felling-on-Tyne Division to CC of Durham, 7, 31 Dec. 1920 (PR, T148/4[924, 980])
104 Superintendent of Felling-on-Tyne Division to CC of Durham, 30 May, 23, 25 Nov. 1921 (PR, T148/5[415, 825, 830])
105 Superintendent of Felling-on-Tyne Division to CC of Durham, 10 Dec. 1920 (PR, T148/4[931])

under surveillance, thus allowing the police to monitor their activities.[106] In an attempt to prevent attacks, likely targets were kept under observation, including railway stations, bridges, collieries, farms and railway signal boxes.[107] 26 members of the Royal Navy were billeted at Addison Colliery in order to protect the government's bonded stores, while soldiers of the Durham Light Infantry were posted on protection duty at the electric power station and flour mills in Dunston.[108] The police discussed the possibility of attacks with the managers of a number of business concerns, including shipbuilders, paint manufacturers, tool companies and collieries. Except for the collieries, all had a number of dedicated watchmen on their premises, while the colliery managers stated that they had workmen on their premises at all times who effectively fulfilled the task of watchmen. Arrangements were made for the police to assist.[109] By July, most collieries had put in place adequate security arrangements.[110] Other precautions taken included advising fuel stations that sales of petrol and benzole 'should be restricted to a minimum during the present emergency'.[111]

Fear that the IRA might attempt to assassinate prominent politicians led the cabinet to authorize increased protection for public buildings in the capital, cabinet ministers and well-known MPs. Such precautions had also been taken in the face of previous episodes of Irish republican violence. In 1867–68, government departments were provided with equipment to combat arson attacks, while precautions were instituted to prevent Fenians using the sewer system as a means of travelling about the capital. In 1884–85, at the height of the bombing campaign, over 1,000 policemen were assigned duties that included the guarding of Westminster Palace and the Abbey, the Tower of London, the Bank of England, St Paul's Cathedral, the British Museum, the National Gallery and the royal palaces, as well as of MPs and their

---

106 Superintendent of Felling-on-Tyne Division to CC of Durham, 30 May 1921 (PR, T148/5[415])

107 Superintendent of Felling-on-Tyne Division to CC of Durham, 26 Dec. 1920, 18 Apr., 1, 29 June 1921 (PR, T148/4[966], T148/5[266, 425, 525])

108 Superintendent of Felling-on-Tyne Division to CC of Durham, 17, 18 Apr. 1921 (PR, T148/5[262, 263, 268])

109 Superintendent of Felling-on-Tyne Division to CC of Durham, 31 Dec. 1920, 11 May 1921 (PR, T148/4[980], T148/5[351])

110 Superintendent of Felling-on-Tyne Division to CC of Durham, 14 July 1921 (PR, T148/5[566–70])

111 Superintendent of Felling-on-Tyne Division to CC of Durham, 12 Apr. 1921 (PR, T148/5[243])

residences.[112] Terence MacSwiney's high profile hunger-strike had resulted in Lloyd George already being provided with a bodyguard. 'Police are convinced that if he dies the Irish will try to kill me', he informed his wife.[113] Following the arson attack two months later, policemen were detailed to patrol inside 28 government buildings in London. The patrols varied in strength according to the size of the building and the likelihood of attacks being mounted against it. Thus, the Ministry of Finance building was guarded by one police constable, the Foreign Office by two, 10 Downing Street three, the Home Office four and the Palace of Westminster by between two and 141. By March the following year, a total of 218 policemen were involved in such work. Some were armed and wore plain clothes. As well as patrolling, the policemen were charged with searching ministers' offices each morning after they had been cleaned. A telephone providing a direct connection to New Scotland Yard was installed in each ministry for use in emergencies. The patrols continued during the truce albeit at a reduced strength. The total cost of these security measures was £51,887 8s. 3d.[114] At the Palace of Westminster, in addition to such patrols, members of the public were excluded from the galleries and the outer lobby. 'Some very old frequenters of the House [of Commons] were at a loss to remember a precedent for so severe a measure of precaution', reported *The Times*, but the arrangements were 'criticised by no one'. Also, preparations were made for the wooden barrier in front of the prime minister's residence to be replaced with an iron gate.[115] Sir Henry Wilson was among the prominent politicians provided with a personal bodyguard.[116]

Another proactive measure designed to frustrate the IRA launching operations in the London area involved the police organizing road blocks. At a

112 Jenkins, *Fenian Problem*, pp. 166–67; Short, *Dynamite War*, pp. 53–54, 106–08, 203, 208

113 David Lloyd George to Mrs Lloyd George, 15 Sept. 1920, reprinted in Kenneth O. Morgan (ed.), *Lloyd George: Family Letters 1885–1936* (Cardiff: University of Wales Press, 1973), p. 193

114 Returns showing number of police employed inside government buildings, n.d.; Inspector Sriffen to HO, 5 Dec. 1920; Commissioner of Police of the Metropolis to USS, HO, 14 Mar.; ?CuwBalloward to Johnson, 27 July 1921 (MEPO, 3/298); 'Note dictated by the Home Secretary', *c.* Aug. 1922 (DLGP, LG/F/45/6/42)

115 *TT*, 30 Nov., 2 Dec. 1920

116 Cabinet Conclusions, 11 a.m., 23 June 1922 (CAB, 21/255); A.F. Moslau to Commissioner of Police, 19 Oct. 1922 (MEPO, 2/1974); 'Note dictated by the Home Secretary', *c.* Aug. 1922 (DLGP, LG/F/45/6/42)

Home Office conference in June 1921, it was decided to construct special posts at the boundary where the roads leading out of the capital crossed into the Home Counties. Each post would consist of five or six policemen. By means of ropes or poles the road would be narrowed, thus forcing motorists to slow down. Between 9 p.m. and 10.30 p.m. each night, such a set-up would allow the police to monitor the traffic leaving London. After 10.30 p.m the traffic in both directions would be affected: 'Cars will be stopped, their number taken and licences seen, and their business discretely ascertained'. Should pursuit prove necessary, motor cycles could be used. So as to avoid too close proximity of posts, their locations would be co-ordinated by the various constabularies. Also, their positions would be varied so as to ensure an element of surprise for motorists. Moreover, it was suggested that police patrols might operate between the barriers.[117] In total, 37 barriers employing 149 policemen were erected inside the Metropolitan area.[118] However, these security arrangements failed to prevent attacks on London's railway infrastructure in the latter half of June. This may have been due to motorists' habit of warning each other of the upcoming obstruction.[119] 'London is now getting a dose of Sinn Fein', Sir Hamar Greenwood observed to the prime minister. 'In my opinion, it will get more, and modern police methods won't meet medieval sabotage.'[120] Nevertheless, police intelligence held that the barricades had 'a very marked effect' on the IRA's plans.[121] On 12 July, the day after the truce came into effect, the barriers and patrols were suspended.[122]

As well as such proactive policies, the police also took a reactive approach. In response to the attacks of November 1920, police in Liverpool, London and Glasgow raided the addresses of people and organizations known or suspected of being connected with the republican movement. Searches were mounted of ISDL offices and private houses.[123] In London, documents were

---

117 'Minutes of a Conference held at the Home Office at 11.0 a.m. on the 10th June, 1921, on the methods of dealing with Sinn Fein outrages' (HO, 144/4645)

118 'SUMMARY of Superintendents' reports showing the positions of barriers, and the number of men manning each ...', 13 June 1921 (MEPO, 3/465)

119 Superintendent 'Y' Division, LMP, to the Commissioner of Police of the Metropolis, 12 June 1921 (MEPO, 3/465)

120 Sir Hamar Greenwood to David Lloyd George, 9 June 1921 (DLGP, LG/F/19/5/1)

121 'RROUK', no. 113, 7 July 1921 (CAB, 24/126)

122 Telegram, 'A.C.A.' to Superintendents of 'A' to 'Z' Divisions, LMP, 12 July 1921 (MEPO, 3/465)

123 *IT*, 1 Dec.; *MG*, 3 Dec; *TT*, 2, 3, 4 Dec. 1920

uncovered revealing that Art O'Brien had supplied money for the importation of weapons into Ireland from Germany.[124] Meanwhile, those on Clydeside led to the discovery a large batch of explosives in a car being driven from the city by Volunteers Henry Coyle and Charles McGinn. The consignment amounted to three cwt (152.4 kg) of gelignite and samsonite explosives in cake form, 300 detonators, two rifles, two bayonets and three revolvers.[125] One of those arrested on Merseyside was Neil Kerr Senior. It was 'almost inevitable' that Kerr's house would be raided, John Pinkman later wrote, given that he was 'a well-known Sinn Féiner and one of the leading lights among Irish nationalists in Liverpool'. In the house, as well as uncovering incriminating documents linking Kerr to the arson attacks, including receipts for bolt-cutters used to break the warehouses' locks, police also found a Volunteer, James McCaughey, and an IRA uniform. Both men were arrested and, along with six others, charged initially with conspiracy to set fires.[126]

Raids such as these became the standard police response to an IRA attack, as they facilitated the requisition of documents and arrest of suspects. On 2 January, for example, a policeman approached a group of men acting suspiciously near a granary in Salford. The party immediately dispersed, but the policeman soon caught up with two people hurrying towards the canal tow-path. The two agreed to accompany him to the station for questioning. However, they suddenly made to escape and when the constable grabbed the collar of one of them he was shot through the wrist and in the chest. 'The police had been aware for some time' that Patrick Flynn, a Wandsworth resident, was 'a member of the Republican Army', explained *The Times*. Searching Flynn's house, the police found bullets in a waistcoat pocket, a patrol tin and photographs of members of the IRA. The four men living there were arrested and charged initially with acting in a manner prejudicial to public safety in contravention of DORR.[127] Due to his prominence, Art O'Brien's offices and lodgings were raided on a number of occasions. His stenographer described one such search on 5 April 1921:

> At about 11.15 a.m. six police officers called here and said they had come to pay us another visit. One of them, Inspector Cosgrave, read a long statement to [O'Brien's office manager] Mr. [Fintan] Murphy,

124 'RROUK', no. 85, 16 Dec. 1920 (CAB, 24/117)
125 'RROUK', no. 84, 9 Dec. 1920 (CAB, 24/116)
126 Pinkman, *Legion*, pp. 40–41; *TT*, 30 Dec. 1920
127 CC of Salford to the USS, HO, 18 Oct. 1922 (FIN, 1/1589); *TT*, 3, 4 Jan. 1921

which was an order for his detention for seven days, under some Emergency Act, and stating that, if at the end of seven days, it did not appear necessary to detain him, and that evidence had again been produced in his favour, he might again be released. When asked if there was any charge, he said that there was none. He [i.e. Murphy] asked if he might wait until the arrival of the clerk, in order not to leave me alone, but though they allowed him to wait some little time, they took him away before Liam's arrival. Two officers left with him, and the other four made a detailed search of the premises, leaving no stone unturned, in the hope, I believe, of finding something of a startling and incriminating nature. They seemed both surprised and disappointed at the result of their work. They even tried to look behind the gas fires. They were quite polite and not in any way offensive, but they were very determined and anxious to do their work thoroughly. Most of the files, which had been taken away before [i.e. in a previous raid], were this time left untouched. They made the entire lot [of other files] into three paper parcels and one of them went for a taxi in which they departed. They already knew my name but they asked Liam for his and took it down. I was not allowed to answer the telephone and they insisted on seeing all callers. ... I answered the telephone once while they were here, but it was a call from Scotland Yard and I was instructed that I was not to do so again.

Murphy was interned in Ballykinlar camp as the authorities associated him with recent attacks in the capital. The documents seized included letters from the Dáil's representative in Paris and Dáil loan applications.[128]

Reflecting on the year 1921, the commissioner of the LMP stated that the 'extension of Sinn Fein activities to the Metropolitan area', along with unemployment and other social troubles, had presented the police with a problem 'of more than ordinary difficulty to deal with'. However, utilizing 'much tact and discretion', the force had discharged its duties 'firmly and judiciously' and thus achieved 'satisfactory results' in maintaining the peace.[129] Was this the case? As we saw in Chapter 3, the IRA was responsible for at least

---

128 Art O'Brien to Michael Collins, 7 Apr. 1921, enclosing O'Brien to 'P[resident de Valera]', 7 Apr. 1921 (DÉ, 2/329); 'RROUK', no. 100, 7 Apr. 1921 (CAB, 24/122)

129 *Report of the Commissioner of Police of the Metropolis for the Year 1921* [Cmd. 1699] H.C., 1922, pp. 11–12

Table 5: Convictions Secured for Incidents of IRA Violence
According to Constabulary Area, 27 Nov. 1920–11 July 1921

Area	No. of incidents	No. of incidents for which convictions were secured
Lancashire	103	49
London Metropolitan Area	44	3
Durham	30	2
Northumberland	18	1
Cheshire	15	2
Kent	9	0
Yorkshire (North Riding)	6	0
Warwickshire	2	0
Essex	1	0
Scotland	11	7
Total	239	64

Sources: Figures compiled from returns to the HO from 20 police units, the LMP and the Scottish Office, Oct.–Nov. 1922 (HO, 144/4645; MEPO, 3/462; FIN, 1/1589); O/C Britain to C/S, 3 June 1921 (RMP, P7/A/19[16-20]); *IT*, *MG*, *The Observer*, *TT*, Nov. 1920–July 1921; membership rolls of Scottish Brigade IRA (EMP, 3/C/13); BMHWS

239 violent incidents in Britain between 27 November 1920 and 11 July 1921. Convictions were secured for only 64 of these. Volunteers, therefore, enjoyed an almost 3.75:1 chance of escaping justice. Therefore, the IRA's cessation of operations, like the Fenians' suspension of their bombing campaign in the 1880s, was motivated by politics rather than by the success of the police in tackling them.

Tables 5 and 6 examine the conviction rates for attacks according to geographical area and type of attack. As we can see, Lancashire saw 103 incidents, with convictions being secured in relation to 49, or 47.6 per cent, of cases, while the London Metropolitan area saw 44 incidents, with convictions in only three cases or 6.8 per cent. In neither area was anyone convicted of involvement in the May 1921 attacks on RIC men and their relatives, one of which led to the death of a householder. Neither was a conviction secured in relation to the deaths of William Ward in November 1920 or Vincent

Table 6: Convictions Secured for IRA Violence
According to Type of Incident, 27 Nov. 1920–11 July 1921

Type of incident	No. of incidents of that type	No. of incidents of that type for which convictions were secured
Attacks on farms and crops	112	12
Attacks on railway and communications infrastructure	42	3
Attacks on warehouses	39	37
Attacks on factories, mills and retailers	19	2
Attacks on timber yards	6	6
Attacks on houses of RIC men and/or their relatives	9	0
Attacks on miscellaneous targets	12	4
Total	239	64

Sources: Figures compiled from returns to the HO from 20 police units, the LMP and the Scottish Office, Oct.–Nov. 1922 (HO, 144/4645; MEPO, 3/462; FIN, 1/1589); O/C Britain to C/S, 3 June 1921 (RMP, P7/A/19[16-20]); *IT, MG, The Observer, TT*, Nov. 1920–July 1921; membership rolls of Scottish Brigade IRA (EMP, 3/C/13); BMHWS

Fouvargue the following April. Scotland, meanwhile, boasted a 63.6 per cent conviction rate, though no one was brought to justice for the death of Inspector Johnston in May.

The geographical variation in conviction rates is accounted for by a couple of factors. Of foremost importance was the nature of the targets attacked in each area. Due to the isolated nature of farms, railways and communications infrastructure, it was difficult for the police to apprehend Volunteers while in the act of attacking them. On learning that the IRA was planning attacks in rural areas where the police were 'not numerous', police intelligence predicted: 'Such a campaign will be difficult to deal with, for nothing is easier [to do] than to fire a [hay] rick or cut a telephone wire'.[130] By the time the police arrived on the scene, the perpetrators had usually long fled. Arson paraphernalia was sometimes found at the site of the farm fires, but

130 'RROUK', no. 94, 24 Feb. 1921 (CAB, 24/120)

it was difficult to link such evidence with specific individuals. For example, a 'quart oil can was found near the spot' where five hay and straw stacks were set alight at a farm in West Molesey, Surrey, on 5 February 1921, noted the police, but 'No arrests were made'.[131] Cheshire police believed that the sawing-through of two telegraph poles and the cutting of the wires attached in Birkenhead on 2 June was 'apparently the work of Sinn Fein agents from Liverpool, as certain tools, found close to the scene and used to commit the damage, were found on enquiry, to have been recently purchased in Liverpool'. Again, however, due to the inability of the police to connect such evidence with specific individuals, no one was ever convicted of these incidents.[132]

The London Metropolitan area suffered ten arson attacks on farms and farm produce between 26 March and 30 April. The comment 'probably attributable to Irish agency' or variations of it appear nine times in a police report, while 'certainly attributable to Irish agencies' appears once. Similarly, in relation to nine incidents of infrastructure sabotage committed between 7 and 16 June, the responsibility of 'Irish agency' was considered to be certain in two instances and probable in the remaining seven. However, no arrests were made in any of these cases and no convictions were secured.[133] It was the same in other parts of England. Kent witnessed four farm fires and five attacks on railways and the communications network and again no convictions were secured.[134] Lancashire saw 19 attacks on infrastructure and 21 farm fires, among other incidents, and convictions were secured in only one and two cases respectively.[135] Thus, while the police suspected the IRA of being responsible for a number of incidents, they lacked the evidence to prove it.

The police found it easier to tackle attacks on property located in urban areas as, in general, they could quickly appear at the scene and on occasion apprehend the culprits. On 15 January 1921, for example, upon approaching a group of 12 men acting suspiciously in the vicinity of the Vacuum Oil Company in Wandsworth, three policemen found themselves at gunpoint.

131 Acting Commissioner of the Police of the Metropolis to the USS, HO, 18 Nov. 1922 (FIN, 1/1589)

132 CC of Cheshire to the USS, HO, 20 Oct. 1922 (FIN, 1/1589)

133 Acting Commissioner of the Police of the Metropolis to the USS, HO, 18 Nov. 1922 (FIN, 1/1589)

134 ACC of Kent to the ASS, HO, 1 Nov. 1922 (FIN, 1/1589)

135 CC of Bootle to the ASS, HO, 27 Oct.; ACC of Liverpool to the USS, HO, 11 Oct.; CC of Manchester to the USS, HO, 3 Nov.; CC of Rochdale to the USS, HO, 18 Oct.; CC of Salford to the ASS, HO, 18 Oct. 1922 (FIN, 1/1589); ACC of Lancashire to the USS, HO, 27 Oct. 1922 (HO, 144/4645)

A struggle ensued, during which shots were fired but no one injured. The would-be arsonists fled, firing at the police, but one, Wilfred Kenny, was later apprehended at the scene in possession of a revolver, ammunition and documents relating to Sinn Féin. 25 barrels had holes bored in them using steel bits, causing the oil to flow out, and bottles of paraffin, wax tapers, cotton wool and other arson paraphernalia were found. Kenny, along with James Moran and Thomas O'Sullivan, was subsequently found guilty of conspiracy to commit arson, possessing firearms and maliciously attempting to set fire to barrels. They were sentenced to four and eight years' imprisonment respectively.[136]

Lancashire witnessed the highest number of attacks in urban areas, with 38 warehouses, six timber yards and nine factories sustaining damage, for which convictions were secured in 37, six and zero cases respectively.[137]

V

As members of a secret revolutionary organization, Volunteers were obviously wary of the police. One tactic they adopted in the event of police attention becoming unbearable was to go on the run. In March 1920, Joe Vize was forced to move from Glasgow to Bothwell. Despite the personal inconvenience, he welcomed the police's intervention to some extent as it had an unexpected effect: 'this little bit of excitement has done wonders, the boys [i.e. gunrunners] are putting more vim into their work and all carelessness is gone in many quarters, something like it was wanted to shake them up'.[138] The following year, after the arrest of a large number of men in connection with arson attacks in the city centre, many of the Manchester Volunteers who were still at liberty moved to London. There, they found accommodation in the homes of sympathizers.[139] The following month, brothers Eamonn and Seán Mooney were forced to leave Glasgow in order to escape the police dragnet following the shooting dead of Inspector Johnston. Accompanied by a fellow Volunteer named Quinn, they spent a few nights with Mick Burke and his wife in

136 Superintendent of Wandsworth Division, LMP, to USS, HO, 27 Oct. 1922 (FIN, 1/1589); *TT*, 17 Jan., 19 Feb. 1921

137 CC of Bootle to the ASS, HO, 27 Oct.; ACC of Liverpool to the USS, HO, 11 Oct.; CC of Manchester to the USS, HO, 3 Nov.; CC of Rochdale to the USS, HO, 18 Oct.; CC of Salford to the ASS, HO, 18 Oct. 1922 (FIN, 1/1589); ACC of Lancashire to the USS, HO, 27 Oct. 1922 (HO, 144/4645)

138 Joe Vize to Michael Collins, 26 Mar. 1920 (RMP, P7/A/11)

139 BMHWS 1678, William O'Keeffe, p. 14; Paddy Daly to Collins, 18 Apr. 1921 (RMP, P7/A/5)

Motherwell. At the house of a Mr Downey and his wife in West-Calder, they met another IRA man on the run, Peter Kilmurray. With the newspapers carrying descriptions of the brothers, the four were forced to move to another place. To avert suspicion, they decided to split into two groups. Seán Mooney and Kilmurray went to Broxburn, where they were accommodated by a Donegal man named Coll and his family, while Eamonn Mooney and Quinn went elsewhere. Mooney and Kilmurray spent a number of weeks at Coll's house before being arrested.[140] The following October, when police uncovered documents implicating Paddy Daly in gunrunning, the Liverpool IRB man adopted the pseudonym of Murray and went on the run. 'I am unknown to the police', he told Michael Collins, 'so I hope to remain so.'[141]

A similar means of escaping police attention was to go into hiding. By the time of the police raid on his office in April 1921, Art O'Brien had been in hiding since the previous November, when he had been warned of police attention and received a threatening letter. At first, he was accommodated by friends, but later he moved into a hotel. Throughout, however, he attempted to continue working as normal as the Dáil's representative in London.[142] This required elaborate security precautions. On one occasion, P.J. Little, an employee of the Dáil's publicity department, accidently related O'Brien's address to 'a most indiscreet and talkative woman'; O'Brien had to distract her in conversation so as to make her forget it. The police 'are getting much keener on tracing me and any little indiscretion may put them on the track', he warned Robert Brennan, Little's superior. Instead of directing visitors straight to him, O'Brien recommended that they be instructed to call at the ISDL office, where they would be redirected to him.[143]

In February 1920, *An t-Óglác* reminded Volunteers that they were to refuse to answer questions asked of them by the police. Giving information, no matter how innocent, constituted 'a recognition of the enemy's authority on the part of Volunteers' and would be treated as a breach of discipline.[144] The following year, while on a tour of the various Volunteer centres, Rory O'Connor was asked by the O/C Sheffield what attitude his men should take

140 Seán (or Séamus) Mooney's statement on the 'Smashing of the Van' incident; membership roll, 'E' Company, 2nd Battalion, Scottish Brigade IRA (EMP, 5/36, 3/C/13)

141 Paddy Daly to Michael Collins, 18 Oct. 1921 (RMP, P7/A/7)

142 Art O'Brien to Collins, 2 Dec. 1920 (DÉ, 2/326)

143 O'Brien to Collins, 24 Mar. 1921, enclosing O'Brien to 'R.O.B', 24 Mar. 1921 (DÉ, 2/329)

144 *An t-Óglác*, Feb. 1920

towards the police in the event of their being arrested. The O/C himself felt that, as soldiers, Volunteers should refuse to defend or excuse their actions, and O'Connor agreed.[145] Thus, the Volunteers in Britain were urged to emulate their colleagues in Ireland by adopting a defiant attitude in their dealings with the police.

Although John Pinkman and his accomplices divulged their names to a railway policeman after being apprehended by members of the public while attempting to escape from the farm fire operation on 9 March 1921, and felt 'terribly ashamed' for having done so, most Volunteers seem to have taken a defiant stance.[146] Arrested in June, Edward Brady underwent weeks of interrogation in Merseyside and at Scotland Yard in London. Determined to avoid giving his interrogators any useful information, he sometimes feigned ignorance of IRA activities or adopted a sarcastic attitude. 'I proved the despair of all my interrogators', he boasted.[147]

In their confrontations with members of the IRA, the police seem to have employed violence only when they came under violent attack. As we saw in Chapter 3, Volunteers sometimes shot at police in order to escape the scene of attacks, while other times they opened fire seemingly with the deliberate intent of inflicting injuries. Fire-fights also took place away from the scenes of arson and sabotage incidents. On 2 April 1921, police investigating arson attacks in Manchester city earlier that day called at the Irish Club in Hulme, headquarters of the city's No. 2 IRA Company. Seeing two men who answered witnesses' descriptions of the arsonists, the police asked that they accompany them outside. The men agreed, but as they left the room they fled. The police then found themselves confronted with two men armed with revolvers. Shots were exchanged and one of the Volunteers, Seán Morgan, was fatally wounded. Police reinforcements arrived and rushed the building. A further shoot-out occurred on a narrow stairway. A second Volunteer was shot and three policemen were slightly wounded. 16 arrests were made and an arsenal of munitions was uncovered. The violence was akin to that of 'an American film serial', commented the *Manchester Guardian*.[148]

Just as defiance often characterized Volunteers' dealings with the police, so it was in their attitude towards the courts. In February 1921, following

---

145 O/C Britain to C/S, 15 Oct. 1921 (RMP, P7/A/29[264–73])

146 Pinkman, *Legion*, p. 53; see Chapter 3

147 Brady, *Secret Service*, p. 105

148 *TT*, 4 Apr.; *MG*, 5 Apr., 16 July 1921; list of ammunition and explosives found at the Irish Club, Erskine Street, Hulme (HO, 144/4645)

their conviction of attempted arson in Wandsworth, Wilfred Kenny, James Moran and Thomas O'Sullivan stood in the dock with arms folded while they were being sentenced. Kenny then sang 'The Soldier's Song'. As they were being led away, they waved to their friends in the gallery and shouted 'Ta Ta'.[149] Awaiting trial, Neil Kerr Senior was reported to be 'in the best spirits imaginable, and absolutely defiant'.[150] When the judge announced the prison sentences on John Pinkman and his four co-accused at their trial two months later, they laughed at him and shouted 'Up the rebels!' as they were led away to the cells.[151] After being found guilty of shooting with intent to cause grievous bodily harm and possessing firearms, William Robinson and three other London Volunteers shouted 'God save Ireland', the defiant declaration of the Manchester Martyrs.[152] Robinson was outraged at the conviction of Jeremiah Minihane for the crime but had a difficult task persuading him to launch an appeal as he 'didn't care 2*d.*' about it.[153]

This defiant attitude was motivated by the belief that the British criminal justice system was prejudiced against the Irish. Such alleged discrimination took a number of forms, including judges' admittance of questionable evidence, fabrication of evidence by the prosecution and harsh sentencing. During the trial of the London Volunteer Michael O'Kelly Simington in October 1920, on a charge of illegally possessing plans of the Irish Office in contravention of the Official Secrets Act, the prosecution repeatedly emphasized the fact that the defendant was a member of the ISDL. Simington's barrister, having failed in his attempt to have such evidence refused admittance, later lamented that the Irish republican flag 'was waved before the faces of the jury, and such an air of treason was created that it was impossible to defend the prisoner'. The ISDL complained that the sentence handed down was 'extremely severe' given the defendant's 'very good character'.[154]

In the run-up to the trial of the Liverpool men charged with involvement in the arson attacks of November 1920, Michael Collins believed that the greatest obstacle to the defendants being found innocent would be

149 *Freeman's Journal*, 19 Feb. 1921

150 Paddy Daly to Michael Collins, 21 Feb. 1921 (RMP, P7/A/4)

151 *TT*, 11 Apr. 1921

152 *TT*, 4 July 1921

153 William Robinson to unknown, *c*. mid-1921 (CAB, 21/255); *TT*, 16 June, 4 July 1921

154 Quoted in David Foxton, *Revolutionary Lawyers: Sinn Féin and Crown Courts in Ireland and Britain, 1916–1923* (Dublin: Four Courts Press, 2008), p. 306; Seán McGrath to Michael Collins, 13 Mar. 1922 (D/T, S8037)

'prejudice'.[155] Art O'Brien agreed, writing that 'anti-Irish prejudice' might blind the authorities to the merits of the men's defence. Moreover, such a risk would be 'decidedly greater before certain judges than before others'.[156] When Neil Kerr Senior, Matthew Fowler and James McCaughey were indeed convicted of conspiracy to murder and commit arson, Paddy Daly complained of 'prejudice', especially in the case of McCaughey, who was 'absolutely innocent' of the attempted murder of the two policemen. (As we saw in Chapter 3, this was actually true. Interned in Mountjoy prison in Dublin, Michael O'Leary admitted that he, not McCaughey, had shot at the policemen. However, the senior IRA leaders in the prison refused him permission to inform the authorities of this.[157]) 'The judge was more of a prosecutor than a judge', he declared, 'and his summing up might well be taken as the final speech of the prosecution. He was sent, without doubt, to obtain a conviction.' Collins agreed.[158]

John Pinkman claimed that the prosecution's case at the initial hearing against him and his fellow would-be arsonists was based on 'a mass of fabricated evidence' given by the police. The only solid evidence presented by the prosecution was a religious medal found at one of the farms targeted for attack, ownership of which was admitted by one of the defendants, it was claimed. The prosecution then maintained that Pinkman and another defendant wore similar medals. Convinced by the evidence, the magistrates ordered the men to be put on trial. Pinkman and his comrades were 'stunned' at having to stand trial for a crime which they 'hadn't been able to commit'. He noted that the judge at the subsequent trial, Rigby Swift, had been a Conservative MP and was appointed to the High Court by Lord Birkenhead, a politician who had opposed Irish home rule. Thus, he implied that his and his comrades' conviction of arson, conspiracy and unlawful possession of firearms owed more to the political prejudices of the judge than to the evidence presented.[159] The ISDL complained that the sentences handed down in the trial of J.P. Connolly and his gunrunning accomplices, including husband and wife David and Kitty Evans, were 'extremely heavy', especially considering that Kitty Evans was in bad health. Moreover, Justice McCardie, who had also presided at the Simington trial, was 'extremely severe in his

155 Collins to Art O'Brien, 5 Jan. 1921 (DÉ, 2/326)

156 O'Brien to Collins, 10 Jan. 1921 (DÉ, 2/327)

157 BMHWS 797, Micheál Ó Laoghaire, pp. 47, 51–52

158 Correspondence between Paddy Daly and Michael Collins, 15, 17 Feb. 1921 (RMP, P7/A/4)

159 Pinkman, *Legion*, pp. 56–57, 59–60; *TT*, 11 Apr. 1921

remarks and stated that Mrs. Evans was as bad if not worse than any of the others'. He also implied that the Evans were not married and made some 'very disparaging remarks' in relation to Irish organizations in Britain.[160]

Objectively, the role of prejudice in securing convictions of Volunteers in Britain is difficult to evaluate. The barrister David Foxton has argued that some judges did make questionable decisions. Justice McCardie's actions in the Simington trial were 'highly prejudicial' but 'scarcely probative', he argues. Sir Alfred Tobin put before the jury 'a very weak case' of conspiracy to murder against Neil Kerr Senior, as did the judge in Jeremiah Minihane's trial. The Court of Criminal Appeal subsequently overturned Kerr's murder conviction but refused to hear Minihane's case. In the case of appeals against deportations, judges delivered adverse decisions 'on very technical and highly questionable grounds'. However, juries adopted a more sceptical attitude towards charges of murder or attempted murder than those related to property offences or conspiracy. 'To this extent', he concludes, 'the presence of a jury in England provided a check on capital convictions which was wholly absent in Ireland.'[161]

It would seem, therefore, that there may have been some substance to republicans' allegations that the criminal justice system in Britain was prejudiced against them. However, it is also likely that accusations of discrimination were a reaction to the adverse political climate in Britain. In Ireland, where the populace was becoming increasingly alienated from British rule, Volunteers used their trials to engage in anti-British defiance. Such exercises were facilitated by sympathetic juries reluctant to convict and disseminated abroad through a largely well-disposed media. Volunteers in Britain, however, endured a harsher climate. It was one where, outside the environs of the sympathetic Irish population and radical circles, the IRA was viewed as a criminal conspiracy terrorizing the loyal population of Ireland rather than as an army of liberation. The extension of its campaign of violence to Britain only reinforced the public's sense of fear and revulsion. Such hostility manifested itself in the courtroom. Judges refused to respect the declarations of Volunteers that their actions were honourably motivated by a desire to draw attention to events in Ireland. Instead, they treated Volunteers as criminals. In February 1921, sentencing Kenny, Moran and O'Sullivan to terms of imprisonment, Justice Lush said that there were 'legitimate' and 'criminal' means of alerting the British public to the actions of Crown forces in Ireland. By resolving to

---

160 Séan McGrath to Michael Collins, 13 Mar. 1922 (D/T, S8037)

161 Foxton, *Revolutionary Lawyers*, p. 334

'cause destruction of a vast amount of property ... [and] to expose a number
of innocent persons to serious [economic] loss and undoubtedly to serious
bodily danger', the defendants had chosen the criminal option and therefore
deserved punishment.[162] At the trial of 19 Manchester IRA men in July
1921 on charges related to arson attacks in the city three months earlier,
Justice Swift noted that a number of the defendants claimed that they were
members of an organization which hoped 'to obtain by force some political
aim'. He, however, refused to engage with that argument. 'All I have to do
is to punish crimes which are committed in this country against the people
of this country', he stated.

> It is obvious that society could not exist if deeds such as you have been
> [found] guilty of were not within the grasp of the law, and if when
> they are proved to have been done there was the slightest paltering or
> hesitation, on the part either of juries or judges, in putting down such
> offences.[163]

Justice McCardie's criticism of the defendants in the Evans trial – that they
had repaid Welsh hospitality with treachery and crime and that their actions
had tarnished the honour of Ireland – was probably motivated by a similar
abhorrence of crime rather than by 'anti-Irish prejudice', for he was the son
of an Irishman.[164]

At least one Volunteer conceded that IRA operations could only
fuel the prejudice their colleagues were allegedly suffering while on trial.
Following Neil Kerr Senior's conviction, Paddy Daly feared that the jury had
been prejudiced by the 'Man[chester] operations', a reference to farm fires
recently mounted by Volunteers.[165] Moreover, Joshua Casswell, a barrister
who defended a number of IRA men, later argued that such violence was
bound to effect a jury's attitude towards the defendants: 'with Irishmen
committing bomb outrages [sic] over here [in Britain] almost every week
purely legal arguments – however technically correct – were not likely to
be extremely efficacious'.[166]

162 *TT*, 19 Feb. 1921
163 *MG*, 16 July 1921
164 *IT*, *TT*, 18 Nov. 1921; A. Lentin, 'McCardie, Sir Henry Alfred (1869–1933)', in
     ODNB, accessed at http://www.oxforddnb.com/view/article/34677 on 17 May
     2010
165 Paddy Daly to Michael Collins, 16 Feb. 1921 (RMP, P7/A/4)
166 Quoted in Foxton, *Revolutionary Lawyers*, p. 334

In contrast to their comrades in Ireland, therefore, there were limits to the defiance exhibited by Volunteers in Britain. As part of their campaign against the British administration, IRA men in Ireland adopted a passive aggressive attitude of 'non-recognition' while on trial so as to undermine the legitimacy of the British courts. Such an attitude consisted of a refusal to give a formal plea to the charge or consent to undertakings such as bail. Such defiance was possible in a climate where, out of fear of or admiration for the Volunteers, juries and sometimes judges often acquitted IRA men of the charges against them.[167] Britain, however, lacked such a climate of opinion and Volunteers recognized that an outright refusal to engage with the courts would do little to prevent their being convicted of the charges against them. Thus, James McCaughey, charged with attempted murder of a policeman, told the court through his barrister that he initially intended 'to refuse to recognize the Court at all' but eventually decided to produce an alibi.[168] Moreover, as Foxton notes, in contrast to the behaviour of their comrades in Ireland, verbal acts of defiance by Volunteers in British courts were performed *after* they had been convicted.[169] In March 1921, for example, Henry Coyle told an Edinburgh court that 'he was a soldier of the IRA and he was proud of it'. However, this declaration was only made after he had been convicted of conspiracy. At the start of the trial, Coyle had, along with his fellow defendants, entered a plea of not guilty.[170]

The cost of defending Volunteers on trial sometimes proved onerous and controversial. Irish societies in Liverpool raised £1,000 to cover the expenses of Neil Kerr Senior's defence.[171] Their counterparts in Glasgow, however, were not so generous when Clydeside men were on trial.[172] In the end, the cost was largely borne by Dublin. Writing to de Valera about the trial of the Erskine Street men, Collins stated: 'In my opinion we are directly in the position that we have to defend such cases as these'. This was because 'on [our] own people in England a very bad impression would be created if the prisoners were undefended'.[173] In this case, Collins advanced £2,500 to cover the cost of hiring a defence team. This money was to be paid back within four months,

167 Foxton, *Revolutionary Lawyers*, pp. 173–78
168 *TT*, 12 Feb. 1921
169 Foxton, *Revolutionary Lawyers*, p. 333
170 Quoted in Foxton, *Revolutionary Lawyers*, p. 312; *IT*, 15 Mar. 1921
171 Paddy Daly to Michael Collins, 19 Jan. 1921 (RMP, P7/A/3)
172 E.g. correspondence between Art O'Brien, Collins and others, Aug. 1921–Jan. 1922 (AÓBP, MS 8445/21)
173 Collins to Eamon de Valera, 11 May 1921 (EdeVP, P150/1377)

but he doubted that it would ever be refunded.[174] By late 1922, around £4,000 in expenses, including trial fees, had yet to be paid in relation to events in Scotland prior to the signing of the treaty.[175]

Overall, between 1918 and the end of 1921, at least 111 people were convicted of offences in relation to the Irish republican movement in Britain. 47 were condemned for gunrunning or illegal possession of munitions, 36 for involvement in the campaign of violence, and an additional 26 for both. The remaining two were found guilty of house-breaking and illegally possessing the plans of a government building.[176] In addition, a minimum of 30 men were deported from Britain and interned in Ireland between December 1920 and the truce.[177]

VI

If defiance characterized the dealings of Volunteers with the police and the courts, it was at its most noticeable in their behaviour in prison. Many were familiar with accounts of the suffering endured by the Young Irelanders and the Fenians in English prisons in the mid- to late-nineteenth century. The hardships of O'Donovan Rossa in particular were the stuff of legend. Sentenced to life imprisonment in 1865 after being found guilty of plotting a rebellion in Ireland, he spent five years in various prisons, where his defiant attitude saw him subjected to a variety of punishments including long periods of solitary confinement and, on one occasion, the manacling of his hands behind his back for 35 consecutive days. Indeed, the privations endured by O'Donovan Rossa and other Fenians gave rise to an amnesty campaign in Ireland which would later become the springboard for the home rule movement.[178] In the popular nationalist history which many Volunteers imbibed in their youth from family, friends and the media, the

---

174 Correspondence between de Valera and Collins, 12 May 1921 (EdeVP, P150/1377)

175 Unknown to the Minister of Defence, 26 Oct. 1922 (DDAF, A/13942)

176 *Freeman's Journal, II, IT, MG, The Observer, TT,* 1918– 1921; Edward Troup to Sir Archibald Bodkin, 21 Jan. 1922, enclosing 'List of Prisoners in Custody for Offences Connected with the Sinn Fein Movement Who Were Convicted in England & Wales'; list of 55 prisoners granted remission on 11 Feb.; list of 14 prisoners granted remission on 1 Apr. 1922 (HO, 144/4645)

177 'RROUK', no. 88, 13 Jan.; 'RROUK', no. 98, 23 Mar. 1921 (CAB, 24/118, 24/121); *Irish Exile,* July 1921; BMHWS 797, Micheál Ó Laoghaire, pp. 47–48

178 McConville, *Irish Political Prisoners,* pp. 123–24, 168–201, 214–75

Figure 3: Republicans from Britain in Ballykinlar Internment Camp, County Down, mid- to late-1921.
Left to right, front row: P. Coyne (Liverpool), M. Horan (Liverpool), Seán McGrath (London), J. Horan (Liverpool), Michael McGrath (London), Joseph Carr (London); back row: McLean (Liverpool), Emmett Fox (London), D. O'Brien (Coventry), M. O'Higgins (London), O'Connor (Liverpool), E. Moran (Liverpool), Hugh Early (Liverpool), R. Duggan (Liverpool), G. Tierney (London) (Courtesy of the National Library of Ireland)

imprisoned Fenian was a heroic figure, a martyr for Ireland tormented by cruel jailors. Some Volunteers, therefore, entered prison infused with feelings of self-righteousness and noble martyrdom. 'A felon's hat is the noblest crown an Irish head can wear', John Pinkman told his mother before he was transported to Walton prison, slightly misquoting a line from a famous nationalistic poem, 'The Felons of our Land'.[179]

As a result, relations between prisoners and prison authorities were often tense. 'You could see the hatred he had for us by the look in his eyes', wrote Pinkman of the doctor in Walton prison.[180] Seán McGrath railed against Irishmen being 'subjected to the whims of heartless gaolers, [and] cruelly

179 Pinkman, *Legion*, pp. 60–61
180 Pinkman, *Legion*, p. 58

punished for the slightest infraction of the iron code of rules concocted with scientific precision for the purpose of breaking the spirit of anyone subjected to them'.[181] The governor of Dartmoor stated that in dealing with Irish prisoners he had carried out his orders 'strictly & I hope fairly'. Nevertheless, the IRA men later claimed that except for about six 'humane and even kindly men', all the warders in Dartmoor treated them brutally. The *Freeman's Journal* speculated that as a result of working in 'the most formidable of English convict prisons', the Dartmoor warder 'seems to lose all feeling', 'grows hard' and becomes 'a lion-tamer'.[182]

'As soldiers of the Irish Republic I ask that we shall be treated as prisoners of war', declared Charles Harding, O/C No. 2 Company Manchester IRA, after he and 15 comrades were convicted of involvement in arson attacks on Manchester city in April 1921.[183] His request was declined. Refused political prisoner status, republicans were often categorized as ordinary criminals, a situation which Volunteers and their supporters outside found scandalous. The *Irish Exile* complained that Irish men were being treated not 'as prisoners of war, but as the worst of criminals' and forced to associate with 'the lowest type of criminals'.[184] The *Freeman's Journal* noted that in Dartmoor, Volunteers rubbed shoulders with 'the most hardened of criminals, thieves, forgers, and murderers of every nationality'.[185] Seán McGrath protested that they had been 'herded with the criminal scum from the purlieus of English cities'.[186]

Like the Easter Rising veterans interned and incarcerated in Britain in 1916–17, it was in their attempts to secure prisoner of war or political prisoner status that imprisoned Volunteers were at their most defiant. In the summer of 1921, Dartmoor prison witnessed a number of such attempts. The first incident saw men refusing to perform their work duties, but the protest soon collapsed. Those who participated in the strike were reprimanded with a three-day bread and water diet. However, the punishment only strengthened the resolve of the strikers and embarrassed the recalcitrants. On 16 July, they launched a second strike. According to the prison governor, the prisoners claimed that, by entering into peace talks with Sinn Féin, the British government had recognized the IRA 'as an army' and that they as 'soldiers' should, therefore,

---

181 *Irish Exile*, Feb. 1922
182 Directors of Dartmoor Prison to the Home Secretary, 14 Feb. 1922 (HO, 144/1734/376829); *Freeman's Journal*, 18 Jan. 1922
183 *MG*, 16 July 1921
184 *Irish Exile*, Dec. 1921
185 *Freeman's Journal*, 18 Jan. 1922
186 *Irish Exile*, Feb. 1922

'be treated as prisoners of war'.[187] 84 prisoners threw off their coveralls and refused to leave the exercise yard. They were then attacked by baton-wielding warders and removed to their cells. Volunteers arrested in England were in a separate exercise yard and Pinkman saw the warders dragging a prisoner towards the punishment cells, all the while beating him 'until he was as limp as a rag doll'. When he and Paddy Lowe made to intervene, however, they too were attacked by the warders. Pinkman managed to escape and made to run into the prison to alert his comrades. However, the gate guard stepped into his path and aimed his rifle at him. Pinkman stopped and raised his hands. The warders then surrounded him and started to beat him with 'batons, boots, [and] fists'. They trussed him up and dragged him to the punishments cells. 'Break his arms ... Break the son-of-a-bitch's arms!' shouted one of the warders. Inside the punishment block, Pinkman was pushed down a steep iron staircase. As he lay on the floor, he was beaten again. 'I tried to cover my head with my arms', he remembered,

> but they kicked the shite out of me. When they finished with me I was nothing but blood from head to toe, and when they threw me in the cell I just lay on the floor thinking I was dying. I crawled close to one of the walls and made an act of contrition.[188]

Joseph Kelly, another prisoner, stated that he was kicked and beaten by the warders while being dragged to his cell. 'At the cell door they amused themselves by shoving me in [to the cell] and dragging me back [out] again, beating me all the time', he remembered. Eventually, he was hurled into the cell and lay on the floor semi-conscious until he was removed to hospital. Later, the warders removed the prisoners' leaders from their cells and beat them. One, Layng, claimed that he too was flung down an iron staircase and forced to run the gauntlet between two lines of warders who beat him with batons, before being thrown down a further flight of stairs. Waking up in a punishment cell 'in a pool of blood', he was removed to the hospital where his head, legs, arms and shoulders were bandaged. He was then sentenced to three months' solitary confinement and 15 days on a bread and water diet. It was also alleged that another prisoner, John Doyle, had his arm broken by the warders.[189]

---

187 Governor of Dartmoor to E. Troup, 27 July 1921 (DLGP, LG/F/45/6/38)
188 *Freeman's Journal*, 18 Jan. 1922; Pinkman, *Legion*, pp. 76–77
189 *Freeman's Journal*, 18 Jan. 1922

While admitting that a 'disturbance' had occurred in the prison on 16 July, the governor of Dartmoor claimed that the prisoners' allegations of violence were 'grossly exaggerated and in many points utterly untrue'. When the warders attempted to remove them to the cells, a small number of prisoners reacted violently. Most, however, 'went quietly but had to be pushed along as they showed passive resistance'. Neither here nor during the removal of the prisoners' leaders to other cells did the governor see the warders employ their batons. Over the course of the following week, the prisoners' leaders received visits from the prison directors and on no occasion did they make any complaint regarding their treatment, though they did protest the government's refusal to treat them as prisoners of war generally. The governor admitted that six prisoners, including Pinkman, Lowe, Layng and Kelly, were admitted to the hospital, but he noted that some warders had sustained injuries too. The allegation that warders broke Doyle's arm was 'utterly untrue'. Indeed, the directors believed that the warders exhibited 'most commendable self-restraint' in dealing with the incident.[190] The peace talks between the British government and Sinn Féin had led to 'a very dangerous spirit' manifesting itself among the Irish inmates, the governor noted on another occasion. The prison authorities believed that republican inmates from Ireland and Britain, numbering 300 in total, would take advantage of whatever opportunities arose to mount more protests. To deal with the situation, they had decided to confine them to cellular labour, with exercise in the yard only in small groups. This, however, was only a stop-gap measure. Anticipating further outbreaks of violence, Dartmoor had already asked Portland prison to transfer to it any warders it could spare, where they would be issued with unloaded carbines. The governor also requested that the Home Office supply a military guard of 50 men for use daily between 7 a.m. and 5 p.m.[191]

After the second work strike collapsed, the prisoners decided to mount a hunger-strike. Hunger-striking held particular resonance in both the pagan and Catholic religions. The hunger-strike as a means of protesting a grievance originated in pre-Christian Ireland where, according to the Brehon Laws, an individual who felt himself ill-treated by another could abstain from food near the offender's residence with the aim of shaming him into reaching some mutually agreeable settlement. With the arrival of Christianity, the hunger-strike became a symbolic fast from food in imitation of Christ. In the

---

190 Directors of Dartmoor Prison to the Home Secretary, 14 Feb. 1922 (HO, 144/1734/376829)

191 Governor of Dartmoor to E. Troup, 27 July 1921 (DLGP, LG/F/45/6/38)

nineteenth century, the 'devotional revolution', the reform in religious practise which saw an increase in the power, prestige and influence of the Catholic Church in Ireland, along with the cultural revival resulted in the virtual fusion of religious and national identity, creating an Irish Catholicism replete with themes of heroic self-sacrifice and stoic self-abnegation.[192] Perhaps influenced also by its use by suffragettes in Britain in 1912–14, in the aftermath of the 1916 Rising the hunger-strike became the weapon of choice of incarcerated nationalists. The death of IRB president Thomas Ashe through botched force-feeding in September 1917 was a significant event in the ascendancy of advanced nationalism in Ireland. Three years later, Terence MacSwiney's death after a 74-day hunger-strike in Brixton prison attested to the grim struggle that raged between the British government and the republican movement for control of Ireland. The moral force of the protest was compelling. By subjecting himself to 'all the horrors of hunger and the dangers of a self-inflicted death', the hunger-striker excited the humane instincts of even implacable foes and wrong-footed the authorities.[193]

During his trial, Charles Harding had hinted at his intention to commence a hunger-strike if his demand for prisoner of war status was declined.[194] Now, refusing to eat their meals, except for bread and water, the hunger-striking prisoners in Dartmoor, including John Pinkman, stayed in their cells. About 12 days into the strike, a visiting monk persuaded the men to end their protest. Having eaten only bread and water for a week and no food at all for the last four days, the men were 'as weak as kittens'. A certain amount of bitterness was caused by the fact that some Volunteers failed to participate in these protests. For some time afterwards, Pinkman refused to speak to such recalcitrants. Eventually, however, he forgave them: 'I came to realise that you can't blame a man if he hasn't got the courage to go through with something like that. Some men are made of steel, others are made of brass – and you can't expect a piece of brass to act like steel.' Others, however, refused to grant such forgiveness.[195]

A similar hunger-strike occurred in Maidstone prison. Volunteers from Ireland had been given prisoner of war status by the prison authorities. Refused similar treatment, the prisoners from Britain, including Harding, went on hunger-strike. 'I am O.K. now in hospital', wrote William Robinson,

192 George Sweeney, 'Irish Hunger Strikes and the Cult of Self-Sacrifice', *Journal of Contemporary History*, 28.3 (1993), pp. 421–23

193 *Hansard 5* (*Commons*), cxxvii, cols 1538–45: T.P. O'Connor (13 Apr. 1920)

194 *MG*, 16 July 1921

195 Pinkman, *Legion*, pp. 70–74

one of the participants, 'but the others are having a rough time.' He requested that London's Irish societies publicize their protest.[196]

Edward Brady remembered that, in their campaign for political prisoner status, IRA men in Mountjoy 'openly and flagrantly' disobeyed the regulations.[197] As a protest against the prison authorities changing the rules in relation to prisoners receiving parcels and letters from outside, they too began a hunger-strike. 'Never till then did I realise the pangs of real hunger', he confessed.

> The third day the sensation of it is hellish – no one but those who have suffered it can possibly conceive what it is like. Then a general weakness supervenes, and the craving subsides. Even the mind suffers intolerably for a while, until one becomes quite unconscious of everything – even of the pain.

After six days, the strike was concluded and the prisoners had their privileges reinstated.[198]

'Escape was the topic of the day, always in the minds of the Volunteers', remembered Michael O'Leary of his time as an inmate in the Curragh internment camp in County Kildare.[199] Indeed, it was the topic foremost on the minds of IRA men incarcerated everywhere in Ireland and Britain. Successful break-outs constituted propaganda coups for the Irish cause and occasioned acute embarrassment on the part of the British authorities. The first successful escape of Volunteers from a prison in Britain occurred at Usk in Monmouthshire, Wales, on 24 January 1919, three days after the Dáil first met and the war of independence began. Four Sinn Féin leaders, including two TDs, climbed over the wall of the prison using a rope ladder fashioned from towels and firewood. They then walked to Newport, where they took the train to Liverpool. There, they were given refuge by sympathizers before Steve Lanigan arranged their passage to Dublin.[200]

196 William Robinson to unknown, *c.* mid-1921 (CAB 21/255); 'List of Prisoners in Custody for Offences Connected with Sinn Fein Movement Who Were Convicted in England and Wales', 19 Jan. 1922 (HO, 144/4645)

197 Brady, *Secret Service*, p. 128

198 Brady, *Secret Service*, p. 143

199 BMHWS 797, Micheál Ó Laoghaire, p. 66

200 Frank Shouldice and George Geraghty, 'The Break-Out from Usk Jail in Wales by Four 'German Plot' Prisoners', in Florence O'Donoghue (ed.), *IRA Jailbreaks 1918–1921* (Cork: Mercier Press, 2010), pp. 38–51; *TT*, 25 Jan. 1919

Michael Collins was alarmed by the incident. He feared that the authorities would react by increasing security at all prisons and thereby frustrate the planned rescue of Eamon de Valera and others from Lincoln jail. In the event, however, as we have already seen, this jailbreak was successful too.[201] On 25 October, the Manchester IRA participated in another victorious rescue, this time at Strangeways Prison. Masquerading as window cleaners, they blockaded the street at the back of the jail and used a prop extension ladder and a rope ladder to spring six men, including D.P. Walsh and Piaras Béaslaí. Béaslaí later wrote that the planning of escape attempts had consumed most of his time since his arrest the previous May for making a seditious speech. From the day of his arrival at Strangeways, he began thinking of ways to emulate the successful flight of 20 prisoners from Mountjoy in late March 1919. Breaking out of Strangeways would prove a tough task, he conceded: '[W]e were in an English city in the midst of a hostile population; but a captive lives on hope'.[202] The rescue was 'a feat of which Volunteers may well be proud', declared *An t-Óglác*.

The affair was planned with a thoroughness and an attention to detail which caused the proceedings to work with the utmost smoothness and success. Needless to say, the most elaborate planning and observations were required to ensure the success of such a daring scheme. The little band of Irishmen who formed the rescue party showed no less cool heroism than that other little band who, in 1867, rescued two Fenian leaders from a prison van in the streets of Manchester. Fortunately, in this case no sacrifice of life resulted, but every man who went into the work of the rescue knew he was taking his life in his hands. The work both inside and outside the prison was carried out to a finish with the utmost precision and promptitude.[203]

A number of other rescues were mooted but never carried to fruition. For example, Volunteer Paddy O'Neill organized and led a rescue attempt on Perth prison in Scotland. 'They penetrated the prison but had to retire [empty-handed]', one veteran remembered.[204]

---

201 Béaslaí, *Michael Collins*, i, p. 266; see Chapter 1
202 Béaslaí, *Michael Collins*, i, pp. 360–72, quote pp. 360–61; BMHWS 847, Patrick O'Donoghue, pp. 7–10; BMHWS 274, Liam McMahon, pp. 13–17
203 *An t-Óglác*, 15 Dec. 1919
204 Cathal Duthie to Eamonn Mooney, n.d. but *c.* 1951 (EMP, 3A/39)

The week after the signing of the treaty, the British government released the internees in Ireland.[205] A month later, an amnesty of all prisoners convicted of offences committed prior to the truce was announced. This amnesty applied only to those convicted of wrongdoing in Ireland and incarcerated there.[206] However, following representations from the Provisional Government, the reprieve was extended to 'prisoners now in custody for offences committed prior to the truce in Great Britain from Irish political motives'.[207] The Tullcross men were released shortly afterwards.[208] Further enquiries by Michael Collins ensured the release of those, such as J.P. Connolly, who had been convicted of crimes committed between the truce and the signing of the treaty.[209]

The prisoners in Dartmoor indulged in one last act of defiance before being released on 14 February. In the exercise yard, one of their number gave the order for the Volunteers to fall in. They 'lined up in three ranks', remembered Pinkman.

> Someone shouted, 'Quick march!' and we marched – yes, *marched* – to the gates saying, 'We came here as soldiers of the IRA, and by God we'll leave as soldiers of the IRA! We'll show these bastards!' The bloody warders just looked at us; they didn't know what to make of us, I'm sure.

Pinkman and his comrades then took the train home to Liverpool, where they were greeted by a pipe band and their O/C, Tom Kerr, himself released from internment in Ireland. Then, with a mixture of excitement and relief, they proceeded to enjoy a feast.[210]

VII

In the months following the Dáil's ratification of the treaty, the police continued to monitor republican activities in Britain. As well as noting the division caused by the agreement amongst the Irish in Britain generally and in political organizations such as the ISDL and Sinn Féin in particular,

205 'RROUK', no. 135, 15 Dec. 1921 (CAB, 24/131)
206 *TT*, 13 Jan. 1922
207 Correspondence between the Home Secretary and Masterton Smith, 11 Feb. 1922; list of 55 prisoners granted remission on 11 Feb. 1922 (HO, 144/4645)
208 S. Duggan to Art O'Brien, 26 Feb. 1922 (AÓBP, MS 8445/16)
209 List of 14 prisoners granted remission on 1 Apr. 1922 (HO, 144/4645)
210 Pinkman, *Legion*, pp. 79–81; original emphasis

police intelligence kept a close eye on the IRA.[211] In late February, it was reported that Volunteers who had arrived in Britain since the truce were being sounded out as to their views on the treaty and 'warned to hold themselves in readiness'.[212] The following week, 'reprisals' were allegedly being contemplated if Joe Robinson, Richard Purcell, J.P. Connolly and other prisoners were not amnestied soon.[213] Shortly afterwards, preparations were underway to send young IRA men across the Irish Sea 'to strengthen the extreme section of the Republican Army' and to supply the outfit with munitions.[214] At the end of March, unrelenting attempts by republicans from Ireland to uncover munitions in Britain led police intelligence to predict 'trouble of a serious nature in Ireland at no very distant date'.[215] By late April, the gunrunning activities of Paddy Daly, Joe Scanlon and James Cunningham had become 'noticeable'.[216]

Intelligence led the police to discover some arms dumps. In February, 6 cwt (304.8 kg) of explosives was found hidden in the back courts and ashbins of Glasgow's East End.[217] As we saw, on 29 April a number of Volunteers were arrested as they attempted to remove munitions from the magazine at the Premier Aluminium Casting Company in Birmingham.[218] Mills bombs and about 80 incendiary bombs with fuses found in Peckham that same month and a small number of hand grenades uncovered in St Helens two months later may also have belonged to the Volunteers.[219]

Police patrols of public buildings and bodyguards for government ministers and other prominent people were removed following the treaty's passage, a decision that proved controversial in the wake of Sir Henry Wilson's assassination in June. '[A]ccording to our information there was never any fear of organized murder by Sinn Feiners in this country' following the Dáil's acceptance of the treaty, the Home Secretary later stated. A flurry of threatening letters to well-known politicians had kept the police busy, he continued, and all known Volunteers had been kept under observation.

211 See Chapter 4
212 'RROUK', no. 144, 23 Feb. 1922 (CAB, 24/133)
213 'RROUK', no. 145, 2 Mar. 1922 (CAB, 24/133)
214 'RROUK', no. 146, 9 Mar. 1922 (CAB, 24/134)
215 'RROUK', no. 149, 31 Mar. 1922 (CAB, 24/136)
216 'RROUK', no. 154, 4 May 1922 (CAB, 24/136)
217 *TT*, 21 Feb. 1922
218 Depositions of Det. Inspt. James McArdell, Det. Sgt. Samuel Price, P.C. Oliver Knee, pp. 7–8, 16–18, 19–20, May 1922 (ASSI, 13/52/2); see Chapter 4
219 *MG*, 22 Apr., 13 June 1922

However, as the entire membership of the IRA was not known to the police, it was impossible to ensure that every Volunteer was kept under watch. Two whose membership was not suspected were Dunne and O'Sullivan. Wilson's killing led to the reinstitution of bodyguards. Special Branch protection was then extended to members of the Northern Ireland government and their associates while in Britain, along with visiting foreign dignitaries such as the King of Serbia.[220] A few hours after Wilson death, the cabinet was told that the police had about 30 'dangerous Irishmen' under surveillance in London. Though these suspects were mainly engaged in propaganda work for the ISDL and seemed to be unconnected with the Volunteers, the cabinet authorized searches of their lodgings and arrests in the event of munitions or 'anything else specially suspicious' being uncovered. That night, the police raided houses in Brixton, Paddington and Bayswater, and uncovered a quantity of arms and incendiary fuses. 16 people were arrested, two of whom, Elizabeth Eadie (sister of Seán Connolly, one of the first rebels killed in the 1916 Rising) and Herbert Wrigley, were later convicted of illegal possession of munitions.[221]

As tensions increased in Ireland, the Provisional Government was alive to the potential threat posed by republicans in Britain. Initially, they attempted to neutralize the menace without the aid of the British authorities. In the summer of 1922, Arthur Nolan, a member of CID, was sent to Glasgow to put a stop to IRA gunrunning there. However, he and an accomplice were arrested by police on the Glasgow to Liverpool train having relieved the Volunteers of a remarkable armoury composed of a machine gun, 27 automatic pistols, a revolver and hundreds of thousands of rounds of ammunition.[222] Embarrassed by the incident, the Dublin government opted hereon in to co-operate with its British counterpart in attempting to frustrate republican activities in Britain. The civil war, therefore, saw former IRA men, now in the employ of the Provisional/Free State government, liaising with their ex-pursuers in the British security services in an attempt to frustrate the activities of their late comrades in the IRA.

As we saw previously, in the early stages of the civil war the National Army employed six men, including Michael O'Callaghan, to stymie Volunteer

220 Cabinet Conclusions, 11 a.m., 23 June 1922 (CAB, 21/255); A.F. Moslau to Commissioner of Police, 19 Oct. 1922 (MEPO, 2/1974); 'Note dictated by the Home Secretary', *c.* Aug. 1922 (DLGP, LG/F/45/6/42)

221 Cabinet Conclusions, 5 p.m. meeting, 22 June 1922 (CAB, 21/255); *TT*, 24 June, 22 July 1922; *IT*, 9 Oct. 1922; *II*, 22 Jan. 1923

222 Telegrams between Mark Sturgis and Alfred Cope, 11.13 a.m., 5.37 p.m., 11 Aug.; 'G.G.W.' to James Masterton Smith, 12 Aug. 1922 (CO, 739/6)

organizational efforts and gunrunning in Scotland.[223] By early 1923, there were at least four agents operating in Britain: H. Conroy and H. Short in Liverpool, F. Saurin in London and O'Callaghan in Glasgow.[224] Like O'Callaghan, at least one of the Liverpool agents was very familiar with his beat, being a veteran of the Merseyside IRA and therefore possessing valuable knowledge about the haunts and *modus operandi* of his former comrades.[225] Conroy and Short investigated the city's Cumann na mBan, for example. They reported that Kitty Furlong 'works in close association with the Irregulars in England and Ireland', was involved in the dissemination of anti-Free State propaganda and aided the IRA in Ireland both financially and otherwise. In order to learn more, they persuaded a woman to join the unit and report back to them on its activities. They thereby ascertained that Furlong also kept the gunrunning records for the local Volunteers.[226] Margaret Leonard and Mary Finan were judged to have been 'extremely active' in persuading the Liverpool outfit to adopt a hostile attitude towards the Free State government and to co-operate with the IRA. Like Furlong, both were said to be involved in weapons-smuggling too.[227] Maura Lively was also concerned with gunrunning. 'It is well known that ammunition is collected in Liverpool for despatch to Ireland and that members of Cumann na mBan assist the men in transferring the parcels from dump to dump', declared Diarmuid O'Hegarty, now the National Army's director of intelligence.[228] The Free State authorities also made use of the services of Neil Kerr Senior to hinder IRA gunrunning on Merseyside.[229]

Some of the agents' reports displayed animosity towards their former colleagues. In Liverpool, Paddy Daly was described as 'a coward': '[He] Has his eyes on cash. Took advantage of [the treaty] Split to get out of Purchases debts'. Meanwhile, Seán Kearns, a propagandist, was an 'awful blackguard'.[230]

---

223 See Chapter 4

224 Director of Intelligence to Minister for External Affairs, 3 Apr. 1923 (NAI, Department of Foreign Affairs file: Provisional Govt./IFS: 141(3): Section D5 no. 4)

225 Intelligence report on Margaret Leonard, n.d. (HO, 144/2904)

226 Diarmuid O'Hegarty to Col. Carter, 10 Apr. 1923 (HO, 144/2865); see Chapter 5

227 O'Hegarty to Carter, 1 May 1923 (HO, 144/2904); Mary Finan's hearing before the Advisory Committee, 16 Apr. 1923 (HO, 144/2866)

228 O'Hegarty to Carter, 1 May 1923 (HO, 144/2904)

229 Memorandum on Neil Kerr Senior, 3 Mar. 1925 (DDAF, A/13648)

230 'List of Republicans in Liverpool and District', n.d. (EO'ML, P17a/182)

Michael O'Callaghan's reports from Glasgow were peppered with resentments from the war of independence period and before. For example, Charles Diamond 'received £40 worth of explosives from me for nothing and sold same to Commandant O'Neill, Citizen Army, at Liberty Hall, for £50 in 1918', he declared. Ambrose Kenny, meanwhile, was allegedly 'expelled [from the Volunteers] owing to misbehaviour (Drunken[n]ess creating disturbance)', and he supposedly embezzled £40 which had been raised to pay the legal defence of a Volunteer on trial.[231]

Intelligence agents sometimes received threats from republicans. In November 1922, the agent in London was 'warned' by the gunrunner Martin Donovan 'that if anyone was arrested in London two [National Army] Officers here [in Ireland] would be shot as well as certain civilians whom he suspected as [i.e. of] giving information'. He got warnings from Art O'Brien and Seán McGrath too.[232] Meanwhile, through an intermediary, agents in Liverpool were ordered by C. Smith, 'a sort of Staff O/C Member of the ruling Inner Circle' of the local IRA, to leave the city 'or take the consequences'.[233] On 3 January 1923, a man named Plunkett was shot at by Volunteers in Glasgow on suspicion of being an agent.[234]

Of course, the British police continued to gather intelligence on the IRA too. At the end of July 1922, it was noted that money was 'not being spared' by republicans in Britain and in continental Europe in their 'anxiety for arms and ammunition'. The police speculated that the money may have been stolen from banks in Ireland.[235] In mid-December, an 'increase' in Volunteer activity was observed: a new O/C Britain had been appointed and 'urgent orders to units have been issued to obtain arms and ammunition'.[236] The following month, 'reliable information' indicated that America was the IRA's largest source of munitions, with a 'lesser quantity' of armaments being procured in Britain and 'no very large quantities' purchased on the continent. The weapons sourced in the US and continental Europe were being smuggled directly to Ireland, though sometimes they followed those procured in Britain by travelling through Liverpool.[237] In February 1923, it was reported that the O/C Britain was visiting Scotland and the north of England in order to

231 List of republicans in Scotland, n.d. (EO'ML, P17a/182)
232 List of active republicans in London, n.d. (EO'ML, P17a/182)
233 'Charges Against Irregulars Living in England', 12 Jan. 1923 (EO'ML, P17a/182)
234 'RROUK', no. 188, 11 Jan. 1923 (CAB, 24/158); *II*, 13 Jan. 1923
235 'RROUK', no. 165, 27 July 1922 (CAB, 24/138)
236 'RROUK', not numbered but actually no. 186, 21 Dec. 1922 (CAB, 24/140)
237 'RROUK', no. 189, 18 Jan. 1923 (CAB, 24/158)

put the IRA 'back on something like its old footing'. New members were being recruited and new companies established. Volunteers were 'being urged to become efficient and ready for any emergency that may arise'.[238] The following month, IRA leaders were 'still active', despite the recent arrest of a number of Volunteers in Liverpool and Glasgow and the seizure of munitions. Moreover, agents in Hamburg were reportedly making a deal to purchase about 1,000,000 rounds of ammunition, and they planned to use sailors to smuggle the consignment to Ireland in small quantities via Glasgow and Merseyside.[239]

Police intelligence also maintained its interest in contacts between republicans and communists. In February 1922, Cumann na mBan members in Britain, 'as fiery and determined as ever', allegedly received instructions from Dublin to work with 'Communists and extreme Labour' to 'cause as much trouble as ever'.[240] In May, Russian Bolsheviks were reportedly hoping to use Ireland as 'the jumping off ground for a European revolution' by means of an agreement between the IRA and the Communist Party of Ireland (CPI).[241]

There were elements of truth in these observations. The CPI, formerly the SPI, had condemned the treaty as a desperate attempt by the British to shore up their disintegrating empire. It, therefore, supported the anti-treatyites and hoped to persuade them to adopt radical social policies. The Comintern commended the CPI's stance, noting that the 'attitude of the proletarian majority' of the IRA demonstrated that the Irish communists were on 'the right path' and represented 'the will of the Irish working class'. The 'proletarian' outlook of the IRA in Ireland seemed to be on full display on 1 May when it issued an agrarian programme ordering local O/Cs to seize particular lands in their areas for re-distribution amongst the people. Moreover, upon the outbreak of the civil war, an estimated 143 ICA members and about 12 men from the CPI's small 'Red Guard' joined the Volunteers in battling the National Army in Dublin.[242] In August, representatives of Mikhail Borodin, the Comintern's agent in Britain, secured the IRA's provisional agreement to a political programme which included such measures as state ownership of heavy industry, transport and banks, land re-distribution and an eight-hour working day. In return, Moscow was

238 'RROUK', no. 192, 6 Feb. 1923 (CAB, 24/158)
239 'RROUK', no. 188, 11 Jan.; 'RROUK', no. 189, 18 Jan.; 'RROUK', no. 196, 8 Mar. 1923 (CAB, 24/158– 24/159); *TT*, 12 Jan. 1923
240 'RROUK', no. 142, 9 Feb. 1922 (CAB, 24/133)
241 'RROUK', no. 157, 25 May 1922 (CAB, 24/136)
242 O'Connor, *Reds*, pp. 50–66; Hanley, 'Irish Citizen Army', p. 41

to provide military, political and economic aid to the republicans.[243] Also, contacts continued between communists and republicans in Britain. In October 1922, police intelligence noted an article in the *Workers' Republic*, the CPI organ, by Patrick Lavin, the secretary of the Scottish Labour College, in which he urged communists to aid the fight for an Irish republic. He quoted Lenin at the Second Congress of the Comintern: 'Direct assistance must be given by all Communist Parties to the revolutionary movements of subject peoples (for example – Ireland)'.[244] In December, Joe Robinson was allegedly in discussions with communists on 'the question of arming', though the police believed that rank and file communists could not be 'depended upon to fight'.[245] They also held that Robinson's Scottish Brigade was receiving munitions from communists.[246]

On 1 July, three days after the outbreak of the civil war, and worried that the IRA in Munster and Connacht would become active once they had received munitions from Britain and elsewhere, the Provisional Government requested that the Royal Navy institute vigilant patrolling of the Irish Sea. Special attention was to be paid to 'small craft such as trawlers and fishing vessels' as they might be involved in the 'picking up of contraband [materiel] at sea'. Also, customs officials were requested to mount a careful examination of all vessels leaving Britain for Southern Ireland, especially colliers and fishing boats.[247] It was imperative that the British did their utmost to assist the Irish authorities, wrote Lionel Curtis, the colonial secretary's adviser on Irish affairs, for the treaty specifically charged them with protecting Irish waters for a period of five years.[248] The British government agreed to the request. By 25 July, Royal Navy patrols consisted of 23 ships: 11 destroyers, five mine-sweepers, four trawlers and three light cruisers.[249] By the end of the month, patrols had stopped and searched ten larger ships and 'a large number' of fishing vessels.[250] Two months later, the force had been reduced to nine

243 O'Connor, *Reds*, pp. 66–68
244 'RROUK, no. 176, 12 Oct. 1922 (CAB, 24/139), quoting *Workers' Republic*, 7 Oct. 1922
245 'RROUK', no. 184, 7 Dec. 1922 (CAB, 24/140)
246 'RROUK', no. 187, 4 Jan.; 'RROUK', no. 188, 11 Jan. 1923 (CAB, 24/158)
247 Telegram, Alfred Cope to Lionel Curtis, 4.31 p.m., 1 July 1922 (CO, 906/21)
248 Curtis to the Secretary of State for the Colonies, 13 Sept. 1922 (CO, 739/3); Alex May, 'Curtis, Lionel George (1872–1955)', in *ODNB*, online edn, May 2006, accessed at http://www.oxforddnb.com/view/article/32678 on 12 Aug. 2010
249 Secretary to the Admiralty to the USS, CO, 25 July 1922 (CO, 739/3)
250 Telegram, Mark Sturgis to Alfred Cope, 29 July 1922 (CO, 739/3)

destroyers, five mine-sweepers, four trawlers and three light cruisers.[251] On one occasion, a mine-sweeper, the *Bodminton*, came under fire while it was patrolling 400 yards (366 m) off-shore at Lackeen, County Kerry. One sailor was wounded and the ship returned fire.[252]

The effectiveness of these patrols was doubted. The Admiralty repeatedly requested permission to reduce the number of ships involved, apparently in the belief that little gunrunning was actually taking place.[253] Seemingly, only three ships were actually found to be smuggling munitions.[254] The Provisional Government, on the other hand, believed that the patrols were 'not doing much good', for the IRA was still receiving munitions from Britain.[255] Lionel Curtis agreed. He held that gunrunning did not involve ships cleared at recognized ports. Rather, he had 'no doubt' but that 'the munitions obtained by the rebels are introduced [into Ireland] in small craft and fishing boats landed at creeks', instancing the Volunteers' landing of weapons by yacht at Howth in July 1914. He therefore proposed that arrangements be put in place for the searching of such vessels for a period of one month.[256] Three months later, frustrated by the British navy's inability to put a stop to IRA gunrunning, the Provisional Government proposed that they themselves might employ 'armed trawlers' to tackle the problem.[257]

The seizure of munitions by police and customs officials during the civil war meant that only a fraction of the materiel that passed through the hands of republicans in Britain actually reached their comrades in Ireland. As we saw earlier, in December 1922 Merseyside police and customs uncovered 12,000 rounds of ammunition and chemicals used in the manufacture of explosives aboard a small steamer plying between Liverpool and Ireland. Moreover, in April 1923 Glasgow police unearthed gelignite and fuse hidden inside a railway tunnel.[258]

---

251 Secretary to the Admiralty to the USS, CO, 16 Sept. 1922 (CO, 739/3)
252 Telegram, Alfred Cope to Winston Churchill, 3.58 p.m., 30 July 1922 (CO, 906/21)
253 Secretary to the Admiralty to the USS, CO, 25 July, 2 Aug., 16 Sept.; Lionel Curtis to the Secretary of State, 21 Sept., 2 Oct. 1922 (CO, 739/3)
254 Secretary to the Admiralty to the USS, CO, 25 July (CO, 739/3); telegram, Alfred Cope to Mark Sturgis, 3.53 p.m., 29 July 1922 (CO, 906/21)
255 Telegram, Cope to Sturgis, 12.19 p.m., 31 July 1922 (CO, 906/21)
256 Lionel Curtis to the Secretary of State for the Colonies, 13 Sept. 1922 (CO, 739/3)
257 Admiralty to L.B. Freeston, 2 Nov. 1922 (CO, 739/3)
258 See Chapter 5

However, the performance of British customs officials came in for criticism. Alfred Cope, the British government's liaison officer with Dublin, instanced two cases where ships cleared by customs in Britain were found to have munitions hidden aboard upon arrival in Ireland. In Sligo, 25 rifles and a quantity of ammunition were found on the SS *Carrickfergus* from Liverpool. 'It is obvious that the conflict must end if the supplies are cut off and as the Irregulars still have good supplies the Customs must be missing the concealments', he complained.[259] The War Office declared that the *Carrickfergus* incident constituted a 'grave irregularity' on the part of both the ship's captain and the Liverpool harbour authorities.[260]

Late 1922 saw an upsurge in political activity by republicans in Britain. Meetings held by the ISDL and Poblacht na h-Eireann in Albain denounced the treaty in vehement terms and pledged support to the IRA.[261] In mid-December, Diarmuid O'Hegarty stated that there existed in British cities 'a considerable number of more or less prominent Irregulars who are engaged in the purchase of arms and explosives and who have possibly other designs for activity in England'. From the point of view of both the Irish and British governments, it was imperative, he concluded, that their activities be stymied.[262] The colonial secretary advised the Irish government that if it could be proven that republicans in Britain were acting in concert with the IRA in Ireland in order to aid the latter's rebellion, then the British government would consider bringing a charge of seditious conspiracy against them. Upon the issue of the relevant warrants in Ireland, 'parties to such conspiracy who by their overt acts or speeches in England showed that they were acting in furtherance of the seditious or rebellious objects [of the IRA in Ireland] could be arrested here [in Britain] and conveyed to Ireland for trial', a Home Office memorandum stated.[263]

Initially, the Irish government declined the offer.[264] In mid-January 1923, however, a British government official informed it of 'a marked increase' in republican activity in Britain and suggested that an intelligence officer travel

259 Telegram, Alfred Cope to Mark Sturgis, 3.53 p.m., 29 July 1922 (CO, 906/21)

260 B.B. Cubbit to Secretary to the Admiralty, 17 Aug. 1922 (CO, 739/11)

261 See Chapter 5

262 Director of Intelligence to Commander in Chief, 14 Dec. 1922 (EO'ML, P17a/182)

263 The Duke of Devonshire to the Irish Governor General, 15 Dec. 1922, enclosing HO memorandum etc. (D/T, S1753)

264 Executive Council Minutes, 2 Jan. 1923 (NAI, Provisional Government/ Executive Council Papers [PG/ECP], G 2/1)

to London to consult with the authorities on the matter. The government agreed to the suggestion and O'Hegarty was sent to the English capital.[265] The information he gleaned made an impression, for soon after his return Dublin requested that the British authorities apprehend the republican activists and deport them to Ireland for internment.[266] In the early hours of 11 March, the police mounted a co-ordinated mass arrest throughout Britain. 33 people were detained in London, 24 in Liverpool and St Helens, eight in Manchester, four on Tyneside and three in Birmingham, along 27 in Glasgow and 11 elsewhere in Scotland. In total, 110 people, including 19 women, were arrested. Later that same day, they were put aboard the HMS *Castor* in Liverpool and taken to Dublin for internment in Mountjoy.[267] In addition, on 6 and 9 April, police in Glasgow arrested two men who had eluded capture on 11 March; they were deported too.[268]

'It is undesirable that the United Kingdom should provide a refuge for men engaged in the promotion of murder and outrage in Southern Ireland', observed one newspaper welcoming the 'combing-out of disaffected Irish from England and Scotland'.[269] Intelligence supplied by Free State agents enabled the police to arrest the most active republicans. At least ten officers in the Scottish IRA were captured, for example, effectively decapitating the outfit.[270] Though regretting that 'a small number of important persons' had escaped the dragnet, including Pa Murray, Billy Ahern, Séamus Reader and Michael Cremin, police intelligence reported that the operation had disrupted the Volunteers 'at a very critical moment', for they had been 'gathering together their forces so as to put their full weight behind the blow to be struck against the Free State this Spring …'.[271] Diarmuid O'Hegarty later stated that the operation was ordered only after 'careful consideration' of the information relating to each individual. The intelligence

265 Executive Council Minutes, 13 Jan. 1923 (PG/ECP, G 2/1)

266 *Hansard 5* (*Commons*), clxi, col. 1044: Home Secretary Bridgeman (12 Mar. 1923); *Hansard 5* (*Commons*), clxi, col. 1191: Attorney General Sir Douglas Hogg (12 Mar. 1923); *Hansard 5* (*Commons*), clxi, col. 2248: Home Secretary Bridgeman (19 Mar. 1923); *Dáil Debates*, vol. 2, cols. 2343–44: President Cosgrave (20 Mar. 1923), accessed at http://historical-debates.oireachtas. ie/D/0002/D.0002.192303200026.html on 14 June 2012

267 *TT*, 13 Mar. 1923; 'RROUK', no. 197, 15 Mar. 1923 (CAB, 24/159)

268 See Chapter 5

269 *Pall Mall Gazette and Globe*, 12 Mar. 1923 (Editorial)

270 Membership rolls of the Scottish Brigade IRA (EMP, 3/C/13); see Chapter 5

271 'RROUK', no. 197, 15 Mar.; 'RROUK', no. 198, 22 Mar. 1923 (CAB, 24/159)

gathered by agents in Britain and the documents seized from suspects upon being arrested provided 'abundant evidence of a widespread conspiracy to import munitions of war into Ireland', he continued. The conspiracy had been successful in that 'thousands of rounds of ammunition, machine guns, revolvers, pistols, wireless apparatus and explosive materials in large quantities' were smuggled to the IRA in Ireland. Members of the Cumann na mBan, ISDL and Sinn Féin clubs had aided the gunrunners by supplying money to buy the munitions and facilities to store them, and some had carried the weapons to Ireland.[272]

In Mountjoy, the deportees found themselves on the opposite side of the prison bars to former comrades. Sorcha McDermott met a soldier whom she had visited while he was imprisoned in London in 1920. 'I know her; she is Sorcha McDermott', she remembered him saying.

> I said "Oh, you do remember me". He said, "You want to die for Ireland". I answered, "There was a time when you did too and don't forget that you gave me your photograph with the words 'freedom or death' after twenty-three days hunger-strike in Wormwood Scrubs", and he went as white as a sheet.[273]

The deportees made numerous complaints of conditions in Mountjoy. Kathleen Brooks claimed that the sentries often fired shots at the women while they were in the exercise yard and at their cell windows. At least one woman was injured by such shooting, she asserted. In addition, she alleged that the prison governor and a group of soldiers had burst into the cell she was sharing one night. Drunk, the governor verbally abused the women while the soldiers brandished their weapons.[274] 'There were frequent threats of shooting if any of the deportees infringed the regulations', Art O'Brien asserted.[275] Questioned on these allegations, the Home Secretary stated that he presumed that the Free State government would ensure the deportees' safety.[276]

As was the case during the war of independence, the mass arrest and deportation of March 1923 was carried out under regulation 14B of the Restoration of Order in Ireland Act 1920 (ROIA). The regulation stated

272 Diarmuid O'Hegarty to President Cosgrave, 3 Apr. 1923 (D/T, S2156)
273 BMHWS 945, Sorcha Nic Diarmada, pp. 11–12
274 Clipping from *The Star*, 15 Oct. 1923 (MEPO, 38/111)
275 Art O'Brien statement, n.d. (AÓBP, MS 8439/4)
276 *Hansard 5* (*Commons*), clxi, col. 2106 (19 Mar. 1923)

that if, 'on the recommendation of a competent naval or military authority or of one of the Advisory Committees', the Home Secretary believed that 'the restoration or maintenance of order in Ireland' was being menaced by 'a person who is suspected of acting, or having acted, or being about to act, in a manner prejudicial to the restoration or maintenance of order in Ireland', then he 'may by order require that person forthwith or from time to time either to remain in or to proceed to and reside in such place as may be specified in the order and to comply with such directions as to reporting to the police, restriction of movement, and otherwise as may be specified in the order'.[277] Art O'Brien applied to the Divisional Court in London for a writ of habeas corpus in order to challenge the legality of the deportation. Following the failure of two requests, he took a case to the Court of Appeal. The court ruled that the British government's powers under ROIA to intern people in the territory of the Free State had been implicitly repealed by the passage through Westminster of the Irish Free State Constitution Act, the legislation which officially established the Free State in December 1922. Therefore, the arrest, deportation and internment operation of March 1923 was illegal. The Law Lords confirmed the judgement by declining to hear the government's appeal against the ruling.[278] In May, the deportees were returned to Britain and released, just two weeks before the civil war in Ireland ended with the IRA dumping its arms.[279]

Prior to this, there had been some doubt about the advisability of the government employing ROIA to intern in Ireland people living in Britain. In December 1920, while he advocated such deportations as a means of breaking the IRA's violent campaign in England, Basil Thomson believed that special legislation would have to be drawn up to authorize them.[280] However, the government believed otherwise, with the Home Secretary stating that 'existing powers', including those under the wartime Defence of the Realm Act, were 'sufficient'.[281] Nevertheless, in June 1921 the cabinet was advised that 'in the opinion of the law officers, regulation 14B of the Restoration of Order in Ireland Regulations is *ultra vires*, so far as it purports to authorize internment and treatment as prisoners of war outside

---

277 *TT*, 10 May 1923; *Hansard 5 (Commons)*, clxi, col. 1189: Home Secretary Bridgeman (12 Mar. 1923)
278 *TT*, 24 Mar., 11 Apr., 10, 15 May 1923
279 *TT*, 14, 18 May 1923
280 Director of Intelligence to the Home Secretary, 2 Dec. 1920 (HO, 317/48)
281 *Hansard 5 (Commons)*, cxxxv, col. 1234 (1 Dec. 1920)

Ireland'.[282] Despite this, however, the British government continued to use ROIA to deport people from Britain.

In May 1923, in order to protect the Home Secretary from being personally sued by the ex-deportees following the Court of Appeal's judgement, the government passed an Indemnity Act. The act also established an Irish Deportees Compensation Tribunal to expiate the former deportees for the indignities they had endured. By March 1924, those deported from England had between them received £37,041 17s. 2d. and those from Scotland £17,098 14s. 10d., though costs had yet to be settled. Art O'Brien received £441, for example, Seán McGrath £210 5s., Denis Fleming £238, Anthony Mularkey £293 and Joe Robinson £415.[283]

By then, O'Brien, McGrath, Fleming and Mularkey were in prison once again. In reaction to its defeat in the Court of Appeal, the government decided to re-arrest a number of the late deportees on criminal charges. In July, with the aid of testimony from National Army officers, the Crown secured a conviction against the four, along with two other men, for assisting the IRA in its conspiracy to overthrow the Irish government. Incarcerated in Wormwoods Scrubs, the prisoners voiced familiar complaints regarding the conditions, the food, the unfriendly attitude of the officials and the fact that prison regulations did little to distinguish between the second division prisoners, the category to which they belonged, and those of the third division and hard labour class.[284]

VIII

It was only with the launching of the IRA's campaign of violence in November 1920 that the activities of republicans in Britain really entered the political and public consciousness. Prior to this, the authorities were aware of gunrunning but did not view its interruption as a priority. Republican links with social agitators had also been noted, and some members of the establishment feared a communist revolution in Britain and Ireland to match that which had taken place in Russia and was threatening elsewhere in war-scarred Europe. Again, however, such links did not lead to concerted

282 Memo to Cabinet, 'Internment of Irish Rebels', 25 June 1921 (CAB, 24/125)

283 G. Stewart King to H.R. Scott, 5 Mar. 1924 (HO, 144/7583)

284 'Conditions Under Which Art O'Brien & Other Irish Political Prisoners Are Serving Terms of Imprisonment in 2nd Division at Wormwood Scrubs', Sept. 1923 (AÓBP, MS 8427/41)

action on the part of the authorities. Yet, following the arson attack on Merseyside, the disruption of the republican movement in Britain became a major concern for the forces of law and order. The approach taken by the police in tackling gunrunning and violence was similar to that used by their predecessors when grappling with similar episodes of Fenian activity in the 1860s and 1880s and included protecting likely targets, acting on intelligence received, sometimes from informers, and monitoring suspicious persons. Such tactics led to the imprisonment and internment without trial in Ireland of some important IRA gunrunners and arsonists. However, the actual number convicted was low. With republican activity continuing despite the arrests, the ruling by Michael Collins that 'the enemy must not be allowed to break up our organisation, no matter whom he takes' was upheld.[285] The treatment which republicans received from the criminal justice system in Britain was reasonable. Unlike their comrades in Ireland, they were not subject to courts martial. Convinced of the righteousness of their cause, they adopted a defiant attitude towards the police, the courts and the prison authorities. Viewing themselves as soldiers rather than criminals, they used hunger- and work-strikes to demand political prisoner status, sometimes successfully. During the civil war, the authorities proved much more successful in disrupting the activities of the IRA. This was due to the co-operation they received from their former enemies in the service of the Provisional/Free State government. The mass arrest and deportation of March 1923 represented the culmination of this relationship.

285 See Chapter 1

Epilogue and Conclusion

On 23 July 1924, Art O'Brien and Seán McGrath were released from Brixton prison, each having served just over one year of their two-year sentences for seditious conspiracy.[1] Two months later, the ISDL held a reception to celebrate the event. After declaring that their trial had been 'a farce', O'Brien insisted that the treaty 'would never bring peace between England and Ireland'. Denouncing the continued partition of Ireland, he stated that peace between the two countries could only be achieved by England getting out of Irish affairs.[2]

By then, however, the ISDL was a mere shadow of its former self. The previous year, C.B. Dutton, O'Brien's stand-in while he was in prison, had contacted 27 branches but received only one encouraging reply. The situation was 'bad', he wrote, and without funds for re-organization it was 'practically hopeless'.[3] In straitened circumstances, de Valera's republican government was unable to finance any re-organization. Moreover, the league's reputation had become rather tarnished. Evidence presented at the conspiracy trial had exposed O'Brien's comfortable circumstances. Recalling the 'greatest difficulty' he had encountered in receiving aid from the INACDF in 1922, William Robinson balked at the revelation that the republican envoy was at the time 'living in luxury at the Grosvenor Hotel, & receiving from the Republic £750 per annum plus £120 weekly for expenses!' Moreover, in the witness box, O'Brien and McGrath had denied any association with the IRA, while the latter also criticized Countess Markievicz's communist politics. 'This was done by avowed Republicans before the common enemy, in order to secure a mitigation of sentence!' thundered a disgusted Robinson.[4]

1 *TT*, 24 July 1924
2 *TT*, 24 Sept. 1924
3 C.B. Dutton to 'P[resident de Valera]', 12 Oct. 1923 (EdeVP, P150/1776)
4 William Robinson to the Secretary, Sinn Féin Re-Organization Committee, 4 Nov. 1923 (EdeVP, P150/1776)

In December 1923, P.J. Rutledge, de Valera's minister for foreign affairs, appointed Brian O'Hannigan as his representative in England.[5] Two months later, a new republican body was founded: the Irish Freedom League of Great Britain. Its aims were 'to assist in securing the Independence of the Irish Nation' and to 'support all organisations having for their object the furtherance of the Irish Language, Irish Pastimes, and Irish Industries; and any movement tending to strengthen Ireland's distinctive Nationality.' Like the ISDL, membership was confined to people of Irish birth and descent and participation in British domestic politics was to be eschewed. O'Hannigan became president of the organization.[6]

O'Brien was unhappy with Dublin's sidelining of the ISDL and himself. More importantly, however, he also complained of having had to bear the majority of the cost of the habeas corpus proceedings against the 1923 deportation, despite de Valera's government having instructed him to initiate them. In total, he claimed that he was owed £2,143 7s. 4d.[7] De Valera disputed this, stating that his government had not authorized the proceedings, that all expenditure after 30 June 1922 'was incurred contrary to instructions' and that O'Brien's accounts had not been audited.[8] The dispute dragged on inconclusively in 1924–25. Leaving politics behind, O'Brien took up the position of managing director of a publishing company.[9]

Seven years later, the quarrel erupted again when the Free State's department of finance reminded O'Brien of a 1923 court judgement against him in a case initiated by Michael Collins concerning the London funds, according to which he was required to hand over £8,755 17s. 1d.[10] Fianna Fáil, de Valera's new political party, had by now come to power in Ireland. O'Brien was bitter towards de Valera, noting that the civil war-era republican government had failed to contest the court case on his behalf. Therefore, he refused to honour the judgement.[11] Instead, he beseeched his friend Seán T. O'Kelly, a government minister, to have the issue resolved once and for all.

---

5 Minister for Foreign Affairs to Brian Hannigan, 10 Dec. 1923 (EdeVP, P150/1776)

6 Pamphlet, 'Irish Freedom League', n.d. (EdeVP, P150/1776)

7 'Matters Requiring Settlement Either By Inquiry Or Other Suitable Way', n.d.; Art O'Brien to Henry Dixon, 28 Apr. 1925 (AÓBP, MS 8438/6)

8 Ernest Pround to Dixon, 29 June 1925 (AÓBP, MS 8438/6)

9 *II*, 13 Aug. 1949 (Obituary)

10 J.J. MacElligott to Art O'Brien, 5 Apr. 1932 (AÓBP, MS 8460/19); *IT*, 30 Nov. 1923

11 O'Brien to the Secretary, Dept. of Finance, 3 May 1932 (AÓBP, MS 8460/19)

However, O'Kelly encountered opposition from de Valera: he 'had no use' for O'Brien, O'Kelly reported sadly. Reacting, O'Brien said that this proved that 'not alone was De V. [sic] no friend of his, but that he was in fact an enemy, and a malicious one at that'.[12] By 1935, however, de Valera had mellowed. On 30 June, O'Brien was appointed Irish minister or ambassador to France, the minister for finance having directed in connection with the court judgement that 'this matter is to be finally abandoned and the amount written off'.[13] When ill-health forced O'Brien's retirement in 1938, he relocated to Dublin, and died there in August 1949.[14]

By then a number of other veterans of the republican movement in Britain had died too. Due to the constraint of space, the fates of Sam Maguire and David Fitzgerald will have to stand for those who took opposites sides in the dispute over the treaty. In January 1923, Maguire, a treaty supporter, returned to Ireland and took up a position in the civil service. However, he soon grew disillusioned with the new regime, contending that the government saw the treaty as an end in itself rather than, as Michael Collins had argued, a means of achieving greater freedom. A group of army officers believed likewise and Maguire became involved in their mutiny in 1924. When the conspiracy was crushed, Maguire was dismissed from his position. Returning to his native County Cork, he died from tuberculosis in 1927. The following year, a group of his friends decided to commemorate him by presenting the GAA with a trophy named in his honour. Ever since, the Sam Maguire Cup has been awarded to the winning team in the GAA's annual All Ireland Senior Football Championship.[15]

Tyneside's David Fitzgerald remained in the IRA after the end of the civil war, helping to re-organize units in the Irish midlands. Arrested in 1925, he was convicted of firearms offences and sentenced to 18 months' imprisonment. A short time into his sentence, however, he was among 19 prisoners

12 'Art O'Brien and Fianna Fail Government', n.d. (AÓBP, MS 8460/19)

13 'Memorandum for the Executive Council on the Proposed Reinstatement in the Civil Service of Mr Art O Briain', 1 May; extract from Executive Council Minutes, 7 May 1935 (D/T, S5735A)

14 *II*, 13 Aug. 1949 (Obituary)

15 Coleman, 'Maguire, Sam'; BMHWS 860, Elizabeth MacGinley, pp. 2–3; meanwhile, the winning team of the GAA's annual All Ireland Senior Hurling Championship receives a trophy named in honour of another London sports enthusiast and IRB member, Liam MacCarthy, who died in 1928: Marcus de Búrca, 'MacCarthy, Liam', in *DIB*, accessed at http://dib.cambridge.org on 1 Dec. 2009

who escaped from Mountjoy. Fitzgerald then returned to organization work, this time in Northern Ireland. Re-arrested in 1929, he served the remainder of his sentence. Fitzgerald was one of a number of IRA leaders who proposed that the achievement of Irish freedom from Britain involved not just political change but also social transformation. In 1931, he was elected National Secretary of Saor Éire (Free Ireland), a political organization dedicated to the achievement of a socialist republic. However, the outfit was quickly banned by the government. By then, Fitzgerald's health was deteriorating badly and he died on 1 September 1933.[16]

As we have seen, IRA violence in 1920–22 was not the first time that Irish politics had caused bloodshed in Britain. Neither was it the last. In the periods 1939–40 and 1972–2001, the IRA returned to offensive operations in Britain. Space constraints prevent detailed treatments of these campaigns. However, a number of parallels and differences can be identified between them and that of the early 1920s. In 1938, C/S Seán Russell, director of munitions during the latter stages of the war of independence, saw a bombing campaign as a means of forcing the British to withdraw from Northern Ireland. Jim O'Donovan, who had advocated 'incendiary and destructive operations in England' during the civil war, drew up an ambitious plan of campaign known as the 'S-Plan' ('S' for sabotage). Public services, such as the electricity network, the postal service and the telephone and telegraph systems, were to be attacked, along with road, rail, sea and air transport. Key industries, including armaments manufacture and power-generation, were to be targeted too, as were hostile newspapers. As in 1920–21, Volunteers were ordered to avoid killing civilians in these attacks. Also, due to the small number of men, operations were to be 'so fool proof and so certain in action as to afford a 10,000:1 margin of safety, i.e. freedom of detection or capture'. Moreover, being home to 'kindred of a common race', Scotland and Wales were to be spared attacks (though an unexploded bomb was discovered on the main Glasgow to Edinburgh railway line in September 1939).[17]

However, the state of the IRA in Britain left a lot to be desired. Languishing since the end of the civil war, a tour of inspection by Moss Twomey in 1938 found the organization to be 'poor and loose, and militarily

16 *An Phoblacht*, 9 Sept. 1933
17 David O'Donoghue, *The Devil's Deal: The IRA, Nazi Germany and the Double Life of Jim O'Donovan* (Dublin: New Island, 2010), pp. 91, 250–77, 292 n. 17

... almost elementary'.[18] In contrast to 1920–21, responsibility for mounting this campaign, therefore, fell mainly to operatives sent from Ireland.

It began on 16 January 1939, with bomb attacks against power stations and electrical infrastructure in London, Manchester and elsewhere. One person was killed. However, the police quickly arrested suspects and captured a copy of the S-Plan, putting the IRA on the back foot. With power stations and similar targets increasing their security, Volunteers were forced to resort to more modest operations. Tube stations, bridges and canals were targeted, so also were cinemas, where tear-gas bombs were set off, and telephone kiosks, where the wires were cut.[19] By the end of the year, 291 attacks had taken place, of which 207 were minor incidents of sabotage, 47 consisted of damage to public or private buildings and 37 involved attempts to disrupt public services. Seven people had been killed, five in Coventry in an incident for which two men were later convicted and executed. Meanwhile, 96 people were injured.[20] Evidence of increased bloodthirstiness, such as a failed attack on crowded West End streets in London, prompted the government to introduce powers to deport suspects to Ireland. Its futility evident to the IRA leadership, the campaign petered out the following year with about a dozen attacks, the last being an explosion at a refuse depot in London on 18 March.[21] 'The bombing campaign was an unmitigated disaster for the IRA', contends the historian Paul McMahon. 96 of its members were convicted of offences, 156 were deported to Ireland, with many others making the journey on their own volition, and most of those who remained in Britain were interned at the outbreak of the Second World War. Moreover, the campaign cost the IRA public support in Ireland, thus allowing de Valera to suppress it during the war.[22]

Events in Northern Ireland in 1968–69 precipitated a split in the republican movement, creating the Officials and the Provisionals. On 22 February 1972, the Official IRA detonated a bomb outside the officers' mess of the British army's parachute regiment in Aldershot, Hampshire, causing

---

18 Quoted in Brian Hanley, *The IRA, 1926–1936* (Dublin: Four Courts Press, 2002), p. 172

19 Paul McMahon, *British Spies and Irish Rebels: British Intelligence and Ireland, 1916–1945* (Woodbridge: The Boydell Press, 2008), pp. 267–70; O'Donoghue, *Devil's Deal*, pp. 129, 132

20 Gary McGladdery, *The Provisional IRA in England: The Bombing Campaign 1973–1997* (Dublin: Irish Academic Press, 2006), pp. 38–40, 266

21 McMahon, *British Spies*, pp. 273–74; O'Donoghue, *Devil's Deal*, p. 124

22 McMahon, *British Spies*, p. 275

the deaths of an army chaplain, five female cleaners and a gardener. Just as the operations of the early 1920s were motivated mainly by anger at events taking place in Ireland, this attack was by way of retribution for the regiment's killing of 13 unarmed protesters in Derry on 22 January ('Bloody Sunday').[23] The Official IRA subsequently backed away from violence. Into the breach stepped the Provisional IRA. Its members contended that attacks in Britain would gain a lot more publicity than operations in Northern Ireland. Also, echoing the reasoning of 1920–21, it was believed that public pressure would force the British government into making concessions, this time in relation to the six counties. Moreover, following Michael Collins, Gerry Adams, president of Provisional Sinn Féin, held that responsibility for 'the problems created' in Northern Ireland by the British government 'must also be shared by the people who elected it and in whose name it governs part of Ireland'.[24]

On 8 March 1973, the campaign began in London with bomb attacks on the Old Bailey, Great Scotland Yard and the Central Army Recruiting Office, causing the death of one person and injuring 265.[25] By the time it agreed to a permanent ceasefire in 1997, the Provisional IRA, relying mainly on Volunteers sent from Ireland, had mounted at least 488 attacks in England; Scotland and Wales were left untouched. Fatalities amounted to 115 and injuries 2,134, while billions of pounds worth of damage was caused to the economy.[26] As in 1920–22, politicians were targeted for assassination, most audaciously when a bomb at the Conservative Party Conference in Brighton in 1984 had the potential to kill the entire cabinet.[27] Provisional Sinn Féin has argued that the bombing campaign played a significant role in motivating the British government's involvement in peace talks, culminating in the 1998 Good Friday Agreement. However, the historian Garry McGladdery contends that bombings in the early- to mid-1990s almost wrecked the peace process. Moreover, as part of the agreement, the Provisional movement was forced to accept Northern Ireland's continued membership of the United Kingdom.[28]

On 1 June 2000, the Real IRA, a Provisional IRA splinter group that rejected the peace accords, exploded a bomb at London's Hammersmith Bridge. The following year, however, the arrest of a number of Volunteers in

23 Brian Hanley and Scott Millar, *The Lost Revolution: The Story of the Official IRA and the Workers' Party* (Dublin: Penguin Ireland, 2009), pp. 173–77
24 McGladdery, *Provisional IRA*, pp. 2, 4, 60
25 McGladdery, *Provisional IRA*, p. 63
26 McGladdery, *Provisional IRA*, pp. 3–4, 214, 216
27 McGladdery, *Provisional IRA*, pp. 125–35
28 McGladdery, *Provisional IRA*, pp. 214–24

London, Liverpool and Yorkshire brought its campaign to an end. In total, nine attacks had been mounted over the course of 18 months, causing injury to eight people.[29]

Since then, the perpetrators of political violence in Britain have been Islamic extremists rather than Irish republicans. On 7 July 2005, 56 people were killed and around 700 wounded when four al-Qaeda members exploded bombs on underground trains and a bus in London. Attempted bomb attacks took place in the capital and Glasgow later that year and in 2007, while major plots were uncovered in 2006 and 2010.[30] The profile of some of those involved in these operations and their motives are familiar from our study of the IRA. Three of the four 7 July bombers were born in Britain to immigrants, while the fourth was raised in Britain. Imbuing radical Islamist ideology, they isolated themselves from mainstream society. In a video released after the bombings, one of the men defended the operation by saying that the British population was 'directly responsible' for the 'atrocities' being committed against Muslims by the British government.[31]

* * *

In June 1921, Michael Collins wrote that, 'in a manner of speaking, our people in England are only the auxiliaries of our attacking forces'.[32] It has been the argument of this book that Collins's observation was correct. Irish nationalism, as we have seen, was not confined to the inhabitants of Ireland. Fenianism in particular was heavily influenced by the millions who emigrated from the time of the Great Famine onwards. Indeed, it was on the initiative of immigrant nationalists in America that the organization was founded in Ireland. A majority of its membership was composed of emigrants. Its most spectacular activities, including bombings and prison-breaks, occurred outside of Ireland. The war of independence and civil war saw Irish nationalism returning home, in the sense that it was republicans in Ireland who were in the vanguard of the fight for freedom. Nevertheless, nationalists abroad once again rallied to the cause. The republican movement in Britain was part of this network of support which the IRA in Ireland required in order

29 McGladdery, *Provisional IRA*, pp. 219–21, 255
30 Jason Burke, *The 9/11 Wars* (London: Allen Lane, 2011), pp. 209, 212, 257, 289, 475
31 Burke, *9/11 Wars*, pp. 210–11
32 See Introduction

to operate successfully. This was most obviously the case in relation to gunrunning. During the war of independence, Fenians and Volunteers in Liverpool, London, Manchester, Glasgow, Birmingham, Newcastle-upon-Tyne and elsewhere smuggled hundreds of firearms, tens of thousands of rounds of ammunition and hundreds of kilograms of explosives to their comrades in Ireland. The IRA there was perennially short of munitions, but these armaments allowed them to mount as many operations as they did against Crown forces. It was also true in relation to the campaign of violence of 1920–21. Outperforming many IRA units across the Irish Sea, Volunteers brought the war in Ireland to Britain itself, thereby, in Seán Ó Murthuile words, 'concentrating the average Englishman's attention of [i.e. on] what was being done in Ireland in his name'.[33] In addition, republican sympathisers in Britain supported the struggle by facilitating the clandestine communications system that kept Dublin in contact with republicans throughout the world, sheltering men on the run, contributing to the Dáil loan and prisoners' charities and agitating in favour of Irish self-determination. The truce of July 1921 was a triumph for those involved in all these activities as it demonstrated that republicans had fought the British state to a stalemate. The civil war saw a small but notable number of men and women from Britain fighting in Ireland in the ranks of the IRA and the National Army. Meanwhile, republicans who remained in Britain sought to continue their auxiliary role, supporting Volunteers in their defence of the republic by smuggling weapons, facilitating communications and raising funds. National Army supporters in Britain worked in a similar role, acquiring munitions and attempting to disrupt the activities of their republican enemies.

Six republicans from Britain were killed in Ireland in the lead up to and during the 1916 Rising. Activities in Britain in the period 1919–23 led to the deaths of 11 people. Five Volunteers were killed. Two, Neil Kerr Junior in September 1920 and Michael McInerney in July 1921, died accidently while handling munitions. One, Seán Morgan, was killed by the police in a shoot-out April 1921. The remaining two, Reginald Dunne and Joseph O'Sullivan, were executed in August 1922 after being found guilty of the murder of Sir Henry Wilson MP two months previously. In turn, the IRA claimed the lives of six people. Three were civilians, William Ward in November 1920, Horace MacNeill in May 1921 and post office clerk Thomas Lovelady in June 1923. The remaining three were the spy Vincent Fouvargue in April 1921, the policeman Robert Johnston the following month and Sir

33 See Chapter 3

Henry Wilson. Finally, fighting in Ireland during the civil war saw the deaths of nine men from Britain.

Much remains to be explored in regard to the activities of republicans in Britain during the Irish Revolution. The approaching centenary might lead to the discovery of new sources. They may well afford us a greater insight into the mentalities of IRA, IRB, Cumann na mBan and Na Fianna Éireann members in Britain and might reveal activities which have gone unrecorded in the sources currently at our disposal. In any event, it is the hope of the author that this book will contribute to the furtherance of knowledge on the subject.

In the introduction, we noted that Iain Patterson accused some of having exaggerated the role which republicans in Scotland and, by implication, in England and Wales, played in the war of independence. Patterson might be correct, but his counter-argument that their contribution to the IRA's victory was 'slight' is an over-reaction. The war of independence and the civil war were ultimately won and lost by the actions of actors in Ireland, but republicans in Britain played a noteworthy role in the drama.

Select Bibliography

Primary Sources

Manuscripts in Ireland

Gaelic Athletic Association Archives
Annual Reports, Balance Sheets and Motions for Congress, 1911–28
Central Council Minutes

Military Archives of Ireland
A Index Files
Bureau of Military History Files
Captured Documents Collection
Michael Collins Papers
Department of Defence Administration Files
Military Secretary Files
Military Service Pensions Collection
National Army Census, 12–13 November 1922
National Army Prisoner Location Books

National Archives of Ireland
Dáil Éireann Files
Dáil Ministry Files
Department of Finance Files
Department of Foreign Affairs Files
Department of Justice Files
Department of the Taoiseach Files
Governor-General Files
Provisional Government/Executive Council Papers

National Library of Ireland
Piaras Béaslaí Papers
Frank Gallagher Papers

Patrick McCormack Statement
William Nelson's Story
Art Ó Briain Papers
Florence O'Donoghue Papers
James O'Donovan Papers
Seán O'Mahoney Papers
George Count Plunkett Papers
John J. Sherlock Statement

University College, Dublin, Archives
Eithne Coyle Papers
Eamon de Valera Papers
Desmond and Mabel Fitzgerald Papers
Sighle Humphreys Papers
Richard Mulcahy Papers
Ernie O'Malley Letters and Notebooks
Maurice Twomey Papers

Manuscripts in Britain

Durham County Record Office
Durham Light Infantry Papers

National Archives, Kew
Admiralty Files
Assizes Files
Cabinet Files
Central Criminal Court Files
Colonial Office Files
Director of Public Prosecutions Files
Foreign Office Files
Home Office Files
Metropolitan Police Office Files
War Office Files

National Archives of Scotland
First World War Files
Police Services General Files

Parliamentary Archives, House of Lords
Andrew Bonar Law Papers
David Lloyd George Papers

Tyne & Wear Archives
Police Files, Dec. 1920–Dec. 1922

Private Papers

Patrick Brennan Papers (in the possession of Patrick Brennan)
Eamonn Mooney Papers (in the possession of Cathleen Knowles-McGuirk)

Published Primary Sources

Books and Articles
'Account of Volunteer 'M'', in Uinseann MacEoin (ed.), *Survivors* (Dublin: Argenta, 1980), pp. 423–29
Barrington, Mary A., *The Irish Independence Movement on Tyneside 1919–1921* (Dublin: Dun Laoghaire Genealogical Society, 1999)
Barry, Tom, *Guerrilla Days in Ireland* (Dublin: Anvil, 1981)
Béaslaí, Piaras, *Michael Collins and the Making of a New Ireland* (2 vols, London: G.G. Harrap & Co., 1926)
Brady, Edward M., *Ireland's Secret Service in England* (Dublin: Talbot Press, 1928)
Brennan, Michael, *The War in Clare: Personal Memoirs of the Irish War of Independence* (Dublin: Four Courts Press & Irish Academic Press, 1980)
Briscoe, Robert, with Alden Hatch, *For the Life of Me* (London: Longmans, 1958)
Childs, Sir Wyndham, *Episodes and Reflections* (London: Cassell & Co., 1930)
Deasy, Liam, *Towards Ireland Free: The West Cork Brigade in the War of Independence 1917–21*, ed. John E. Chisholm (Cork: Royal Carbery Books, 1973)
Good, Joe, *Enchanted by Dreams: Journal of a Revolutionary*, ed. Maurice Good (Dingle: Brandon, 1996)
Jones, Thomas, *Whitehall Diary, iii: Ireland 1918–1925*, ed. Keith Middlemas (London: Oxford University Press, 1971)
McArthur, John, 'The Recollections of John McArthur', in Ian MacDougall (ed.), *Militant Miners: Recollections of John McArthur, Buckhaven; and Letters, 1924–26, of David Proudfoot, Methil, to G. Allen Hutt* (Edinburgh: Polygon Books, 1981)
Morgan, Kenneth O. (ed.), *Lloyd George: Family Letters 1885–1936* (Cardiff: University of Wales Press, 1973)
Nelson, William, '"Q" Company', *An tÓglach*, 2.2 (1966), p. 12
Nunan, Ernie, 'The Irish Volunteers in London', *An tÓglach*, 1.12 (1966), p. 4
Ó Briain, Art, 'Gaedhil Thar Sáile: Some Notes on the History of the Gaelic League of London', *Capuchin Annual*, (1944), pp. 116–26

O'Brien, William, *Forth the Banners Go: Reminiscences of William O'Brien as Told to Edward MacLysaght* (Dublin: Three Candles, 1969)

O'Connor, John T. ('Blimey'), 'Some Have Come from a Land Beyond the Sea', *An tÓglach*, 1.12 (1966), pp. 4–6

O'Donoghue, Florence, *No Other Law* (Dublin: Anvil, 1986)

O'Malley, Ernie, *On Another Man's Wound* (Dublin: Anvil, 2002)

O'Rahilly, The, *The Secret History of the Irish Volunteers* (Dublin: Irish Publicity League, 1915)

Phelan, Jim, *The Name's Phelan: The First Part of the Autobiography of Jim Phelan* (Belfast: Blackstaff, 1993)

Pinkman, John, *In the Legion of the Vanguard*, ed. Francis E. Maguire (Cork: Mercier Press, 1998)

Report of the Labour Commission to Ireland (London: Caledonian Press, 1921)

Ryan, Mark, *Fenian Memories* (Dublin: M.H. Gill & Son, 1945)

Shouldice, Frank, and George Geraghty, 'The Break-Out from Usk Jail in Wales by Four 'German Plot' Prisoners', in Florence O'Donoghue (ed.), *IRA Jailbreaks 1918–1921* (Cork: Mercier Press, 2010), pp. 38–51

Skinnider, Margaret, *Doing My Bit for Ireland* (New York: The Century Co., 1917)

'Statutes of the Communist International, 4 August 1920', in Rex A. Wade (ed.), *Documents of Soviet History, ii, Triumph and Retreat 1920–1922* (Gulf Breeze, Fl.: Academic International Press, 1993), pp. 109–13

Thomson, Basil, *My Experiences at Scotland Yard* (New York: Doubleday, Page & Co., 1923)

Wallace, Martin, 'Reginald Dunn and Joseph O'Sullivan', *An tÓglach*, 1.7 (1963), p. 1

Zinoviev, Grigori, 'Zinoviev on the World Revolution: Opening Address to the Second Congress of the Comintern, 19 July 1920', in Rex A. Wade (ed.), *Documents of Soviet History, ii, Triumph and Retreat 1920–1922* (Gulf Breeze, Fl.: Academic International Press, 1993), pp. 96–101

Parliamentary Papers

Parliamentary Debates

Dáil Éireann debates, accessed at http://historical-debates.oireachtas.ie

The Parliamentary Debates, 5th Series, *House of Commons*, 1917–23 (vols. cx–clxiv, London, 1917–23)

The Parliamentary Debates, 5th Series, *House of Lords*, 1919–23 (vols. xxxiii–lv, London, 1919–23)

Command Papers

Articles of Agreement for a Treaty Between Great Britain and Ireland [Cmd. 1560], H.C. 1921

Census of England and Wales 1911, ix, Birthplaces of Persons Enumerated in Administrative Counties, County Boroughs, etc, and Ages and Occupations of Foreigners [Cd. 7017], H.C. 1913

Intercourse between Bolshevism and Sinn Féin [Cmd. 1326], H.C. 1921

Report of the Commissioner of Police of the Metropolis for the Year 1921 [Cmd. 1699], H.C. 1922

Report on the Twelfth Decennial Census of Scotland, vol. iii [Cd. 7163], H.C. 1913

Return Showing by Monthly Periods the Number of Murders of Members of the Royal Irish Constabulary and of the Dublin Metropolitan Police, and of Soldiers, Officials, and Civilians, and the Number of Political Outrages of Persons and Property in Ireland from the 1st Day of January, 1919, to the 30th April, 1920 [Cmd. 709], H.C. 1920

Return Showing by Monthly Periods the Number of Murders of Members of the Royal Irish Constabulary and of the Dublin Metropolitan Police, and of Soldiers, Officials, and Civilians, and the Number of Political Outrages of Persons and Property in Ireland for May and June 1920 [Cmd. 859], H.C. 1920

Return Showing the Number of Serious Outrages in Ireland Reported by the Royal Irish Constabulary and the Dublin Metropolitan Police During the Months of October, November and December, 1920 [Cmd. 1165], H.C. 1921

Sessional Papers

Reports of His Majesty's Inspectors of Constabulary for the Year Ended the 29th September 1921, H.C. 1922 (5)

Other Parliamentary Papers

Epitome of the Reports from the Committee of Public Accounts on the Appropriation Accounts for the Years 1922–23 to 1933–34, Inclusive, and of the Minutes of the Minister for Finance Thereon (Dublin: Stationary Office, 1937)

Statutes

Statute Laws accessed at www.opsi.gov.uk

Newspapers

An t-Óglác (1918–23)
An Phoblacht
Daily Telegraph
Éire: The Irish Nation
Evening News (London)

Forward (Glasgow)
Freeman's Journal
Glasgow Herald
Glasgow Observer and Catholic Herald
Irish Exile
Irish Independent
Irish Times
Irish Volunteer (1914–16)
Liverpool Courier
Liverpool Echo
Manchester Guardian
Newcastle Daily Chronicle
Newcastle Daily Chronicle, North Mail
Pall Mall Gazette
Pall Mall Gazette and Globe
Pall Mall and Globe
Poblacht na hÉireann (Scottish edition)
The Observer
The Times

Census

1911 Census of England and Wales accessed at www.1911census.co.uk/
1911 Census of Ireland accessed at www.nationalarchives.ie/

Other Web Resources

Jarrow ISDL Minute Book, 'Report of Reception given to Returned Prisoners', 24 Feb. 1922, accessed at http://www.donmouth.co.uk/local_history/ira/conroy_reception.html on 25 Apr. 2012

National Archives Historical Currency Convertor, accessed at http://www.nationalarchives.gov.uk/currency/default0.asp#mid on 6 Nov. 2012

Interviews

Cathleen Knowles-McGuirk (6 Aug. 2009)

Secondary Sources

Books and Articles

Andrew, Christopher, *The Defence of the Realm: The Authorised History of MI5* (London: Allen Lane, 2009)

Augusteijn, Joost, *From Public Defiance to Guerrilla Warfare: The Experience of Ordinary Volunteers in the Irish War of Independence 1916–1921* (Dublin: Irish Academic Press, 1996)

Augusteijn, Joost, 'Motivation: Why did they Fight for Ireland? The Motivation of Volunteers in the Revolution', in Joost Augusteijn (ed.), *The Irish Revolution, 1913–1923* (Basingstoke: Palgrave, 2002), pp. 103–20

Bearman, C. J., 'An Examination of Suffragette Violence', *English Historical Review*, 120.486 (2005), pp. 365–97

Boyle, Mark, 'Towards a (Re)Theorization of the Historical Geography of Nationalism in Diasporas: The Irish Diaspora as an Exemplar', *International Journal of Population Geography*, 7.6 (2001), pp. 429–46

Brown, Stewart J., '"Outside the Covenant": The Scottish Presbyterian Churches and Irish Immigration, 1922–1938', *Innes Review*, 42.1 (1991), pp. 19–45

Burke, Jason, *The 9/11 Wars* (London: Allen Lane, 2011)

Campbell, Fergus, *Land and Revolution: Nationalist Politics in the West of Ireland 1891–1921* (Oxford: Oxford University Press, 2005)

Clarke, Peter, *Hope and Glory: Britain 1900–2000* (London: Penguin, 2004)

Clutterbuck, Lindsay, 'The Progenitors of Terrorism: Russian Revolutionaries or Extreme Irish Republicans?', *Terrorism and Political Violence*, 16.1 (2004), pp. 154–81

Clutterbuck, Lindsay, 'Countering Irish Republican Terrorism in Britain: Its Origin as a Police Function', *Terrorism and Political Violence*, 18.1 (2006), pp. 95–118

Coleman, Marie, *County Longford and the Irish Revolution 1910–1923* (Dublin: Irish Academic Press, 2003)

Coleman, Marie, 'Maguire, Sam', in James McGuire and James Quinn (eds), *Dictionary of Irish Biography* (Cambridge: Cambridge University Press, 2009), downloaded from http://dib.cambridge.org on 1 Dec. 2009

Coleman, Marie, 'Robinson, Séamus', in James McGuire and James Quinn (eds), *Dictionary of Irish Biography* (Cambridge: Cambridge University Press, 2009), downloaded from http://dib.cambridge.org on 1 Dec. 2009

Coleman, Marie, and William Murphy, 'Mellows, William Joseph ('Liam')', in James McGuire and James Quinn (eds), *Dictionary of Irish Biography* (Cambridge: Cambridge University Press, 2009), downloaded from http://dib.cambridge.org on 1 Dec. 2009

Colley, Linda, *Britons: Forging the Nation 1707–1837* (New Haven: Yale University Press, 1992)

Comerford, R.V., 'Patriotism as Pastime: The Appeal of Fenianism in the Mid-1860s', *Irish Historical Studies*, 22.86 (1980), pp. 239–50

Coogan, Tim Pat, *Michael Collins: A Biography* (London: Hutchinson, 1990)

Cooney, John, 'The Irish Republican Brotherhood in Scotland: The Untold Stories of Andrew Fagen and Michael O'Carroll', in T.M. Devine and J.F. McMillan (eds), *Celebrating Columba: Irish-Scottish Connections 597–1997* (Edinburgh: John Donald, 1999), pp. 137–54

Coyle, Stephen, *High Noon on High Street: The Story of a Daring Ambush by the IRA in Glasgow in 1921* (Glasgow: Clydeside Press, 2008)

Curran, Joseph M., 'The Decline and Fall of the IRB', *Éire-Ireland*, 10.1 (1975), pp. 14–23

Curtain, Nancy J., *The United Irishmen: Popular Politics in Ulster and Dublin, 1791–1798* (Oxford: Clarendon Press, 1994)

Darwin, John, *After Tamerlane: The Rise and Fall of Global Empires, 1400–2000* (London: Allen Lane, 2007)

Davies, Sam, "A Stormy Political Career': P.J. Kelly and Irish Nationalist and Labour Politics in Liverpool, 1891–1936', *Transactions of the Historic Society of Lancashire and Cheshire*, 148 (1999), pp. 147–89

de Búrca, Marcus, 'MacCarthy, Liam', in James McGuire and James Quinn (eds), *Dictionary of Irish Biography* (Cambridge: Cambridge University Press, 2009), downloaded from http://dib.cambridge.org on 1 Dec. 2009

Delaney, Enda, 'Narratives of Exile and Displacement: Irish Catholic Emigrants and the National Past, 1850–1914', in Terence Dooley (ed.), *Ireland's Polemical Past: Views of Irish History in Honour of R.V. Comerford* (Dublin: University College Dublin Press, 2010), pp. 102–22

Dolan, Anne, 'Killing and Bloody Sunday, November 1920', *Historical Journal*, 49.3 (2006), pp. 789–810

Eliot, T.S., *The Waste Land and Other Poems* (London: Faber & Faber, 1940)

Elliott, Marianne, 'The "Despard Conspiracy" Reconsidered', *Past & Present*, 75 (1977), pp. 46–71

Elliott, Marianne, 'Irish Republicanism in England: The First Phase, 1797–9', in Thomas Bartlett and D. W. Hayton (eds), *Penal Era and Golden Age: Essays in Irish History 1690–1800* (Belfast: Ulster Historical Foundation, 1979), pp. 204–221

Fanning, Ronan, *Fatal Path: British Government and Irish Revolution, 1910–1922* (London: Faber & Faber, 2013)

Farrell, Michael, 'Frank Fitzgerald and the Arms Crisis of 1922', *Magill*, 6.6 (1983), pp. 31–35

Farry, Michael, *The Aftermath of Revolution: Sligo 1921–23* (Dublin: University College Dublin Press, 2000)

Finlay, Richard J., 'Nationalism, Race, Religion and the Irish Question in Inter-War Scotland', *Innes Review*, 42.1 (1991), pp. 46–67

Fitzpatrick, David, *Politics and Irish Life 1913–1921: Provincial Experience of War and Revolution* (Cork: Cork University Press, 1998)

Fitzpatrick, David, 'The Geography of Irish Nationalism 1910–1921', *Past & Present*, 78 (1978), pp. 113–44

Fitzpatrick, David, 'Irish Emigration in the Later Nineteenth Century', *Irish Historical Studies*, 22.86 (1980), pp. 126–43

Fitzpatrick, David, '"A Peculiar Tramping People": The Irish in Britain, 1801–70', in W.E. Vaughan (ed.), *A New History of Ireland, Vol. V: Ireland Under the Union, Vol. I, 1801–70* (Oxford: Clarendon Press, 1989), pp. 623–60

Fitzpatrick, David, 'The Irish in Britain, 1871–1921', in W.E. Vaughan (ed.), *A New History of Ireland, Vol. VI: Ireland Under the Union, Vol. II: 1870–1921* (Oxford: Clarendon Press, 1996), pp. 653–702

Foxton, David, *Revolutionary Lawyers: Sinn Féin and Crown Courts in Ireland and Britain, 1916–1923* (Dublin: Four Courts Press, 2008)

Gallagher, John, 'Nationalisms and the Crisis of Empire, 1919–22', *Modern Asian Studies*, 15.3 (1981), pp. 355–68

Gerwarth, Robert, 'The Central European Counter-Revolution: Paramilitary Violence in Germany, Austria and Hungary after the Great War', *Past & Present*, 200 (2008), pp. 175–209

Githens-Mazer, Jonathan, *Myths and Memories of the Easter Rising: Cultural and Political Nationalism in Ireland* (Dublin: Irish Academic Press, 2006)

Griffiths, Kenneth, and Timothy E. O'Grady, *Curious Journey: An Oral History of Ireland's Unfinished Revolution* (London: Hutchinson, 1982)

Hanley, Brian, *The IRA: 1926–1936* (Dublin: Four Courts Press, 2002)

Hanley, Brian, 'The Irish Citizen Army after 1916', *Saothar: Journal of the Irish Labour History Society*, 28 (2003), pp. 37–47

Hanley, Brian, and Scott Millar, *The Lost Revolution: The Story of the Official IRA and the Workers' Party* (Dublin: Penguin Ireland, 2009)

Hart, Peter, *The IRA and Its Enemies: Violence and Community in Cork, 1916–1923* (Oxford: Clarendon Press, 1998)

Hart, Peter, *Mick: The Real Michael Collins* (London: Macmillan, 2005)

Hart, Peter, 'The Geography of Revolution in Ireland', in Peter Hart, *The IRA at War 1916–1923* (Oxford: Oxford University Press, 2003), pp. 30–61

Hart, Peter, 'The Social Structure of the Irish Republican Army', in Peter Hart, *The IRA at War 1916–1923* (Oxford: Oxford University Press, 2003), pp. 110–38

Hart, Peter, 'Operations Abroad: The IRA in Britain', in Peter Hart, *The IRA at War 1916–1923* (Oxford: Oxford University Press, 2003), pp. 141–77

Hart, Peter, 'The Thompson Submachine Gun in Ireland Revisited', in Peter Hart, *The IRA at War 1916–1923* (Oxford: Oxford University Press, 2003), pp. 178–93

Hart, Peter, 'Michael Collins and the Assassination of Sir Henry Wilson', in Peter Hart, *The IRA at War 1916–1923* (Oxford: Oxford University Press, 2003), pp. 194–220

Hart, Peter, 'Ethnic Conflict and Minority Responses', in Peter Hart, *The IRA at War 1916–1923* (Oxford: Oxford University Press, 2003), pp. 241–58

Hart, Peter, 'Collins, Michael (1890–1922)', in H.C.G. Matthew and Brian Harrison (eds), *Oxford Dictionary of National Biography* (Oxford: Oxford University Press, 2004), online edition, Jan. 2008, accessed at http://www.oxforddnb.com/view/article/32506 on 15 July 2010

Hart, Peter, 'The Fenians and the International Revolutionary Tradition', in Fearghal McGarry and James McConnel (eds), *The Black Hand of Republicanism: Fenianism in Modern Ireland* (Dublin: Irish Academic Press, 2009), pp. 190–204

Hay, Marnie, *Bulmer Hobson and the Nationalist Movement in Twentieth Century Ireland* (Manchester: Manchester University Press, 2009)

Hay, Marnie, 'The Foundation and Development of Na Fianna Éireann, 1906–16', *Irish Historical Studies*, 36.141 (2008), pp. 53–71

Hopkinson, Michael, *Green against Green: The Irish Civil War* (Dublin: Gill & Macmillan, 2004)

Hopkinson, Michael, *The Irish War of Independence* (Dublin: Gill & Macmillan, 2004)

Hopkinson, Michael, 'From Treaty to Civil War, 1921–2', in J.R. Hill (ed.), *A New History of Ireland, Vol. VII: Ireland, 1921–1984* (Oxford: Oxford University Press, 2003), pp. 1–30

Inoue, Keiko, 'Dáil Propaganda and the Irish Self-Determination League of Great Britain during the Anglo-Irish War', *Irish Studies Review*, 6.1 (1998), pp. 47–53

Inoue, Keiko, 'O'Brien, Arthur Patrick Donovan', in James McGuire and James Quinn (eds), *Dictionary of Irish Biography* (Cambridge: Cambridge University Press, 2009), downloaded from http://dib.cambridge.org on 1 Dec. 2009

Jackson, Daniel M., *Popular Opposition to Irish Home Rule in Edwardian Britain* (Liverpool: Liverpool University Press, 2009)

Jeffery, Keith, *Field Marshal Sir Henry Wilson: A Political Soldier* (Oxford: Oxford University Press, 2006)

Jeffery, Keith, and Peter Hennessy, *States of Emergency: British Governments and Strikebreaking Since 1919* (London: Routledge & Kegan Paul, 1983)

Jenkins, Brian, *The Fenian Problem: Insurgency and Terrorism in a Liberal State, 1858–1874* (Toronto: McGill-Queen's University Press, 2008)

Jung, Patrick, 'The Thompson Submachine Gun During and After the Anglo-Irish War: the New Evidence', *Irish Sword*, 21.84 (1998), pp. 190–218

Kautt, W.H., *Ambushes and Armour: The Irish Rebellion 1919–1921* (Dublin: Irish Academic Press, 2010)

Kennedy, Padraic C., 'The Secret Service Department: A British Intelligence Bureau in Mid-Victorian London, September 1867 to April 1868', *Intelligence and National Security*, 18.3 (2003), pp. 100–127

Kinvig, Clifford, *Churchill's Crusade: The British Invasion of Russia, 1918–1920* (London: Continuum, 2006)

Kissane, Bill, *The Politics of the Irish Civil War* (Oxford: Oxford University Press, 2005)

Laffan, Michael, *The Resurrection of Ireland: The Sinn Féin Party, 1916–1923* (Cambridge: Cambridge University Press, 1999)

Leeson, D.M., *The Black and Tans: British Police and Auxiliaries in the Irish War of Independence, 1920–1921* (Oxford: Oxford University Press, 2011)

Lentin, A., 'McCardie, Sir Henry Alfred (1869–1933)', in H.C.G. Matthew and Brian Harrison (eds), *Oxford Dictionary of National Biography* (Oxford: Oxford University Press, 2004), accessed at http://www.oxforddnb.com/view/article/34677 on 17 May 2010

Longford, The Earl of, and Thomas P. O'Neill, *Eamon de Valera* (London: Hutchinson, 1970)

Lowe, W.J., 'The Chartists and the Irish Confederates: Lancashire, 1848', *Irish Historical Studies*, 24.94 (1984), pp. 172–96

Lynch, Robert, *The Northern IRA and the Early Years of Partition 1920–1922* (Dublin: Irish Academic Press, 2006)

MacFarlane, L.J., 'Hands Off Russia: British Labour and the Russo-Polish War, 1920', *Past & Present*, 38 (1967), pp. 126–52

Malcolm, Joyce Lee, *Guns and Violence: The English Experience* (Cambridge, Mass.: Harvard University Press, 2002)

Manela, Erez, *The Wilsonian Moment: Self-Determination and the International Origins of Anti-Colonial Nationalism* (Oxford: Oxford University Press, 2007)

Marchington, James, *Handguns & Sub-Machine Guns: Semi-Automatic Pistols & Revolvers* (London: Brassey's, 1997)

Matthews, Ann, *The Kimmage Garrison, 1916: Making Bill-Can Bombs in Larkfield* (Dublin: Four Courts Press, 2010)

May, Alex, 'Curtis, Lionel George (1872–1955)', in H.C.G. Matthew and Brian Harrison (eds), *Oxford Dictionary of National Biography* (Oxford: Oxford University Press, 2004); online edn, May 2006, accessed at http://www.oxforddnb.com/view/article/32678 on 12 Aug. 2010

McConville, Seán, *Irish Political Prisoners, 1848–1922: Theatres of War* (London: Routledge, 2003)

McFarland, E.W., *Ireland and Scotland in the Age of Revolution: Planting the Green Bough* (Edinburgh: Edinburgh University Press, 1994)

McFarland, Elaine W., 'A Reality and Yet Impalpable: The Fenian Panic in Mid-Victorian Scotland', *Scottish Historical Review*, 77.2 (1998), pp. 199–223

McGladdery, Gary, *The Provisional IRA in England: The Bombing Campaign 1973–1997* (Dublin: Irish Academic Press, 2006)

McGuire, Charlie, *Sean McLoughlin: Ireland's Forgotten Revolutionary* (Pontypool: Merlin Press, 2011)

McHugh, John, 'Maclean, John (1879–1923)', in H.C.G. Matthew and Brian Harrison (eds), *Oxford Dictionary of National Biography* (Oxford: Oxford University Press, 2004); online edn, May 2006, accessed at http://www. oxforddnb.com/view/article/37721, on 13 Oct. 2010

McLoughlin, Barry, *Left to the Wolves: Irish Victims of Stalinist Terror* (Dublin: Irish Academic Press, 2007)

McMahon, Paul, *British Spies and Irish Rebels: British Intelligence and Ireland, 1916–1945* (Woodbridge: The Boydell Press, 2008)

Meyer, Rudolf, Josef Köhler and Axel Homburg, *Explosives* (Weinheim: Wiley-VCH, 2007)

Moody, T.W., *Davitt and Irish Revolution, 1846–82* (Oxford: Clarendon Press, 1984)

Morgan, Kenneth O., *Consensus and Disunity: The Lloyd George Coalition Government, 1918–1922* (Oxford: Clarendon Press, 1979)

Mulligan, Adrian N., 'A Forgotten 'Greater Ireland': The Transatlantic Development of Irish Nationalism', *Scottish Geographical Journal*, 118.3 (2002), pp. 219–34

Mulligan, Adrian N., 'Absence Makes the Heart Grow Fonder: Transatlantic Irish Nationalism and the 1867 Rising', *Social & Cultural Geography*, 6.3 (2005), pp. 439–54

Noonan, Gerard, 'Supplying an Army: IRA Gunrunning in Britain during the War of Independence', *History Studies: University of Limerick History Society Journal*, 12 (2011), pp. 80–92

Noonan, Gerard, 'Republican Terrorism in Britain, 1920–1923', in David Fitzpatrick (ed.), *Terror in Ireland 1916–1923* (Dublin: Lilliput Press, 2012), pp. 236–48

O'Beirne-Ranelagh, John, 'The Irish Republican Brotherhood in the Revolutionary Period, 1879–1923', in D.G. Boyce (ed.), *The Revolution in Ireland, 1879–1923* (Dublin: Gill & Macmillan, 1988), pp. 137–56

Ó Catháin, Máirtín Seán, *Irish Republicanism in Scotland 1858–1916: Fenians in Exile* (Dublin: Irish Academic Press, 2007)

Ó Catháin, Máirtín Seán, 'A Land Beyond the Sea: Irish and Scottish Republicans in Dublin, 1916', in Ruan O'Donnell (ed.), *The Impact of the 1916 Rising: Among the Nations* (Dublin: Irish Academic Press, 2008), pp. 37–48

Ó Catháin, Máirtín, 'A Winnowing Spirit: Sinn Féin in Scotland, 1905–38', in Martin J. Mitchell (ed.), *New Perspectives on the Irish in Scotland* (Edinburgh: John Donald, 2008), pp. 114–26

Ó Catháin, Máirtín, 'Michael Collins and Scotland', in Frank Ferguson and James McConnel (eds), *Ireland and Scotland in the Nineteenth Century* (Dublin: Four Courts Press, 2009), pp. 160–75

Ó Catháin, Máirtín, "The Black Hand of Irish Republicanism'?: Transcontinental Fenianism and Theories of Global Terror', in Fearghal McGarry and James

McConnel (eds), *The Black Hand of Republicanism: Fenianism in Modern Ireland* (Dublin: Irish Academic Press, 2009), pp. 135–46

O'Callaghan, John, *Revolutionary Limerick: The Republican Campaign for Independence in Limerick, 1913–1921* (Dublin: Irish Academic Press, 2010)

O'Connor, Emmet, *Syndicalism in Ireland 1917–1923* (Cork: Cork University Press, 1988)

O'Connor, Emmet, *Reds and the Green: Ireland, Russia and the Communist Internationals, 1919–43* (Dublin: University College Dublin Press, 2004)

O'Connor, Emmet, 'Waterford and IRA Gun-Running, 1917–22', *Decies: Journal of the Waterford Archaeological & Historical Society*, 57 (2001), pp. 181–93

O'Day, Alan, 'Varieties of Anti-Irish Behaviour in Britain, 1846–1922', in Panikos Panayi (ed.), *Racial Violence in Britain, 1840–1950* (Leicester: Leicester University Press, 1993), pp. 26–43

O'Donoghue, David, *The Devil's Deal: The IRA, Nazi Germany and the Double Life of Jim O'Donovan* (Dublin: New Island, 2010)

O Grada, Cormac, 'Fenianism and Socialism: The Career of Joseph Patrick McDonnell', *Saothar: Journal of the Irish Labour History Society*, 1.1 (1975), pp. 31–41

O'Halpin, Eunan, *The Decline of the Union: British Government in Ireland 1892–1920* (Dublin: Gill & Macmillan, 1987)

O'Halpin, Eunan, *Defending Ireland: The Irish State and Its Enemies Since 1922* (Oxford: Oxford University Press, 1999)

Owens, Gary, 'Constructing the Martyrs: The Manchester Executions and the Nationalist Imagination', in Lawrence W. McBride (ed.), *Images, Icons and the Irish Nationalist Imagination* (Dublin: Four Courts Press, 1999), pp. 18–36

Parkinson, Alan, *Belfast's Unholy War: The Troubles of the 1920s* (Dublin: Four Courts Press, 2004)

Patterson, Iain D., 'The Activities of Irish Republican Physical Force Organisations in Scotland, 1919–21', *Scottish Historical Review*, 72.193 (1993), pp. 39–59

Porter, Bernard, 'Piatkoff, Peter (*fl.* 1910)', in H.C.G. Matthew and Brian Harrison (eds), *Oxford Dictionary of National Biography* (Oxford: Oxford University Press, 2004), online edn, Sept. 2010, accessed at http://www.oxforddnb.com/view/article/92479, on 13 Oct. 2010

Putkowski, Julian, 'The Best Secret Service Man We Had: Jack Byrnes, A2 and the IRA', *Lobster 94: Journal of Parapolitics*, 28 (1994), pp. 1–38

Ramón, Martha, *A Provisional Dictator: James Stephens and the Fenian Movement* (Dublin: University College Dublin Press, 2007)

Rosen, Andrew, *Rise Up Women!: The Militant Campaign of the Women's Social and Political Union 1903–1914* (London: Routledge & Kegan Paul, 1974)

Roth, Andreas, 'Gun Running from Germany to Ireland in the Early 1920s', *Irish Sword*, 22.88 (2000), pp. 209–20

Routh, Guy, *Occupation and Pay in Great Britain, 1906–60* (Cambridge: Cambridge University Press, 1965)

Sellwood, A.V., *Police Strike–1919* (London: W.H. Allen, 1978)

Short, K.R.M., *The Dynamite War: Irish-American Bombers in Victorian Britain* (Dublin: Gill & Macmillan, 1979)

Skinnerton, Ian, *The British Service Lee: Lee-Metford and Lee-Enfield Rifles and Carbines 1880–1980* (London: Arms & Armour Press, 1982)

Squires, Mike, 'Saklatvala, Shapurji (1874–1936)', in H.C.G. Matthew and Brian Harrison (eds), *Oxford Dictionary of National Biography* (Oxford: Oxford University Press, 2004), online edition, accessed at http://www.oxforddnb.com/view/article/35909, on 14 June 2010

Steiner, Zara, *The Lights that Failed: European International History 1913–1933* (Oxford: Oxford University Press, 2005)

Sweeney, George, 'Irish Hunger Strikes and the Cult of Self-Sacrifice', *Journal of Contemporary History*, 28.3 (1993), pp. 421–37

Takagami, Shin-inchi, 'The Fenian Rising in Dublin, March 1867', *Irish Historical Studies*, 29.115 (1995), pp. 340–62

Townshend, Charles, *The British Campaign in Ireland 1919–1921: The Development of Political and Military Policies* (London: Oxford University Press, 1975)

Townshend, Charles, *Political Violence in Ireland: Government and Resistance Since 1848* (Oxford: Clarendon Press, 1983)

Townshend, Charles, *Easter 1916: The Irish Rebellion* (London: Allen Lane, 2005)

Townshend, Charles, 'The Irish Republican Army and the Development of Guerrilla Warfare, 1916–1921', *English Historical Review*, 114.321 (1979), pp. 318–45

Wheatley, Michael, *Nationalism and the Irish Party: Provincial Ireland 1910–1916* (Oxford: Oxford University Press, 2005)

Whelehan, Niall, *The Dynamiters: Irish Nationalism and Political Violence in the Wider World, 1867–1900* (Cambridge: Cambridge University Press, 2012)

White, Laurence William, 'O'Connor, Roderick ('Rory')', in James McGuire and James Quinn (eds), *Dictionary of Irish Biography* (Cambridge: Cambridge University Press, 2009), downloaded from http://dib.cambridge.org on 1 Dec. 2009

White, Lawrence William, 'Skinnider, Margaret (Ní Scineadóra, Máighréad)', in James McGuire and James Quinn (eds), *Dictionary of Irish Biography* (Cambridge: Cambridge University Press, 2009), downloaded from http://dib.cambridge.org on 1 Dec. 2009

Index